KU-325-473

DISPOSED OF
BY LIBRARY
HOUSE OF LORDS

PREHISTORIC WALES

*Frances Lynch, Stephen Aldhouse-Green
and Jeffrey L. Davies*

SUTTON PUBLISHING

First published in 2000 by
Sutton Publishing Limited · Phoenix Mill
Thrupp · Stroud · Gloucestershire · GL5 2BU

Copyright © Frances Lynch, Stephen Aldhouse-Green and Jeffrey L. Davies, 2000

All rights reserved. No part of this publication may be reproduced, stored in a retrieval system, or transmitted, in any form, or by any means, electronic, mechanical, photocopying, recording or otherwise, without the prior permission of the publisher and copyright holders.

Frances Lynch, Stephen Aldhouse-Green and Jeffrey L. Davies hereby assert the moral right to be identified as the authors of this work.

British Library Cataloguing in Publication Data
A catalogue record for this book is available from the British Library

ISBN 0-7509-2165-X

Typeset in 10/13pt Sabon.
Typesetting and origination by
Sutton Publishing Limited.
Printed in Great Britain by
Bookcraft, Midsomer Norton, Somerset.

CONTENTS

LIST OF PLATES

LIST OF ILLUSTRATIONS

PREFACE

This book has had a long and rather chequered period of gestation. It was conceived in 1989 by Jeff Davies and Chris Arnold as a successor to Taylor's edited volume *Culture and Environment in Prehistoric Wales* which had summarised the state of knowledge in 1980, but the new one was intended to have an extended chronological range, matching that of the earlier synthesis *Prehistoric and Early Wales*, brought together in 1965 by Idris Foster and Glyn Daniel. However, after several vicissitudes the work has now emerged in a changed form as two complementary volumes, this first one covering prehistory, with a second one dealing with Roman and post-Roman Wales written by the 'original' editors. All the authors involved are grateful to Sutton Publishing for this expansion of the brief and their faith in the project, and to their editors Rupert Harding and Sarah Cook.

While the delays and the long period over which some of the chapters have been written may have caused frustrations, there have also been advantages in the postponement since the last few years have seen many important discoveries and significant long-term projects coming to fruition, whose results can now be incorporated in a book which, it is hoped, will fill the long-apparent need for a convenient textbook on Welsh prehistory. To this end the authors were asked to write within a standard framework and to provide a comprehensive bibliography so that readers could tap the full wealth of evidence available. Evidence has been at the forefront of the approach, in the belief that it is the necessary foundation to any worthwhile interpretation of life in the past.

The individual authors are each beholden to several friends and colleagues for information, help and advice. Stephen Aldhouse-Green would like to thank Martin Bell, Jill Cook, Roger Jacobi, Nicholas Barton, Rick Shulting, Stephanie Swainston and Elizabeth Walker, who all generously provided information concerning their current research programmes; David Jenkins who provided information on Llyn Aled Isaf, and John Kenyon and the staff of the Library of the National Museum and Galleries of Wales who provided excellent research facilities. He acknowledges the help of Andrew David, Miranda Aldhouse-Green and Joshua Pollard who read drafts of the text, to its considerable improvement. Frances Lynch would like to thank Jeff Davies, George Williams and especially Peter Crew and Peter Northover for much help with the text and for generously providing information about unpublished work. Jeff Davies would like to thank several individuals for unstinting access to new information and for discussing a number of issues with him. Among these are members of staff of the four Welsh Archaeological Trusts, especially Mr George Williams to whom special thanks must be extended, and also the staff of the RCAMHW at Aberystwyth, particularly Mr Toby Driver, who were all most helpful.

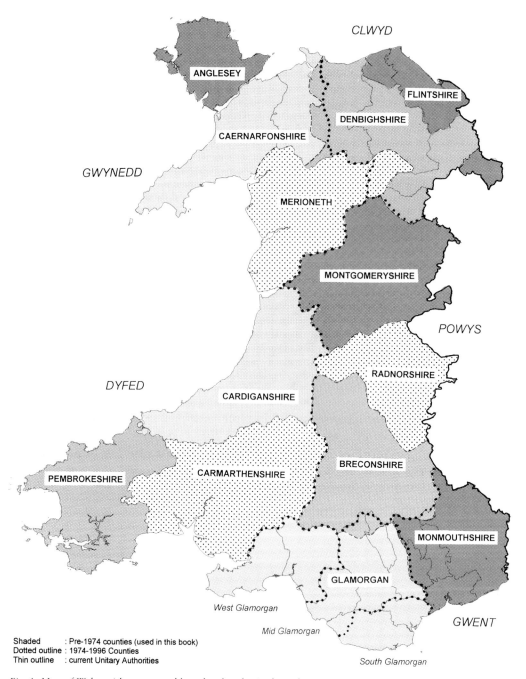

Fig. 1. Map of Wales with county and later local authority boundaries.

For help with illustrations Stephen Aldhouse-Green is indebted to Richard Brewer, Tony Daly, Jackie Chadwick and Evan Chapman of the Department of Archaeology and Numismatics of the National Museums and Galleries of Wales, and also to Jeff Wallis (Oxford) and Anne Leaver of the University of Wales College, Newport. Frances Lynch would like to thank Tony Daly, Carol Greenway, Heledd Owen and Emrys Jones for assistance with computer scanning; Tass Rees for printing out the texts and, particularly, Chris Martin of CPAT for providing the map information and for creating the distribution maps. She is also most grateful to Bill Britnell, Ken Murphy, Peter Crew and Mick Sharp for the provision of photographs. Jeff Davies would like to thank Chris Musson and Terry James who gave a great deal of assistance with the selection, preparation and presentation of some of the aerial photographs reproduced in this book; Chris Martin for help with distribution maps and Charles Green who prepared many of the line drawings for Chapter 4. He is particularly grateful to the University of Wales, Aberystwyth, for money from the David Hughes Parry Award to finance these illustrations.

For permission to use and reproduce illustrations, all three authors are grateful to those acknowledged in the individual captions.

NOTE ON ADMINISTRATIVE DIVISIONS

Wales was divided into counties in 1282 and these divisions remained reasonably stable until 1974 when they were amalgamated into larger units which were then deconstructed in 1996. The historic counties are the ones that are best known and are embedded in the archaeological literature; it was therefore decided to retain them in this book. To facilitate correlations, a map showing all three periods of division is provided.

DATING SYSTEMS

All dates in Chapter 1 are expressed in years BP; all dates in Chapters 2–4 are expressed in calibrated calender years BC (cal BC). Radiocarbon dating, developed in 1946 by Willard Libby, has enabled an objective, worldwide chronology to be established for the prehistoric period, but since the 1960s it has been realised that 'radiocarbon years' diverge from true calendrical years by an amount which varies over time and tends to fluctuate at certain critical periods. By comparing the radiocarbon results with other absolute, chronometric dating systems, mainly dendrochronology (tree-ring dating), it has been possible to establish a calibration curve. Radiocarbon dates to which this calibration has been applied are denoted 'cal BC'; these are more accurate than previous radiocarbon results but they remain, inevitably, imprecise. They do, however, provide a band of dating within which the correct date is (98 per cent) likely to lie.

Where individual dates are quoted the laboratory result (with laboratory reference number) is given in radiocarbon years BP (Before Present, i.e. 1950), followed by the calibrated range (calculated by the computer program devised by Stuiver and Kra in 1986). Generalised dates also conform to this range and centuries are noted as 'cal BC' to make that explicit. However, where dendrochronological or archaeomagnetic dates are quoted they are given as BC because they do not require calibration. The calibration curve does not reach far back into the Palaeolithic so dates in Chapter 1 are given in radiocarbon years BP, as is the convention for Quaternary and palaeobotanical studies.

Fig. 2. Chronological chart with a summary of Welsh prehistory.

Chapter	BC	Period	Climate	Settlement	Artefacts	Industry	Ritual and Death	BP
CHAPTER 1	225 ka	Lower Pal.	Cold (See Fig. 1.2) Glacial	Pontnewydd, Coygan, Paviland	Handaxes Levallois, Triangular handaxes, Blade technology	Hunting, Fishing, Gathering	'Red Lady' burial	
	50 ka	Mid Palaeolithic						
	26 ka	E. Upper Pal.						
	21–13k							
	10 ka	Mesolithic	Warm and dry	Nab Head/Rhuddlan, Waun Figlen Felin	Microliths		Kendrick's Cave dec. bone, Rhuddlan pebbles	12 ka
CHAPTER 2	4,400	Early Neolithic	Warm and wet	Large wooden houses, Llandegai, Gwernvale	*Pottery: shouldered bowls*, Stone axeheads, Leaf-shaped arrowheads	Farming	Monumental Tombs, Portal Dolmens, Cotswold–Severn cairns, Small Passage Graves, Large Passage Graves, ? Cursus	5,600
	3,600	Middle Neolithic		Clegyr Boia	*Peterborough ware*	Stone quarrying		4,800
CHAPTER 3	2,900	Late Neolithic	Drier and warm	Small round houses, Trelystan, Walton	*Grooved ware*, Beakers, Copper axes, halberds	Copper mining, Copa Hill	Henge Monuments, Timber circles, Early individual graves, Standing Stones, Ring Cairns, Stone Circles, Round barrows/cairns, Cemetery mounds	4,300
	2,300	Early Bronze Age		Stackpole, ?? Class II huts, Burnt mounds	*Food Vessels*, *Collared Urns*, Acton Park bronzes, Cemmaes bronzes	Parys Mt., Great Orme		
	1600	Middle Bronze Age						
	1400							
	1300			Plank built round houses, Glanfeinion, Gwent Levels	*Plain jars: Rhuddlan*, Penard bronzes	? Gold mining	Kerb Cairns	3,200
CHAPTER 4	1100	Late Bronze Age	Wet and cold	Palisaded hilltops, Breiddin, Dinorben	Guilsfield/Wilburton metal, *Plain jars: Breiddin*, Carp's Tongue bronzes, Llyn Fawr metalwork		Some secondary burials In barrows	2,900
	800	Early Iron Age		Hillforts & Concentrics, M.Y Gaer, M. Hiraddug, Moel y Gerddi, Small enclosures, Collfryn, Dan y Coed, Bryn Eryr	*Malvernian pots*, La Tène metalwork		Votive sites: Llyn Fawr	2,700
	700		Warmer and drier					
	400	Middle Iron Age				Salt trade	Renewed interest in Standing Stones, Inhumations	
	50	Late Iron Age		Sudbrook, Lesser Garth	*Llanmelin style*, *SW Decorated pots*, *Thrown pots*, Enamelled metalwork	Iron industry in north	Votive sites: Llyn Cerrig Bach	2,000

Fig. 2. *Chronological chart with a summary of Welsh prehistory. Pottery traditions are shown in italics; site names are indented; BC dates are calibrated BC; BP dates are radiocarbon years expressed as Before Present (to obtain a bc date subtract 1950); ka means 1000 years ago. The traditional Three Age System is emphasised by shading; the chapter divisions of this book cut time differently.*

ONE

PALAEOLITHIC AND MESOLITHIC WALES: PART I: THE PALAEOLITHIC PERIOD

Stephen Aldhouse-Green

[God] made from one blood the whole race of humankind to dwell upon the entire face of the earth . . .

Acts of the Apostles 17:26

INTRODUCTION

The opening quotation states two profound truths with which modern archaeologists would generally agree: first, that all humankind is ultimately related and secondly, that it was in the nature of humans that they would eventually colonise the earth. Anthropologists view this global expansion as a biological imperative. Advances in molecular biology reveal to us how relatively recent, and probably temporary, are the present racial groupings of the world and equally enable us to perceive – against a vast canvas of several million years – the nature of humanity. It is essential here to view humans as part of the animal kingdom. Indeed, for the period when humans lived as hunters, scavengers and gatherers, no other approach is remotely useful.

Wales was first inhabited around a quarter of a million years ago. The people of this period, within the last Ice Age (or Pleistocene), lived by hunting, by scavenging the kills of other carnivores, by gathering wild foods and, possibly only over the last 50,000 years or so, by gathering shellfish or fishing. Even after the Ice Age ended, the hunting and gathering way of life continued in the progressively warmer and increasingly forested conditions of the early Postglacial (Holocene) period. The hunter-gatherer period only came to an end towards 6,000 years ago when farming was introduced to the British Isles. Both the geology and archaeology of the earlier prehistoric periods have much to tell us both about our world and ourselves. The climatic secrets locked in the polar ice cap and in deep sea sediments help us to understand the history of climate and thereby to predict its future. The fossilised bones of our ancestors and the DNA they contain reveal the story of our evolution. The settlement sites of hunters and gatherers enable us to understand the very different societies and social networks of Neanderthals and Modern Humans. But the story of the Welsh past must properly begin with the origins of the human race.

HUMAN EVOLUTION AND THE COLONISATION OF EUROPE

The ancestors of the genus *Homo* can be traced back to between 4 and 5 million years. The story begins, however, as far back as 70 to 80 million years ago with the emergence of primates which represent, in biological terminology, an order whose members are all ultimately related. The primates became differentiated within the class of mammalia through characteristics such as the development of stereoscopic vision and grasping feet. The former made possible effective visual hunting strategies while the latter favoured not only tree-climbing, for gathering and self-defence, but ultimately the use of the hands for tool-making. The order of primates includes a superfamily, the *Hominoidea*, whose members include both apes and hominids. This superfamily, at the present day, is divided into three families: hominids, pongids (the great apes) and hylobatids (lesser apes). Included among the great apes are chimpanzees, gorillas and orang-utans. Strictly speaking, only orang-utans should be differentiated from the family of hominids which should logically include humans, chimpanzees and gorillas as equal members (Klein 1989).

Our closest relatives are the chimpanzees from whom we diverged between 8 and 5 million years ago and with whom we share about 98 per cent of our genes. Our modern understanding of chimpanzees shows that they are – like ourselves and some other species – tool-makers with a complex social system, equipped with a good geographical, faunal and botanical knowledge of their territories, and with the ability to communicate using language (Peterson & Goodall 1993). McGrew (1991) stressed such similarities and saw in chimpanzees a potential model of the origins of human culture. Recently the debate has seen a dramatic development with the appearance of an authoritative study of the behaviour of chimpanzee communities at seven separate sites in Africa (Whiten *et al.* 1999). This revealed a scale of cultural variation exceeded only by the human species. Culture is often defined in different ways by archaeologists, anthropologists and life scientists. For archaeologists working in the field of human origins, culture may be defined as 'the non-genetic transmission of habits . . . [such that] one community can readily be distinguished from another by its unique suite of behavioural characteristics' (de Waal 1999). This definition does not presuppose the mechanisms by which culture is passed on, whether through copying, teaching or the use of language. Indeed, it is now clear that 'culture', in the sense of the development of stone tools, is likely to be a development that pre-dates the appearance of the first human by perhaps half a million years (Wood & Collard 1999a).

It is, of course, easier to apply concepts of culture to living, or historically attested, communities whether chimpanzee or human. Traditional usage by prehistorians has involved the concept of a contemporary set of artefact types recurring within the same region. Such patterns occur throughout prehistory but archaeologists tend now to avoid the term 'culture' because of a recognition that such patterns need not simply equate with distinct geographical communities but may be more complex in origin, perhaps relating to specialist, age, gender, priestly or other status groups operating within, or across, the boundaries of self-recognising cultural communities. The recognition of cultural behaviour by our closest living relative, the chimpanzee, is important here. Queen Victoria was perhaps prescient in her comment, made during a visit to London Zoo, that chimpanzees looked 'painfully and disagreeably human' (Jones 1996, xiv). Our modern perspective has tended to be human-centred with the success or failure of other species judged in relation to our own perceived superiority. When looked at with the time depth that only archaeology and palaeontology can give, we can see instead that humans, above all other animals, are actually characterised by a self-interested opportunism which has led to a remorseless depletion, degradation and destruction of our environment (Kingdon 1993, 11–12, 324; Flannery 1994). We see this in the destruction of the world's flora and fauna, as well as in the humanly created 'greenhouse effect', which could, through melting of the polar ice caps, cause a massive dislocation to the world's coastlines and climate.

It is perhaps most useful to pick up the evolutionary story (**Fig. 1.1**) around 4.5 million years ago when the Australopithecines, the immediate ancestors of the genus *Homo*, appeared in eastern Africa (Wood 1994; Wood & Collard 1999b). The Australopithecines can themselves be divided into a number of species of which one may finally have evolved into *Homo* around 2 million years ago. They were essentially apes with some human characteristics, notably upright walking, but not speech. Brains were ape-sized but their enhanced ratio of brain to body size is indicative of some reorganisation of the brain (Conroy 1997, 176). Generally rather smaller than modern humans, especially the females, the difference in size between the sexes (dimorphism) – adult size range varies from 1.00–1.70 metres – may have had profound consequences for a social structure almost certainly unlike our own. The direct evidence of the footprints of Australopithecines from Laetoli in Tanzania at 3.6 million years ago shows that they

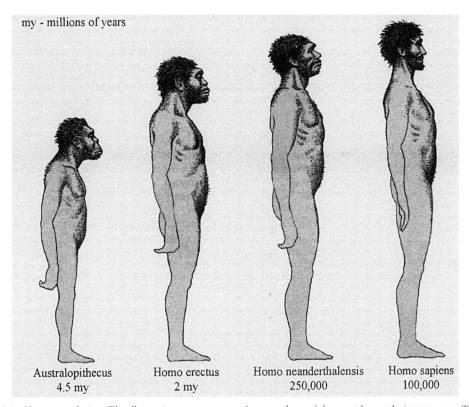

Fig. 1.1. Human evolution. The illustration presents some key members of the complex evolutionary story. The contrasts between the Australopithecines and Homo *are considerable in comparison with the differences between species of* Homo. *Since bodies were not deliberately buried before the late Pleistocene, much of the early part of the human story has to be pieced together from very incomplete remains. Based on Boaz & Almquist 1999, 213. (By permission of Prentice Hall, Inc.)*

walked fully upright with the striding gait characteristic of modern humans, even though they remained adapted to arboreal climbing (Spoor *et al.* 1994). The configuration of the Australopithecine face certainly remained ape-like, however, with nostrils pointed outwards rather than downwards, as with *Homo*.

Archaeologists often discuss the impact of humans on the environment both in later prehistory and in historic times. It is important to understand, however, that for much of the period of human evolution – down, in fact, to the Postglacial period in Wales – the nature of the impact was reversed. Changes in global climate led to regional climatic changes which in turn influenced vegetation, the composition of local fauna and, indeed, the very presence or absence of humans in the landscape. Such climatic changes seem to have played a role in determining the course of human evolution itself. About 2.5 million years ago the climate in eastern Africa became much drier and the plains expanded, favouring species like the early hominids whose bipedal gait adapted them for life on the savanna. It is at this time that the earliest evidence for making stone tools appears (Steele 1999), although it is unclear which of the three hominid species then living was actually involved.

With the arrival of *Homo erectus* at around 1.9 million years ago we enter a world that is broadly familiar to us. These humans walked and certainly looked a lot like us, even though the issue of the origins of language remains hotly contested (Boaz & Almquist 1999, 266–72). But humans are not attested in Britain before around 500,000 years ago and, in Wales, not until around 250,000 years ago. Accordingly the details of earlier hominid evolution need scarcely detain us further here. One key fact, however, is that *Homo erectus* was the first human to spread beyond Africa. In this migration *Homo* was following the earlier expansion into Eurasia of lions and hyaenas (Kingdon 1993, 2). The details of the spread of *Homo* into Europe are far from clear. The suggestion has been made that the existence of a large form of hyaena, *Pachycrocuta brevirostris*, combined with the presence of the spotted hyaena effectively excluded humans from much of the continental mainland because humans were unable to compete with such effective scavengers (Turner 1992). This hypothesis would see humans, certainly before the Middle Pleistocene, as primarily scavengers rather than hunters. We can infer from the evidence of kill sites at Boxgrove, and from the recovery of wooden spears at Schöningen in Germany, that hominids were skilled hunters by half a million years ago or soon after (Dennell 1997). It is, however, unclear to what extent hunting played a significant part in food procurement before this time.

Boxgrove man has been identified as *Homo heidelbergensis*, the earliest species known from northern Europe (Roberts *et al.* 1994). The discovery at Boxgrove of a fragment of leg bone from an adult male reveals that this example of Heidelberg man was exceptionally robust, around 1.80 metres in height and with a 'physique somewhere between a light heavyweight boxing champion and a rugby half-back' (*Independent* newspaper, 22.6.94). From these European populations of *heidelbergensis*, there developed an archaic human lineage among whose members Neanderthal characteristics may be detected from 250,000 years ago or earlier (Rightmire 1997).

'Classic' Neanderthals (*Homo neanderthalensis*) had appeared by the Last Interglacial (*c.* 125,000 years ago) and finally died out around 30,000 years ago, following an overlap of at least several thousand years with anatomically modern humans (*Homo sapiens*) in regions of western Europe. Such a long period of overlap triggers many questions about the nature and interrelationship of Neanderthals and modern humans. Indeed both groups actually overlapped by as much as 70,000 years in the Middle East (Allsworth-Jones 1993) where the modern humans moving north from Africa, where they evolved more than 100,000 years ago, encountered Neanderthals perhaps displaced from Europe by the intense cold of the last glaciation. The question of how, or whether, Neanderthals and modern humans had remained as separate communities over such a long period of time has been a focus of ongoing – often bitter – debate in the anthropological community. It has been suggested that there may have been cultural or linguistic barriers to interbreeding, or that the Middle East populations may never even have met (Trinkaus & Shipman 1993, 415). The matter seemed to be resolved by the recovery from the bones of the original Neanderthal skeleton of DNA whose pattern had little in common with that of modern humans (Ward & Stringer 1997). Most recently, however, the discovery in December 1998 of an ochre-covered Upper Palaeolithic ceremonial burial at the rock shelter of Lagar Velho in Portugal has resulted in the apparent identification of both Neanderthal and anatomically modern human features in the skeleton (Duarte *et al.* 1999). Given the radiocarbon age of the burial at *c.* 24,500 BP, this is evidence that – in this part of Europe at least – Neanderthals not only interbred with anatomically modern humans but also survived as an identifiable population until well past 30,000 BP. It has become increasingly clear that the extinction of Neanderthals must be seen as a complex process taking over 10,000 years, with areas at the margins of their distribution – including Wales – being potential areas of late survival (Pettitt 1999). However, even this hypothesis may require modification, for a new review of the evidence has shown late survival of Neanderthals not only in geographically marginal areas but even in the European heartland of Croatia, where remains from Vindija have now been dated at 28,000 BP (Smith *et al.* 1999). Moreover, it is argued that anatomically modern humans cannot be shown to have been present in Europe earlier than 32,000 BP, raising the real possibility that the earlier Aurignacian 'industry' at least – generally interpreted as a proxy for modern humans – was actually made by Neanderthals. If one cannot equate culture specifically with humans, it is perhaps even less likely that we can equate phases of material culture with particular hominid types. It none the less remains the case that the appearance of the famous cave and mobiliary art in western Europe has not been dated radiometrically earlier than 32,000 BP and it is therefore valid to argue that this should be associated with the spread of modern humans into Europe.

We may recognise the existence of three human types in Ice Age Wales: early Neanderthals at Pontnewydd Cave, *c.* 225,000 years ago; classic Neanderthals at Coygan Cave, *c.* 50,000 years ago; and fully modern humans at Paviland Cave around 26,000 years ago (Aldhouse-Green & Pettitt 1998). The Pontnewydd fossils comprise mostly jaw fragments and teeth, and our picture of these hominids must therefore be based largely upon discoveries elsewhere.

Neanderthals would have been different in appearance from ourselves: heavily muscular and stocky in build, with tall narrow 'pulled-forward' faces with strong brow-ridges, large noses and receding chins (**Pl. 1**). The jaw projected so far forward that there was space for a gap, known as the retromolar space, between the wisdom teeth (the third molars) and the upright part of the lower jaw. Various scholars have interpreted Neanderthal biology as reflecting an adaptation to the cold conditions of Ice Age Europe where they had evolved. Thus the facial arrangements (the long broad nose and puffed out cheeks) may have developed to warm cold air before it entered the lungs and the relatively short lower arms and legs would likewise have encouraged conservation of body heat. Alternatively, the facial morphology of Neanderthals may have been a response to the very considerable use they made of their teeth, attested by evidence of massive wear. It would seem that Neanderthal hands were more powerful but less controlled than our own and so use was made of the jaws as a vice to extend the use of the hands. At present we cannot be certain whether these features are a response to cold adaptation rather than to facial stress induced by use of the jaws for gripping. Again, as probably in all palaeolithic populations, there would have been a marked difference in size and muscularity between males and females. Overall height was probably only a little less than at the present day.

CLIMATE AND ENVIRONMENT

Throughout the Pleistocene period the climate played a determining role. Humans, like other carnivores, were at the mercy of environmental change. Ice Age hunters appear either to have been unable or, more likely, to have chosen not to operate in dense forest or under severe climatic conditions. Rather the hunters favoured conditions of open steppe where their prey was exposed on the grassy plains. In some geologically suitable areas humans could use caves as vantage points, meeting and storage places, as well as for shelter and security. Such occupation is unlikely to have involved regular use of caves beyond the daylight zone at the entrance before the Upper Palaeolithic when the earliest lamps were developed (Beaune 1987, 36–9; Beaune & White 1993).

The Pleistocene period saw a series of successive warm and cold phases, but much of the period was neither temperate nor glacial. Even when temperate conditions reappeared – as in the milder interludes (interstadials) of glacial phases – forest may not have had time to recolonise the land. True temperate periods (interglacials), with a climate rather like that of the present day, were actually somewhat rare and shortlived. A duration of 10,000 years would not be atypical and contrasts with the cold phases that lasted many tens of thousands of years.

The successive changes of the later Pleistocene are best viewed in the form of a diagram (**Fig. 1.2A**) which conveys something of its complexity. For much of this period sea-level (**Fig. 1.3**) was a great deal lower than now because much of the water from the world's oceans was locked up in expanded polar ice caps and also in upland glaciers. At these times Britain was physically part of Europe and sites in Wales (**Fig. 1.4**) were distributed on the north-westernmost margin of the Eurasian landmass. Early Neanderthals are known to have been present at Pontnewydd Cave in Wales, probably during a part of the temperate phase (Oxygen Isotope Stage 7a) that lasted from *c.* 225,000–186,000 years ago. It has not been possible to disentangle the Pontnewydd story in detail because all of the bones and artefacts were retrieved from secondary contexts, in this case the debris flows which filled the cave-system (Green 1984a). A few bear and horse bones display butchery marks and so must have been contemporary with a human presence. So, too, may rhinoceros, wolf, leopard and bison. Study of the fauna as a whole would suggest a possible environment of open steppe, neither fully temperate nor glacial (Currant 1984).

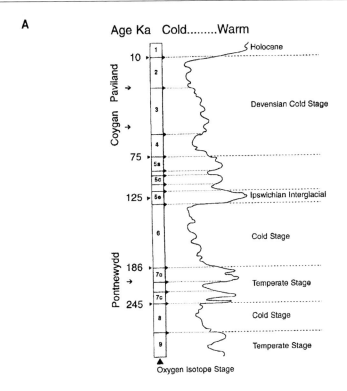

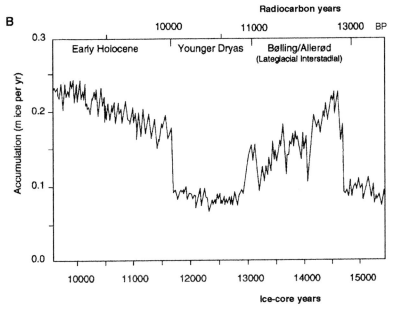

Fig. 1.2. Changing climate in Ice Age Wales: the last 250,000 years. (A): The oxygen isotope sequence is based on evidence preserved in fossil marine organisms. The ratio of Oxygen-18 to Oxygen-16 (O^{18}/O^{16}) in their shells preserves a record of past global ice-volumes from which Ice Age climates may be inferred. After Green & Walker 1991. (B): The climate of the Late Glacial 13,000–10,000 BP based on the evidence of the Greenland ice cores. Ice is laid down in annual layers and so provides a very detailed record of climatic oscillations through oxygen isotope and other analyses. After Barton 1997, 119.

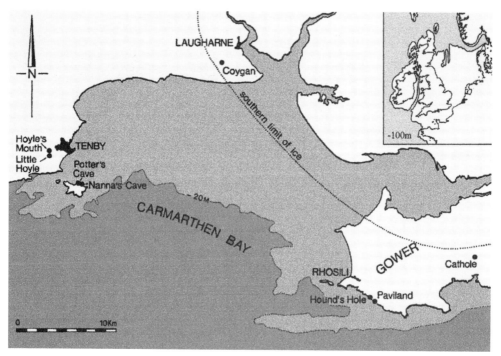

Fig. 1.3. Ice Age sea-levels. The caves of Carmarthen Bay and Gower in relation to former sea-levels and the limit of Last Glaciation ice, c. 18,000 BP. Sea-level lay at –80 metres when the 'Red Lady' was buried in Paviland Cave. During the glacial maximum, it fell to over 100 metres. (Inset): Even in the Early Mesolithic, it lay as low as –35 metres. Ice Age sea-levels were greatly lowered because so much water was locked up in glacial ice. In Scotland there were ice sheets over a mile thick. Britain became a peninsula of Europe. (By permission of the National Museum of Wales)

Classic Neanderthals were present at Coygan Cave around 50,000 years ago. Coygan Cave was primarily a hyaena den site (Aldhouse-Green *et al.* 1995) but the few artefacts present probably pre-date the phase of carnivore occupation. Coygan has become the type site for characteristic assemblages of carnivores and herbivores, of which mammoth, woolly rhinoceros, horse and spotted hyaena are especially typical (Currant & Jacobi 1997). This was an assemblage of high diversity, with an important component of large herbivores, which must have provided abundant game for the small population of Neanderthals who exploited it. The environment was one of abundant but arid grassland. The first Neanderthals to recolonise the British peninsula during the last glaciation would

(Opposite) *Fig. 1.4. Wales in the Palaeolithic period – principal sites.* Stray finds of handaxes: *A Narberth; B. Rhosili; C. Rhiwbina; D. Penylan; E. Blaenafon; F. Sudbrook; G. Sedbury Cliffs; H. Lavernock.* Palaeolithic caves and open sites: *1. Kendrick's Cave; 2. Ogof Tan-y-Bryn; 3. Cefn Cave; 4. Pontnewydd; 5. Cae Gwyn; 6. Ffynnon Beuno; 7. Lynx Cave; 8. Porth-y-Waen; 9. Breiddin; 10. Arrow Court; 11. Priory Farm Cave; 12. Hoyle's Mouth; 13. Little Hoyle; 14. Potter's Cave; 15. Nanna's Cave; 16. Ogof-yr-Ychen; 17. Coygan; 18. Worm's Head Cave; 19. Hound's Hole & Goat's Hole caves, Paviland; 20. Long Hole; 21. Cathole; 22. New Radnor; 23. Gwernvale; 24. King Arthur's Cave; 25. Ty-llwyd, Llanishen; 26. Uphill caves; 27. Gough's Cave. (By permission of the National Museum of Wales)*

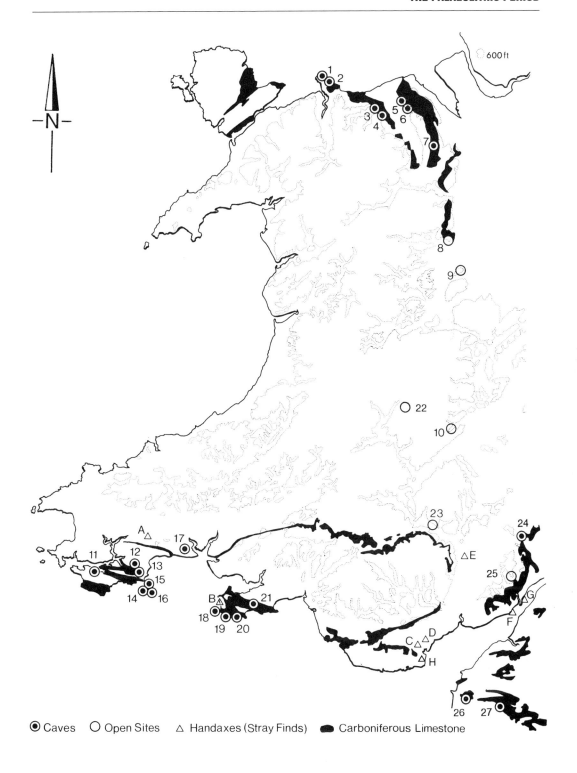

● Caves   ○ Open Sites   △ Handaxes (Stray Finds)   ● Carboniferous Limestone

apparently have come into a landscape empty of fellow humans but teeming with game. On the killing grounds of the Welsh plains life may have been easy.

The first anatomically modern humans arrived in Britain *c.* 30,000 BP and the Early Upper Palaeolithic was played out against a background of deteriorating and sharply oscillating climate. The scale of the climatic downturn is witnessed by the recovery, during excavation at Little Hoyle, Pembrokeshire, of the bones of a breeding population of Barnacle geese dated *c.* 22,800 BP. These geese now breed no nearer than eastern Greenland. Wales, like England, seems to have been largely or wholly deserted by humans during the period from *c.* 21,000 to 13,000 BP (Aldhouse-Green & Pettitt 1998) which saw the growth, spread and retreat of ice sheets; at their height these covered virtually all of Wales, from *c.* 20,000–18,000 BP, with ice at times up to 300 metres thick. The climate became complex in detail after *c.* 13,000 BP. The period from 13,000 to 11,000 BP is known as the Late Glacial or Windermere Interstadial with an initial, thirteenth millennium, phase known as the Bølling (**Fig. 1.2B**). During the middle of the thirteenth millennium, summer temperatures of 17°C were comparable with those of the present day, although the environment remained open. The later part of the Interstadial from 12,000 to 11,000 BP, also known as the Allerød, saw the expansion of birch woodland. The Windermere Interstadial was terminated by a severely cold phase called the Loch Lomond Stadial or Younger Dryas (11,000–10,000 BP). Small glaciers actively reformed in Wales in Snowdonia, on Cader Idris and on the Brecon Beacons. The environment became one of subarctic desert.

The Welsh botanical evidence for the Pleistocene has been reviewed by Caseldine (1990, 23–31) and almost all relates to the last glacial (or Devensian) cold stage. Long Hole is an important site because its pollen sequence seems to extend from perhaps 80,000 to 10,000 BP. The bulk of the evidence is focused, however, on the period known as the Late Glacial (13,000–10,000 BP). Here the open landscape of the 13th millennium BP was characterised by *Gramineae*, *Cyperaceae*, *Rumex* and *Artemisia* with a thermal peak associated with the spread of junipers around 12,500 BP. At Llanilid in South Wales the beginning of the Windermere Interstadial has been dated to *c.* 13,200 BP, with its thermal maximum at around 12,500 BP. There followed a long cooling phase with a significant environmental change marked by the development of closed birch forest from around 11,700 BP. This woodland shows an abrupt decline at around 11,400 BP, with the onset of the Loch Lomond stadial dating to *c.* 11,000 BP (Walker & Harkness 1990).

SETTLEMENT AND SUBSISTENCE

During much of the Palaeolithic occupation of Britain the sea-level was low: the Bristol Channel, Cardigan Bay and the Irish Sea were all plains, and sites now on the sea's edge – such as Paviland Cave or the caves of Caldey – would have lain many miles from their contemporary coastline (**Figs 1.3–1.4**). The Palaeolithic period in Wales (225,000–10,000 BP) lacks any sites with certain evidence of structures, or even of undisturbed hearths and living-floors. In some cases caves were selected for occupation but we cannot generally say with confidence what their precise function actually was, whether for use as dwellings or as places for storage, protection, burial or ritual. If not sites themselves, were they elements in larger encampments? Caves maintain a constant temperature all year round – about 10°C at the present day – and so are cool in summer and warm in winter. Some caves can, however, be very damp with extensive roof-dripping, but sites vary according to local ground conditions and such dripping is unlikely to have occurred under conditions of continuous permafrost. Glacial and periglacial action has probably destroyed much of the evidence of settlement during the Palaeolithic period. If we look, however, at the use of caves by Mesolithic hunters (Green 1989a) we see that cave-use was just one element of a much wider pattern of landscape exploitation. But here again we must pose a question: can we compare cave-use by modern humans with a potentially different pattern of use by Neanderthals – people, after all, of different physique, social history and, probably, communication skills, operating in a treeless landscape and competing for food with a range of large carnivores.

Open sites   Palaeolithic finds in England frequently occur in association with river gravels. Acheulian finds, principally handaxes perhaps a quarter of a million years old, were found at Sudbrook in the gravels of the Severn Estuary (Green 1989b; Wymer 1996). Also in the Bristol Channel area a flint handaxe has been found on the beach at Rhosili in Gower (Green 1981a). Another handaxe, this time of a sub-triangular form comparable with examples made by Neanderthals in Britain and believed to date to *c.* 50,000 BP, comes from Lavernock near Cardiff (Aldhouse-Green 1998a). It thus forms part of the earlier palaeolithic distribution of finds along the South Wales littoral (**Fig. 1.4**), as does the only putatively Early Upper Palaeolithic find. The latter, from Reynoldston in Gower, comprises a bifacially retouched piece susceptible of interpretation as a leaf-point. An alternative view, that the artefact may represent a Bronze Age flint dagger (Green 1984b), cannot be altogether excluded, but the fact that the artefact appears – on the basis of a colour photograph – to possess the staining characteristic of inclusion in river gravel renders such an interpretation less likely.

During the Late Upper Palaeolithic – the only part of the palaeolithic where there has not been a later substantive phase of glaciation – sites and stray finds are distributed along the northern and southern coasts of Wales and along the Welsh Marches. In other words they have a broadly lowland distribution on the margins of the Welsh massif. The principal elements in the fauna at this time were wolf, red fox, arctic fox, bear, wild cattle, elk, horse, red deer and mammoth. The latter seems to have become extinct by 12,000 BP. Reindeer reappear in the cold conditions of the Loch Lomond Stadial. If red deer followed a migratory pattern of winter/lowland and summer/upland movements, there is no palaeolithic evidence from Wales to show that the hunters exploited them in their summer pastures. However, spring and autumn migrations were especially important because of the size of the herds involved. Such migration intercept sites may include Llanishen in Monmouthshire (Green & Walker 1991, 36), Gwernvale (Healey & Green 1984), New Radnor (Aldhouse-Green 1998b) and the Breiddin (Green & Wainwright 1991). Finds are also attested from contiguous lowland areas in England, namely Arrow Court, Herefordshire (Campbell 1977) and Porth-y-Waen, Shropshire (Britnell 1984).

Cave sites   Where caves are concerned, the earlier phases are attested at only a few sites. Thus the Lower Palaeolithic is represented only by Pontnewydd, and the Middle Palaeolithic only by Coygan and Paviland. The Early Upper Palaeolithic has at least four sites – Paviland, Hoyle's Mouth, Ffynnon Beuno and Cae Gwyn – if doubtful finds from

Nottle Tor and Long Hole are excluded (David 1990, 19–22). The Late Upper Palaeolithic sees a further increase to a total of ten sites: Paviland, Cathole, Little Hoyle, Nanna's Cave, Potter's Cave, Priory Farm Cave, Kendrick's Cave, Ogof Tan-y-Bryn, Cefn and Lynx Cave. With the exception of Hoyle's Mouth, with nearly 400 finds, no other site has produced more than a couple of dozen finds. Within the Late Upper Palaeolithic there are four sites with explicit thirteenth-millennium (Creswellian) occupation (Paviland, Hoyle's Mouth, Nanna's Cave and Cathole) and four with diagnostic twelfth-millennium (Final Palaeolithic) artefacts (Paviland, Priory Farm Cave, Nanna's Cave and Potter's Cave). A bone point from Lynx Cave finds a close parallel at Coniston Dib, Yorkshire, dated to 11,210 ± 90 BP (OxA-2847) (pers. comm. R.M. Jacobi).

In August 1999 Nick Barton of Oxford Brookes University and Catherine Price of University of Wales College, Newport, conducted a new survey and excavation of Priory Farm Cave and I am indebted to Dr Barton for the following account.

> The cave provides one of the most westerly records of Lateglacial human occupation in the British Isles. In 1906–7, excavations at the entrance revealed a small assemblage of flint and chert artefacts of Final Upper Palaeolithic type including four characteristic 'penknife points'. The presence of these presumed projectile points implies that the site was used for hunting purposes although amongst the tools was also a burin, an implement typically associated with the working of bone and antler. The excavation showed that substantial stratified deposits survived outside the entrance and, from the small area examined, significant numbers of very small chips of struck flint debris were recovered. From their stratigraphic position and degree of patination, it is clear that they are of Final Upper Palaeolithic type. They also prove quite clearly that the existing collection of tools was not part of a deliberately hidden cache, as some have suggested (David 1991, 152), but was no doubt a result of *in situ* manufacturing activity. The newly examined deposits also contain rich small vertebrate faunas which will help in understanding the nature and intensity of climatic changes at the end of the last Ice Age.

The only fixed points for settlement within the succeeding millennium, 11,000–10,000 BP, are art objects from Kendrick's Cave, dated to *c.* 10,600 and 10,000 BP and discussed further below; and also a date on a cut-marked ungulate bone from Gower, radiocarbon dated to 10,625 ± 80 BP (OxA-6500). The context of the latter find was the Neolithic Parc le Breos Cwm chambered tomb, but Whittle & Wysocki (1998, 147–8, 176–7) believe that the bone probably originated in the nearby Cathole Cave. Nearby, on the Gower coast, radiocarbon dates recently obtained from Foxhole Cave (Aldhouse-Green 1997; in press) attest the existence of contemporary fauna of this period.

ARTEFACTS

Lower Palaeolithic: Pontnewydd Cave (*c.* 225,000 BP)

Certain types predominate among the range of artefacts found (**Pl. 2**). These include handaxes probably used, on the basis of microwear studies elsewhere, as multi-purpose butchery tools. Experimentation shows that these were particularly effective at skinning large game (Jones 1980). Sharp flakes, probably used for cutting up meat, were produced using Levallois prepared-core techniques, methods which permit the production of flakes, blades and triangular points, each removed with a single blow from a carefully shaped core. All types of Levallois products are present at Pontnewydd, with the points possibly used to tip spears or javelins. Finally stone scrapers were used in the cleaning and preparation of hides, perhaps for clothing, bedding or shelter-covers.

The commonest raw materials used were rhyolite, fine silicic tuff, other tuffs, feldspar-phyric lava, ignimbrite and flint. All these rocks have been moved by natural glacial or periglacial action, often from quite distant sources, in the form or boulders, cobbles or pebbles to the vicinity of the cave. There is evidence of the deliberate selection of raw materials by the Pontnewydd hominids, based on the varying sizes of the cobbles or pebbles available, as well as on the flaking characteristics of the different rocks (Green 1988). Handaxes and other heavy duty tools were preferentially made of rhyolite and feldspar-phyric lava; scrapers, by contrast, show high incidences of the use of flint and fine silicic tuff. There is some evidence that fine silicic tuff – which, of all the volcanic rocks, most closely approaches the flaking qualities of flint – was brought to the site in the form of roughed-out cores. It seems that these cores were later removed from the site after use by the tool-makers for re-use elsewhere. All other raw materials seem to have been readily available at or near the cave and to have been worked on the spot and then abandoned. This is attested partly by the character of the scrapers which generally display less refinement than the constraints of the raw material would strictly require (Newcomer 1984), evidence of resharpening being generally absent. None the less, using volcanic rocks it would have been more difficult to produce thin elegant handaxes. Likewise, greater numbers of Levallois flakes might have been produced were it not for the relatively intractable nature of much of the raw material. What is clear, however, is that the knappers were possessed of considerable skill and were clearly able to discriminate between the properties of the different rocks.

There is no evidence from earlier Palaeolithic Wales for trade or exchange, apart from fine silicic tuff at Pontnewydd, but in this case transport may have been very local since glacially derived pebbles are involved and the rock is known to occur in the pre-archaeological levels in the cave itself. This evidence for only a very local traffic in raw materials during earlier palaeolithic times is consistent with what is known from Europe, where 50 kilometres would normally be the limit of such transport (Stringer & Gamble 1993, 174).

Middle Palaeolithic: Coygan Cave (c. 50,000 BP)

The most significant finds come from Coygan Cave and comprise three triangular handaxes of a type called *bout coupé*. Such handaxes are generally recognised as belonging to a phase of the Mousterian. The name, derived from the type site of Le Moustier in France, has been widely used to describe the material equipment of Last Glaciation Neanderthals. It has long been recognised that the distinctive handaxe type may belong to a single chronological horizon. *Bout coupés* occur most commonly in southern England with a scatter in northern France. The evidence from Coygan, combined with continental dating evidence, suggests that these types should belong within a maximum range of 64,000 to 38,000 BP (Aldhouse-Green *et al.* 1995). As in the case of Pontnewydd, the Coygan handaxes are made from raw materials available locally. In addition, several discoidal cores are present at Paviland Cave, from a context likely to be no older than earlier to middle Devensian and therefore Mousterian (pers. comm. S. Swainson).

Upper Palaeolithic (30,000–10,000 BP)

We see here very significant differences in artefact types, technology and raw materials (**Fig. 1.5**). Upper Palaeolithic flint-knapping generally utilised a technology based upon the production of parallel-sided blades which served as blanks for a whole range of tool types including end-of-blade scrapers, burins and blunted-back spearheads and knives (the blunting being designed to enable insertion of the artefact into a slotted haft). Whereas there had been few significant changes in tool types over thousands of years, the Upper Palaeolithic saw myriad changes. As far as lithic technology was concerned, this multiplication of tool types was largely a consequence of the development of blades as blanks for the production of a range of implement forms. Such equilibrium shifts may seem dramatic but new ideas may stimulate complete changes in aspects of material culture and do not necessarily imply cognitive advances or population replacements (Yellen 1998, 195). Even so, for the first time in archaeology, we may see the rapid technological change with which we are so familiar today. The explanation of this technological explosion is a contentious issue but many believe that it bears witness to intellectual differences between modern humans and Neanderthals. Alternatively, and perhaps more plausibly, it may arise from a cultural shift fired by the interaction of two intelligent human species.

Upper Palaeolithic culture in its broadest sense is defined by distinctive lithic and bone/antler technologies and by its practices of art and ceremonial burial (discussed later). The key lithic types represented in Wales may best be described under the following headings:

Leaf-points (**Fig. 1.5A**)   These artefacts comprise a range of bifacially worked foliate points generally produced on blades. Their cultural context is unclear. It seems likely on the basis of continental stratigraphy and chronology that some, perhaps even all, are Mousterian and were manufactured by Neanderthals perhaps as early as 40,000 BP, but a recent review of their chronology in Britain showed that none could actually be demonstrated as certainly older than 29,000 or younger than 27,000 BP (Aldhouse-Green & Pettitt 1998). A case can also be made out, on the basis of their co-occurrence with Aurignacian material at Ffynnon Beuno and Paviland, that such leaf-points – whatever their cultural origins in Europe – became part of the equipment of Aurignacian hunters in Britain, thereby replacing the bone spearpoints which are characteristic of the continental heartland but which are conspicuous largely by their near-absence from the British peninsula, save only a sole example from Uphill in Somerset.

Aurignacian (**Fig. 1.5B–D**)   The British Aurignacian is represented at only a few sites in Britain, all clustered along the western seaboard and thereby suggesting an origin in western France rather than in the Low Countries. Kent's Cavern is the only notable site outside Wales. Paviland is by far the richest site in Britain and is used here, along with

(Opposite) *Fig. 1.5. Upper Palaeolithic artefact types in Wales and the Marches.* Artefacts: *A. leaf-point; B–C. Aurignacian busked burin and nosed scraper; D. Aurignacian end-scraper; E. Gravettian Font Robert point; F–G. Creswellian Cheddar points; H. Final Palaeolithic penknife point; I–J. Late Upper Palaeolithic burin and end-scraper; K. barbed antler point.* Findspots: *A–B. Ffynnon Beuno; C, E–J. Paviland; D. Caë Gwyn; K. Porth-y-Waen.* Source of illustrations: *A–B, E–J. National Museum of Wales; C–D. Jeff Wallis; K. after Britnell 1984.*

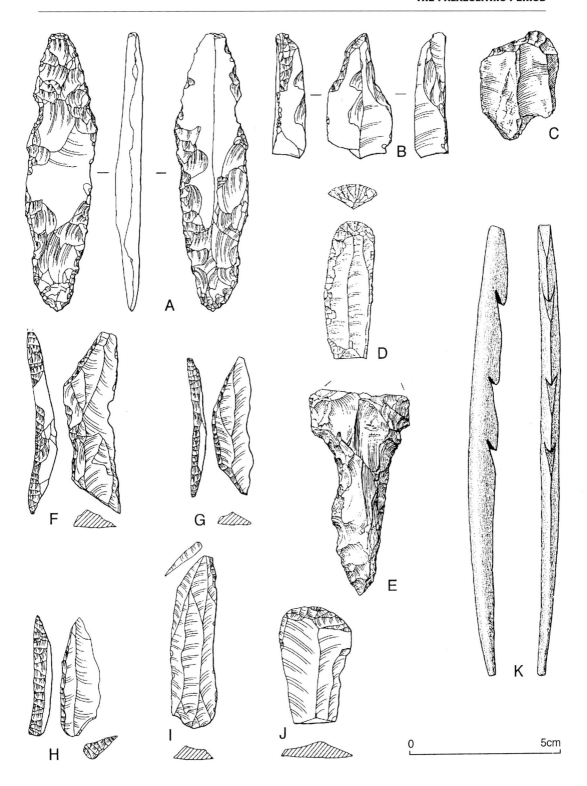

Ffynnon Beuno and Hoyle's Mouth, to illustrate the characteristic forms. These include a highly distinctive form of engraving tool, the busked burin (or *burin busqué*), whose working edge is formed by the intersection of a burin facet with a series of spalls 'stopped' by a notch. Also diagnostic are nosed and carinated scrapers. On the basis of French dating an age of 32,000–30,000 BP might have been suggested for the Aurignacian in Britain. However, the Paviland dating programme would favour an age after 30,000 in Wales, perhaps *c.* 28,500 BP (Aldhouse-Green & Pettitt 1998). This interpretation is now supported by the date of *c.* 28,000 BP for an Aurignacian lozengic bone point from Uphill, Somerset (R.M. Jacobi in Oxford Upper Palaeolithic Conference lecture, December 1999). The British occurrences may represent a relatively shortlived episode.

Gravettian (**Fig. 1.5E**)   The Gravettian is recognised in Britain by distinctive tanged artefacts, some clearly spearpoints known as *Font Robert* points and dated to *c.* 28,000–26,000 BP in France. Welsh examples are known from Paviland and, possibly, Cathole caves. The Gravettian spanned the long period of climatic downturn (*c.* 28,000–21,000 BP). Groups were probably small and highly mobile, and with far-flung social networks. The ceremonial burial of the 'Red Lady' of Paviland is now securely dated to the Gravettian, *c.* 26,000 BP, and is discussed below.

The Last Glacial Maximum   The Gravettian was succeeded by a period, 21,000–13,000 BP, which lacks any substantive evidence for human presence in Britain. The only hint of such a presence comes from Little Hoyle Cave near Tenby where an ungulate bone associated with fragmentary flint artefacts produced a radiocarbon age of 17,600 ± 200 BP (OxA-1026). This bone showed no trace of human modification and may have been residual from an older context. Even so, its location in the south-west of Wales, a region of maritime climate, where large game in the form of horse or bovid was present, is clearly a potential context also for human hunters.

Late Upper Palaeolithic (**Fig. 1.5 F–G, H–K**)   This was a complex period in terms both of climate and human activity. It is currently divided into three main groupings: Creswellian, Final Palaeolithic, and Ahrensburgian/Long Blade Industries.

The Creswellian has been dated to *c.* 12,900–12,000 BP. Whereas the richest Early Upper Palaeolithic site in Britain had been Paviland Cave, the focus moves in the Lateglacial period to Gough's Cave, Cheddar. The only relatively rich Welsh site is now Hoyle's Mouth, Pembrokeshire. The latter's assemblage serves to illustrate the main lithic types (David 1991). These include two characteristic forms of backed artefact, the trapezoidal Cheddar and angled Creswell points, end-scrapers on blades, as well as burins and piercers. Blades are typically curved in longitudinal profile with a preferred flaking direction; striking platforms were often carefully facetted and detached with an antler hammer (Barton 1999). Raw materials are generally of high quality, transported from potentially distant sources.

The Final Palaeolithic has been described by Barton & Roberts (1996). Assemblages with characteristic 'penknife points' have been dated to 12,000–11,300 BP, while dates on bone and antler points and harpoons range from 11,700–10,700 BP (Barton 1999, 18, 26) down to the onset of the coldest phase of the Younger Dryas when Britain may once again have been abandoned. Typical forms of the Final Palaeolithic include curved back points (and the variant with additional basal truncation known as the 'penknife point'), short end-scrapers, thumbnail scrapers and truncation burins. Lithic raw materials are generally of poorer quality than in the Creswellian, being derived from secondary fluviatile and other sources.

The Ahrensburgian/Long Blade Industries belong to the very end of the Younger Dryas. They are not known in Wales. Typical finds include examples of rare Ahrensburgian tanged points or large blades, typically in excess of 12 centimetres in length and sometimes with characteristic bruised edges resulting from heavy duty use (Barton 1989). Occupation using these items of material culture is attested no closer to Wales than Doniford Cliff on the Somerset coast (Barton 1999, 31). Doniford is within sight of Gower, where Foxhole Cave (excavated by the author in 1997) has yielded both early and late eleventh-millennium BP dates on fauna from the lowest level reached, suggesting that further work may be productive.

Long-distance transport develops dramatically with the arrival of anatomically modern humans in Europe. Transport distances of 120 kilometres are perfectly plausible, with some raw materials – such as flint from the Holy Cross Mountains, Poland, and fossil amber from the Black Sea – 'traded' over 400 kilometres or 700 kilometres respectively (Stringer & Gamble 1993, 208). Such traffic in raw materials was doubtless facilitated by expanded social networks, but these networks may themselves have developed as a response to the need for appropriate raw materials for the production of blade-blanks.

Whereas local rocks, generally volcanic, were used in the Lower and Middle Palaeolithic, from the Upper Palaeolithic onwards flint or chert is favoured, perhaps because – here evoking the timeless principle that 'size matters' – copious supplies of pebbles suitable for making artefacts were available in the extensive fossil and active Pleistocene shorelines exposed by the lower sea-levels of the Ice Age. In the Early Upper Palaeolithic (30,000–21,000 BP) raw materials seem to have been substantively local and were probably derived in many cases from the fossil strandlines of the Last Interglacial, or else from exposed glacial deposits of the Irish Sea drift including flint, cherts and occasional pebbles of volcanic rocks (Campbell & Bowen 1989). The 'Red Lady' burial in Paviland Cave presents comparable evidence of movement of materials, for perforated sea-shells placed with the burial must have come from the contemporary coast which then lay over 30 kilometres away, at *c.* 80 metres below modern sea-level. In the Creswellian phase of the Late Upper Palaeolithic (12,900–12,000 BP) flint was clearly imported. Indeed, given the comparability of the Hoyle's Mouth Upper Palaeolithic industry to that at Gough's Cave, Cheddar (David 1991, 149), it is possible that the flint component of the Hoyle's Mouth material derived from the same (probably Wiltshire) source. In the Final Upper Palaeolithic, local materials again seem to have been favoured, perhaps a consequence of the increasingly wooded environment making both raw material sources less visible and long-distance contacts harder to maintain.

RITUAL AND DEATH

It is generally accepted that explicit evidence for some kind of religious belief is not attested before the earliest deliberate burials occur, and perhaps not even then. We can only identify religious belief archaeologically where that belief has either resulted in direct or indirect evidence of ritual practice. It need not follow, however, that absence of such evidence implies absence of belief. Our own concepts of religion are circumscribed by our own experience. A simple view (Armstrong 1993) sees religion as being, in essence, a perception of life as mysterious and sacred. Such a view has enabled people to show compassion for each other, with caring attested archaeologically, for example, through the evidence of last glaciation Neanderthals who, having suffered injury in life, have clearly been sustained by the help of their comrades (Trinkaus 1983, 422–3). There are very few dated palaeolithic burials, deposits or accumulations from Wales but all are of some importance.

Pontnewydd Cave

Around twenty Pleistocene human finds have been recovered representing at least three (two adults and one child) and perhaps as many as six separate individuals. The remains were found near the base of the Lower Breccia debris flow on the south side of the East Passage and within the South-East Fissure. The bones are locally interstratified with a fauna, including remains of hibernating bears, which had accumulated *within* the cave (pers. comm. Andrew Currant). However, the evidence does not shed any light on the nature of the original context and mode of deposition, for the bones give no indication as to the manner of death of the hominids involved. Thus, cut-marks, suggestive perhaps of cannibalism or defleshing rites, are absent. The bones are not meat-bearing and so may have been present through discard by carnivores, although purely taphonomic factors – the type of bones surviving being the most durable – could also be invoked. The key factor is that the remains were localised, with one exception, to a small part of the cave and so may represent a single accumulation, later dispersed. The occurrence of human remains is so rare at this period that chance accumulation does not provide a reasonable explanation. It is likely, therefore, that we are dealing with the disposal of a group of, perhaps related, individuals over a relatively short space of time. Such a disposal could be *formal*, in the case of either deliberate burial or disposal after ritual practices, or *informal* if the bodies were simply discarded in a convenient place. Such disposals could have occurred simultaneously after a catastrophic event, whether natural or humanly caused, such as warfare; or successively in the case either of burials spread over some years; or as a carnivore accumulation, whether or not the carnivores were animal or human.

Paviland

The so-called 'Red Lady' of Paviland (**Pl. 3**) was excavated in January 1823 by Dean Buckland and marks the earliest discovery of a fossil human known to science (1823, 88–9). The skeleton is now known to be that of a male aged about 25, buried in an extended position. The bones were stained with red ochre and Buckland deduced that the body had been 'entirely surrounded or covered at the time of its interment with this substance'. Close to the thigh were two handfuls of the shells of *Nerita littoralis* deliberately pierced for suspension. By the ribs were forty to fifty fragments of small cylindrical ivory rods of a kind generally interpreted as blanks for beads, although a ritual function for such wands cannot be excluded. Also of ivory were fragments of one or (probably) two bracelets.

Paviland is the richest Early Upper Palaeolithic site in the British Isles and the 'Red Lady' is Britain's only ceremonial burial of that age. Excavations in the nineteenth and early twentieth centuries, combined with the action of the sea, removed virtually all of the cave's sedimentary sequence but did not result in a detailed identification and record of the cave's deposits. As part of a new definitive study of the site and its finds, over forty samples have now been radiocarbon dated (Aldhouse-Green & Pettitt 1998). A total of nine dates relate directly to human presence, compared with only two such dates from all other British Early Upper Palaeolithic sites. Thus Paviland currently holds the key to the understanding of the chronology of human activity and settlement during this period in Britain as a whole.

The results present a narrative of human presence in the British Early Upper Palaeolithic, a narrative with a chronological and episodic structure. The story begins with a perhaps limited Mousterian presence and leaf point phase recognisable archaeologically but not through dated samples. The main phase of settlement follows and can be identified as Aurignacian but the inference of the samples dated is that it is late by comparison with the continental sequence, falling as late as c. 28,500 BP, perhaps because of long-lived Mousterian settlement on the British peninsula or because of the lack of a demographic imperative to continued Aurignacian expansion. The age of the ceremonial burial of the so-called 'Red Lady' has now been conclusively resolved. The skeleton has been redated to 25,840 ± 280 BP (OxA-8025), a result wholly consistent with an earlier determination of 26,350 ± 550 BP (OxA-1815). Later activity is attested by ivory-working as late as 21,000 BP. Falling between these ages, at c. 23,000 BP, is a group – perhaps once a deposit – of bone spatulae (**Fig. 1.6C**) of a type seemingly unknown in western Europe but with generic parallels as far afield as the Eastern Gravettian. The Late Upper Palaeolithic period, following the glacial maximum, is attested by artefacts belonging to the period 12,900–11,000 but the absence of radiocarbon dates, supported by the small number of finds, suggests that occupation at this period was sparse. The reason for this probably lay in the simple fact that by this time the cave was largely filled up with scree and debris (Aldhouse-Green 1997) and little living space remained.

As recently as 1986 it was suggested that the British Early Upper Palaeolithic came to an end at around 27,000 BP. The Paviland dating programme now demonstrates that humans were present in Britain, albeit perhaps episodically, right down to the edge of the last glacial maximum. It is argued here that the unusual and special nature of the evidence – the ceremonial burial, the unique spatulae, the ivory objects, and the continuation of visits to the site during a period of extreme climatic downturn (at a period when virtually no other evidence is known of human presence in Britain) – suggests that the cave, or perhaps the hill containing it, may have been of ancestral or religious significance and so perhaps an object of pilgrimage. Certainly the Gower plateau must have been visible for some distance from the Bristol Channel plain, as it is now from the sea. The Paviland stretch of the Gower plateau would have formed the southernmost part of the Welsh upland massif and would therefore have been the first place to be seen and reached by travellers from the territories to the south. Certainly when it is viewed from the modern sea during a summer sunset, with the sky ablaze with red, the effect is dramatic.

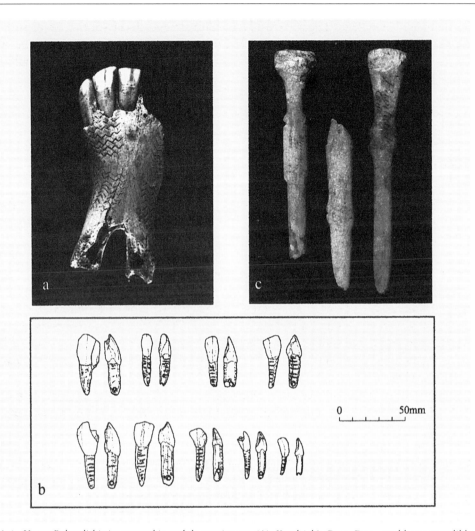

Fig. 1.6. *Upper Palaeolithic iconographic and decorative art. (A): Kendrick's Cave. Decorated horse mandible. By permission of the Trustees of the British Museum. (B): Kendrick's Cave. Decorated animal teeth – probably wild cattle, cervid and red deer. By permission of the National Museum of Wales. (C): The Paviland 'spatulae'. If parallels in eastern Europe and Russia are valid, these spatulae may be interpreted as schematic female figurines with the head symbolised by the articular end of the bone, the breasts/buttocks by the medial swelling, and perhaps a belt by the opposed notches which may once have held a decorative binding (Aldhouse-Green & Pettitt 1998). (By permission of the National Museum of Wales)*

The burial represents a single event in the history of this cave, but such an event is rare even on a European scale. The European evidence has been reviewed as a whole by Binant (1991a; 1991b) and twenty-seven Upper Palaeolithic burials have been listed as having colorant present in the grave. Study of a well-excavated multiple Upper Palaeolithic burial at Dolní Vestoniče in Moravia shows clearly that here the ochre was carefully placed and cannot represent secondary redisposition (Jelinek 1992, 212–13). In addition we may note that the child burial from Lagar Vehlo was ochre-stained. Even so, the Paviland burial lacks the wealth of adornment identified at Sunghir in Russia or the Grotta delle Arene Candide in Italy (Aldhouse-Green 1998a). The 'Red Lady' may reflect continental burial practice for persons of special status but the ritual was arguably impoverished, perhaps because the mourners were far from their normal territories on a seasonal hunting expedition and/or visiting a distant, perhaps ancestral, cave imbued with sanctity from a divine revelation – for the secular and the sacred were but one in the ancient world.

Kendrick's Cave, Great Orme, Llandudno

This site has produced the only examples of portable Late Upper Palaeolithic art from Wales (**Fig. 1.6A–B**). One item, a horse jawbone decorated with incised zig-zag lines has been radiocarbon dated to 10,000 ± 200 BP (OxA-111) and so lies at the very interface of the Palaeolithic and Mesolithic. From the same site came nine perforated teeth, probably of wild cattle and red deer, with incised decoration on the roots. A date on one of these teeth of 10,580 ± 100 BP (OxA-4573) is not far removed from the determination on the decorated horse jaw and renders their original association more plausible. It had been suggested that these finds were grave-goods associated with one or more, or even all, of four human skeletons found at the time (Sieveking 1971). Other finds from the site include four engraved and ochre-stained tallies. Such spaced groups of incisions on bone or ivory have been interpreted as simple tallies, lunar calendars or gaming pieces and comparable examples are known at Gough's Cave, Cheddar.

Kendrick's Cave is the subject of current research by Jill Cook and Roger Jacobi of the British Museum, and I am indebted to them for the following account which puts this material into context.

Kendrick's Cave was named after Thomas Kendrick who dug out most of the deposit in AD 1880. He encountered a limestone breccia 1.5–2.0 metres in thickness, sealed by stalagmite, and found, near the base of the breccia, bones of at least four human individuals, two perforated bear canines and a decorated horse mandible. In subsequent excavations, flint artefacts and decorated and perforated cervid teeth were recovered. Below this, in cave-earth up to one metre thick, were bovid bones. A decorated and perforated badger canine was found by Melvyn Davies in 1977.

Recent research, including radiocarbon date estimates, suggests that there were several phases of human activity in and around the site. The earliest of these took place during the Late Upper Palaeolithic around 12,000 and 10,000 BP. Human burials date to the former and the decorated horse mandible and badger tooth to the latter. Unlike some of the human bone from Late Upper Palaeolithic contexts at Gough's Cave, there is no evidence for intentional dismemberment of the corpses or deliberate bone breakage. A bovid tibia is slightly older than any of the human bone and a flint blade has a striking platform of a form known in Creswellian assemblages.

Metacarpals of roe deer coloured with red ochre and marked with grouped incisions have been associated with the Kendrick's Cave finds, although there is no evidence that they came from the cave itself. A radiocarbon estimate for one of these is close to that of the Upper Palaeolithic burials.

This extraordinary group of finds is without parallel in north-west Europe. Particularly surprising is evidence for human activity precisely at the Pleistocene/Holocene boundary so far away from evidence of coeval settlement.

SOCIAL STRUCTURE AND NETWORKS

There is little that can be said definitively on the question of social structure. Population would have been very low with, for example, perhaps at most one or two thousand Palaeolithic hunters in Wales (Gamble *et al.* 1999). Group size is likely to have been small and based on the extended family or perhaps several families grouped together. Although settlement is attested by stray finds, not a single actual house-site can be identified in Wales throughout this long period and the population seems likely to have been dispersed and highly mobile. Evidence of status is rarely seen but is clearly attested in the Upper Palaeolithic at Paviland and Kendrick's Cave.

The few Lower and Middle Palaeolithic sites present no evidence for expanded social networks. I have suggested elsewhere (Green 1981b) that the size of the surviving cave-entrance at Pontnewydd might suggest occupation by a group of half a dozen persons at most, if occupation were actually restricted to the cave itself – an inherently unlikely and ultimately untestable assumption. The Welsh Aurignacian – and there is little more than the Welsh Aurignacian in Britain as a whole – is seen at Paviland (principally), but also at Ffynnon Beuno and Hoyle's Mouth. The industry was clearly made by a group exploiting mostly local raw materials (Campbell 1977). The Aurignacian thus presents the picture of a group, or groups, resident for some time in Wales. By contrast the succeeding Gravettian seems to be attested in Britain by little more than individual finds – as at Paviland and Cathole in Wales – and, of course, by the isolated but dramatic event of the interment of the 'Red Lady'. Even here, the ochre and other pigments present – if all are truly coeval with the burial – are local, being derived from no further than the Vale of Glamorgan (Tim Young *in litt.*). Perhaps the nature of their presence was no more than task-specific expeditions, whether sacred or profane. Perhaps, however, a shift in religious thinking had taken place and caves had become places that were largely avoided, as in the case of post-Pleistocene Australian Aborigines (Spate 1997). In these circumstances, given the rarity of open sites and the lack of opportunities afforded by them for the build-up of thick accumulations of deposits, a Gravettian presence would inevitably be much less visible.

Britain was recolonised after the Last Glacial Maximum some time at or after 12,900 BP. Sites in Wales, both north and south, are more numerous and settlement along the Welsh Marches is attested by a scatter of stray finds (**Fig. 1.4**). In the same area a barbed antler spearpoint (**Fig. 1.5K**) from Porth-y-Waen, Shropshire, dated to 11,390 ± 120 BP (OxA-1946) represents a casual hunting loss (Britnell 1984). The Creswellian phase is characterised by exchange networks or by 'embedded procurement' (the collection of raw materials in the natural course of seasonal movements) which provided high-quality flint as raw material for artefacts. In the succeeding Final Palaeolithic of the twelfth millennium BP, such materials seemed to have become less available and the impression is one of smaller scale and more localised communities. During the cold Younger Dryas phase of the eleventh millennium BP, Wales seems to have been largely abandoned with a human presence attested only at Kendrick's Cave and Parc Cwm, Gower.

PART II: THE MESOLITHIC PERIOD

INTRODUCTION

As we have seen, the evidence for human settlement in Wales during the final, Younger Dryas, phase of the Last Glacial is scanty. The radiocarbon dates of the Kendrick's Cave decorated teeth and horse mandible are divergent, but it may be that the teeth were 'heirlooms' when they were deposited in around 10,000 BP. It is now known (Lewis 1991; Barton 1999) that forms of microlith – the hallmark of the Mesolithic – are found in association with the late eleventh millennium Long Blade/Ahrensburgian industries which marked the inception of the resettlement of Britain following the end of the coldest phase of the Younger Dryas. It may be, therefore, that this resettlement is the event which truly marks the initiation of the period of largely postglacial activity characterised as the Mesolithic.

The main events of the Mesolithic were its progressive afforestation; a change from broad blade to narrow blade microlith forms at around 8,700 BP, the latter event marking the boundary between the Early and Late Mesolithic; a progressive rise in sea-level leading to the drowning of the English Channel and the consequential insulation of Britain, c. 8,500 BP, with all the concomitant social implications arising from this loss of land; and finally, for almost the first time in history, growing evidence for the human management of the landscape itself.

In England, the earliest sites conventionally termed Mesolithic – for example Thatcham and Star Carr – have produced radiocarbon dates close to 9,700 BP. In Wales the earliest dating comes from the Nab Head, Pembrokeshire, but lies closer to 9,200 BP, with ages of 9,210 ± 80 BP (OxA-1495) and 9,110 ± 80 BP (OxA-1496). There seems no reason why Wales should have remained an 'empty quarter' of the British Isles for 500 radiocarbon years and it may be just a matter of time before earlier sites are found. None the less dates for other 'early' material are all relatively late. David (1990, 104) has discounted the very late dates for Trwyn Du (8,640 ± 150 BP (Q-1385) and 8,590 ± 90 BP (HAR-1194)) and Rhuddlan. However, Berridge (in Quinnell & Blockley 1994, 127), while concurring in the rejection of the Trwyn Du dates, has argued cogently that a determination of 8,739 ± 86 BP (BM-691) from Rhuddlan, on a discrete sample of carbonised hazelnut shells securely stratified within the fill of pit J104, is not in doubt and, indeed, 'may be one of the most secure from any Mesolithic site in Wales'. Radiocarbon dates from Daylight Rock likewise fall neatly into this 9,200–8,700 BP time range with results of 9,040 ± 90 BP (OxA-2245), 9,030 ± 80 BP (OxA-2246) and 8,850 ± 80 BP (OxA-2247).

The earliest radiocarbon determinations from Wales for the appearance of Late Mesolithic forms come from Prestatyn, Flintshire (Clark 1938; 1939). Here, a Late Mesolithic industry produced dates of 8,700 ± 100 BP (OxA-2268) and 8,730 ± 90 BP (OxA-2269), each on a single hazelnut shell (David 1990, 179). Recently, a secure Late Mesolithic context at Madawg rock shelter in the Wye Valley produced an age of 8,710 ± 70 BP (OxA-6081) on a charred sloe stone stratified at the same level as a narrow blade, scalene triangle microlith (Barton *et al.* 1997).

CLIMATE AND ENVIRONMENT

It is interesting that, unlike during the last interglacial 125,000 years ago, hunters were present in the increasingly forested conditions of the present Flandrian Interglacial which began 10,000 years ago. Two, perhaps convergent, factors may account for a human presence in Britain during the Mesolithic: first, and perhaps most significantly, the world population was larger than ever before and so could not easily retreat as in previous periods to more favoured areas; secondly, for the first time the hunters and gatherers were modern humans like ourselves, and their communication skills, level of technology, adaptability and their use of fire for clearing vegetation are probably relevant to their ability to live in forested landscapes. The distribution map of sites (**Fig. 1.7**) suggests, however, that the more open areas – coasts and rivers – were favoured, and in this the hunter-gatherer preference for open areas mirrors the apparent Pleistocene situation.

The rising and fluctuating sea-levels of the Mesolithic are of particular relevance for human settlement in the early Holocene and will be considered below in the context of the archaeology. But sea-level was only one of the variables involved, for vegetation and temperature must also be considered. During the mid-eleventh millennium BP summer temperatures were as low as 10°C (Atkinson *et al.* 1987). The transition from the Pleistocene to the Holocene fell around 10,000 BP and within as little as twenty years temperatures may have risen to present-day levels (Alley *et al.* 1993). The spread of juniper followed by birch generally characterises the earliest (Pre-Boreal) phase of the Holocene. At Llangorse Lake this transition is dated to 9,920 ± 65 BP (SRR-3463) and is marked by the development of birch woodland (Walker *et al.* 1993). The Mesolithic period is often characterised in vegetational terms by pollen zones (**Table I**).

Approximate dates	Pollen zone	Vegetation	Climate
10,000–9,300 BP	IV. Pre-Boreal	birch, juniper, pine	rapid warming
9,300–8200 BP	V. Early Boreal	hazel, birch, pine	warming
8,200–7,500 BP	VI. Late Boreal	oak, elm	warm and dry
7,500–4,500 BP	VII. Atlantic	oak, elm, lime, ash, alder	warm and wet

Table I. Vegetational changes during the Mesolithic period. Based on Parker & Chambers (1997).

The spread of hazel by 9,300 BP even to upland habitats in Wales is important, for the first occupation of Waun Fignen Felen in upland south Wales coincides with the first appearance of hazel there (Barton *et al.* 1995, 101). Hazel shows a consistent presence on Welsh and British Mesolithic sites in the form of hazelnut shells which have clearly been deliberately burnt to improve their eating qualities, and in some cases have been stored in pits in considerable quantity as at Staosnaig in the southern Hebrides (Mithen & Lake 1996, 138–42). From Prestatyn, too, there is a record of the discovery of 'large numbers of fragments of hazelnut shells, clearly broken by human agency' (Clark 1939). A carbonised hazelnut shell is known from a late phase of occupation at the site of Goldcliff in the Severn Estuary where it has been dated to 5,415 ± 75 BP (OxA-6682). The occupation at Waun Fignen Felen falls into the period of maximum upland summer warmth from

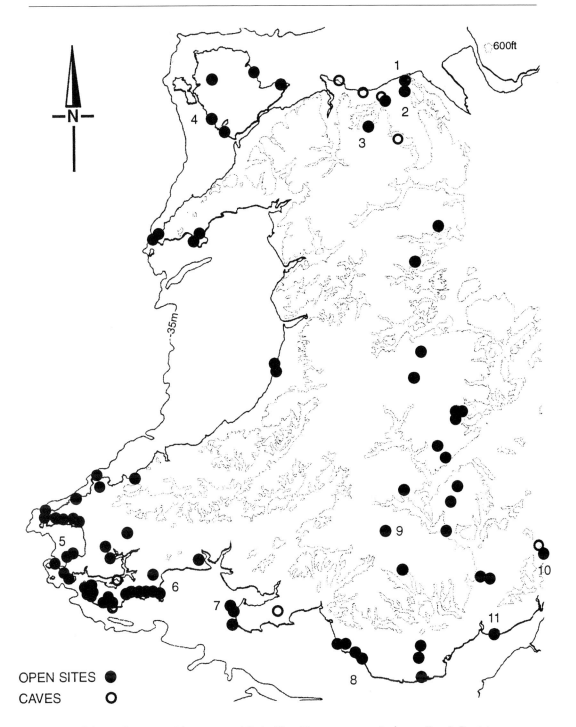

Fig. 1.7. Mesolithic settlement in Wales – sites and finds. The –35 metre contour is shown. Key: 1. Prestatyn;
2. Rhuddlan; 3. Brenig; 4. Trwyn Du; 5. Nab Head; 6. Daylight Rock; 7. Burry Holms; 8. Ogmore; 9. Waun Fignen
Felen; 10. Madawg Rockshelter; 11. Goldcliff. (By permission of the National Museum of Wales)

9,000–8,000 BP (Simmons 1996, 16–17). It has been suggested that the deliberate use of fire to manage the landscape for hunting fostered the spread of hazel – a relatively fire-resistant species – although it may equally be argued that fires may have developed spontaneously more readily in the warmer conditions of the early Holocene (Parker & Chambers 1997, 39). Whilst there are known Mesolithic sites where human presence is not attested by charcoal or pollen evidence preserved in local sedimentary sequences (Caseldine 1990, 36–7), evidence from Goldcliff would lend support to a scenario of the deliberate use of fire in the British later Mesolithic (Bell *et al.* 1999, 60).

From 8,500 BP a mixed oak forest 'wildwood' vegetation of oak, elm, lime, ash and alder progressively became established. Between 8,800 and 4,500 BP, temperatures actually rose even higher than at the present day, to 17 or 18°C, during the favourable conditions of the Postglacial Hypsithermal or climatic optimum (Simmons 1996, 10). The palaeobotanical evidence for the environment of Wales during the Mesolithic has been fully reviewed by Caseldine (1990, 33–42).

Woodland had blanketed Britain as a whole to heights in excess of 300 metres above modern sea-level by the 8th millennium BP. A height of 530 metres is attested at Waun Fignen Felen with a fully treeless landscape only cutting in, in southern Wales, above 700 metres. Between 9,000 and 7,000 BP as much as 80 per cent of the south Wales landscape was blanketed with trees (Simmons 1996, 17–19). There would, therefore, have been comparatively little open ground. It is well known that red deer and wild cattle prefer a mixture of grassland and open woodland and it is therefore in more open conditions that herds of such herbivores would have been found by Mesolithic hunters. These conditions would have obtained in the coastal regions – where the strandlines would also have offered an attractive and seemingly inexhaustible supply of raw materials for stone tools – and in the river valleys, where beavers may have had a part to play in opening up the vegetation (Simmons 1996, 130–1).

SETTLEMENT AND SUBSISTENCE

The Postglacial rise in sea-level, following the end of the Ice Age 10,000 years ago, took place globally primarily as a consequence of melting glacial ice (eustatic rise), and led to the successive formation and submergence of the landscapes now exposed or buried by the vicissitudes of coastal erosion and deposition. Around 9,100 BP, shortly after the inception of the Mesolithic in Wales, sea-level (**Fig. 1.7**) may have lain at around –35 metres (Heyworth & Kidson 1982). By around 8,500 BP the Straits of Dover had been breached, the North Sea Plain flooded and Britain had become an island (Preece 1995). Finally, by 7,000 BP or so the coastline had stabilised to roughly where it is now, although continuing episodes of transgression, regression and human reclamation create a complex picture.

We cannot underestimate the potential of the coastal environment for Mesolithic settlement. No coastal Mesolithic shellfish middens are known in Wales, perhaps because the Mesolithic shorelines are now largely lost to sea-level rise or marine erosion, apart from a possible deposit within Nanna's Cave on Caldey and at the open site of Abersoch, Lleyn (Caseldine 1990, 41). The food value of such accumulations needs to be understood: 150,000 cockles are equivalent in calorific value to a single carcass of red deer. Accordingly shellfish are likely to have formed only a seasonal element in a varied diet. None the less marine resources as a whole, perhaps especially fish whose exploitation is directly attested at Goldcliff, were clearly important, as analysis of stable isotope ratios of $\alpha^{13}C$ and $\alpha^{15}N$ indicate. Evidence of diet is preserved in human bone and the relevant ratios are now routinely measured when radiocarbon dating is undertaken. Determinations demonstrating an important marine component in the diet within the time range *c.* 8,600–7,800 BP have so far been made on Mesolithic human remains from Potter's Cave, Daylight Rock and Ogof-yr-Ychen, all on Caldey (Schulting pers. comm; 1998; Schulting & Richards in press). A slightly later measurement from Pontnewydd Cave of 7,420 ± 90 BP (OxA-5819) has yielded a result indicative of a terrestrial diet (Aldhouse-Green *et al.* 1996). Again, and geographically more relevant, dating of Postglacial human teeth/bones at Foxhole in Gower has yielded a later Mesolithic result of 6,785 ± 50 BP (OxA-8316) with ^{13}C and ^{15}N ratios (respectively –20.0 and 11.3) clearly indicative of a meat-eating terrestrial diet; in this respect, these results are comparable with those from the Neolithic burials from Parc le Breos Cwm (Richards 1998) and from Foxhole and Hoyle's Mouth (Aldhouse-Green in press). Clearly it would be unwise to draw conclusions from only two later Mesolithic results but the Foxhole measurement speaks, at the very least, of greater variation in diet in Gower – perhaps precipitated by a combination of the drowning of the former coastal plain below the Gower cliffs and a more aggressive territoriality, engendered by the same process, which further restricted access to the coast. Such territoriality is likely to have been a product of the development of communities increasingly defensive of land and resources, a demographic process perhaps driven in part by the displacement from 7,000 BP of communities from southern England to Wales as a consequence of the spread of lime forests (Jacobi 1987, 165–6). Lime seems to have become established in the lowlands of eastern Wales by 6,000 BP, but did not achieve corresponding densities in western Wales (Caseldine 1990, 34).

The grazing offered by the coastal peat fens and saltmarshes accommodated abundant wild cattle and deer, attested by hoof-prints and actual remains. Apart from the special wetland preservation conditions provided by such coastal deposits, faunal remains are also preserved in the calcareous conditions provided by limestone caves. Otherwise, sadly, such remains are not generally preserved in Welsh archaeological sites. We may note red deer, wild pig, aurochs (wild cattle), brown bear, beaver, and wild cat or marten from King Arthur's Cave in the Wye Valley (Taylor 1927); wood-mouse and bank vole from the nearby Madawg rock shelter, consistent with charcoal evidence for deciduous woodland (Barton *et al.* 1997, 73); aurochs, wild pig, fox, cervid and dog at Potter's Cave, Caldey (Lacaille & Grimes 1955); red and roe deer, fox, wolf, bear and several species of bird, but from a less than secure context, at Ogof Garreg Hir, Pembrokeshire (Davies 1989, 81); and roe deer and red fox from Cathole, Gower (Campbell 1977, vol. II, 73–4, layers C–D). Securely stratified material has been recovered from Goldcliff in the Severn Estuary: there, mammals include red deer, roe deer, wild pig, wolf and otter, with aurochs and red deer hoof-prints also attested; coot and possibly mallard are the bird species represented; and fish include principally eel and goby, with smelt, three-spined stickleback and flatfish also present (Bell *et al.* 1999). Probable cervid hoof-prints – as also those of wading birds – are known from Uskmouth (Aldhouse-Green *et al.* 1992, 16).

In coastal sites plant resources – whether in the form of timber for building, withies for basketry or peat for fuel – are likely to have been important. The materials available would also have included abundant reeds for thatching. Seas and rivers offered rich resources (David 1990, 279–87). Sea-fishing was best in spring/early summer when many species were close to shore. Seals were most vulnerable in September/October when the females were shorebound with their pups. Cockles, mussels and oysters, too, are likely to have offered a rich harvest. On the rivers, salmon and eels would have presented a seasonally important resource. The potential contibution of vegetable foods to the hunter-gatherer diet must not be understated (Clarke 1976), but there is little direct evidence apart from carbonised hazelnut shells which – if eaten fresh – may suggest exploitation of hazel in the months of August or September; alternatively, the nuts might have been charred and stored or made into a paste for future consumption. The potential scale of the harvest was enormous. It is necessary to set this against a possible population range of 6,000–27,000 people in Britain as a whole, or perhaps only some 400–1,800 people for the whole of Wales, an area of 20,763 km² with likely population densities of between 0.02 and 0.09 persons per km² (Gamble *et al.* 1999, 3). Locally, of course, densities would have varied, with much higher figures possible in estuarine situations, perhaps of the order of 3 to 10 persons per square kilometre. These very small human population levels compare with that of other carnivores (fewer than 8,000 each of wolf and lynx for Britain as a whole) but may be contrasted with the likely numbers of herbivores with as many as 1,500,000 red deer, 1,000,000 roe deer, 1,350,000 wild pig and 100,000 aurochs present (Yalden 1999, 74).

Much of the focus of recent Mesolithic studies – following Grahame Clark's work at Star Carr – has been to seek to interpret the upland and lowland patterning of Mesolithic sites as reflecting seasonal movements in the hunting of red deer (Clark 1972). In Wales, too, the evidence of beach pebbles used as raw material for artefacts has been interpreted as indicating movements between upland and coast as, for example, in the case of the Glamorgan uplands and a coastal site like Ogmore in the Vale of Glamorgan (Jacobi 1980, 195). Theories of large-scale seasonal migrations by red deer in the Mesolithic are now largely discounted in the case of woodland or low-relief environments, but significant movements are likely to have occurred in Wales where the altitudinal variations are extreme (Legge & Rowley-Conwy 1988, 38).

Such contrasting upland and coastal patterns would be especially visible in the Later Mesolithic. Before that, sea-level was still relatively low and sites which now appear coastal actually lay inland. In fact these sites would have lain on the often low hills edging former coastal plains whose rich resources could have been exploited by the hunters and gatherers. Moreover, many sites located actually on those plains must now lie beneath the seas surrounding the Welsh coasts. Marine erosion, too, had yet to cut into the Last Glaciation screes and hillslope deposits which had become banked up against ancient cliffs dating back to the high sea-levels of the Last Interglacial 125,000 years ago. For example, a site like the Nab Head (**Pl. 4**) in Pembrokeshire, now on a headland surrounded by sheer cliffs, probably lay – at the time of its occupation – on a hill with gently sloping sides and, therefore, with easy access to a coastal plain perhaps 6 kilometres in width (David 1990, 170–1).

Coastal peat beds in Wales – reflecting temporary periods of marine retreat (regression) – generally date from around the later Mesolithic or younger and follow the long period of postglacial rise in sea-level. Older peat deposits are known but are often to be found only in sub-marine contexts because of the rapid inland movement of the shores of the Irish Sea, Cardigan Bay, the Bristol Channel and the Severn Vale. Accordingly, we would expect the bulk of the evidence from the modern inter-tidal zone to be generally of that age or younger. We see direct evidence of coastal exploitation at Uskmouth in Gwent, dated to the seventh millennium BP, where footprint trails (**Fig. 1.8**) made by four humans – three adults and a child – are contiguous with areas of animal prints among which those of cloven-hooved animals, probably deer, are very frequent (Aldhouse-Green *et al.* 1992, 16). Uskmouth has also yielded a perforated red deer antler mattock comparable in type to one found in coastal deposits at Splash Point, Rhyl, dated respectively to 6,180 ± 80 BP (OxA-4574) and 6,560 ± 80 BP (OxA-1009) (Aldhouse-Green & Housley 1993). These are the

only two such finds from the whole of Wales and their contexts of discovery suggest their possible use for digging, perhaps for shellfish, in soft coastal sediments.

The results of Martin Bell's excavations at Goldcliff are of great importance here for they cast light both on the nature of Mesolithic settlement and its seasonal dimension (Bell *et al.* 1999). The settlement areas identified are located on the once dryland margins of the perimeter of Goldcliff Island, originally several times larger than the present peninsula. This is not a single site but, rather, a series of 'overlapping activity zones' formed as a result of cyclic reoccupation of the edges of an island, fringed with dense reed swamp, whose interior seems to have comprised deciduous oak woodland. No house-sites were found, nor constructed hearths, and the artefactual assemblage retrieved was limited in its typological range. The one posthole located was tentatively identified as part of a drying frame for the smoking of fish. The size evidence presented by the bones of eels and smelt is suggestive of occupation in the winter/spring, an interpretation

Fig. 1.8. Uskmouth: Mesolithic footprint trail. The prints are those of an adult, probably male, about 1.70 metres in height, and with size 8 feet, walking barefoot along the foreshore. He was moving slowly, at about 3–4 kilometres per hour, probably because of the treacherous conditions underfoot (Day in Aldhouse-Green et al. 1992, 36). (Photograph by courtesy of Derek Upton)

supported by the seasonal data presented by the remains of wild pig. Study of bone modification shows that red deer, wild pig, roe deer and otter bones all had humanly made cut-marks consistent with filleting. A large number of the fish bones had been burnt, presumably on Mesolithic barbecues, and burning was observed on bird bones also.

The site had been buried first by estuarine clay and, later, by peat. Widespread occurrences of charcoal at a consistent horizon in the peat, extending for 800 metres around the periphery of the island, may reflect the deliberate burning of vegetation to open up the environment for grazing animals which were then targeted by the hunters. The main phase of occupation at the site is radiocarbon-dated to between *c.* 6,760 ± 80 BP (date on a cut-marked deer bone) and 6,420 ± 80 BP (date on charcoal). The occupation took place during a phase of marine regression when peat was formed, although human footprints preserved in the sediments overlying and underlying the peat, attest exploitation of the environment at a time when it consisted of saltmarsh. In the centuries following the occupation, the site was inundated by marine transgression and later, by 5,920 ± 80 BP, bog began to form. These events marked the end of the site as an area of significant Mesolithic activity.

As we have seen, the distribution of sites overall (**Fig. 1.7**) shows a marked lowland focus. Important earlier sites (Rhuddlan, Trwyn Du, Aberystwyth, the Nab Head, Daylight Rock and Burry Holms) all fall into this category. Waun Fignen Felen (Barton *et al.* 1995), with early and late Mesolithic phases, is exceptional in its upland location. In the later Mesolithic the lowland coastal focus remains but important upland sites now occur, for example at Brenig in the heart of the Hiraethog moorland of Denbighshire (Lynch 1993) and on the Glamorgan uplands (Stanton 1984a). On the basis of fieldwork in the Black Mountains of south Wales, Tilley (1994, 111–17) has defined a number of situations in which sites occur: these include sites near former small lakes, on river terraces, with views across valleys, and near passes at heads of valleys.

Mellars (1976a) has identified three categories of site, based on the percentages of tools present – the latter defined as microliths, scrapers, denticulates and tranchet adzes/axes:

- 88–97 per cent of tools are microliths. Generally small specialist sites, chiefly hunting/kill sites, on high moorland.
- 30–60 per cent of tools are microliths; typically 25–50 per cent are scrapers; axes and denticulates are present. Multi-purpose sites generally on lower ground.
- High percentage of scrapers. Specialist sites concerned with hide-processing.

In Wales Mesolithic sites generally fall into the categories of task sites – generally kill sites or lithic exploitation sites. Of these types of site, the lithic exploitation sites represent an addition to Mellars's list. Here, David's study (1990, 243–7) of the Mesolithic of south-western Wales has demonstrated that many of the extensive coastal scatters probably represent raw material exploitation. Such sites are characterised by extensive testing and knapping of small pebbles of flint, chert and occasionally rhyolite, derived fom the local beaches. Sites are generally close to the modern coast and their positioning may relate to springs or streams. Individual sites often display close spacing and may coalesce, covering several hectares. In these assemblages cortical flakes and pebble fragments are dominant while rare microliths and low-quality blade cores none the less show a consistent presence. It is clear too that the site of Goldcliff is likely to represent a series of transitory sites where hunting groups sought wild pig in the reedswamps and, sometimes, killed a red deer at greater distance and brought back selected parts of the carcass to their shoreline campsite. They used the lithic materials available in the local gravels to repair or replace their arrows. In one instance two microlithic barbs of an arrow seem to have remained within a wild pig carcass and to have been roasted with it. Hitherto, only one possible kill site had been known, at Lydstep in Pembrokeshire and, according to one reading of the evidence, this may have involved the poaching of a Neolithic domesticated pig by Mesolithic hunters. A pair of microliths – perhaps components of the armature of a Mesolithic arrow – was found in a context suggestive of the arrow having been embedded in the neck of a pig whose status, wild or domesticated, is not wholly clear (David 1990, 290–1). This kill site – or death site if the pig survived the attack but carried the remains of the arrow embedded in its neck – is dated to $5,300 \pm 100$ BP (OxA-1412) and so clearly lies at the very interface of the Mesolithic and Neolithic.

Upland sites are well attested in Wales, with forty-nine listed by Jacobi in 1980. For the most part these sites are of Late Mesolithic date (Reynier 1998). The majority seem to represent seasonal hunting locations and do not present evidence of year-round exploitation of the (mostly upland) hinterland of Wales. Their tool inventories are different and processing equipment, in particular tranchet adzes, burins and bevelled pebbles, are generally absent (Barton *et al.* 1995, 95–100). The nature of the occupation is well illustrated by the evidence from Waun Fignen Felen. The excavator (Barton *et al.* 1995, 107–11) believes that the sites, represented by small lithic scatters of the order of 20–35 m², were hunting sites, perhaps for marsh birds and waterfowl, some possibly occupied only for a few minutes and all located at the eastern (upwind) end of the lake at a point where use of the Haffes gorge could allow a hunter to approach unseen to within 300 metres of the lake. The importance of the site, as a 'persistent place', is shown by the fact that the lake was episodically revisited over several millennia.

Apart from Goldcliff (Bell *et al.* 1999) and Waun Fignen Felen (Barton *et al.* 1995), modern excavations of Mesolithic sites have been conducted at the Nab Head (David 1990), Rhuddlan (Quinnell & Blockley 1994), Trwyn Du (White 1978), Brenig (Lynch 1993), Burry Holms (Walker 1999), Gwernvale (Britnell & Savory 1984), Hoyle's Cottage near Tenby (Aldhouse-Green 1996) and Ogmore in the Vale of Glamorgan (Hamilton & Aldhouse-Green 1998). Recording, collecting and limited excavation has also taken place at Llyn Aled Isaf on Mynydd Hiraethog, Denbighshire (Brassil 1991a, 51–3; Jenkins 1991) and at sites in the Glamorgan uplands (Stanton 1984a). The sum tale of knowledge from these sites is indicative of very transient settlement, with no certain examples of Mesolithic houses yet known from Wales.

The Nab Head I (Early Mesolithic) produced no certainly coeval structures but the Nab Head II (Late Mesolithic) produced a number of features. These included three concentrations of artefacts which collectively surrounded an 'empty area' around 5 metres in diameter, a size comparable with the diameters of Mesolithic houses at Mount Sandel in Ireland, dated to *c.* 9,000 BP (Woodman 1985). It is tempting to interpret the Nab Head plan as indicative of a house-site surrounded by discard zones of artefacts, burnt flint and charcoal. It is interesting that the burnt materials lay at a slightly greater distance from the putative house-site than the artefacts. Also identified was a shallow pit with tightly packed angular stones above a fill of burnt soil and charcoal dated to 7,360 ± 90 BP (OxA-860), and finally a flint scatter associated with a possible hearth dated to 6,210 ± 90 BP (OxA-861) (David 1990, 210–12). Rhuddlan produced post-holes which could have formed windbreaks or even parts of the curved walls of small huts. Just such a structure was preserved in the anaerobic conditions of the inter-tidal zone at Frainslake in Pembrokeshire: here a probable Late Mesolithic flint scatter was associated with a windbreak of gorse, birch and hazel which 'ran in a gentle curve for 4–5 yards' (Gordon-Williams 1926). Brenig produced hearth-sites in the form of re-used 'fire-pits' and, again, a possible windbreak (Allen in Lynch 1993, 22). Llyn Aled Isaf produced hearths, stake-holes and grooves, evidently relating to some kind of shelter (David 1990, 193–4). Gwernvale produced a hearth-site dated to 6,895 ± 80 BP (CAR-118). No other certainly Mesolithic features were found there but an extensive flint industry was plausibly focused in part on an earthfast stone 0.70 metres high referred to by Britnell (1984, 50; pl. 13b; figs 30, 58) as a 'natural monolith'. A Mesolithic burin was actually found embedded in a crevice in the top of the monolith. The Glamorgan uplands sites (Stanton 1984a, 50, 57–65) produced evidence of flint scatters related to hearths but with no substantive evidence of structures. Indeed, we must see Mesolithic Wales as occupied by mobile hunting groups who may have ranged widely and whose *modus vivendi* generally did not lend itself to settlement sufficiently sustained in one place to lead to the construction of semi-permanent shelters.

Whereas the Palaeolithic environment was typically very open, the Mesolithic landscape became thickly wooded with settlement probably focused in the coastal areas and river valleys. It is clear, however, that the contemporary peoples were well able to open up and control landscapes through the use of fire (Mellars 1976b). Such evidence in Wales is seen at Goldcliff, discussed above; at Moel-y-Gerddi in north-west Wales, where charcoal was found in a level with high incidences of grasses, sedges and wetland herbs, dated to 7,510 ± 95 BP (CAR-664) (Chambers & Price 1988; Chambers *et al.* 1988); at Waun Fignen Felen where charcoal in sediments dated to around 7,400–7,100 BP has been interpreted as reflecting the use of fire to manage not woodland but rather heathland in order to improve grazing for red deer and other potential game (Barton *et al.* 1995, 105); and at Llyn Aled Isaf where charcoal collected in 1995 from a horizon in a colluvial deposit yielding flint artefacts produced an age of 7,365 ± 65 BP (AA-15213) (Lascelles 1995), superseding a younger result published by Jenkins (1991). However, it is important to restate that fires may have developed naturally more often in the drier conditions of the Postglacial Hypsithermal and that the presence of humans at these sites may reflect a desire to take advantage of the possibilities for hunting created by a natural event of this kind. Except where the contextual evidence is of a high order, as at Goldcliff, it would be unwise to use uncritically the presence of charcoal unaccompanied by artefacts as a barometer of human presence.

ARTEFACTS

In general Mesolithic artefacts are smaller than Upper Palaeolithic examples – perhaps as a consequence of progressively diminishing access to raw materials, because of the rise in sea-level taking place in tandem with the change from Upper Palaeolithic tundra to a soil-covered forested Mesolithic landscape. Just as Upper Palaeolithic sites are more numerous than earlier Palaeolithic sites so, too, are later Mesolithic sites in comparison with earlier Mesolithic sites. Here, Healey (in Lynch 1993, 17) has noted 66 later assemblages compared with only 17 earlier ones. A technological break occurs around 8,700 BP with the introduction of narrow blade microliths, contrasting with earlier broad blade industries which differ in both artefact size and typology. A figure of 8 millimetres conventionally marks the broad blade/narrow blade boundary in England. However, a slightly lower figure may be appropriate for Wales (Stanton 1984a, 50), probably because of the almost uniformly low quality of the raw materials used. A small percentage of broad blade microlith forms is typically present on Late Mesolithic sites but it is often unclear whether these products are genuinely contemporary with the Late Mesolithic assemblage. The fact, however, that these forms are often of reduced size when they occur in late contexts suggests that they may be genuinely of Late Mesolithic age (Pitts & Jacobi 1979, 169–70).

Early Mesolithic (Fig. 1.9)

Archery had been developed by the end of the Upper Palaeolithic and small backed implements, probably generally used as arrow armatures or as inserts for composite knives, are known as 'microliths' by archaeologists. Barbed antler and bone spearpoints continued in use, and antler mattocks now appear and may have been used as tools for digging in soft sediments. The typological range includes a number of characteristic items. These include broad blade microliths shaped into obliquely blunted point, scalene and isosceles triangle forms. In the manufacture of microliths the bulbar end of the blade-blank has been deliberately removed by the microburin technique. Other implements include tranchet adzes, probably used for woodworking, in which the blade has been typically resharpened by means of a sideways or 'tranchet' blow, producing a characteristic sharpening flake. Awls were used *inter alia* for perforating hides for the making of clothing, tents, etc.; particularly important for Wales is the *mèche de foret* (or drill-bit), found in large numbers at the Nab Head and Daylight Rock and almost certainly associated with stone bead production. Convex end-scrapers, made on flakes or blades, were used in the preparation of hides. Burins were engraving tools used to work bone and antler, and rare microdenticulates or 'saws' could have been used in the manufacture of organic products.

Late Mesolithic (Fig. 1.10)

The Nab Head, Pembrokeshire, is a well-excavated site with important Early and Late Mesolithic phases (Nab Head I and II respectively). The site produced not only the range of Early Mesolithic tools described above, but a characteristic range of Late Mesolithic forms as well (David 1990, 209–27). Artefacts of all kinds totalled 31,797 from an area of 195 m². The full reduction sequence was present with single platform cores typical; neatly made prismatic or pyramidical cores were rare, probably because of the low quality of the raw materials used. Indeed, the mean core height of only 28 millimetres reflects the small size of the beach shingle used for knapping. Of the narrow blade microliths present,

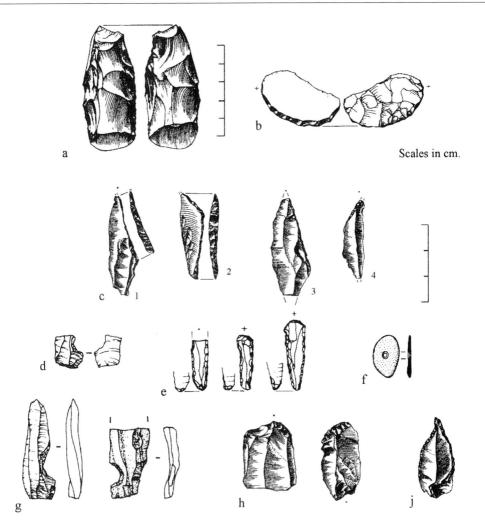

Fig. 1.9. Early Mesolithic artefact types. A. tranchet adze; B. tranchet adze sharpening flake; C. broad blade microliths: 1–2 large scalene triangles, 3–4 obliquely blunted points; D. microburin; E. mèches de foret (drill bits), probably used in bead-manufacture; F. mudstone bead; G. blades notched prior to microburin snap; H. end-scrapers; J. piercer. C, F, H and J: Waun Fignen Felen site 8, after Barton et al. 1995; A, B and E: Nab Head, after Jacobi 1980; D and G: Rhuddlan, after Berridge in Quinnell & Blockley 1994.

66 per cent are scalene triangles and 12 per cent are convex-backed pieces. The great majority of the microliths and all the microburins recovered display, respectively, rightward points and right-hand notches, plausibly reflecting the handedness of the knappers (David 1990, 218). In contrast to the Early Mesolithic, denticulates form a consistent part of Late Mesolithic assemblages, totalling 11 per cent at the Nab Head. Convex end-scrapers were also consistently present, but were less neatly made than at the Nab Head I Early Mesolithic site. Pebble tools become important in the Late Mesolithic, especially bevelled

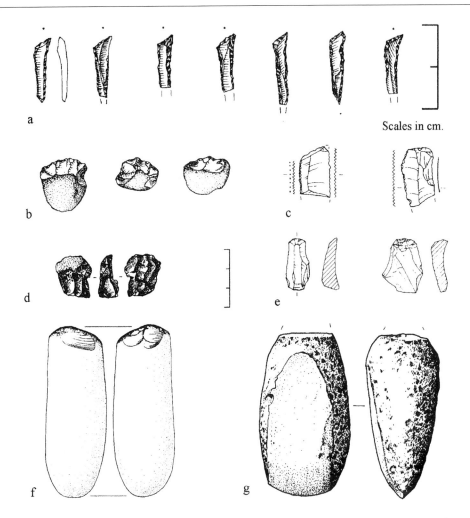

Fig. 1.10. Late Mesolithic artefact types. A. narrow blade microliths; B. denticulate scrapers; C. denticulates; D. blade core; E. end-scrapers; F. bevelled pebble; G. pecked and ground axe with affinities to axes from the Nab Head. A: Waun Fignen Felen after Berridge et al. 1995; B: Nab Head II after David 1989; C and E: Brenig, after Healey in Lynch et al. 1993; D: Merthyr Mawr, after Stanton 1984; F: Frainslake, after Jacobi 1980; G: Ogmore, drawing by Anne Leaver.

pebbles, once known as 'limpet scoops' or 'limpet hammers'. These are selected natural elongated flat-sided pebbles, very occasionally completely unmodified, but typically with one or both ends first flaked, then abraded or bevelled. Occasionally there are percussion marks on the sides from use as hammers or anvils. The Nab Head II site also produced a stone 'macehead' or ring and four ground stone axes. The latter, hitherto regarded as an exclusive Neolithic type, are of distinctive form, being elongated pebbles ground or pecked over most of their surfaces, with a blade-edge which may be flat-polished on one surface and which sometimes has a distinct winged or expanded form (David 1989). An axe of this type has recently (1999) been excavated from the Late Mesolithic site of Ogmore. Two unstratified finds from Goldcliff of flaked axes or adzes of volcanic tuff, combined with stratified finds of what may reasonably be interpreted as flakes from the axe manufacturing process, indicate that these products continued to be manufactured in the Late Mesolithic, at least into the seventh millennium BP (Barton in Bell *et al.* 1999, 46–8).

There is evidence for traffic in Early Mesolithic perforated stone beads of the type well known from the Nab Head (David 1989, 245). The Nab Head itself has produced no fewer than 690 artifically perforated natural mudstone pebbles. This artefact type occurs also at Palmerston Farm and Freshwater East in south-west Wales but more importantly at Waun Fignen Felen (**Fig. 1.9F**) in the Black Mountain range of Breconshire (Barton *et al.* 1995, 92). Here, the presence of broken beads and a flint drill-bit (*mèche de foret*) suggest on-site manufacture. Large numbers of *mèches de foret* occur at the Nab Head, thereby identifying the site as a potential focus for the manufacture and dissemination of the beads. There is parallel evidence for transport of special items, in this case cowrie shells for use as necklaces or in fringing clothing or bags, from King Arthur's Cave and Madawg rock shelter in the Wye Valley. At the latter site the beads were excavated from a Late Mesolithic context with dates of 8,710 ± 70 BP (OxA-6081) and 6,655 ± 65 BP (OxA-6082). Their origin is marine and so they must have been collected from the contemporary shoreline of the Bristol Channel (Barton *et al.* 1997).

During the Mesolithic period, we see evidence of exchange, or perhaps 'embedded procurement', in the frequent occurrence of beach pebble flint on inland sites, as at Rhuddlan (Berridge in Quinnell & Blockley 1994, 95). None the less lithic raw materials tend to be substantively local in both Early and Late Mesolithic contexts. Thus, black Gronant chert originating in the limestone on the east side of the Vale of Clwyd was used locally in north-east Wales where its distribution extends from Prestatyn to Llyn Aled Isaf in the Hiraethog moorland (Lynch 1993, 17; Healey in Lynch 1993, 24–5). It formed 84 per cent of the Rhuddlan assemblage. Mesolithic assemblages in north-east Wales are characterised by their predominant use of this local chert (Sargent 1923), in contrast to Neolithic and Bronze Age sites where flint (presumably deliberately imported) is predominant. At Rhuddlan the remainder of the raw materials comprises flint (15 per cent) and rhyolite (less than 1 per cent). A similar picture occurs in south Wales. Thus, at Nab Head I (Early Mesolithic) as much as 98.8 per cent of the lithic raw material was beach pebble flint (David 1990, 148). At the Early Mesolithic Palmerston Farm site, also in Pembrokeshire, 97.6 per cent of the artefacts were of beach pebble flint (David 1990, 124). Recently Barton has reviewed the evidence for long-distance transport of raw materials by groups colonising or exploiting the uplands of Wales (Barton *et al.* 1995). In the Early Mesolithic at Waun Fignen Felen, both beach pebble flint and a fine-grained greensand chert of cretaceous age were exploited. Greensand chert seems to have been exploited preferentially during the Early Mesolithic of Somerset and Devon, probably drawing on local sources in Somerset, both *in situ* and in the form of river gravels. The nearest sources to Waun Fignen Felen seem to lie at least 80 kilometres distant. However, the cretaceous greensand chert present need not have originated in the English sources quoted, since the raw material is readily available in the beach shingles of west and south Wales (David 1990, 149).

In the Late Mesolithic local chert was dominant at the site of Hendre near Rhuddlan (Manley & Healey 1982). In south-east Wales the Late Mesolithic assemblages of the Glamorgan uplands are dominated by the use of beach pebble flint, almost certainly from the coast of the Vale of Glamorgan, but with an admixture of local materials, most notably carboniferous chert. Again 'embedded procurement' (the collection of raw materials during regular seasonal movements) rather than exchange between groups, is perhaps the most likely explanation for this distribution. At Goldcliff, flint, chert, tuff and quartzite were all exploited, with the most likely immediate source being the marine and fluvial gravels of the Severn Estuary (Allen in Bell *et al.* 1999, 38–9). These raw materials seem to have been used primarily for the production of laminar flakes – rather than true blades – for the production of microliths. The manufacture of flakes rather than blades is characteristic of some late Mesolithic industries and may have chronological significance (Bell *et al.* 1999, 40, 59). It is noteworthy that the local carboniferous chert at Waun Fignen Felen was exploited during the Late Mesolithic only, suggesting that exchange networks were less reliable or mobility was reduced. At Waun Fignen Felen also greensand chert is absent from the Late Mesolithic assemblages, a lacuna that may reflect resource availability in the Bristol Channel *or* a change in territorial range (Barton *et al.* 1995, 107). At Brenig it seems that Gronant chert may have been heated in order to improve its flaking qualities (Healey in Lynch 1993, 24).

Elsewhere in Britain there is evidence for an increasing focus on local lithic sources from around 8,000 BP (Jacobi 1987, 164–5). In Wales there is no evidence from the raw materials of long-distance exchange beyond Wales. Extended raw material networks had flourished in the open landscapes of the early Windermere Interstadial; they were not to reappear until the arrival, or development, of the first farming communities.

RITUAL AND DEATH

In Britain as whole the incidence of disposal of human remains in caves increased during the Mesolithic. Across the Bristol Channel, the Mendip sites of Gough's Cave and Aveline's Hole are well known (Barham *et al.* 1999). At Gough's Cave a nearly complete skeleton has been dated to 9,100 ± 100 BP (OxA-814). Far more dramatic was the 'cemetery' found within Aveline's Hole where seemingly some eighty burials, all of presumptive Mesolithic date, were found. Of these, two found together (Davies 1924) were slightly ochre-stained and were accompanied by grave-goods including pierced teeth of giant deer, pig and red deer. The root of a horse incisor was perforated and decorated with parallel incisions in the manner of the Kendrick's Cave teeth. Radiocarbon dates for human material from Aveline's Hole range from 9,114 ± 110 BP (BM-471) to 8,740 ± 100 BP (OxA-1070). We may note instances of Mesolithic human remains from Wales which may once have been burials. These include remains of one or two individuals from Paviland Cave, represented by several bones and dated to 7,190 ± 80 BP (OxA-681), but without associated artefactual evidence. Other sites include Ogof-yr-Ychen, Potter's Cave and Daylight Rock on Caldey; Worm's Head and Foxhole, Gower; and Pontnewydd Cave, Denbighshire. Of these results, that from Worm's Head (8,800 BP) alone falls into the Early Mesolithic, while the other determinations are of Late Mesolithic age (range of results, *c.* 8,600–6,800 BP).

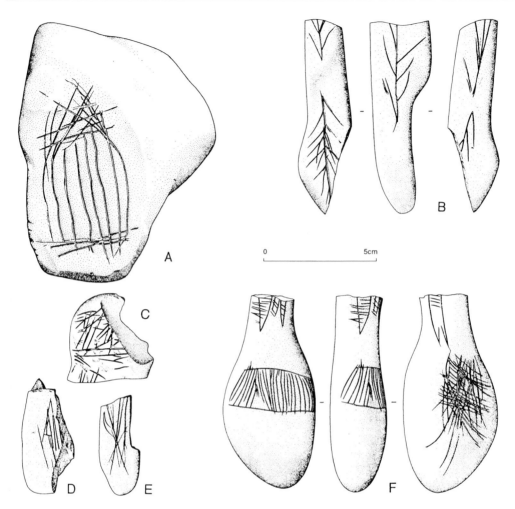

Fig. 1.11. Decorated Mesolithic pebbles from Rhuddlan. After Roberts & Berridge in Quinnell & Blockley

In the context of Mesolithic ritual we should consider the evidence of the engraved stones from Rhuddlan, where a series of six pebbles, decorated with incised lines forming both geometric and apparently random scratch patterns, was recovered (**Fig. 1.11**). Mesolithic art of any kind is rare in Britain but it occurs in northern Europe and the Rhuddlan pieces are comparable with such material. It cannot be said, at present, whether such 'art' is likely to have had symbolic significance or whether it was simply decoration. At least one design could represent a simple house structure or fish basket. There is also an engraved stone from the Nab Head (David 1990, 167) where Jacobi (1980, 160) has speculatively interpreted the large numbers of beads as possibly having once been sets of jewellery derived from burials. A so-called figurine from the site of the Nab Head (Gordon-Williams 1926, 94–9) was believed by the late W.F. Grimes to have been a fake and a modern reassessment is clearly desirable (David 1990, 164–6). It may be relevant to note here the fact that the beads from Waun Fignen Felen (Barton *et al.* 1997) were of an unusual spotted mudstone whose significance is as likely to be magical as aesthetic. The recognition of a dozen pieces of red ochre at Prestatyn hints at the adornment of bodies or perhaps of items of personal equipment (Clark 1939).

In Wales the focus of the Mesolithic settlement at Gwernvale close to a 'natural monolith', itself apparently consciously incorporated into the later megalithic tomb, may not be fortuitous.

SOCIAL STRUCTURE AND NETWORKS

The Mesolithic population seems likely to have been dispersed and highly mobile and, while elsewhere in Britain it has proved possible to identify 'social territories' from analysis of regionally varying microlith typology (but see Jacobi 1987), the more restricted nature of Welsh Mesolithic assemblages and the low quality of the lithic raw materials do not readily lend themselves to this approach (David 1989). The recent consensus on Mesolithic settlement patterns has been to envisage bipolar seasonal movements between differing environments, usually characterised as coast/inland or lowland/upland with winter settlement often involving larger social aggregations and typically based in lowland areas.

Wales has great numbers of Mesolithic sites but securely stratified material and organic finds are rare. Accordingly doubts must often remain about the reliability of association and interpretation of different kinds of evidence. Fragmentary human remains are preserved in caves and provide information about the chronology of human presence, the patterning in time of such human disposals (they can hardly be called burials), and the diet of the humans involved. We can scarcely make the kind of social inferences which are possible where true Mesolithic cemeteries are found, whether at Aveline's Hole, Mendip, or elsewhere (Schulting 1996). Most lithic material seems to have been substantially local – increasingly so as the period progressed – or, else plausibly acquired in the course of a seasonal round. The scale of distance involved in the transport of lithic materials, a maximum of 80 kilometres in the case of Waun Fignen Felen (Barton *et al.* 1995, 105) – or 100 kilometres in the case of the perforated beads – easily falls within the range of mobility of forest-living hunter-gatherers, where an annual territory might cover 28,000 km^2 with a diameter of 170 kilometres. However, a forest model would not be appropriate for groups essentially exploiting open coastal and riverine areas, and in that case figures for open country hunter-gatherers – territory size and diameter with respective ranges of 2,500–5,500 and 60–85 kilometres – might be more appropriate (Aldhouse-Green 1998a, 143).

The interior of Mesolithic Wales still looks painfully empty on the distribution map (**Fig. 1.7**) and study of the material equipment of upland sites at Waun Fignen Felen and elsewhere suggests that the full range of home base equipment is lacking, and that task groups perhaps of younger men – or maybe just lovers (Jacobi 1987) – were either exploiting untouched resources in the warm summers of the climatic optimum or else were breaking away temporarily, in the manner of Bushman groups, to relieve social tensions built up during a long winter aggregation (Guenther 1997, 181). Even the very large surface collections of lithics from the Walton Basin of Radnorshire yielded a surprisingly small Mesolithic component (Gibson 1999a, 77). Analysis of the results of surface collection undertaken in recent years as part of the Royal Commission on Ancient and Historical Monuments' Uplands Survey will be an important analytical tool in testing whether or not the lands of the Welsh interior were largely unoccupied at this time.

The process of re-peopling Postglacial Wales may be relevant here. It would seem that there is no evidence for a human presence in Wales before *c.* 9,200 BP, half a millennium later than in England. But Scotland does not seem to have been settled before 8,500 BP and there was clearly therefore no overriding demographic imperative leading to the establishment of human groups throughout the British Isles. Wales may simply have been colonised late and with hunter-gatherer groups strongly focused on the coastal plains.

Another important question to emerge from this survey is the issue of whether there is evidence for increased territoriality in the later Mesolithic. Much more data needs to be collected but dietary evidence, derived from analysis of human skeletal material, is suggestive of the possibility that access to marine resources was restricted, at least locally – perhaps because of the forcing mechanisms of loss of substantive areas of coastal plain, with consequential encroachment of the sea right to the foot of the cliffs in many areas, and increased population density. The restriction of greensand chert – obtained from or via coastal regions – to the Early Mesolithic only at Waun Fignen Felen may reflect precisely the same situation. It is intriguing to speculate, too, whether the failure of the early Neolithic people, buried in the Gower chamber tomb of Parc le Breos Cwm, to exploit marine protein as part of their diet (Richards 1998) may not reflect the continuing control of coastal resources by indigenous groups, particularly perhaps where such features as steep cliffs added a natural measure of control. By contrast, the data from Goldcliff, a seventh-millennium site located on the margin of the mud-flats of the Severn Estuary and coeval with the isotopic data from Foxhole suggestive of a terrestrial diet, do not argue for ubiquitous heightened territoriality at this period. Indeed, interpretation of the nature of settlement at Goldcliff (Bell *et al.* 1999, 63) suggests that it may reflect a pattern of high residential mobility with transitory encampments. By contrast, the wide artefactual range from the Nab Head is suggestive of homebase status but Barton and Bell (Bell *et al.* 1999, 63) raise the suggestion that the site may be no more than a 'persistent place' where visits taking place over millennia, as the radiocarbon determinations would indicate, have created a palimpsest whose original elements can no longer be retrieved. What is clear is that patterns of mobility will have varied both regionally and over time and much more data, reflecting activity across contemporaneous landscapes, will have to be accumulated and assessed before we can develop a real understanding of the nature of patterns of Mesolithic land use in Wales.

CONCLUSION

In examining evidence for the settlement of Wales by hunter-gatherers, we began with some aspects of the story of human evolution. Some understanding of the nature of humanity can be deduced from this evidence, linked to assessment of strictly archaeological data and informed by our knowledge of recent hunter-gatherer and pre-industrial farming societies. Such lives need not be viewed as full of unremitting toil. Hunter-gatherers did not know 'poverty', if defined as a relative lack of material possessions, for this condition is a social status. It is doubtful, too, that hunger was known on anything like its present global scale. In general hunter-gatherers probably 'worked' 20 to 35 hours per week and early farmers the same or slightly more (Sahlins 1974, 35–7, 97). It is indeed a paradox that the amount of work actually increases with the development of culture.

Humans had moved out of Africa by at least one, possibly almost two, million years ago and by 500,000 years ago or so they had entered north-western Europe. The settlement of Wales appears to have been intermittent until around 10,000 years ago when the Ice Age ended. We know that Wales was first settled by early Neanderthals at Pontnewydd Cave 225,000 years ago and that classic Neanderthals must have been present at Coygan Cave around 50,000 years ago. The arrival of modern humans at around 30,000 BP or soon after led to an expansion of settlement which none the less remained sparse and intermittent during the Upper Palaeolithic period. Wales was apparently abandoned from around 21,000 until after 13,000 BP during the maximum of the last glaciation. People probably lived in groups of one or more extended families. The technology of Modern Humans saw relatively rapid developments with some evidence of long-distance transport in raw materials and decorative items. Burials took place at Paviland at around 26,000 BP and perhaps at Kendrick's Cave nearer to 12,000 BP.

The Mesolithic saw a continuation of the hunter-gatherer way of life until the development of farming in Wales. The evidence so far available suggests that there may not have been a continuous human presence in Wales until c. 9,200 BP, half a millennium later than in England. Settlement then focused on the coastal plains and only limited exploitation of the uplands took place, probably by specialist hunting groups. Lithic raw materials were available to the coastal dwellers in the form of fossil and active strandlines in which flint, chert and occasional flakeable volcanic rocks were readily available. Even in the Late Mesolithic, upland Wales seems to have remained virtually empty with more repeated, but still only small-scale, visits by hunting parties. Perhaps, however, the primary purpose of these groups was social rather than exploitative – holiday groups rather than hunting groups – breaking away for a time, to 'chill out' as it were, away from the tensive and frictive stresses of life among the larger social aggregations of the lowlands or coast. There is evidence that such social stress was heightened in the later Mesolithic. The sea, once accessible from the coastal plains, now lay in many areas at the foot of forbidding cliffs and there is some tentative evidence from these areas – in the form of isotopic ratios preserved in human bone – that some groups, perhaps denied access to the sea by others, moved to a fully terrestrial diet, lacking the component of marine protein seen in earlier Mesolithic people in Wales. Such an interpretation would find support in complementary evidence that lithic resources, too, were more local in origin. This would imply – locally at least – reduced territorial range and reduced mobility, but with more rigid boundaries in the period immediately before the *adventus* of the first farming communities. The evidence from Goldcliff, however, shows that hunter-gatherers there with access to coastal resources may have exploited them through a highly mobile lifestyle based on 'short-term transitory encampments' and that established models of Mesolithic groups – seasonally migrating between winter residential bases on the coastal plains, summer encampments for the hunting of deer or aurochs in the uplands, and spring bases in the coastal and estuarine regions (Bell *et al.* 1999, 63) – may be oversimplified.

Two

THE EARLIER NEOLITHIC

Frances Lynch

INTRODUCTION: THE FIRST FARMERS

The adoption of a farming economy is perhaps the most fundamental change which can affect any prehistoric population. It is a change that is almost impossible to reverse and one whose consequences deeply affect not only material life but also philosophical attitudes. It is not surprising, therefore, that the nature of the evidence surviving from this period differs greatly from that of preceding eras and raises new problems of social interpretation.

Hunting territories must have been clearly defined within the minds of their users, but, like the ecological niche in the animal world, it may have been a multi-layered land, used by several groups at different times: a concept of ownership necessarily much more fluid than that demanded by farmers with a year-round commitment to land whose products and fertility they will actively mould to their own requirements. The stability of settlement which the production of crops implies eventually gives rise to new features in the archaeological record: to substantial houses, to the manufacture of pottery (heavy and breakable, pottery is an inconvenience to mobile groups), and, most conspicuously, to the construction of monumental tombs.

Unlike some more densely populated areas of England, Wales has produced good evidence for substantial Neolithic houses which seem to have been isolated farmsteads. No enclosures or village groups of any size can be recognised at this period and, indeed, such a dispersed settlement pattern is characteristic of the region almost up to the present day. The absence of large centres of population may have reduced the need for formal political structures to absorb inter-personal stress and dispute – hence the lack of early communal monuments such as the causeway camps of Wessex and the reliance on the family-orientated tomb, alone, as the focus for community identity.

Wales contains a variety of megalithic tombs. Their distribution, mainly in the western lowlands with fertile soil and soft climate, emphasises the agricultural concerns of their builders, while their architectural differences indicate the diversity of their cultural backgrounds. Decay and destruction have left many too badly damaged to classify, but three main families may be recognised among the better preserved sites: the Cotswold-Severn group initially settled in Breconshire and the Bristol Channel region, and maintaining contacts to the east; the Portal Dolmens, with several regionally dominant groups; and the scattered Passage Graves whose connections lie in the Irish Sea province and Atlantic Europe. The inter-action of these tomb-builders provides an index of the gradual amalgamation of initially disparate populations, producing by the Middle Neolithic a more unified cultural scene on to which renewed eastern contacts imposed further change.

One of the unifying factors during the Middle Neolithic is undoubtedly the exchange of goods, most clearly exemplified in the 'axe trade'. The Neolithic farmers are believed to have been essentially self-sufficient, in contrast to the Bronze Age when obvious dependence on rare resources and international trade networks are thought to have generated inequalities in society. Analysis of raw materials, however, has shown that self-sufficiency was never absolute and in the dispersal patterns of stone axes we can see tangible evidence for cross-connections between quite distant groups and regions.

The mechanism by which a hunting economy was transformed into a farming one has been hotly disputed and the role of the indigenous population, whose manipulation of their prey was becoming increasingly sophisticated, has been widely debated, as has the degree of stability in the lifestyle of the earliest farmers (Dennell 1983; Barker 1985; Whittle 1997). Since Britain had been an island for some two thousand years before the first incontrovertible evidence for farming appears (not earlier than 5,000 cal BC) the introduction of alien elements – crops or animals – must be more deliberate than in mainland Europe where the process of borrowing and copying (acculturation) can be easily imagined (Kinnes 1988). The appearance of non-native crops and animals (notably sheep) must imply colonists, even if their numbers were small; their origin must lie in Europe, northern or Atlantic Europe. So far neither chronology nor cultural connections have pointed to specific homelands on the continent nor to any primary landfall in these islands.

Dates for Neolithic sites – tombs or settlements – are as early in Wales as elsewhere in Britain, though Ireland may have some priority (Herne 1988, Table 2.3). Fronting the highway of the Irish Sea, access from Atlantic Europe was easy and the similarity of cultural strands in northern and western Wales and in Ireland confirms that traffic up and down and across that waterway was frequent, especially in the earlier part of the period. South-eastern Wales and the Vale of Glamorgan show links with the lands across the Severn, notably the Cotswolds. It is perhaps surprising that the distinctive culture of Devon and Cornwall has little impact on the north shore of the Bristol Channel, an isolation which is maintained into the Bronze Age.

Evidence for earlier Neolithic activity is so closely associated with tombs that it is difficult to know how to treat those areas without them. Were these areas, central Wales and the north-east, devoid of population or did they support groups without a tomb-building tradition? If the latter, where did these groups come from? In the north-east there is evidence for a Mesolithic population with, perhaps, an alternative, cave-burial system. It is possible, therefore, that the indigenous population may have remained dominant and the full Neolithic cultural package was never absorbed. In the tree-choked valleys of central Wales an absence, or certainly sparseness, of population in the Early Neolithic may be real; the region may not be opened up until the Late Neolithic when many significant new trends become apparent there. It is these two eastern regions of Wales which then show the strongest links with northern and central England, links which eventually extend westwards to eclipse the Irish connection which had dominated the earlier part of the period.

CLIMATE AND VEGETATION

The late fifth millennium cal BC was a period of considerable environmental change but the difficulty is to distinguish among these changes the artificial from the natural. The climate had declined from its post-glacial optimum and is normally characterised as being relatively warm but wet, favouring the growth of deciduous woodland in all but the most exposed sites. Climate, however, is never uniform over a country such as Wales. The frost-free winters of the western peninsulae – Pembrokeshire, Lleyn and Anglesey – which allow a longer growing season, and their relatively sparse tree cover, because of the salt-laden winds, can be seen to influence settlement throughout prehistory (Webley 1976, Fig. 1).

The coastline of these peninsulae, and especially the flatlands of the Severn and Clwyd estuaries and the sweep of Cardigan Bay, were in a process of change at the beginning of this period when the post-glacial rise in sea-level reached its maximum (Taylor 1980a). The extent of land-loss is difficult to measure but the presence of drowned forests around much of the Welsh coast is witness to its reality (Rippon 1996, 14–24) (see **Fig. 1.7**). Much of the crucial evidence of the transition to a farming life may have been lost here.

The nature of the natural tree cover can be established through pollen studies (Simmons & Tooley 1981, Fig. 4.1). These show some significant differences between north and south Wales: the south-west is dominated by hazel, in contrast to alder which is the commonest shrub in the north. Birch and oak were the main trees, with oak and lime particularly strong in mid-Wales. Pine was virtually non-existent and elm was rare. The density of this woodland and the altitude to which it grew are the subject of debate (Taylor 1980a, 124; Price & Moore 1984). It is possible that the tree-line might have been at 600 metres and sheltered valleys would undoubtedly have been densely choked.

Association between forest clearance, especially the loss of elm, and the beginning of agriculture has long been a tenet of archaeological interpretation but in recent years the link has been questioned on several fronts (Groenman van Waateringe 1983). The elm decline is a widespread, almost synchronous and easily recognisable phenomenon in many pollen sequences. Affecting only one tree species it was judged to be man-induced, unrelated to climate change; since the elm prefers good soils it might have been used by early farmers as a guide to the better land in new territory; in addition its leaves could have been used for cattle fodder. However, the recent experience of elm disease and the discovery of disease-carrying beetles in prehistoric Britain suggest an alternative explanation; the recognition of earlier forest clearances indicating that Mesolithic man also opened the woodland cover, probably to lure his prey, and the occasional discovery of cereal pollen in pre-elm decline contexts have all combined to undermine the automatic assumption that the reduction in elm pollen marks the initial development of farming in any district.

However, it remains true that any serious agricultural activity, whether pastoral or arable, demands the clearance of dense woodland and some impact in the pollen record may be expected. A great many pollen sequences are available from Wales (Caseldine 1990, Fig. 11) but they tend to be from the upland areas, whereas the earlier Neolithic sites lie in the lowlands, and few of them are well dated. Some cores are radiocarbon dated, but horizons within them may be dated by interpolation, which is of doubtful value.

In broad terms the evidence suggests that there is a good deal of interference with the natural tree cover around about the end of the fifth millennium cal BC; the appearance of cereal is extremely limited and may not belong to cultivated grasses; *plantago lanceolata*, a meadow plant, is more common and it has been suggested that the earliest farming was largely pastoral, a conclusion which might suggest either that Mesolithic peoples were themselves initiating change, or that our evidence is simply coming from areas which were more suited to that form of husbandry (Caseldine 1990, 43–5). The problems of chronology, pollen dispersal and the likelihood of variation from place to place make it impossible to be dogmatic about the processes which had undoubtedly wrought significant changes in the landscape by the Late Neolithic.

Environmental evidence more directly associated with Neolithic monuments normally provides only a snapshot, not the developing sequence which can be gained from deep peats. However, evidence from under the multi-phase cairn at Trefignath, Anglesey, does provide a picture of expanding farmland, confirmed by the sequence from the nearby bog (Greig in Smith & Lynch 1987). Soil under the earliest cairn contained pollen indicative of oak woodland in the vicinity, but grassland immediately around the site; soil beneath the later cairn showed that the woodland by then had been greatly reduced. Pollen from beneath the cairn at Dyffryn Ardudwy, Merioneth, from the turves in the mound at Barclodiad y Gawres, Anglesey, and snails from the soil beneath Bryn yr Hen Bobl, Anglesey, all suggested that the tombs were quite closely surrounded by woodland (Dimbleby in Powell 1973; Godwin in Powell & Daniel 1956; Hemp 1935, 279–81). Soils beneath the cairn on Mynydd Troed, Breconshire (Crampton & Webley 1966), suggested a more open environment, as do the lake sediments in Llangorse Lake nearby, but this situation is not closely dated (Jones *et al.* 1985). Clearly conditions were variable across the country and earlier Neolithic clearances are likely to have been small and perhaps short-lived (Chambers 1982).

No ploughed surface of this date has been found in Wales and direct evidence for cultivated crops is not large. Pollen of cereals and celtic bean have come from Trefignath; charred emmer wheat has been found at Gwernvale, Breconshire, and in a pit dated to the Middle Neolithic at Plas Gogerddan near Aberystwyth (Caseldine 1990, 47). Late Neolithic sites produce similarly limited evidence but add barley to the list of cultivars. Not surprisingly, wild foods, crab apples, hazelnuts and blackberries were collected.

Most of the soils in Wales are acidic and bone does not survive well so the complementary evidence for animal husbandry is equally thin. Only cattle bones were found at the settlement of Clegyr Boia in Pembrokeshire (Williams 1952); elsewhere cattle, sheep/goat and pig have all been found (Caseldine 1990, Table 4), but not in sufficient numbers to allow any discussion of their relative importance in the economy. The appearance of sheep (or goat, the bones are difficult to differentiate) is significant because it is not native to western Europe and is one of the major indicators of new arrivals. Just as wild fruit was collected, so hunting was not neglected and deer bones have been found at several sites (Caseldine 1990, Table 4). Evidence for fishing and wildfowling is more difficult to find, but fish bones were among those in the 'ritual stew' from Barclodiad y Gawres which provides a fascinating insight into the variety of animals caught and cooked, but is unlikely to be typical of everyday diet during the Neolithic in Wales (Powell

& Daniel 1956). Analysis of lipid residues on late pottery from the Walton Basin has hinted at surprisingly specialised diets among some groups but the study is too limited for wide conclusions to be drawn at this stage (Charters, Evershed *et al.* 1997).

POPULATION

The size of a population is an element of basic data which is fundamental to any serious assessment of the achievements and problems of an age. In prehistory, unfortunately, it is impossible to provide even an estimation of absolute numbers based on any objectively measurable factor and even statements about relative numbers are little more than assumptions and educated guesses (but see Smith 1992). This is especially frustrating because so many social and economic developments, regional differences and, indeed, political events will have sprung from changes in population pressure.

The elements which might form the basis of calculations of absolute figures are the number of settlements and their size (the equivalent of the household or taxpayer in later assessments and censuses); the number of burial monuments and the bodies therein (a calculation never attempted for later periods because of its inherent difficulty); and the workforce needed for the construction of monuments (a calculation only relevant to a limited area). Even where possible (Pétrequin *et al.* 1998), such counts are subject to major uncertainty because we cannot be sure for how long a prehistoric farmstead was in occupation, a monument under construction or a tomb in use. Add to this the perennial problem of differential survival and the incompleteness of our knowledge and it is obvious that the goal is unattainable.

Wales, apart from Flintshire, does not possess the invaluable population baseline provided by Domesday Book, but there are lay taxation returns from the thirteenth century. Even these, though, do not deliver firm figures (Williams-Jones 1976). Bede, writing in the eighth century, provides a figure of 960 'familiae' or households (perhaps, at a conservative estimate, 4,000 people) for Anglesey and 300 for the Isle of Man, an island of the same size but much less fertile (Colgrave & Mynors 1991, 163). Regional fluctuation therefore might be considerable. The sixteenth-century population of Wales has been estimated as 300,000 when the population of England and Wales was thought to be 3,000,000–4,000,000 (Dodd 1972, 80) – a ratio of 1:10. A very, very tentative estimate of Neolithic population numbers in England has suggested 23,000 (Atkinson 1968) which would give Wales 2,300. It is difficult to know what to make of such figures in the light of the monuments and finds that we have, bearing in mind that these represent almost 2,000 years of history.

The construction of a megalithic tomb demands a great deal of muscle power (but some of it might be animal) so these monuments must imply at least temporary population groups of reasonable size, but they might, like harvesters and shearers of another age, be gathered from some distance (Startin & Bradley 1981). None the less the distribution of tombs can obviously highlight concentrations of population, though their absence should not necessarily imply desertion. The distribution of the more workaday stone axe is perhaps a better touchstone and a thin scatter can be found covering all parts of Wales but with a clear lowland and valley preference (**Fig. 2.1**).

Environmental evidence showing only relatively small clearings within the general woodland cover would suggest a scattered population, unevenly distributed. Both monuments and

Fig. 2.1. Distribution of megalithic tombs and stone axeheads in Wales.

artefacts demonstrate a strong preference for Anglesey, Pembrokeshire and the Glamorgan and Monmouthshire coasts, but certain valleys and basins were also attractive. The most notable of these is the Talgarth Basin with its concentration of Cotswold-Severn tombs. Although the lack of a detailed chronology precludes proof, this distribution gives the impression of an expanding population, moving into the side valleys and eventually on to higher ground where human interference first becomes apparent in the Late Neolithic (Chambers 1982).

The expansion of occupied areas in the Late Neolithic and Early Bronze Age is discussed in the next chapter. Here one need only comment that, though we do not know the absolute size of the Early Neolithic population, it can be confidently stated that the population, after more than a thousand years of settled farming, had prospered and expanded considerably by the middle of the third millennium cal BC.

Skeletal survival in Wales is not good; the soils are generally acidic and in most of the western tombs cremation is the preferred rite. Any information about the physical appearance of the first farmers, therefore, comes largely from the tombs of Breconshire where inhumation was practised (Lynch 1986a). They were people of small stature (about 1.5–1.64 metres tall) who lived an active life, developing well-marked muscle channels and flattened shin bones owing to squatting rather than sitting. Their skulls were dolichocephalic with a cephalic index of about 74; the skulls were often notably thick, the brow-ridges prominent and the jaw very muscular, probably as a result of a rougher diet and the fact that they had an edge-to-edge bite – the only important characteristic in which they differed in appearance from modern man. A computer-generated portrait of a man buried at Pen yr Wyrlod illustrates this point well (Walker 1996).

Skeletons with these same characteristics are found in the south of England and in France and Spain and the type has been dubbed 'Mediterranean' or 'Iberian', emphasising the undoubted contacts with the continent at this time. However, the type is very close to what we know of the native Mesolithic population in Europe and Britain, though the latter is an extremely small sample, with none from Wales. Any question of new colonists at the beginning of the Neolithic cannot be argued from skeletal evidence, though at the end of the period more robustly built people with broader heads have been recognised in graves with Beaker pottery, leading to belief in a renewed invasion then. Less weight is now given to the physical contrasts because of the gap of more than a thousand years which separates the two populations, but the discovery that DNA may survive in many bones has opened new avenues of research (Lynch 1986a; Richards *et al.* 1993).

Evidence for the health of this population can relate only to those troubles which impact upon the skeleton, such as rheumatism, osteo-arthritis and broken and badly mended bones (Manchester & Roberts 1995). All these troubles have been recorded among the early Welsh population, many of whom also suffered from bad teeth. The adoption of a cereal diet with stone-ground flour led to rapidly worn-down teeth and also to caries. The number of burials from Welsh tombs is too small to allow statistically valid conclusions about life expectancy (see list in Lynch 1986a), but figures derived from the much larger ossuaries of Orkney suggest that few of the population would have lived beyond forty and that there would have been a very high rate of infant and child mortality (Hedges 1987, 174–84). The nine full-term foetuses from Pant y Saer tomb in Anglesey well illustrate the risks of childbirth (Scott 1933, 224–7).

SETTLEMENT

The distribution pattern of earlier Neolithic activity has already been mentioned. It is essentially lowland and almost certainly reflects interest in suitable farming lands (Webley 1976). Unfortunately the distribution of sites of permanent or substantial habitation is very much more restricted than that of 'activity' in the broad sense. Recent debates have stressed this point, suggesting that the earliest farmers were more mobile than we might imagine (Whittle 1997). Only three sites have produced good structural evidence; some half-dozen others have yielded some post-holes, pottery and pits, while the discovery of a few sherds, flints or radiocarbon dated hearths at several other sites provides only a tantalisingly fleeting glimpse of what might be either a transitory camp or a long-established farm.

The most substantial (though not the earliest) Neolithic settlement in Wales is that on the rocky summit of Clegyr Boia near St David's in Pembrokeshire (Baring-Gould 1903; Williams 1952). This prominent flat-topped rock provides just over 0.25 hectares of defensible space standing 45 metres above the coastal plain. In later prehistoric or Dark Age times it was surrounded by a stone rampart but there is no evidence that it was defended or even enclosed during the Neolithic. One of the early houses stood close to the edge of the plateau and was covered by the later rampart.

There had been at least three wooden houses on the hilltop; details of the hut found in 1902 are vague, but plans of the two found during the later excavation could be reconstructed. One is undoubtedly rectangular, 7 x 4 metres, levelled into the rock, with a ridged roof supported on a central line of four posts and resting on rock at the back and on a post-built wall at the front. This wall may have been completed in turf, draining into a stone foundation. The doorway in the centre of this long wall was fronted by two rock-cut steps leading down into the central depression in which there was a hearth or cooking pit in a rock crevice and a midden filling a very large hollow. Three other external hearths had been found in 1902. The second house, which had been burnt down, was discovered beneath the later rampart and the plan is probably incomplete. It has often been reconstructed as a circular building because the occupation layer and spread of burnt debris is approximately circular, but the two rows of post-holes (4.6 metres long, 3 metres apart) conform to a rectangular plan.

House 1 would seem to be complete, a single-roomed building of comparatively small size; House 2 might have been part of a more complex structure. Joining sherds demonstrate that they were both in use at the same time and that the midden was contemporary with them. The often-quoted parallel for this settlement is Lough Gur in Co. Limerick where a defensible (but undefended) peninsula was occupied by several single-roomed houses of rectangular plan (O'Riordain 1954; Grogan & Eogan 1987). Lough Gur was occupied over a very long time and it is uncertain how many of the houses were strictly contemporary but they were never closely packed in the manner of European villages. The same seems to be true both of Clegyr Boia and of the few other sites, such as Tankardstown, Co. Limerick, and Lismore Fields in Derbyshire, where more than one building has been found (Darvill & Thomas 1996, 45, 102).

The day-to-day activity of the occupants of Clegyr Boia is not very well documented. Animal bones did not survive in large numbers so the fact that they were exclusively cattle

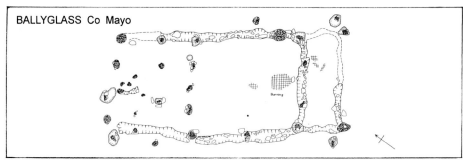

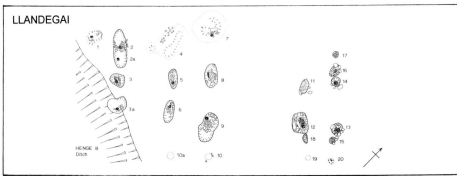

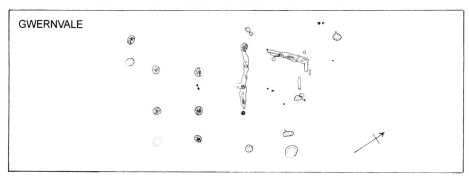

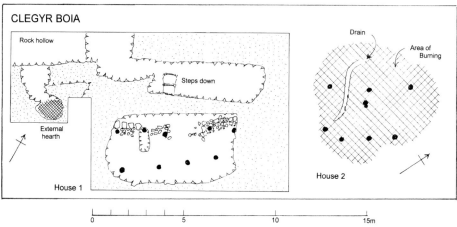

is probably not significant; no evidence of arable farming was recovered, though the surrounding land would have been suitable. Two stone axes, one of them made of local Pembrokeshire stone, demonstrate wood-working, confirmed by the presence of large timber buildings. A quantity of pottery was found, principally in the midden. It included both fine and coarse wares, and bowls and cups of different sizes, suggesting a variety of domestic uses: storage, communal cooking and individual eating.

The style of pottery (undecorated shouldered bowls), like the rectangular house, is common to the Irish Sea area (see **Fig. 2.5**). The form here, however, is considered a later type than the true carinated bowl seen at Llandegai (Herne 1988) which, with the single decorated rimsherd (Williams 1952, Fig. 11), would suggest a Middle rather than Early Neolithic date. Such a date would also be appropriate to Lough Gur and this might suggest that single-roomed houses should be seen as a simplification of earlier plans (Darvill & Thomas 1996).

Post-holes and a putative clay bank or wall found beneath a cairn at Mount Pleasant, Nottage, Glamorgan, have been interpreted as another single-roomed house of approximately rectangular plan (Savory 1952; 1980a). The pottery with decorated rims might support a similar Middle Neolithic date.

The best preserved of the earlier Neolithic houses in Wales is that found during the excavation of Henge B at Llandegai near Bangor, Caernarfonshire (Houlder 1968; Lynch 1989). The occupation levels within the house had been lost but deep post-holes defined a tripartite building 6 metres wide and 13 metres long. It was almost identical in size and design to the much better preserved example from Ballyglass, Co. Mayo, which had a small compartment at one end, a large central room with a hearth, and a section at the other end with many posts, perhaps supporting a raised floor (O'Nuallain 1972). This design, in various sizes, can be found all over Europe.

No other buildings were found in the vicinity, but not far away was a large sunken hearth associated with Neolithic pottery like that from the post-holes of the house and more sherds of the same kind were found in a nearby pit (see **Fig. 2.5**). The loss of the occupation levels meant that only material which had been incorporated in the post-packing survived. The most significant finds were a broken axe polisher, part of a Graig Lwyd axe and several pieces of high-quality black flint, together with sherds of undecorated carinated bowls and charcoal which provided a date of 5,240 ± 150 BP (NPL-223) = 4,400–3,700 cal BC (Houlder 1976, 58).

Excavations at Llandegai were extensive but no other house was found, nor was any enclosing ditch visible on the air photograph which had revealed the archaeological importance of the site (Houlder 1968). The unit of settlement, therefore, would seem to be the single large farmhouse which could have housed an extended family. As at Clegyr Boia there was an external hearth and pits, and domestic debris was scattered around. No evidence for the farming base of the community survived, but the discovery of an axe-polishing stone suggests that they were actively involved in the production – at least the

(Opposite) *Fig. 2.2. Plans of Neolithic houses: Ballyglass, Co. Mayo (after O'Nuallain 1972); Llandegai, Caerns. (after Lynch 1989); Gwernvale, Brecs. (after Britnell and Savory 1984); Clegyr Boia, Pembs. (after Williams 1952).*

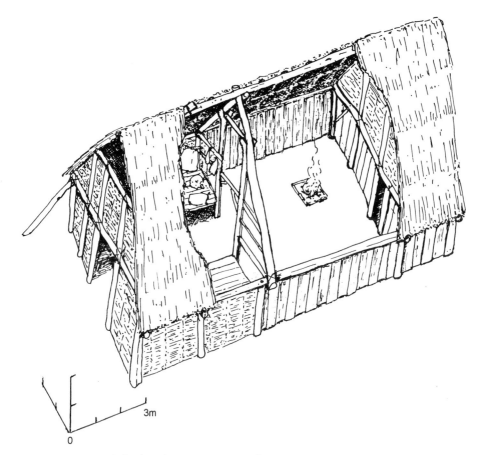

Fig. 2.3. Reconstruction of Llandegai house. (Frances Lynch)

finishing – of stone axes from Graig Lwyd some 16 kilometres distant to the north. A similar range of finds came from the vicinity of the cairn at Bryn yr Hen Bobl, Anglesey, but the nature and date of the settlement is uncertain (Hemp 1935; Gresham 1985).

The wooden building found beneath the east end of Gwernvale cairn on a river terrace above the Wye was even more fragmentary than that at Llandegai. It can be interpreted as a house of the same kind but the situation is complicated by the possibility that the southern group of post-holes may be a ritual building associated with the tomb (Britnell & Savory 1984, 50–5, 138–42). Like the Irish houses, the northern section was built of a combination of deeply set posts and plank walls with a shallow trench foundation. The building was 5.5 metres wide but its complete length is uncertain. Pottery, a rubbing stone and an axe-polisher were found among the post-packing and more pottery, flint scrapers, several leaf-shaped arrowheads, fragments of eight axes, charcoal and carbonised emmer wheat were found in pits scattered along the river terrace for some 30 metres westward (see **Fig. 2.6**). Bones from cattle, sheep, pig and deer were also present. Charcoal from one of the pits beneath the cairn gave a date of 5,050 ± 75 BP (CAR-113) = 4,000–3,700 cal BC.

Another possible rectangular house has been recognised among the features excavated at Moel y Gaer, the Iron Age hillfort near Rhosesmor in Flintshire (Britnell 1991, 55). A radiocarbon date and pottery from shallow pits confirm Neolithic activity on the site. Like Llandegai the house would seem to have been isolated and undefended.

Other sites lack structural evidence. Scattered sherds and pits beneath the initial cairn at Trefignath, Anglesey, combine with environmental data to suggest agricultural settlement on the spot at about 3,900 cal BC (Smith & Lynch 1987, 10–14). Little more can be said about the pits within Coygan Camp which produced an undecorated rimsherd, leaf arrowheads and part of a Pembrokeshire axe with a radiocarbon date of 5,000 ± 95 BP (NPL-132) = 4,000–3,630 cal BC (Wainwright 1967). Other sites with Neolithic radiocarbon dates, such as Ty Mawr, Anglesey (Lynch 1991, 345), or pottery, such as Gwaenysgor and Dyserth in the north-east (Lynch 1969, 172–3) and Llanelwedd, in mid-Wales (Lynch 1984a, 108–9) have provided no structural evidence and consequently the nature and duration of occupation is uncertain. The discovery of occasional Neolithic sherds in caves shows that these natural shelters were still used, but the evidence is sparse (Lacaille & Grimes 1961; Dawkins 1874).

Pollen evidence has shown that woodland was cleared intensively, if not extensively, during the Neolithic, but the agricultural landscape which must have surrounded the settlements has not survived to us (Rippon 1996, 21). Unlike other areas such as the west of Ireland (Caulfield 1983) and the Somerset Levels (Coles & Coles 1986) where evidence for organised land-use has survived beneath a blanket of peat, there are no field walls or bog trackways which can be ascribed to the Neolithic in Wales.

One of the features of Neolithic life, if not settlement, in many parts of England and the continent is the construction of enclosures with banks and ditches which may survive to this day. Most of the French and German farming villages were surrounded by substantial palisades which seem to be defensive. In Britain only the south-western peninsula can produce comparable defended settlements (Mercer 1981; Dixon 1988); elsewhere the interrupted banks and ditches surround hilltops whose use is much more problematic. In the south of England and the Midlands several causeway camps survive as earthworks but air photography has revealed many more. The absence of unambiguous traces of permanent settlement within these enclosures, their apparent rarity and the strangeness of some of the evidence from the ditch-fills has led to a great deal of debate about the role of these sites in the lives of the communities who built them (Mercer 1990). Most authorities reject the idea that these are totally straightforward villages and suggest that they were centres of political and/or religious power, the beginning of a centralising tendency in society and the embryo of chiefdoms recognisable in certain parts of the country at a later date (Renfrew 1973).

If these enclosures are public monuments, fulfilling some kind of political role in the organisation of society, it is not surprising that they are not found all over the country. Greater densities of population, such as that in Wessex, are likely to need more complex rules and structures to deal with competition for resources and power, but a simplistic application of this model would be unwise in view of the absence of causeway camps or other types of Neolithic enclosure from well-populated Yorkshire. However, what we know of settlement patterns and settlement units in Wales (and in other parts of western

Britain and Ireland), would suggest a scattered population, united at the level of the family or lineage and focused upon the family tomb; consequently 'political' enclosures with a wider remit are unlikely to have formed part of their lives, at least in the Earlier Neolithic.

Claims for such a site in Anglesey are unconvincing but the recent campaign of excavation in the Walton Basin (Radnorshire) has revealed a totally unexpected range of later Neolithic enclosures which suggest that major public monuments of the southern English type might have existed in this densely occupied part of Wales (Gibson 1999). The mysterious wooden platform at Abercynafon (Breconshire) is another non-funerary site which hints at public rituals in this south-eastern region at this time (Earwood & Thomas 1995).

COMMUNICATIONS

Throughout history the seaways around Wales have proved essential to contact, exchange and settlement. In the Early Neolithic, with its coastal settlement pattern and its obvious cultural links with Ireland, traffic in the Irish Sea must have been busy and the seaworthiness of the boats must have been of great significance. Unfortunately no evidence for boats of this date has survived. Because of the need for quite large vessels to carry animals and human pioneers it is thought that many may have been built on the lines of the Irish *curragh* – a light wooden frame with a skin covering (Case 1969). This type of boat is much more seaworthy and flexible as to size than the heavy dug-outs which are known to have been used in Mesolithic rivers and continued to be made and used at much later dates. Inevitably the evidence for these light but strong boats is very elusive at any date.

Despite its dangers, sea travel around the coasts must have been a great deal quicker and easier than taking the hunters' trails through the densely wooded interior. Eastward movement must have been possible, however, and the establishment of the Cotswold-Severn tomb-builders in the Talgarth Basin demonstrates that river valleys could soon become lines of communication. The distribution of stone axes, clustering at certain coastal depots and along major river valleys, suggests that different means of transport might be used in the course of a journey; the scale of exchange would lead to the establishment of regular routes. These routes would be largely dictated by geography but reinforced by human choice and need (Webley 1976). At this period it is not possible to pinpoint these paths with the precision which becomes possible in the Bronze Age (p. 95) except to mention the worn track that leads eastwards from the Graig Lwyd axe factory and which must pre-date the Early Bronze Age monument known as Druid's Circle near Penmaenmawr (Griffiths 1960, 313).

ARTEFACTS

Stone Axes

The polished stone axehead is the quintessential artefact of the Neolithic period. It was one of the most important tools of the early farmers in their battle against the native woodland and as such was invested with symbolic and ritual roles in addition to its practical use (Shotton 1972). Its virtual indestructability makes it the commonest find from this period and petrological study has revealed a sophisticated exploitation of natural

Pl. 1. *The Neanderthals. The scene shows Neanderthals outside a cave sited with a wide view across open tundra. Activities shown (right to left) are: knapping a handaxe, straightening a spearshaft, scraping a skin, creating a fire. The skin shelter is resonant of the structure in the Grotte du Lazaret near Nice. The bear's skull was shown to evoke the possibility of ritual but its depiction was actually tongue in cheek, since the evidence for Neanderthal bear cults had already been discounted by the time of the drawing. The image was created in about 1980 by Gino D'Achille for the National Museum of Wales from a brief prepared by Stephen Green in consultation with Christopher Stringer. (By permission of the National Museum of Wales)*

Pl. 2. Pontnewydd Cave: artefacts. Top row (left to right): handaxe, Levallois flake, handaxe; middle row: two side-scrapers, handaxe; bottom row: handaxe, discoidal core, handaxe (length of the latter 11.6cm). (By permission of the National Museum of Wales)

Pl. 3. Paviland Cave: reconstruction scene. The painting was made at a time when the burial was believed to have been Aurignacian. The corpse is shown, for artistic convenience, in an impossibly shallow grave and red ochre is being poured over the body in the form of a powder. Two mourners hold spears tipped, respectively, with a flint leafpoint and an Aurignacian bone point. Others hold ivory rods, depicted much longer than the surviving fragments, which are interpreted here as magical wands. They may, instead, simply have been blanks for the manufacture of ivory beads. The open tundra of the Bristol Channel plain is glimpsed through the cave-entrance. Originated in about 1980 by Gino D'Achille working from a brief prepared by Stephen Green. (By permission of the National Museum of Wales)

Pl. 4. The Nab Head: reconstruction scene.
The scene is set in around 9,000 BP, on the
coastal plain below the Early Mesolithic site of
the Nab Head, St Brides Bay, Pembrokeshire
(the wooded hill seen in the left background). A
range of activities is being undertaken including
manufacture of a tree trunk canoe using a
tranchet adze, making barbed antler points,
smoking fish and meat over fires, practising
archery and, in the distance, sea-fishing from
boats. Painted c. 1980 by Giovanni Caselli
working from a brief devised by Stephen
Green. (By permission of the National Museum
of Wales)

(Above right) Pl. 5. Graig Llwyd rough-outs
and polished Neolithic axehead: stages of
manufacture. (Photo Douglas Madge, UWB)

(Right) Pl. 6. Some of the large flint flakes from
the Late Neolithic Penmachno hoard,
Caernarfonshire. These are undoubtedly mined
flints imported into Wales. (Photo Frances
Lynch)

Pl. 7. Pentre Ifan, Pembrokeshire: view of chamber and forecourt. (Photo Frances Lynch)

Pl. 8. Tan y Muriau, Caernarfonshire: massive capstone on Portal Dolmen at west end of cairn. (Photo Frances Lynch)

Pl. 9. *View of Passage Grave chamber, Carreg Samson, Pembrokeshire. (Photo Frances Lynch)*

Pl. 10. *Ruined megalithic chamber, uncertain classification, at St David's Head, Pembrokeshire. (Photo Frances Lynch)*

Pl. 11. *Entrance to Bronze Age mines on the Great Orme, Llandudno. (Photo Frances Lynch)*

Pl. 12. *Cross section of the burnt mound at Graeanog, Caernarfonshire. (Photo Peter Crew)*

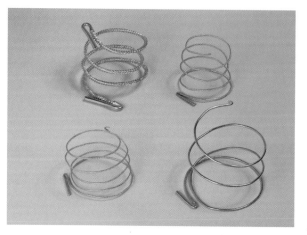

Pl. 13. *Llanwrthwl hoard of gold torcs. (By permission of the National Museum of Wales)*

Pl. 14 Kerb Circle at Moel Ty Uchaf, Merioneth. (Photo copyright Mick Sharp)

Pl. 15 Cairn Circle, Bryn Cader Faner, Merioneth. (Photo Richard Broad)

Pl. 16 Ring Cairn without upright stones at Cwm Cadlan, Breconshire. (Photo Frances Lynch)

Pl. 17 Well-preserved round barrow in Wentwood Forest, Monmouthshire. Since this photograph was taken the trees have, sadly, been felled and the mound damaged. (Photo Frances Lynch)

Pl. 18 Standing Stone beside the Ffordd Ddu trackway along the north flank of Cader Idris, south Merioneth. (Photo Frances Lynch)

resources and a countrywide network of exchange which has altered our perceptions of 'subsistence' farmers.

The qualities of stone desired by implement-makers are homogeneity (able to be shaped and chipped in any direction), strength to resist accidental fracture and capacity to produce a sharp edge either by chipping or by polishing (Pitts 1996). Flint, a silicate occurring only in chalk, is the most popular tool-making material but in Wales is not easy to find. Many igneous rocks have the same qualities as flint but are less brittle and make exceptionally good, heavy axeheads; however, they are more difficult to flake and so are unsuitable for small tools.

Unlike flint these igneous rocks are petrologically distinctive, so tools made from them can be traced back to their point of origin and sometimes the very quarries at which they were made can be identified. Because of the scale of production these sites have become known as 'axe factories', though it should not be forgotten that almost 50 per cent of axes cannot be so 'grouped' or traced and must have been made on an *ad hoc* basis from any pebble that seemed suitable (Briggs 1977). It should also be remembered that petrological ascriptions are sometimes less certain than many would wish (Davis 1985).

Five rock sources used on a relatively large scale during the Neolithic have been identified in Wales, two in the north and three on the Preseli Mountains in the south-west (Clough & Cummins 1988). In the north the Neolithic quarries have been identified and excavated. The southern 'factories' have not been located but the recent discovery of flakes and 'rough-outs' (axes chipped to shape but not yet polished) in fields some distance from the outcrops suggests that glacial erratics brought down by the ice may have been exploited, rather than the parent rock (David & Williams 1995).

The largest and best-known axe factory in Wales was at Graig Lwyd, Penmaenmawr, where a volcanic plug of augite granophyre forms a still-impressive headland (Warren 1922; Williams *et al.* 1998). The early workings were first recognised in 1919 by Hazzeldine Warren who found numerous flakes and 'rough-outs' on the north-eastern flank of the hill where the igneous rock projects through the surrounding shale to form low cliffs. He concluded that the axe material was quarried from such exposures all around the mountain. More recent excavation has confirmed this view but also identified points where the work may have involved some digging out of stone and where detached boulders may have been used (Muckle & Williams 1993).

The axe factory on Mynydd Rhiw on the western tip of Lleyn is exceptional in that no outcrop of the axe material is known; it had to be obtained from quarry pits some 3 metres deep (Houlder 1961a). In this case the axe material is not the igneous rock, an unsuitable dolerite, but the immediately adjacent shale, its laminations fused by the heat of the volcano. Four quarry pits run in a line across the northern end of the hill, each accurately sited to drop down on to the narrow band of suitable rock. They were dug in succession, each filled with the upcast from the next.

At both these sites, and at similar 'factories' in the Lake District (Bradley & Edmonds 1988), the artefactual evidence consists of scatters of small flakes, some half-finished or broken 'rough-outs', and hammerstones, large ones for quarrying and smaller ones for shaping the axes. In the hands of an expert the production of a 'rough-out' takes some fifteen minutes, but the final polishing is a much longer process lasting from two to four days (Torrence 1986) (see **Pl. 5**). This was not done on the open mountainside, where no evidence of any built shelters has been found.

The many rough-outs found in Caernarfonshire and Anglesey and the discovery of axe polishers and flakes of Graig Lwyd stone at Llandegai (Houlder 1976) and Bryn yr Hen Bobl (Hemp 1935) suggest that the final polishing may have been 'farmed out' to others within a radius of 30 to 50 kilometres (Jope 1952; Sheridan 1986). These finishers would also have made the long wooden handles. Rare survivals (Savory 1971c) show that these normally had a hooked or swept-back head.

Stone axes were probably produced at more than twenty centres in western Britain, though only eight actual working sites have been recognised. They were made for perhaps two thousand years, yet they hardly vary. Apart from the difference in cross-section occasioned by flaked (lenticular) or pecked (circular) manufacture there is little variation from factory to factory and it is difficult to detect any development through time (Pitts 1996). The Graig Lwyd axes (Group VII), the commonest in Wales and the third largest group in Britain, are always completely polished and have a pointed oval cross-section; they are very consistent as to shape and size which suggests very competent or perhaps professional manufacture. Because of the nature of the raw material, axes from Mynydd Rhiw (Group XXI) are usually thin and narrow and often only the blade is polished. The Preseli rocks, Group XXIII and its sub-group XIII, are granular and do not flake, so must be shaped by pecking; these axes have a more circular cross-section.

Petrology has revealed the dispersal pattern of these axes from their centres of manufacture, but it cannot identify the mechanisms of this trade (Bradley & Edmonds 1993). Ethnographic parallels show that in some regions the exploitation of quarries is formalised and ritualised, with working restricted to certain groups and times, but that in others the situation is much more casual, with people coming to make axes whenever they needed them (Burton 1984). A study of the hammerstones used at the Lakeland quarries has suggested that two distinct groups exploited the stone there (Bradley & Suthren 1990), but similar work has not yet been done in Wales. The mechanisms of dispersal are also poorly understood; were the axes formally traded, perhaps by a merchant class (an economic niche which might have been filled by the descendants of more mobile hunters) or did they simply pass from hand to hand between neighbours? Definite answers cannot be given; the situation almost certainly changed through time and may have varied regionally.

The dispersal of Cornish axes to south-eastern England has suggested a deliberate seaborne 'trade', probably belonging to the later half of the period (Cummins 1974), but this confident interpretation has recently been questioned (Berridge 1994). Despite the fact that the pattern of Group VII (Graig Lwyd) axes has been claimed to demonstrate hand-to-hand movement (Cummins 1979) there is some evidence in Wales to support the 'commercial' scenario. In the Prestatyn area, beneath the Flintshire hills which form a landmark within the north Irish Sea Basin, and at Merthyr Mawr Warren on the coast of south Wales, axes from a variety of factories have been found in sufficient quantities to suggest depots from which deliberate export might be organised (Houlder 1961a, 138).

Only Graig Lwyd was a major producer on a country-wide scale. It dominated the local market (75 per cent of north Welsh axes were made there) but its products reached the Peak

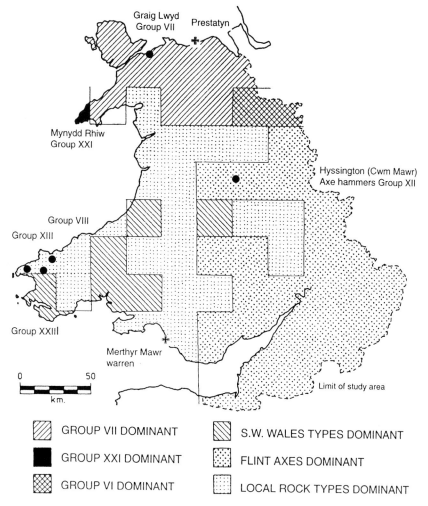

Fig. 2.4. *Generalised distribution of 'axe factory' products showing 'factories', rock sources and possible depots (from Darvill 1989 with additions).*

District, Yorkshire and the English Midlands in significant numbers (Clough & Cummins 1988, Map 7). The other Welsh 'factories' had much more limited markets (*Ibid*. Maps 8, 12 & 18). The petrological identification of Group VIII (from Ramsey Island or Preseli) is rather problematic but the pattern of dispersal within south Wales is convincing. It is important in the south-west, where it provides over a quarter of the axes, and in the south-east where it is rivalled by flint axes from southern England. The two other Preseli groups (XIII and XXIII) are very small, as is Mynydd Rhiw (Group XXI) although its products are quite widely dispersed within Wales and it occurs at the depot sites. Despite the availability of good local stone the products of other 'factories' were used in Wales (Group VI from Langdale mainly in Powys and Group I from Cornwall along the south coast); in eastern Wales the contribution of flint axes was significant (Darvill 1989).

The study of axes from datable contexts can give some chronological depth to this picture (Clough & Cummins 1988, 246–60). Flakes of Group XXI and Group VIII stone have been found at the Mesolithic site of Trwyn Du, Anglesey, indicating that the qualities of these two rocks may have been first recognised by the native hunting population who, though their exploitation of stone was on a small scale, certainly carried good raw materials for considerable distances (see p. 36 above). The identification of Mynydd Rhiw stone in a Mesolithic context is interesting in view of the suggestion that the personal tools of the miners there had Mesolithic traits and that axe traders might have had a hunting ancestry (Houlder 1961a, 136–9).

It can be shown that three of the five grouped rocks from Wales were being exploited in the Early Neolithic (around 4,000 cal BC). Graig Lwyd stone (VII) occurs at the Llandegai house; Mynydd Rhiw (XXI) was used for a pendant from the tomb at Dyffryn Ardudwy (Powell 1973, 26); and one of the axes from the dated pit at Coygan was Group VIII. Other early contexts, Gwernvale and Din Dryfol, produced axes made of ungrouped stone. Group XXIIIb occurs at Clegyr Boia, perhaps a Middle Neolithic site. Only Group XIII, the Preseli bluestone whose main products are shaft-hole implements of Bronze Age type, has no dated context.

The exploitation of Groups VII and VIII continued for a long time. An axe polisher of Group VIII stone covered a burial in the henge monument at Llandegai (Houlder 1976, 59; but see David & Williams 1995, 453) and a macehead of Late Neolithic type found at Windmill Hill in Wiltshire was made from Group VII stone (RCAHMW 1956, xlix). On the basis of these admittedly few dated finds it is possible to argue that it was Mesolithic geologists who first recognised the quality of these rocks, and their exploitation for large tools expanded with the development of farming. Dispersal at this period was probably restricted. The widespread trade in these axes may have begun gradually and did not develop seriously until the Middle to Late Neolithic (Smith 1979). The context of Group VII axes outside Wales is, where datable, late: the Cairnpapple Henge, the West Kennet Avenue, the upper levels of the Windmill Hill ditches and two instances of peat finds at Late Neolithic horizons (RCAHMW 1956, xlix). The same is generally true of Group VIII (David & Williams 1995, 453–4).

English axes in Wales are poorly dated, but none occurs in positively early contexts and their frequency in the Severn Valley, which sees little activity until the later Neolithic, would suggest that they belong to that horizon. It is interesting that Cornish axes should be so rare. There are none from the early groups and even Group I is poorly represented. Its context is likely to be contemporary with the later Beakers: a brief horizon when traffic across the Bristol Channel seems to have been brisk.

The dispersal of stone axes is normally spoken of as a 'trade' but this is a term which conceals our ignorance of the true motivation of the exchange (Edmonds 1995). Whatever its nature, however, this exchange is tangible evidence for contact between distant areas. It provides a background against which it is easy to visualise the adoption and adaptation of new ideas in the realms of religion and politics which we may glimpse behind the changes made to many of the tombs in the later half of the Neolithic. The attraction of these specialised natural resources may have been a spur to movement in this period and some of the links which were established through this 'trade', particularly to northern England, grew yet more important in later centuries.

Flint Implements

Flint implements and other personal goods of the earlier Neolithic in Wales are neither common nor distinctive. The only objects worthy of special note are a perforated sheep bone, perhaps a flute, from the tomb at Penywyrlod (Britnell & Savory 1984, 27–8) and the stone discs from Pant y Saer, Ty Isaf and Penywyrlod. Similar discs are an unexplained feature of several burial chambers in Britain and Brittany.

Scrapers, which are notoriously difficult to date, must be the most common tool but they have seldom been found in contexts that could provide information of either date or function. It is normally assumed that they were used in the preparation of skins to make leather clothing, but we have no direct evidence of such clothing. Because of the burial traditions of the period we know virtually nothing about their trinkets or personal decoration.

The only small artefact which can be confidently ascribed to the earlier Neolithic is the leaf-shaped arrowhead (Green 1980). These may be found as chance finds, on settlements such as that beneath Gwernvale cairn and occasionally inside megalithic tombs. In this last context it is difficult to know whether the arrowhead was deliberately placed in the tomb or had entered it with one of the corpses, for, though there are no overt weapons and no certain defences in Neolithic Wales, evidence from southern England shows that the bow and arrow might be used in warfare as well as in hunting (Green 1986).

Pottery

The manufacture of pottery is one of the significant new features of the Neolithic. Its weight and fragility imply a settled existence and its capacity for variation in shape, fabric and decoration has attracted a train of historical interpretation. Believed to be a highly traditional home-based craft, pottery has been used to identify origins, ancestral groupings, cultural borrowings and the passage of time. In many cases this burden of meaning may be too heavy for the evidence to bear, but of all Neolithic artefacts pottery is the most sensitive to change and therefore warrants discussion.

Early Neolithic pottery has been found in both domestic and ritual contexts in Wales. In both, the range of pot-types is similar: a wide, relatively shallow round-bottomed bowl is the most common container; small cups may exist, but are rare; and there is some evidence for the existence of flat-based storage jars made in coarser fabrics. Domestic assemblages have come from Trefignath, Llandegai and Gwaenysgor in north Wales (Smith & Lynch 1987; Lynch 1976; 1969), Gwernvale and Llanelwedd in mid-Wales (Lynch 1984a) and Clegyr Boia, Coygan and Stackpole Warren in the south (Williams 1952; Wainwright 1967; Benson *et al.* 1990). Occasional sherds have been found in several megalithic tombs but significant deposits have come only from Dyffryn Ardudwy, Carreg Samson, Carreg Coitan, Ty Isaf and Gwernvale (Powell 1973; Lynch 1975a; unpubl.; Grimes 1939; Britnell & Savory 1984). This last site, with well-stratified deposits from pre-cairn settlement, tomb use and tomb closure, is especially important.

In the north well-fired, undecorated carinated bowls made in a vesicular, gritless fabric are dominant. These belong to a widespread family; analogues may be found in Devon and Cornwall, Ireland and northern England where they can be shown to belong to an early horizon (Herne 1988). In Wales the style has been dubbed 'Irish Sea Ware' because

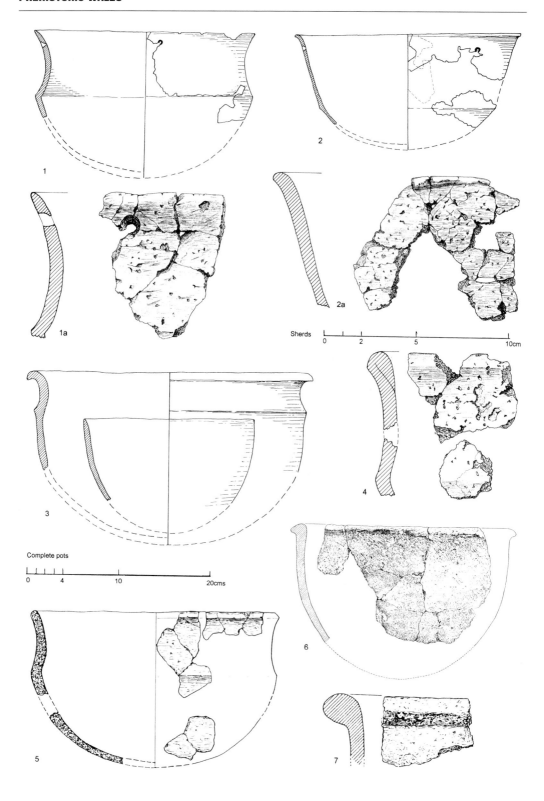

Sherds

0   2   5   10cm

Complete pots

0   4   10   20cms

of its association with tombs and houses similar to those in Ireland (Lynch 1976). Radiocarbon dates from Llandegai and Trefignath confirm the early horizon; the end date is more debatable (Savory 1980a, 221; Herne 1988, 12) but there is no positive evidence for late survival.

Associated with the fine carinated bowls in the north there are a few heavily gritted sherds from straight-sided jars. These are similar to Lough Gur Class II and Kilhoyle pots from Ireland which are normally considered Late Neolithic or later in date (Case 1961). However, they occur at the dated site, Trefignath (Smith & Lynch 1987, 74–7) and at Dyffryn Ardudwy where sherds were stratified beneath the blocking of the eastern chamber with a carinated bowl (Powell 1973, 17).

The settlement beneath the cairn at Gwernvale has produced the largest assemblage of Early Neolithic pottery from Wales (Lynch 1984a). Two styles may be recognised, both used by the same community around 3,900 cal BC. One is an open carinated bowl very similar to those from north-west Wales; the other is an unshouldered hemispherical bowl with a heavier, more emphatic rim. This type does not occur in early contexts in the north, but it is notably associated with the Cotswold-Severn tombs in south-east Wales, occurring in some quantity at Ty Isaf (Grimes 1939) and recognisable in the few sherds from Tinkinswood, Parc le Breos Cwm, Penywyrlod and from chamber 2 at Gwernvale itself (Lynch 1969, Fig. 60).

This shape, and particularly its heavy rim, has been compared to Abingdon Ware, a Middle Neolithic style reflecting the increasing taste for decoration on pottery in south-east England (Lynch 1976; Savory 1980a, 220; Case & Whittle 1982, 30–3). The early date for Gwernvale may cast some doubt on this comparison but the association with tombs having eastward links suggests that it does indeed stem from a south-eastern context (but see Herne 1988, 18). The appearance of more heavily decorated rims on hemispherical bowls at a later horizon – Carreg Coitan, Pembrokeshire, with a radiocarbon date of c. 3,500 cal BC (Barker 1992, 20–1), Mount Pleasant (Savory 1952) and Stackpole Warren (Benson et al. 1990) – may be a development of this style within south Wales. Its appearance in north Wales is limited, but it may be recognised in a Middle Neolithic horizon at Pant y Saer, Anglesey (Lynch 1991, 81–2).

The relatively large quantity of pottery from the settlement at Clegyr Boia, Pembrokeshire, is difficult to date. Shape and fabric are broadly similar to the northern Irish Sea Wares (Lynch 1976) but the rather straighter profile, prominent lugs and high shoulders suggest a slightly different background. It has been suggested that shouldered bowls, such as the Clegyr Boia ones, should be distingished from the carinated ones and recognised as a Middle Neolithic style (Herne 1988). The wide curved lugs on many bowls are reminiscent of Hembury Ware from Devon and Cornwall, an early style which may be long-lived in that region (Herne 1988, 17). It has a surprisingly limited impact in south Wales. This revision of Clegyr Boia would place emphasis on the single decorated rim (Williams 1952, Fig. 11) and equate the settlement with that at Stackpole Warren and the occupation of caves on Caldey Island (Lacaille & Grimes 1961).

(Opposite) *Fig. 2.5. Earlier Neolithic pottery from Wales. 1–2 Dyffryn Ardudwy, Mer.; 3 Clegyr Boia, Pembs. (after Williams 1952); 4 Llandegai, Caerns.; 5 Trefignath, Ang.; 6–7 Ty Isaf, Brecs. (from Grimes 1939).*

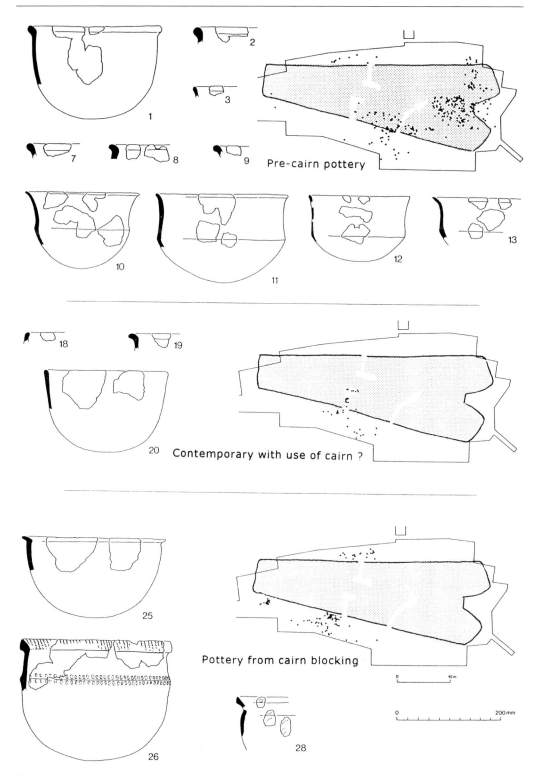

Pre-cairn pottery

Contemporary with use of cairn ?

Pottery from cairn blocking

Fig. 2.6. *Gwernvale, Brecs.: summary of pottery phasing (from Britnell and Savory 1984).*

The presence of simple bowls at an early horizon at Coygan (Wainwright 1967) and in the tomb at Carreg Samson (Lynch 1975a) demonstrates that there was no uniformity of shape among the Early Neolithic pottery of Wales, but it was all entirely undecorated. A taste for decoration appeared first in south Wales and during the Middle Neolithic was restricted to light incision on the rim. Heavily textured pottery with impressed decoration on rim and body – the Peterborough series familiar in the south of England – belongs to a later horizon, though one that radiocarbon dates now suggest is rather earlier (perhaps 3,400–2,500 cal BC) than was previously believed (Gibson & Kinnes 1997). Significantly, it is associated with the closure of the chambers at Gwernvale (Britnell & Savory 1984) and Trefignath (Smith & Lynch 1987) and with jet belt sliders at Gop, Flintshire (Dawkins 1902).

Analysis of Early Neolithic pottery has shown that, for the most part, it is locally made (Jenkins in Smith & Lynch 1987) but in southern England the extensive use of gabbroic pottery from Cornwall indicates that this should not be an automatic assumption. Recognition of a 'trade' in pottery has considerable social implications which it would be premature to consider at this stage (D.A. Jenkins pers. comm.).

TOMBS

Introduction

The great stone tombs which still stand among our modern fields are the most obvious relics to survive from this period and are the subject of the most intense debate (Lynch 1997). They occur all over western Europe at this time and have been interpreted as the product of anxiety about continued fertility of land, animals and human groups arising from the shift to an active responsibility for food production. This argument, however, is perhaps undermined by the simplicity of burial customs among the earliest farmers, the villagers of the Danube Valley. An alternative suggestion, that the preponderance of monumental tombs on the peripheries of Europe stems instead from the traditions of the indigenous Mesolithic hunters, has a convincing geographical base but philosophically they must be the product of a post-transitional phase (Clark 1980; Sherratt 1990). In the absence of previous traditions of monumental burial, either in east or west, the phenomenon of these great tombs, in stone or in earth and wood, which are found all around the Atlantic façade from Portugal to Sweden, may never be satisfactorily explained. Settlement patterns and density of population may hold some of the keys: the eastern farmers owned complex ritual equipment, lived in large villages where there may have been religious buildings not so closely associated with human burial; and their religious activity may have been more multi-facetted. In the west, scattered communities of much smaller size may have found the family tomb a more appropriate focus, and may have needed a more visible and secure symbol of continuity.

In the past the similarities between these monuments were stressed and they were seen as evidence for a broad sweep of colonists reaching Britain from the south; now the complexity of chronology and individual cultural backgrounds has encouraged regional perspectives in which external stimulae are less important, though the Europe-wide dilemma remains (Joussaume 1988). Like other cultural attributes, these monuments differ in design, making it possible to recognise regionally distinctive groups through variations in the plan of burial chambers and in the shape of covering mounds or cairns. Excavation has also revealed differences in burial rituals and ceremonial behaviour, so these monuments embody a great deal of cultural distinctiveness. Occasionally composite structures may be recognised which incorporate features from more than one tradition, an indication of movement and exchange of ideas on a scale which must be historically significant, though its full interpretation will elude us (Corcoran 1972).

These monuments are artefacts of great complexity. Their very scale necessitated a great investment of time and effort on the part of the communities who built them, and their meaning must have been powerful. They are traditionally spoken of as 'tombs' because human bones are regularly found in them (normally the remains of several individuals, as in some family vault), but this may be but a small part of their religious role. The recognition that a monument might have been the focus of activity for perhaps a thousand years, yet contains relatively few bones, or perhaps have been altered externally without the provision of new burial space, has led to the realisation that the monument itself was important – that it may have become a symbol of the desired permanence of the community, a visible link with the ancestors and a guarantor of legitimacy in that territory (Renfrew 1976). Such insights are not susceptible of proof but they help to broaden our appreciation of the role of these monuments in society.

As well as variation in chamber and cairn design there are differences in burial system. In Wales the western tombs contain cremated bone and the south-eastern ones unburnt bone, but in both there is evidence for multiple burial; the ancestors are a group rather than individuals for the bones are mixed and anonymous without differentiation of wealth or status. Men, women and children may be found and none has any personal possessions with them. The fragmentary and disarticulated condition of the unburnt bones suggests that burial was a multi-stage ritual; bones were brought into the chamber after exposure and defleshing elsewhere and perhaps later used as talismans and cult objects. A little pottery, in Wales usually ceremonially broken, may be found in the chambers or at the entrances. Because the stone chambers could be used and re-used over a long period it is difficult to use such pottery to argue for a date of building, but in most groups it is possible to suggest construction of the first tombs in the Early Neolithic with interest, but probably not continuous burial, being maintained to the late fourth millennium cal BC and beyond.

In Wales there are three main families: the complex Cotswold-Severn group in the south-east which has connections in the Cotswolds and eventually extends its influence to north Wales; the Portal Dolmens and other simple stone 'boxes' to be found in the west; and the sparse scatter of simple Passage Graves up the Irish Sea coasts (see **Fig. 2.1**).

Cotswold-Severn Tombs

These tombs may be discussed in three geographical sections. The Glamorgan and Monmouthshire coastal group includes monuments of quite varied design, the range of variation – simple terminal chambers, transepted terminal chambers and laterally chambered cairns – being similar to that seen in the Cotswold and Wessex regions

(Opposite) *Fig. 2.7. Cotswold–Severn tombs in Wales. Hatching denotes formal blocking. (After Lynch 1997.) Scale 1:400.*

PIPTON

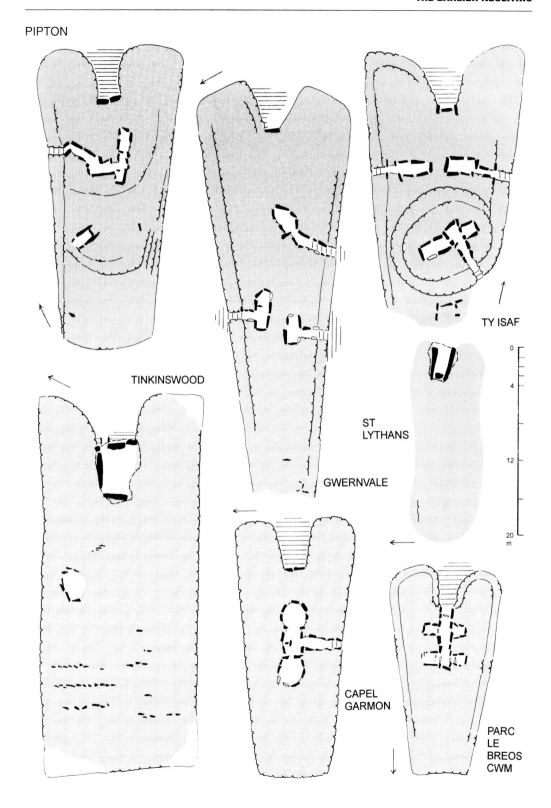

TINKINSWOOD

TY ISAF

ST
LYTHANS

GWERNVALE

CAPEL
GARMON

PARC
LE
BREOS
CWM

Fig. 2.8. Parc le Breos Cwm, Glamorgan. View of front of cairn; walling is original but rebuilt. (Photo: copyright Mick Sharp)

(Corcoran 1969). The Breconshire group, centred on Talgarth, have uniquely complex ground plans combining transepted or angled chambers in a laterally organised cairn. The plans look derivative of the Cotswold and southern groups but their dates seem to be as early as their putative progenitors. Finally a group of cairns in north Wales, which seem to stem from this Breconshire group, may be seen to impact upon already established tomb-building traditions (Lynch 1976).

The Glamorgan/Monmouthshire group includes cairns in Gower with transepted terminal chambers like Parc le Breos Cwm and Penmaen Burrows; simple terminal chambers like Tinkinswood, St Lythans and Portskewett; and cairns of uncertain plan like the newly discovered one at Thornwell (Maylan 1991) and the ruined monument at Garn Llwyd which are probably laterally chambered. All these diverse chambers are united by being set within exceptionally carefully built and neatly walled cairns, normally markedly trapezoid in plan. What we know of the burial system (disarticulated unburnt bone) and funerary equipment is also broadly uniform across the chamber types. Tinkinswood was excavated early in this century (Ward 1915; 1916), Parc le Breos in the nineteenth century

Fig. 2.9. Tinkinswood chambered cairn, Glamorgan, single terminal chamber and forecourt. Horizontal dry-walling is original; herring-bone walling is restoration after the 1916 excavations. (Photo: copyright Mick Sharp)

and again in 1960. The recent publication (Whittle & Wysocki 1998) has provided a full discussion of the weathered and disarticulated bone and a series of radiocarbon dates indicating use between 3,700 and 3,300 cal BC (broadly contemporary with similar monuments elsewhere), with some later burials in the passage.

Early views on the history of this group of tomb-builders stressed the similarity of the transepted chamber plan to those in western France and saw them as colonisers from France moving up the Severn Estuary (Piggott 1962). More recently, the complexity of their architectural inspiration has led to the view that the unique mixture of influences occurred within Britain, combining the formality of earthen long barrow mound design with at least two traditions of continental chamber architecture, the lateral passage graves like Barnenez, and the Pornic transepted chambers from the mouth of the Loire (Corcoran 1969, 73–104). Such an amalgam would most likely have been fused in the Cotswolds and Wiltshire, with the Welsh examples representing a secondary expansion. The recent recognition of two earthen long barrows of English type near Welshpool demonstrates the proximity of groups building in wood and in stone. Limited excavation at the Lower

Luggy long barrow confirmed the presence of a façade trench with oak posts and provided radiocarbon dates centred on 3,700 – 3,300 cal BC (Gibson *forthcoming* in *Studia Celtica*).

The Breconshire tombs are quite clearly a regional variant (Britnell & Savory 1984). Though each is distinct, their very eccentricity of plan is a unifying factor. Like the main group, they have carefully walled trapezoid cairns but none has a terminal chamber; all the forecourts lead to a blind portal and the chambers are entered from the side. These chambers may be simple rectangular boxes with passage access, or more complex polygonal, T-shaped or transepted structures. At Arthur's Stone, Pipton, Gwernvale and probably Little Lodge the passage is angled; at Ty Isaf and Gwernvale the laterals are paired, as they normally are in the Cotswolds, but at others the plan is not so balanced. Despite ingenious attempts (Corcoran 1969, 84–6), it has not been possible to explain this complexity of plan by suggesting that they are the result of multi-period building. The various chambers, all built at the outset, may have been intended for different purposes, and variation in the skeletal content hints at this (Britnell & Savory 1984, 5), but it cannot be demonstrated convincingly.

The blind portals and the mixture of chamber plans have suggested that this group was late, the final stage in a development from transepted terminal chambers (Grimes 1960, 90), the product of a splinter group developing in isolation within its own enclosed region. However, though this argument is typologically attractive, neither radiocarbon dating nor artefact chronology support it. Two recently excavated tombs, Penywyrlod (Talgarth) and Gwernvale have both produced radiocarbon dates close to 3,900 cal BC (as early as any from the Cotswolds and slightly earlier than those from Parc le Breos), while decorated pottery associated with the final closure of Gwernvale is of a type primary to some transepted sites in Gloucestershire (Darvill 1982, 22–5). We are forced therefore to admit that these tombs were among the earlier examples, emerging at a formative period when ideas were fluid and might be adopted from a variety of sources. The most recently and extensively excavated tomb, Gwernvale, demonstrates that the individual monument might be used successively (the end of the chamber passages skilfully concealed on each occasion) over a period of more than 800 years, bringing its life well into the Middle Neolithic. The decision to close it was a formal one and elaborate structures were built to block both the chambers and the ceremonial forecourt.

With twelve monuments within 200 square kilometres, all belonging to the same tradition, the Breconshire tombs form the most culturally cohesive group in Wales. Moreover their influence can be seen in more distant areas where some tombs were built entirely within the Breconshire style and others show adaptation by people who had originally followed different traditions. This period of expansion would seem to belong to the Middle Neolithic but the mechanism is less clear. Is this a movement of settlers? 'Pure Breconshire tombs' such as Capel Garmon, Tyddyn Bleiddyn and perhaps Tyn y Coed and Ystum Cegid Isaf might suggest this (Lynch 1969, 143–7); whereas Carneddau Hengwm and Tan y Muriau, where additions were made to Portal Dolmens, might be explained as existing communities

(Opposite) *Figs 2.10 and 2.11. Gwernvale, Breconshire: (above) high quality walling on cairn edge and outer passages; (below) blocking in passage of north chamber. (Photos: courtesy of Bill Britnell)*

adopting new ideas (Lynch 1976). Either case demonstrates the mixing of traditions which, it can be argued, is a feature of this period in many parts of Britain (Scott 1969, 182–91) and may be either the result or the cause of the development of long-distance trade.

Portal Dolmens and Rectangular Chambers

The Portal Dolmen is dominant in most parts of north-west Wales and in the Nevern Valley in north Pembrokeshire; in the rest of the south-west, as far east as Gower, it occurs alongside other tombs, Passage Graves and chambers of unspecific design. Its absence from Anglesey, an island with a variety of Early Neolithic monuments, is difficult to explain.

The Portal Dolmen belongs to a very widespread family of monuments in which the burial chamber is a more or less simple 'box', for which there is no need to evoke external models (Scott 1969, 180–2). The wooden long barrow chambers in England and the Clyde cairns of south-west Scotland are other members of this same family in which variation develops in the treatment of the entrance – the point of contact between the worlds of the living and the dead (Lynch 1997, 16–21).

Portal Dolmens are arguably some of the most exciting megalithic structures in these islands (see **Pl. 7**). The classic form is architecturally very distinctive with a tall, H-shaped portal fronting a single rectangular chamber covered by what is often an exceptionally massive sloping capstone (see **Pl. 8**). The impressive chamber is set in a relatively small cairn whose shape may be variable. Since these tombs are often on lower slopes, in agricultural land, the cairn seldom survives, but both round and long cairns are known. They do not have the precise delineation of the Cotswold-Severn ones. Classic examples, like the West Chamber at Dyffryn Ardudwy and Gwern Einion in Merioneth can be found in both north and south but in the south the portal is less often closed by a tall slab (Lynch 1969; 1972a).

In Ireland, where there are monuments very similar to the Welsh ones, it was argued that such non-functional entrances must indicate a late date. It was believed that the Portal Dolmen developed there from the more elaborate Court Cairn, then spread to the south-east and thence across to Wales (De Valera 1960). This logical argument was upset by the discovery of Early Neolithic pottery (**Fig. 2.5**) associated with the *closure* of the West Chamber of Dyffryn Ardudwy and by the recognition that early wooden chambers are similarly closed (Shand & Hodder 1990). An alternative view has gained ground which recognises the Portal Dolmen as an early monument type, but perhaps too sophisticated and too widespread to lie at the very beginning of the local sequence (Lynch 1969; Powell 1973; ApSimon 1985/6). As in Scotland the earliest tombs should perhaps be sought among the simpler stone boxes, of which there are examples in Anglesey and in Pembrokeshire.

Recent excavations in Anglesey, which contains no classic Portal Dolmens, have shown that two of the rectangular gallery structures – the Long Graves – are of early date and the product of multi-period building, stone box graves being built one in front of the other (Smith & Lynch 1987) (**Fig. 2.12**). At Trefignath the box chambers followed the

(Opposite) *Fig. 2.12. Portal Dolmens, Rectangular chambers and Small Passage Graves. Multi-period construction differentially shaded; hatching denotes formal blocking. (After Lynch 1969; 1972; 1976; 1991.) Scale 1:300.*

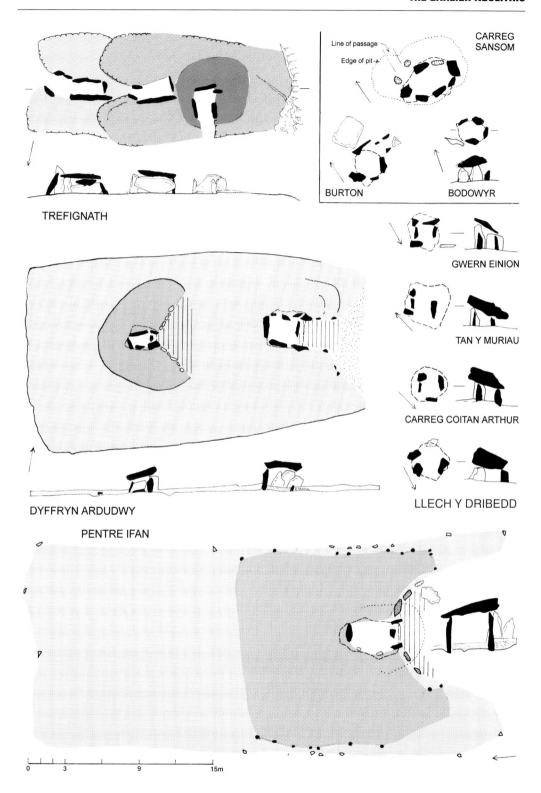

CARREG SANSOM

Line of passage

Edge of pit

BURTON

BODOWYR

TREFIGNATH

GWERN EINION

TAN Y MURIAU

CARREG COITAN ARTHUR

DYFFRYN ARDUDWY

LLECH Y DRIBEDD

PENTRE IFAN

0   3   9   15m

construction of a tomb which has been interpreted as a small Passage Grave, an indication of the complexity of early settlement on the island. Though they have tall portals, neither box chamber looks like a Portal Dolmen and they recall instead the earlier Clyde chambers (Scott 1969). At Din Dryfol the second chamber had a wooden portal, adding another element to the range of structural ideas available. To claim that Din Dryfol and the central chamber at Trefignath are ancestral to an early and already architecturally confident tomb like Dyffryn Ardudwy West Chamber cannot be totally convincing, but it does demonstrate the range of broadly similar, if regionally distinguishable, funerary options available to those sailing regularly across and up and down the Irish Sea, where similarity of pottery and house-building traditions confirm their mutual familiarity.

The excavation of Dyffryn Ardudwy in 1960 transformed our understanding of the Welsh Portal Dolmens (Powell 1973). The classic chamber at the west end of the cairn was shown to be the primary monument, which was originally covered by a circular cairn. The very small chamber and the absence of cremated bones in its interstices suggested that the funerary rite might have been single inhumation, but this unusual conclusion has not been confirmed, largely because these conspicuous and accessible tombs have been so thoroughly robbed in the past. However, the early date, clearly demonstrated by the pottery incorporated in the blocking in the forecourt, has now been generally accepted (ApSimon 1985/6). The West Chamber was superceded by a much less classic structure – still rectangular but without high portals and with a much lower closing slab. This was covered by a rectangular cairn which engulfed the early tomb.

Although it lacks distinctive architectural features, the East Chamber at Dyffryn Ardudwy is still recognisably within the Portal Dolmen tradition. It gives credence to the assimilation into this group of a variety of undistinctive structures having little more than rectangularity of plan and lack of an entrance passage to link them with the tradition (Lynch 1972a). In the absence of excavation not very much can be said about sites such as Maen y Bardd, Bachwen and Rhoslan, Caernarfonshire (Lynch 1969); some might be early progenitors, some might be late 'degenerates' like Dyffryn East Chamber. In the south there seems to be a preference for multiple chambers among the low boxes, as Cerrig y Gof and Trellyffaint (Lynch 1972a; Barker 1992).

Carreg Coetan Arthur near Newport in Pembrokeshire, with Middle Neolithic dates and decorated pottery, suggests that not all later tombs lack architectural distinction (Barker 1992, 19–21). At this time, too, the Portal Dolmen-building communities seem to feel free to absorb new ideas and to adapt their tombs, perhaps for new ceremonial, perhaps for enhancement of the old. The most striking instance of this is Pentre Ifan in the Nevern Valley where an imposing façade, it can be argued, was added to an early Portal Dolmen (Lynch 1972a). Such façades had long been common in the north of Ireland where a well-defined court was the setting for ceremonies outside the tomb. Ceremonies certainly took place in front of Portal Dolmens but there are only two Welsh examples of tall façades. In Scotland the idea was copied more widely (Scott 1969, 182–91).

In the north changes and adaptations were more common and perhaps more serious. Though there has been no excavation to confirm it, it is probably at this time that the Portal Dolmen cairn at Carnedd Hengwm South was enlarged and its neighbour built entirely in the Cotswold-Severn style (Lynch 1976). We can know nothing of any trauma which may have accompanied these changes, but it is noticeable that it is these box chambers, whether in Scotland or in Wales, that are most frequently adapted and changed (Corcoran 1972) and which show evidence for very long survival. Perhaps a certain religious flexibility is the key to this survival.

Passage Graves

Passage Graves can be distinguished from the various box-like structures already discussed by the presence of a clearly defined passage between the burial chamber and the outer world. The entrance to this passage has neither the architectural nor perhaps the symbolic impact of the doorway into the Portal Dolmen or other tombs where a forecourt is provided as a focus for external ceremony. These architectural and, by implication, philosophical differences have always encouraged the belief that there was a sharper divide between those groups who built Passage Graves and those who built the various 'enhanced boxes' previously known by the generic term 'gallery grave' (Daniel 1941). The Passage Graves also have much more uniformity across Europe than the various regionalised 'galleries', a uniformity which may still encourage ideas of introduction.

Wales contains two groups of Passage Graves. The first is a scattered group of seven small isolated monuments found in west Wales and in Anglesey; the second is represented by distinctive monuments of late date in north Wales.

The scattered group, epitomised by Carreg Samson, Pembrokeshire (Lynch 1975a), have polygonal chambers and, where the evidence survives, short passages (**Fig. 2.12** and **Pl. 9**). They can be compared to similar monuments in Brittany and up both sides of the Irish Sea to the Western Isles and beyond. Chronological evidence from Brittany (Boujot & Cassen 1993), Broadsands in Devon (Radford 1958), Carreg Samson (Lynch 1975a) and Achnacreebeag in Argyll (Ritchie 1970) suggests that they belong to an early horizon but only in Scotland does the style develop and the monuments remain the focus of continued interest. Further south the scattered and isolated distribution of these tombs suggests that the communities who built them did not prosper or were absorbed by others whose ideas of tomb-building differed. The secondary position of the Passage Grave at Achnacreebeag shows that other tomb-building traditions co-existed, while at Trefignath the primary Passage Grave is incorporated into a cairn with a different style of chamber (Smith & Lynch 1987) so this group of tombs may be interpreted as the product of a religious tradition which failed to develop.

The later Passage Graves are exceptional structures. Barclodiad y Gawres in Anglesey is a decorated cruciform Passage Grave comparable in every way to the famous monuments of the Boyne Valley in Ireland (Powell & Daniel 1956; Eogan 1986). Beneath the round cairn is a long passage leading to a corbelled chamber with three side-chambers, the right-hand one with an additional annexe. Cremated bone had been placed in the side-chambers and the annexe but not in the central chamber where a fire had burned, quenched in ceremonies which involved a 'magic stew' of frogs and mice. This exceptional survival is a vivid insight into the nature of funerary ceremony, as are the decorated stones, though we cannot read the message of either. Five stones are decorated with abstract designs lightly pecked into the surface, visible only in oblique light. Art is a surprisingly rare adjunct to megalithic tombs, occurring only in Iberia, Brittany and Ireland and each region has its own circumscribed style (Shee-Twohig 1981).

Barclodiad must have been built by people with very close ties to Ireland, people who must have come across in the Middle Neolithic. They were not alone, for decorated stones survive from a similar tomb in Calderstones, Liverpool (Forde Johnston 1957), and it is possible that the great cairn at Gop, Flintshire, covers another (Dawkins 1902). Its scale is comparable to those on the Boyne and much larger than any later monument.

The question of megalithic tombs in the Late Neolithic is a difficult one to pin down because, with re-use always a possibility, it is seldom possible to date the construction of a tomb. During the Late Neolithic new forms of burial were being adopted in some areas (see p. 122) but in both north and south Wales there is evidence that many tombs were still in some sort of use. Sherds of Late Neolithic pottery have been found in several monuments, but at Gwernvale this was certainly a period of formal closure (Britnell & Savory 1984, 90–3). In Anglesey, by contrast, it can be shown that one tomb at least, Bryn Celli Ddu, was actually built during this period (Hemp 1930; O'Kelly 1969).

This is an unusual monument: a Passage Grave with a simple polygonal chamber and a long passage covered by a round cairn which overlies a henge monument (see pp. 129–31). This relationship proves its Late Neolithic date, but typologically the Passage Grave looks much earlier and it is possible to argue (though not to prove) that the obliteration of the henge was an act of antagonistic revival, with earlier traditions reinstated in their purest form (Lynch 1991, 94–5). The use and subsequent burial of a decorated monolith in the centre of the henge and behind the burial chamber seems to have been part of ceremonies to rededicate the site. The decoration on the stone, like the plan of the chamber, harks back to Early Neolithic models, but from Brittany not Ireland.

Proof of the late date of Bryn Celli Ddu arises from exceptional circumstances; other monuments on Anglesey may well be contemporary but the evidence is less compelling. Burial chambers with minimal architectural finesse – such as Lligwy (Lynch 1991, 88–90) – contain bones and Late Neolithic pottery without any admixture of early material and it can be argued that they lie at the end of the tomb-building traditions. Similar monuments, dubbed 'sub-megalithic' (propped capstones, enlarged rock hollows and so on), also exist in Pembrokeshire where several megalith-building traditions had flourished and were deeply rooted, but there none is datable (Barker 1992) (see **Pl. 10**). None the less the general conclusion is tenable that in the most densely occupied areas of the west the old religious and social traditions retained their power.

In other areas where megalithic tombs had never been built the situation is less easy to assess. In north-east Wales, east of the Clwyd, there are caves used for multiple inhumation burial (Dawkins 1874, 149–57; Aldhouse-Green et al. 1996). The excavations are early and the evidence is difficult to assess, but at Gop Cave some burials certainly belong to the Late Neolithic, for they were accompanied by jet belt sliders – the appearance of personal belongings being a portent of things to come (Dawkins 1902). Cave burial occurs in many areas and at several periods; it seems to be a matter of convenience rather than cultural preference, but in this instance it may reflect the strength

(Opposite) *Fig. 2.13. Barclodiad y Gawres, Anglesey. Decorated stone in the main chamber (orthostat 22). (Photo: copyright Mick Sharp)*

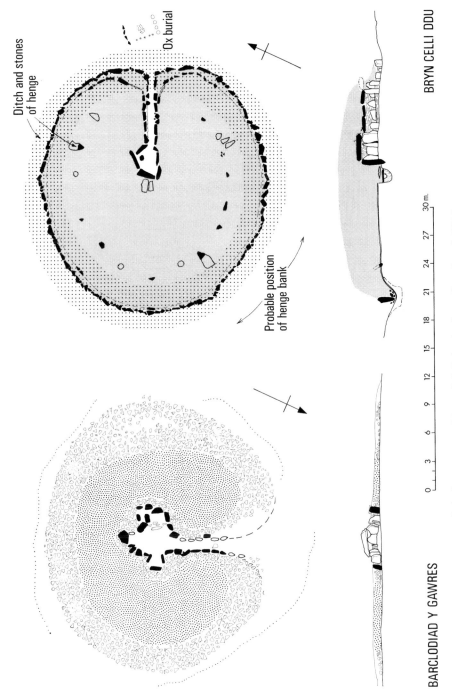

Ditch and stones of henge

Ox burial

Probable position of henge bank

BRYN CELLI DDU

BARCLODIAD Y GAWRES

0   3   6   9   12   15   18   21   24   27   30 m.

Fig. 2.14. Later Passage Graves: Barclodiad y Gawres and Bryn Celli Ddu, Anglesey (from Lynch 1976).

of the pre-existing Mesolithic population, adopting a Neolithic economy but not following the religious practices of the farmers, perhaps largely colonists, on the western coasts. Other areas where tombs were not built may have remained largely unexploited until the Late Neolithic.

SOCIETY

A settled life and commitment to the land is one of the essential characteristics of the farming communities of the Neolithic and the most significant difference from their predecessors. But at the beginning of the period the economic gulf between hunters and farmers may not have been enormous and we cannot be certain how many of the latter were newcomers and how many were gradual converts to the new way of life. Certainly there was room enough for two societies to occupy Wales for many centuries (Junker 1996).

Those centuries were times of considerable change for man and his environment. Some, such as the inexorable rise in sea-level, were beyond control; others, like the gradual clearance of woodland, were the results of man's own activities. After two thousand years or more the worked land may have been damaged, but an enormous potential for expansion remained, an expansion seen very clearly in the following centuries. During the earlier Neolithic there were scattered concentrations of population occupying the coasts and the lowlands; however, though they differed in important ways which suggest different origins and a different web of contacts, they were not completely isolated from each other. In time contacts with more distant regions developed, as the dispersal of stone axes shows, and eastern connections began to eclipse the western influence which had earlier linked western Wales so firmly to Ireland.

Everything that we can know about the social life of the period emphasises the importance of the group rather than the individual. The houses are large, big enough for an extended family of several generations, but these houses are not grouped into large villages so that the occupants remain as a family and it is family relationships which must have dominated the power structure of settlement.

In religion the same pattern emerges. The megalithic tombs are some of the largest and most grandiose structures built, certainly in prehistory; they represent an impressive investment of time and energy demanding a well-directed workforce, yet they do not commemorate one single individual but rather a group of anonymous ancestors, stripped of personal identity and status. Within the tombs are bones of men, women and children and, though at some well-preserved sites there are hints that some bones may be treated differently, familiar hierarchies of gender and age are not recognisable.

The fact that the nature of control within Neolithic societies is hidden from us should not lead us to think that a power structure did not exist. It may be invisible because it was so all-pervasive (Benedict 1934, 57–78). The absence of defences and overt weapons suggests that society was peaceful. This lack of aggression and competition may be because small populations did not put pressure on their resources and had room for manoeuvre and expansion, but it may also have a more structural explanation. The erection of the great tombs, the successful achievement of great communal projects, does not suggest a society of happy individualists, but rather a disciplined populace with a willingly accepted common purpose. Authority is the key to such control and it may be effectively exercised through religion, providing rituals for all aspects of daily life and guaranteeing success if followed faithfully.

Such societies tend to be dominated by those who know the rituals and taboos, to be ruled by priests and elders, and to put store on conformity to the norms of the group. What we know of Neolithic society suggests that it may have been of this kind: very traditional, very conservative, and with a system of control which did not need force, because fear of the displeasure of gods or ancestors would be a more effective restraint. In the Late Neolithic this consensus starts to crack and new configurations of power begin to emerge.

THREE

THE LATER NEOLITHIC AND EARLIER BRONZE AGE

Frances Lynch

INTRODUCTION

In 1932 Sir Cyril Fox identified an essential dichotomy within Britain based on the division between the Highland and Lowland Zones. In the former, to which most of Wales unquestionably belongs, he saw a basic conservatism leading to the long survival here of traditions more rapidly abandoned in richer areas (Fox 1932). While the universal application of this principle may be questioned, his view does seem to be supported by a study of the social and religious trends in Wales during the Late Neolithic and Early Bronze Age.

In south-eastern England at this time the social changes are profound and long-lasting. In the past these changes have been associated with the users of Beaker pottery, believed to be invaders from the continent. But this interpretation has been questioned and the historical model now evoked is perhaps more akin to the deep internal pressures for change in Henry VIII's reign than to the external events of the Norman Conquest. Very few institutions or families came through the sixteenth century unchanged and this seems to be the case with the centuries around 2,500 cal BC.

Nevertheless it can be argued that Wales, where old traditions were not moribund, was less affected by this pressure for change than other areas; the new ideas, though present, had a less permanent impact. The resulting ethos of the Early Bronze Age in Wales therefore does not provide the sharp contrast with the preceding centuries which can be recognised in other regions, notably Wessex, where the individual warrior chieftain stands out above the crowd. Such differences, glimpsed through burial customs, suggest that Britain was divided into regions with quite separate social and political histories, despite the similarity of much of their material culture.

For example, the normal burial monument in Bronze Age Wales is, as elsewhere, the round barrow or cairn covering cremated bones often contained within a large pottery vessel. The style of these urns demonstrates both a broad conformity to national styles and some regional preferences which hint at particular cultural allegiances.

Despite the Highland conservatism, Bronze Age ceremonial monuments in Wales adopt the open, circular design which begins to dominate the scene with the Late Neolithic henges whose distribution within Wales suggests an external origin. The purpose of these enclosures is obscure; their association with rituals of death and perhaps fertility is much less obvious than that of the earlier megalithic tombs but their successors among the ring cairns maintain a link with burials which suggests that basic religious ideas had not changed fundamentally.

The appearance of henges and of decorated pottery in 'English' styles along the northern and southern coasts and up the Marches of Wales is indicative of the increasing power of eastern influences during this period. In North Wales the links are with northern England, the southern Pennines and Yorkshire, providing trade goods and sharing ceramic and architectural styles which imply a similarity of ideas and customs. In the south-east and the Vale of Glamorgan long-established links with the Cotswolds and Wessex are maintained, providing this area with some of the accoutrements of a society more sharply stratified than can be recognised in the rest of Wales. In Central Wales new religious ideas take early root, but social stratification is less apparent. The Irish connection, which had been so strong in the earlier Neolithic, seems to have diminished, except in the technological sphere and on the western coasts, where sea connections would always persist, even if new eastern contacts had taken a hold.

Good agricultural land is not plentiful in Wales and what there is was fully exploited during the earlier Neolithic as the lowland distribution of megalithic tombs demonstrates. After more than a thousand years these farming populations must have increased and some of their lands may have been over-used. These pressures, allied to a favourable climate, led to an expansion into the previously under-exploited upland regions where the presence of numerous ceremonial and burial monuments attest to a great deal of interest and activity, although the settlement bases remain elusive. This shift of settlement in the Late Neolithic and Early Bronze Age can be paralleled in other parts of Britain but our inability to recognise the farms of this period in Wales is frustratingly unlike the situation elsewhere.

The mineral resources of Wales had also been successfully exploited by pre-Bronze Age populations. With the coming of metallurgy a whole new range of minerals became important in north Wales and in mid-Wales, a newly significant area. The availability of copper and lead ores led to the development of an important new production industry which in the Middle Bronze Age became a leader in its field and the centre of a far-flung network of exchange.

Wales, a land of fragile upland environments and high rainfall at the best of times, may be expected to have suffered a serious economic crisis at the end of the Middle Bronze Age when the climate began to deteriorate, threatening the viability of upland agriculture. In the absence of extensive evidence for settlement in the hills it is difficult to judge the severity of the impact, but it is at this time that defended sites first appear, implying some serious changes in a society where previously stress and aggression had not been especially apparent. This changed situation is discussed in the next chapter.

CLIMATE AND VEGETATION

The period under discussion in this chapter coincides with a gradual decline from the optimal climatic conditions of the Boreal and Atlantic periods but is still considered to be a time of favourable weather. Though the summers were cooler in this Sub-Boreal period they were drier and, though the winters were severe, the lapse rates (the altitudinal temperature differentials) were gentler, giving higher ground more agricultural potential, at least in summer (Taylor 1980a).

In southern England it is claimed that this period is one of agricultural crisis with much previously cleared and worked land abandoned to scrub and weeds. In Wales, however, the evidence for these difficulties is much less clear. None the less there are vegetational changes which almost certainly reflect man's changed use of the land. It is in the centuries around 2,500 cal BC that many upland pollen sequences show a period of deforestation to be followed in many cases by the beginning of soil podsolisation and the growth of blanket peat (Caseldine 1990, 55–66). This evidence reveals the beginning of upland agriculture containing within itself the seeds of its own destruction almost before it had begun! There is a good deal of uncertainty and discussion about the date of the initiation of upland peats in Wales: in the Black Mountains it is as early as 6,400 cal BC (Cloutman 1983); on Copa Hill, Cardiganshire, perhaps as late as the Late Bronze Age (Timberlake & Mighall 1992). But it is generally agreed that the process is triggered by deforestation and that is normally considered to be anthropogenic, especially when it coincides with other evidence for human activity, such as the appearance of new monuments in these upland landscapes.

The nature and extent of the forest which previously existed in these uplands is not entirely clear. Taylor (1980a, 124) believes that in the Atlantic period, the treeline could have reached 600 metres OD but such high-altitude woodland would not have been thick. On Hiraethog, a moorland less than 600 metres high, tree pollen amounted to less than 16 per cent of the pollen counted (Hibbert 1993) and it is possible that much of this pollen may have derived from trees which were growing in the surrounding valleys (Price & Moore 1984). The range of trees present is that familiar to us today (except the American sycamore so widely planted in the nineteenth century because of its resistance to wind). Oak, ash and birch appear most frequently in the pollen record and among the charcoal found on archaeological sites, though here one must remember the bias of human selection, for oak was certainly the preferred wood for cremation pyres. Even in their natural state the upland plateaux and ridges must have been fairly bare, with woodland concentrated on the slopes and valley bottoms.

Human activity in the uplands is demonstrated by the number of ritual and burial monuments built on the high moors and in mountain passes rather than by the fields and houses of their builders which remain strangely elusive. A glance at Fig. 2.1 shows the contrast with the distribution of similar structures of an earlier age but it should not be thought that the old lands were deserted. Many barrows can be found in the valleys of the Alyn and the Teme, and wooden sanctuaries are emerging in the Severn and Tanat valleys, while the rich Vale of Glamorgan clearly retained a large, even expanded, population.

Because the climate shift in the middle of the third millennium cal BC is not one of dramatic improvement it is likely that the pressure to expand into new lands was essentially cultural, the response to human population pressures and to some change in farming practice which encouraged greater use of upland grazing. Because of the severe winters the uplands would only be really attractive to farmers in the summer and this

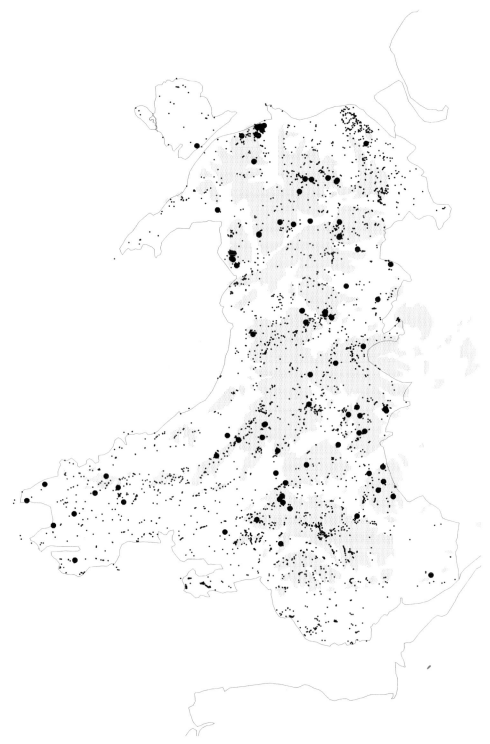

Fig. 3.1. Map of Bronze Age burial sites (•) and stone and timber circles (●) in Wales (from information on Welsh Archaeological Trusts' sites and monuments records).

suggests that their use may have been largely transhumant, providing summer grazing for herds based in the valleys and on the lowland.

It has long been assumed that the Bronze Age distributions implied such a pastoral economy but it is still very difficult to demonstrate it from factual evidence in view of the virtual absence of settlement and of animal bones, which cannot survive the acid soils. However, microwear analysis of flints in the Walton Basin may be relevant, hinting at a shift from vegetable to meat cutting in the centuries around 2,700 cal BC (Donahue in Gibson 1999a, 100–12). Cattle may be expected to have been the major economic support of the system; the predominance of sheep in the uplands is a modern phenomenon but the quantity of sheep teeth in Tooth Cave, Gower, reminds us of their presence in the Bronze Age (Higgs & Yealand 1967). Since the best evidence for pastoral farming in the Bronze Age is the eventual scale of upland forest clearance it is probable that sheep, which are a most effective brake to regeneration, must have been present in some numbers. The numerous red deer antlers used by miners in both north and mid-Wales are another product of the uplands, a natural resource which should not be forgotten.

Cereal pollen is noticeably more common in Bronze Age than in Neolithic contexts and several of these are found in the uplands. It has been found in peats on Plynlumon, Llyn Mire, Nant Helen near Ystradgynlas, on the Berwyns and at Brenig on Hiraethog (Caseldine 1990, 57). In this last case the cereal pollen came from turves used to construct burial monuments; there was no sign of arable farming in the pollen from beneath the barrows anywhere in the head of the valley and it is likely that the turves had been brought from elsewhere (Hibbert 1993), just as the wheat grain imprint on the sherd from Fan y Big relates to its place of manufacture rather than to its upland findspot (Briggs et al. 1990). The need therefore is to identify the exact source of cereal pollen, for cereal-growing should imply year-long occupation. Such activity is not inconceivable, for carefully enclosed Bronze Age fields are found on Dartmoor and on the Cheviots, but so far the expected permanent farmsteads have not been found in the Welsh uplands. The cereal pollen, however, encourages the search.

The lowland economy is scarcely better documented but evidence for arable farming is much more secure. At Stackpole on the Pembrokeshire coast plough-marks of Early Bronze Age date have survived within small embanked fields (Benson et al. 1990) and burnt grain has been found at several sites, though often in religious contexts rather than at the farms themselves. Barley is the commonest crop (Caseldine 1990, 59), being dominant at Stackpole, Welsh St Donats in the Vale of Glamorgan and at Four Crosses in the Severn Valley and present with wheat at Rhuddlan in the north and at Marlborough Grange and Pond Cairn in the Vale. Oats, the mainstay of later Welsh diet, has been found in the Berwyns (Bostock 1980). Complementary evidence for animal husbandry remains rare because of the poor survival conditions for bone. The later Bronze Age settlement on the limestone at Coed y Cymdda, Glamorgan, produced eight cattle bones, one sheep bone and two deer antlers. The contemporary marshland site at Caldicot on the Gwent Levels adds pig and wildfowl to the range of food resources (Caseldine 1990, 64).

Despite the number of Bronze Age monuments and the quantity of finds from the period, the deep pollen sequences from lakes on Anglesey and Lleyn and from lowland bogs like Tregaron suggest that the woodland clearances were still relatively small and temporary and that widescale permanent clearance did not affect the lowlands until the Iron Age (Lynch 1991, 341). The situation in the uplands is uncertain but the impact of deforestation must have been more serious since soils there were more vulnerable. Evidence from beneath many barrows shows that even before the rainfall increased, soils were being degraded by acidification and podsolisation (Keeley in Lynch 1993). The almost universal establishment of blanket peats by the tenth century cal BC signalled the end of any serious possibility of woodland regeneration just as it destroyed the viability of the pastoral farming which had kept it at bay under more favourable climatic conditions.

POPULATION

All that has been said about the difficulty of estimating the size of the population during the Neolithic may be repeated for the Bronze Age. Settlements are almost non-existent, and though burial monuments are far more common it is still probable that these were built for only a minority of the population at irregular intervals and, in any case, contain a variable number of burials, so any exercise of direct counting for the country as a whole would be pointless (Lynch 1993, 149).

The distribution of later Neolithic material (**Fig. 3.2**) reveals the beginning of the move to the uplands and by the full Bronze Age it can be seen that the 'gaps' on the earlier Neolithic map which represent the highest moorlands have almost all been filled with *some* evidence of human activity. Pastoral farming, however, cannot support the same density of population as arable, so the ritual landscape of the hills may have been thinly peopled, as it has always remained. However, pollen evidence from the lowlands does indeed show an increase in arable activity in the Bronze Age, so we may confidently postulate a significant increase in population.

An estimate of Bronze Age populations for England and Wales, based on the shaky foundation of burial monuments (Atkinson 1972; Green 1974) is 100,000 to 200,000; in the light of the sixteenth-century AD ratio of 1:10 (p. 46), Wales's share of that total might be 10,000–20,000, a figure which is comparable to the population of the Falkland Islands (a landmass of much the same size) in 1980. The Welsh Bronze Age population would have been more evenly distributed and occupied the land for longer, so its impact will naturally be more evident on the landscape. At the end of the Middle Bronze Age population levels are believed to have been drastically reduced (Burgess 1985), but the increase in bronze tools in the Late Bronze Age suggests that they may have quickly recovered.

For most of the Bronze Age the burial tradition was cremation so nothing can be said about the physical appearance of this population. At the beginning of the period, however, there is a phase of inhumation burial when physical characteristics can be studied. These graves also contain Beaker pottery and it has been claimed that they belong to invaders recognisably part of an alien population because of a difference in skull shape. The historicity of this invasion has been questioned in recent years and the significance of the 'round skull' has been demoted because the contrast with the 'long skulls' of the Early Neolithic is no longer understood to be immediate, but rather separated by almost a millennium. Of the nineteen relevant burials from Wales, sixteen contain broad-headed individuals, the three exceptions being in Anglesey (Lynch 1986a). Subsequent British populations tend to be long-headed but the history of these changes is intermittent because succeeding generations preferred to cremate the dead, and in the Late Bronze Age the burial record is virtually non-existent.

Any Bronze Age expansion of population is believed to be internally generated. The idea of large-scale introductions of new peoples into Wales or into Britain has been abandoned (Clark 1966), though this does not preclude small-scale movements of perhaps influential groups who open new contacts and stimulate new activity. The Bronze Age is a period of technological and social change during which exchange networks spread right across Europe so that, though the bulk of the population may have been fixed and settled, nowhere was totally isolated from change and movement at certain levels of society.

SETTLEMENT

Evidence for Late Neolithic domestic sites is rather more tenuous than for the earlier period; house plans are more elusive and what buildings there are seem to be less substantial (Darvill in Darvill & Thomas 1996). The unit of settlement remains the unenclosed farmstead; there are still no true villages and the sites are undefined, even by a light fence. Where evidence survives, the houses are circular and much smaller in floor area than before, presumably designed for a smaller family unit. This important difference applies to both lowland and upland sites, so it is not a matter of the difference between the summer hut and the permanent base. The reduction in size might imply a single-generation rather than multi-generation home or may be a question of farming practice, for animals and storage may have occupied sections of the large Neolithic buildings. The circular plan, whether built in wood or stone, remains dominant in Britain for the rest of the prehistoric period and beyond.

Apart from this general circularity of plan, our knowledge of Late Neolithic house structures is uncertain. There was an enormous wooden structure on the top of the hill at Capel Eithin, Anglesey, but it was probably not domestic; a curved section of foundation trench there, suggesting a 4 metre diameter house or hut, is possibly more typical (Lynch 1991, 341; White & Smith 1999, 29–41). At Cefn Caer Euni and at Cefn Cilsanws, both upland sites, stake-holes suggested some lightweight wooden structures but their plans were unclear (Lynch 1986b, 83–7; Webley 1958). At the former site there was an open, informal hearth but at Trelystan hearths were much more carefully built and were inside neat wattle huts (Britnell 1982, 139–42). These huts were also 4 metres across – a medium-sized room in which the hearth occupied a good deal of the available floor space, and would have restricted indoor working. Recent work in the Walton Basin, Radnorshire, has revealed a similar lightly built house associated with Grooved Ware (Gibson 1999a, 36–43).

Most sites reveal only scatters of sherds, flint tools and small pits with charcoal and broken pottery, assumed to be evidence of settlement but telling us little of the fundamental economy. They can establish, however, distribution and chronology and, less certainly, cultural affiliation. Such evidence, found in the south-east, the Severn Valley, north-east Wales and Anglesey, suggests, from the preferred style of pottery (Grooved Ware and Beaker traditions) an increasing contact with the east and the growing importance of the Marches where earlier occupation had been sparse.

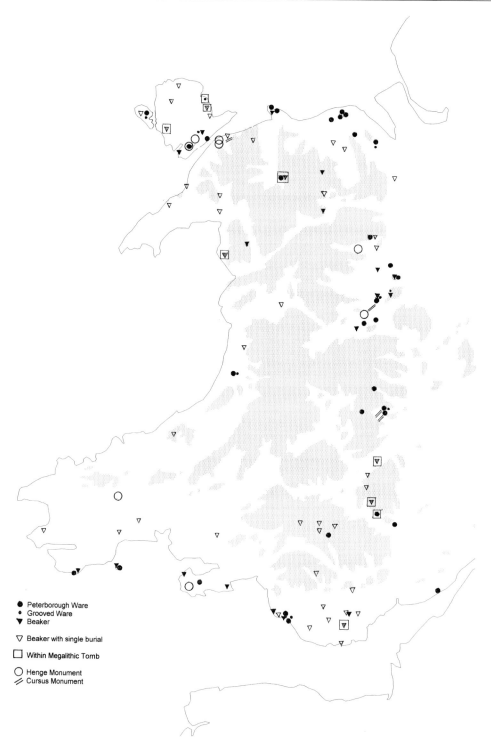

Fig. 3.2. Map of findspots of Peterborough pottery (from Gibson 1995), Grooved Ware and Beaker pottery, together with Beaker burials, henges and related monuments.

Most of this evidence has been found during modern development or excavation of more visible structures, so it cannot be considered an unbiased sample. Nevertheless it is interesting that, though most of these sites were re-used later, almost without exception they were new sites in the later Neolithic – if one may identify that period by the presence of decorated pottery with an eastern connection. Some were in shifting landscapes such as the dune sites on Newborough Warren, Anglesey, or Merthyr Mawr Warren and Ogmore in the south. But others – such as Capel Eithin, Anglesey (Lynch 1991, 341), and Marcher sites like Collfryn and Four Crosses (Gibson 1995a) – are in normal agricultural situations. The exceptions are Bryn yr Hen Bobl, Anglesey, where there had been earlier occupation under the tomb (Gresham 1985), Stackpole in Pembrokeshire, where a few developed Irish Sea Ware sherds were found (Benson *et al.* 1990, 209–11), and some of the caves on the Great Orme and on Caldey Island where the attraction of shelter would be perennial. This lack of continuity, even in the lowlands, taken with the changes in house plan and pottery style and a shift in agricultural emphasis, would suggest that many aspects of life were seriously disrupted at this period, for whatever cause.

The more straightforward phenomenon of expansion, taking up new opportunities in the previously under-exploited uplands, has already been discussed. It is less obvious in settlement than in burial but can be demonstrated by discoveries in Merioneth at Crawcwellt, on Hiraethog at Brenig 51, on Cefn Caer Euni, on Long Mountain at Trelystan and from the hilltops later occupied by the forts of Moel y Gaer, Breiddin and Ffridd Faldwyn. In south Wales the finds from Cefn Cilsanws near Merthyr Tydfil and the dated structure at Cefn Glas in Rhondda Fach (Clayton & Savory 1990) are testimony to occupation alongside the numerous cairns in the Glamorgan uplands.

All the sites mentioned above have produced later Neolithic material, either decorated wares, Beaker pottery or distinctive flint implements. Domestic sites of the full Early Bronze Age are virtually unknown. Rescue excavations at the Atlantic Trading Estate, Barry, Glamorgan, produced evidence for a surprisingly large plank-built round-house with sherds (perhaps partly residual) of Beaker, Food Vessel and Collared Urn as well as Middle Bronze Age wares (Sell 1998). The best-documented and dated example, however, is that on Stackpole Warren on the south coast of Pembrokeshire where a substantial round-house produced a quantity of Collared Urn sherds (Benson *et al.* 1990). Debris from the destruction of the first house there produced radiocarbon dates of 3,570 ± 70 BP (CAR 475) = 2,140–1,740 cal BC and 3,350 ± 70 BP (CAR 100) = 1,880–1,550 cal BC. For some reason we have not yet found, or perhaps not recognised, the farms which were occupied during the first half of the second millennium cal BC. By about 1200 cal BC the record of settlement begins to pick up again, revealed by radiocarbon dates rather than by artefacts, but it is still very thin, except in the Gwent Levels where intensive archaeological work has been carried out (Bell & Neumann 1997). The circular structure beneath the cairn, Brenig 6, demolished before 3,070 ± 90 BP (HAR 536) = 1,452–1,240 cal BC may or may not have been a house – it was bare of finds but had had a fire at its centre – yet it was similar in many ways to that at Stackpole and to an Iron Age structure further up the Brenig Valley (Lynch 1993, 158–61). This structural continuity across a period of crisis is worthy of note.

The Bronze Age settlement on Stackpole Warren, Pembrokeshire, provides the fullest picture of earlier Bronze Age houses and economy, but some problems of structural

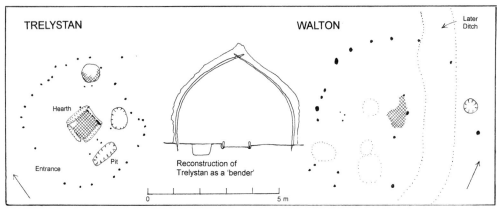

TRELYSTAN

Hearth

Entrance

Pit

WALTON

Later
Ditch

Reconstruction of
Trelystan as a 'bender'

0   5 m

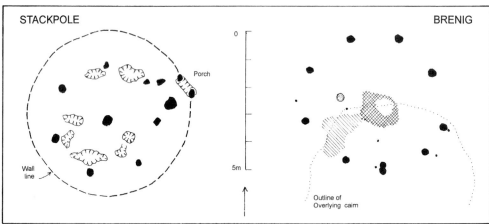

STACKPOLE

Porch

Wall
line

BRENIG

0

5m

Outline of
Overlying cairn

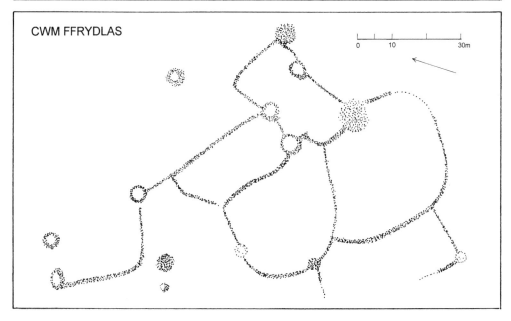

CWM FFRYDLAS

0   10   30m

interpretation remain (Benson *et al.* 1990). Features of various dates survive on this sandy coastal plateau, which seems to have seen activity of some kind or other from the middle Neolithic to the Roman period and beyond, though short phases of abandonment may intervene from time to time. There are burial and ritual monuments from the earlier Bronze Age, as well as houses and fields. The main area of excavation was around the Devil's Quoit where a sequence of settlement, ritual activity, agriculture, burial use and renewed occupation was discovered. The first occupation phase was characterised by perhaps three round wooden houses standing within a few metres of each other and broadly dated by a scatter of Beaker and Collared Urn sherds.

The most complete house was built in a hollow 0.4 metres deep with a long porch on the north-east side. It was defined by a ring of seven substantial posts 4.2 metres in diameter but they seemed to lie outside the wall-line. The porch was 1.6 metres long and 1 metre wide and was built over a sloping ramp. In the centre of the hollow there was a deeper pit which had held a hearth but a central post had later been inserted there, suggesting that the house had been radically redesigned at some stage. The suggested reconstruction therefore is that the original house, a light plank structure built over a hollow possibly covered by a wooden floor, was burnt down (sometime between 1,900 and 1,600 cal BC) and replaced by the bigger post-ring house with a wall (6.5 metres in diameter) set outside the edge of the hollow and with a central post replacing the original hearth.

The finds consisted of sherds from perhaps forty-five Beakers and thirty-four Collared Urns, together with flints, animals bones and sixty-three cereal grains which were mainly barley. About 100 metres to the west other excavations revealed an area of plough-marks, perhaps the edge of a field. Beaker and Urn sherds in the soil suggested it had been worked at a time when the nearby houses were occupied. Sherds and radiocarbon dates from other sites on the Warren showed that the area had continued in occupation and use into the Later Bronze Age and, after a phase of sand invasion, through the Iron Age into the Roman period, suggesting an essential continuity and stability of population from the late Neolithic onwards in an area of reliable and varied food resources.

The focus of excavation at Stackpole had been the standing stone known as the Devil's Quoit. The house, stratified beneath a spread of loess soil, was discovered accidentally. Circular structures have been found in loose association with other standing stones, as at St Ishmaels (Williams 1989) and Rhos-y-Clegyrn (Lewis 1974), both in west Wales, but the purpose of these buildings is far from clear. Their shape, however, underlines the fact that Bronze Age constructions, of whatever kind, were almost invariably round.

The excavations on Stackpole Warren produced evidence for another prehistoric phenomenon which has been the centre of much discussion in recent years (Buckley 1990). This is the 'mound of burnt stone': the debris of cracked pot-boilers, charcoal and burnt earth resulting from the process of heating stones in order to boil water. At Stackpole and Dan y Coed in west Wales and Ty Mawr, Anglesey, the stones were intermingled with

(Opposite) *Fig. 3.3. Plans of round-houses: Trelystan, Mont. Plan and reconstruction (after Britnell 1982); Upper Ninepence, Walton, Rads. (after Gibson 1999a); Stackpole, Pembs. (after Benson* et al. *1990); Brenig 6 (after Lynch 1993); Cwm Ffrydlas, Bethesda, Caerns. (after RCAHMW 1956).*

other settlement debris – amorphous heaps tossed into the corner of farm enclosures – and dated from the Iron Age or Romano-British period. When burnt stone is found with normal domestic rubbish it is usually of this date and should be distinguished from the more puzzling Bronze Age mounds which occur in wet spots, in marshes or beside streams, at some distance from recognisable living sites (Barber 1990).

These 'mounds of burnt stone' occur in upland north-west and south-west Wales; in south Pembrokeshire and Carmarthenshire their distribution is particularly dense (Cantrill & Jones 1911). There are several in Anglesey but very few in Glamorgan, some have been found in recent fieldwork in Breconshire (RCAHMW 1997) but none has yet been recorded from eastern Wales, though there are several in the English Midlands (C. Martin, pers. comm.). They are recognisable as mounds 10–20 metres in diameter and up to 1.5 metres high, very often kidney-shaped in plan and composed of the characteristic burnt and broken stones (**Pl. 12**). The preferred siting is beside a stream or in a marsh since water is essential. They may occur singly or in groups of four or five but are never closely associated with signs of settlement.

Early work on these mounds identified them as cooking places, the components of which were a wooden trough, a large hearth and a heap of stones, the hearth and the trough eventually becoming surrounded by the ever-increasing mound of burnt stone which could not be used more than a few times before it shattered into useless fragments. Experiments and ethnographic parallels have demonstrated that heating stones in the fire and shovelling them into the trough full of water is an effective way of cooking large joints of meat and these open-air kitchens are normally believed to have been used by hunting parties (O'Kelly 1954). The remote position of these sites, often on open moor or on the edge of a marsh, would support such an interpretation, for their distribution is echoed by that of flint arrowheads and of small Middle Bronze Age spears, suggesting that hunting had become a distinct and perhaps exclusive social activity (Bradley 1978, 83–4). Datable artefacts have very seldom been found at these sites but sufficient radiocarbon dates are now available to show convincingly that most of them belong to the Bronze Age (Brindley *et al.* 1990).

However, although the interpretation of these mounds as cooking sites is the most widely preferred explanation, it must be admitted that few of the Welsh sites have all the classic features. The wooden trough is seldom present; Cantrill found only one in south Wales (Cantrill & Jones 1911, 259) and though one is recognisable at an unexcavated site near Bethesda, Caernarfonshire (RCAHMW 1956, Fig. 143) only one has been found at any of the recently excavated mounds (Kelly & Williams in Buckley 1990). The well-made hearth is equally rare; two were found in 1912 in Anglesey (Lynch 1991, 281–2) but others have been more problematic.

Apart from the trough excavated under difficult conditions at Nant Porth, Bangor (Davidson 1998), recently excavated sites in both north and south Wales have proved to be very unstructured and confusing. Both high kidney-shaped mounds and low amorphous spreads of stone have been found to cover irregular pits, some with evidence of burning, some without, but all filled with the ubiquitous burnt and cracked stones in a matrix of charcoal and burnt earth. The discovery of a piece of slag in one in Anglesey (White 1977; Lynch 1991, 363) hints at a connection with metalworking but the link is tenuous and there are various activities for which hot water would be necessary. Activity was often recurrent and at Graeanog one site was re-activated after a lapse of several centuries with a new pit cut into the old mound (Kelly 1992b). However, at most sites the pits became obsolete and were buried beneath the accumulating mound of debris. Most of these irregular pits and mounds have proved to belong to the earlier Bronze Age but they can have a wide date range – from Late Neolithic to the early centuries AD – and it is likely that they also had a wide range of functions.

The field clearance cairns scattered over the upland moors present a different series of problems and uncertainties (Ward 1989). In their case the agricultural nature of the activity is universally agreed but the dating is more problematic. These cairns are small heaps of unburnt stone less than 3 metres across and normally under 0.5 metres high. They are the product of surface stone collection but the exact purpose of this land improvement is not entirely clear for they are often quite closely spaced and would obstruct a plough-team. Perhaps these fields were cultivated with a hoe, or the stones may have been removed to improve the quality of grazing; it has been claimed that the heaps of stone retain the heat of the sun and would help to raise the soil temperature (Fleming 1976, 368). These cairns are found on the high moorland, often in the vicinity of hut circles and field walls (though this is not always the case). It is this upland distribution rather than any positive dating by artefacts or radiocarbon testing which suggests that they belong to the earlier Bronze Age. Since this is assumed to be the period of greatest agricultural use of the uplands the argument is reasonable but not incontrovertible.

The same level of argument applies to the huts and fields with which these clearance cairns are often associated. In other parts of Britain such huts, whether associated with regimented fields as on Dartmoor (Fleming 1989) or with irregular enclosures as on Bodmin or the moors of northern England (Johnson & Rose 1994; Hart 1981), have been convincingly dated to this period. Unfortunately in Wales this has not yet been achieved. Most authorities would agree that the round huts associated with irregular enclosures classified as Class II in the scheme devised by W.E. Griffiths (1950) and adopted by the Royal Commission in Caernarfonshire (1964) are the most likely candidates for a Bronze Age date. These occur in the uplands above 300 metres and also in lowland situations where they are often overlain by more substantial enclosed homesteads (for example, Din Lligwy, Anglesey). In the uplands the huts average about 5 metres in diameter and their stone walls are very poorly built, suggesting that they may be little more than dumped reinforcements for a wooden wall, as in the Bronze Age huts of Arran (Barber 1982). They occur in groups (from four to twenty-eight in number) and are surrounded by irregular stone-walled enclosures, the huts often incorporated along the line of the wall (see Cwm Ffrydlas, Fig. 3.3). The area thus enclosed may be up to 5 hectares in extent but the economic basis of the settlements remains problematic; there is little sign of lynchetting within the fields and the ground is at present inappropriate for arable, but it is noticeable that these settlements occupy relatively warm micro-climates within a generally inhospitable environment.

The distribution of these hut settlements within Wales has not been consistently mapped. They are often very emphemeral, half-buried in peat, and were seldom noted by early fieldworkers. The first thorough study was that of the Royal Commission in

Caernarfonshire, where such settlements are very common on the fringes of Snowdonia. Merioneth has also produced good evidence (Bowen & Gresham 1967) and more may be expected on Hiraethog and the Berwyns, where serious searching is only now beginning, though here platforms for wooden huts may be all that remains.

In the south, however, these stone huts seem to be genuinely rare. About twenty small groups are known on the uplands of south Breconshire and north Glamorgan and a few have been recorded on the southern slopes of the Preseli range (RCAHMW 1976, 72–8; Leighton 1997; Chris Martin (CPAT) and Ken Murphy (DAT) pers. comm.). Alternative forms of structure must fill the niche, whatever its date, and in eastern Wales it is easy to imagine that this alternative was wood, the standard building material in this part of the world until the railways distributed Ruabon brick.

In 1964, when the type was first discussed, there had been no modern excavation of any Class II site so no direct evidence of date was available. Since then a large settlement of this class at Crawcwellt near Trawsfynydd in Merioneth has been investigated and proved to be a specialised ironworkers' settlement of the second century cal BC (Crew 1989; 1998) (see pp. 163, 210). For those who were hoping for evidence to show that these unenclosed huts with irregular fields were indeed Bronze Age in date this has been a disappointment, though it does not disprove the general contention which must await further excavations for its demonstration. It should be remembered that at Crawcwellt ephemeral traces of earlier Bronze Age settlement and a burial cairn occurred within the area covered by later features. Such a simple structural type must have had a long currency and many sites will need to be tested before its full date range can be satisfactorily known.

Intensive analytical field survey of the kind carried out on Bodmin (Johnson & Rose 1994) has not yet begun seriously in Wales, but would undoubtedly prove fruitful. The work on Bodmin revealed several types of remains: cairns and circles; small curvilinear accreted fields with some evidence for lynchetting, suggesting cultivation; and large boundaries dividing the landscape into blocks. Huts of varying sizes occur with the fields and a few with the boundaries, while some smaller ones are isolated. A study of superimposition and robbing in certain areas showed that the accreted fields and their medium-sized huts were often overlain and robbed to build boundaries and larger huts, suggesting that a period of permanent cultivation had been followed by a change to pastoralism with perhaps seasonal occupation. The completely isolated huts and the ritual monuments are difficult to place within this sequence but the monuments are likely to belong to the earlier phase and the isolated huts might be of any date. It is assumed by analogy with the unusually rigorous land organisation of Dartmoor (Fleming 1989) that the bulk of these remains belong to the Bronze Age and represent the remains of pre- and post-'crisis' agriculture. The patches of rather haphazard enclosure seen on Bodmin and the 'wandering walls' which denote partition rather than containment are similar to those recognised, if not fully understood, in Wales.

The simple assumption that any upland settlement which appears to have an agricultural base must be Early Bronze Age in date because the fertility of this land was destroyed after 1,300 cal BC is obviously simplistic. Agricultural systems such as those of Dartmoor and the Cheviots can be shown to have collapsed at about this date and climatic history would suggest that others would have done as well, but abandonment would not have been absolute. Excavation and radiocarbon dating of very impoverished-looking

Fig. 3.4. Bernard's Well Mountain, Pembs. Undated upland settlement of stone-built circular huts and related enclosures. (Copyright, Dyfed Archaeological Trust)

settlements on the edge of Hiraethog have shown that they were in occupation during the critical centuries (Manley 1990) and the presence of Iron Age sites in the uplands, perhaps encouraged by some improvement of the weather in the second century cal BC (Taylor 1980a, 125; Simmons & Tooley 1981, 261), shows that the correlation of altitude and date of settlement is not a simple one.

The centuries 1,300–1,000 cal BC undoubtedly saw changes to the settlement pattern in Wales and from this time the archaeological record picks up, running through to the Late Bronze Age and even to the Iron Age in some places. The availability of radiocarbon dating at sites producing few artefacts has revealed that certain structural types, such as the Class III concentric enclosures in north Wales, may have Late or even Middle Bronze Age antecedents (see p. 163). The double enclosure at Sarn Meyllteyrn in western Lleyn has provided dates of 3,000 ± 70 BP (Washington 1288) = 1,430–1,050 cal BC for burnt material overlying one of three round-houses and an archaeomagnetic date of 1,150 ± 60 BC for a hearth; artefacts were very limited and not chronologically distinctive (Kelly 1990; 1991; 1992a).

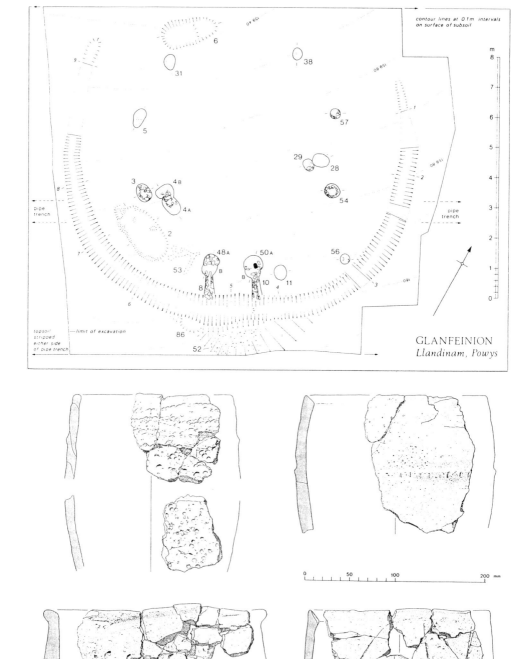

Fig. 3.5. *Glanfeinion, Montgomeryshire. Middle/Late Bronze Age house plan with a selection of pottery (from Britnell et al. 1997).*

The use of wood and the absence of enclosure have made small settlements invisible unless modern development intervenes. The discovery, during pipe-laying operations, of the 9 metre diameter round-house in the valley bottom at Glanfeinion near Llandinam (Montgomeryshire) is a case in point (Britnell *et al.* 1997), as are the discoveries at Barry (Sell 1998) where the size of the house suggests a Middle rather than Early Bronze Age date, and on the Gwent Levels where wooden houses have been revealed at several locations along the shore of the Bristol Channel.

At Chapel Tump on the Levels two large but incomplete circular buildings were identified; at Rumney Great Wharf a substantial post-built structure 5 metres in diameter was exposed and scatters of pottery and stone tools were found nearby; at Redwick four rectangular buildings were found; and at Caldicot settlement debris, including some military finery and part of a boat, was thrown into a creek (Whittle 1989; Allen 1996; Bell & Neumann 1997; Nayling & Caseldine 1997). Sherds indicate a later Bronze Age horizon and radiocarbon dates suggest an occupation lasting from 1,500 to 950 cal BC and perhaps beyond. The very unusual rectangular structures at Redwick were associated with cattle hoofmarks, as were the similar Iron Age ones at Goldcliff, and may represent some specialist agricultural activity related to salt-marsh grazing (Bell & Neumann 1997, 103–4). Though the Gwent Levels may be expected to have suffered increased flooding and several sites were abandoned, the region as a whole, like coastal Stackpole, shows some continuity across this period when upland settlement became more precarious.

COMMUNICATIONS

In the Early Neolithic the sea routes from the west seem to have been the most significant but from the Late Neolithic onwards eastern contacts grow in importance and routes across the mountainous interior must have been pioneered and maintained. Such routes, directed towards the Severn and Wye valleys, are geographically determined but, in the absence of engineered roads, difficult to identify on the ground.

However, at some points Bronze Age monuments cluster so thickly along mountain trackways that it is reasonable to claim that they must have been a focus for regular traffic at the time. The first such route leading to the Severn was identified from monuments and finds along the Kerry and Clee ridgeways in mid-Wales (Chitty 1963). A more northerly west–east route was found by Gresham and Irvine (1963) and connections to the Wye were discussed by Webley (1976). In Merioneth two lengths of road can be more precisely mapped through the proliferation of cairns and standing stones (Bowen & Gresham 1967, 56–9; Lynch 1984b, 34–6), and on Penmaenmawr a well-worn track clearly pre-dates the Bronze Age circle (Griffiths 1960). These tracks must have served principally the local community but would have linked into the long-distance routes which, as the exchange of commodities demonstrates, were in constant use throughout the period.

Though the opening up of the interior made land travel easier, boats must have remained crucial to any serious transport of goods. Substantial flat-bottomed boats of Bronze Age date have been found in the Humber Estuary (Wright 1990) and also in the Channel at Dover where wrecked cargoes have also been found (Muckleroy 1981; Parfitt 1993). The discovery of planks from similar sewn boats in the Gwent Levels at Caldicot and Goldcliff shows that shipping in the Bristol Channel must have been comparable in scale and design (Bell 1992) (see pp. 177–8). Two oak coffins buried beneath the cairn on Disgwylfa Fawr (Green 1987) are believed to echo the shape and style of the dug-out canoes which had been used since Mesolithic times and continued to serve on inland waters for many centuries to come. A similar longevity may be assumed for skin boats like the Teifi coracles but the evidence is inevitably elusive.

MINING AND METALLURGY

Wales is a land with considerable mineral resources: copper, lead and gold can all be found here. Copper is extensively found in north-west and mid-Wales; lead in mid-Wales and also in the north-east; and gold in more limited but quite rich veins in mid-Wales and the south-west. Modern mining of all these deposits was assumed to have destroyed any evidence of earlier working, but recently an astonishing wealth of evidence has been recognised and confirmed as Bronze Age in date by a gratifyingly consistent series of radiocarbon dates (Crew & Crew 1990). This new work has sprung from the campaign of investigation undertaken by Oliver Davies in the 1930s (Davies 1937). In the absence of radiocarbon dating he was unable to provide a chronology for the fire-setting and stone hammers that he found. The recent campaigns have reopened many of his trenches, obtaining large samples of well-buried charcoal which have produced radiocarbon dates running from about 2,000 to 500 cal BC.

On the north slope of Parys Mountain, Anglesey, Davies identified an early spoil heap which has now been dated to the Early Bronze Age, and a stone hammer found in one of the underground galleries indicates that the prehistoric mine was extensive (Jenkins 1995). Roman copper ingots are known from the area (Livens 1970) but so far no material of Roman date has been obtained from any unequivocal context related to the mines.

Copa Hill near Aberystwyth has a copper lode in an area known mainly for its lead ores (Timberlake & Switsur 1988; Timberlake 1990; 1993; 1995; Timberlake & Mighall 1992). Old spoil heaps covered with broken hammer stones were recognisable among the heaps of sharply fractured modern waste and have now provided a series of Bronze Age dates. Examination of a large opencast at the top of the hill has indicated that it is essentially prehistoric, though reworked in places. In the centre was a vertical shaft crossed by a hollowed tree trunk over 4 metres long by which excess water was drained away. This channel, which has been dated to 3690 ± 90 BP (BM2908)=2,200–1,950 cal BC, is a relatively late feature since it lies on spoil in the bottom of the deep opencast (Timberlake 1995, 40). It was later buried by more spoil from continued mining.

Hammerstones have been recorded at a great number of mining locations in mid-Wales – an indication of the probable extent of early mining in the area (Thorburn 1990). The fullest evidence, however, for the nature and scale of the industry has come from the north, from the mines on the Great Orme above Llandudno (Lewis 1990; Dutton & Fasham 1994).

The copper is present there as a visible green malachite in a band of dolomitised limestone running across the headland. In the vicinity of the veins of metal this parent rock is very soft and can be scraped away with any sharpened bone. The metal-bearing shales are nearly equally soft so the nature of the geology here almost certainly explains the scale of the prehistoric workings which are now known to extend for at least 6 kilometres at more than 30 metres below the surface.

The initial working seems to have been by open trench mines running in from the naturally exposed cliffs of the Pyllau Valley (see **Pl. 11**). Behind the pierced screen of these cliffs the mine opens out into an enormous opencast area (which may be a collapsed chamber), the full extent of which has not yet been established. Below this is a series of underground galleries, intercut by nineteenth-century shafts and galleries but distinguishable from them by the rounded nature of their fire-licked and stone-hammered walls. The fill of these galleries contains innumerable bone tools, perfectly preserved and stained green by the mineral salts; where they had to mine through areas of harder rock, there are also charcoal and broken hammerstones. Charcoal from these galleries has provided nine radiocarbon dates between about 1,800 and 600 cal BC, demonstrating production through most of the Bronze Age. The galleries are terrifyingly cramped and narrow, perhaps suggesting the use of child labour, but the design of the mine is technologically sophisticated.

The discovery of Bronze Age mines has added to the interest and urgency of analytical programmes on the copper and bronze implements produced. A major study has been made of the Welsh bronze tools but the full results are not yet available, though the broad outlines of metallurgical development can be discerned. Allied to typological studies this analysis has greatly refined our knowledge of the development of alloys, has helped to define workshop traditions and has encouraged the meaningful discussion of ore source identification (Northover 1980; 1982).

The background to the Welsh bronze industry lies outside Britain, in mainland Europe and in Ireland. The two-thousand-year long development of metallurgy from an exotic luxury to an essential commodity for all tools and weapons need not be rehearsed here. By the mid-third millennium cal BC, when metal first reached Britain, central Europe was undoubtedly a major producer and is the likely source of the daggers found in rich graves in southern England. But in Ireland the preponderance of copper axes and moulds suggests an independent industry, perhaps derived from the far south-west of Atlantic Europe where an early flowering of metallurgy is known at certain restricted sites (Burgess 1979a; Craddock 1979; Sheridan 1983). Central Europe (via England) and Ireland both played a part in the establishment of the Welsh industry, but the Irish role is predominant.

Both the analysis of the copper, which has significant antimony levels, and the shape of the axes suggest that the earliest metal goods in Wales, such as the hoard from Moel Arthur (Forde Johnston 1964) (**Fig. 3.7**), were imports from Ireland where a single copper source dominated the industry. However, local ores may soon have been used, for the thin-butted copper axe from Llandderfel is probably of north Welsh metal (Northover 1980, 232) and by the time bronze was in regular use analysis shows that mining must have expanded, for a variety of copper ores were available.

Bronze is an alloy of copper and tin which is much harder and tougher than copper alone, and it became the standard metal in the twenty-second century cal BC and the production of effective weapons and tools expanded enormously (Needham *et al.* 1989). At least four regional industries can be recognised in Wales through their preference for differently derived copper ores. In Glamorgan, as in southern England, metals of ultimately European origin were used. In south-west and central Wales a copper with low arsenic content was preferred, while in north Wales and the Marches two different metal

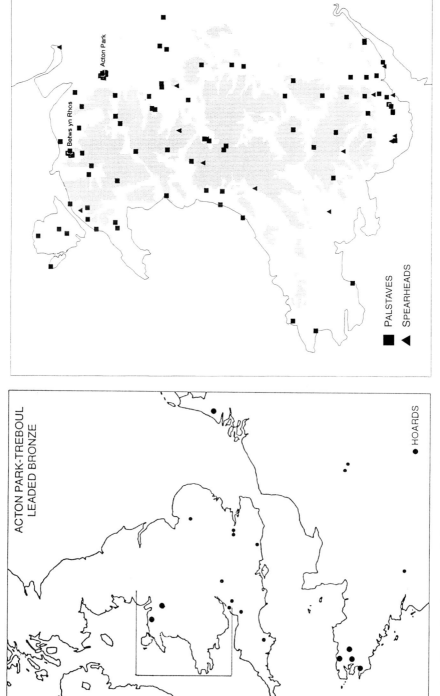

Fig. 3.6. *Maps of implements made from Acton Park metal in Britain and Europe; in Wales. Analysis has been selective outside Wales. (From information supplied by Dr Peter Northover.)*

sources were available, one of which (C in the Northover scheme) was possibly local to the region (Northover 1980; 1982).

Towards the end of the Early Bronze Age the Welsh metal industry enters a most significant and enterprising phase characterised by the production of tools of the Acton Park Complex, named after a hoard from Wrexham (Burgess 1964; 1980a, 261–2; Schmidt & Burgess 1981, 119–25; Northover 1982, 54–9). Both design and metallurgy are innovative and successful and the products can be found all over southern Britain and along the continental coasts from north Germany to Brittany. The metal-mix is particularly interesting because it is the first occasion when lead is added to the tin bronze, probably by the co-smelting of galena with chalcopyritic ores. Both minerals are available in north Wales and the impurity pattern suggests that the copper source may be the Great Orme where a hearth has produced slag with a relevant nickel content (P. Northover pers. comm.). Only very small amounts of material have been recovered from this site, demonstrating the difficulty of locating such production stations.

The proportion of lead in the Acton Park metal is 1–3 per cent but may occasionally be as high as 7 per cent; tin, which must have been imported, is high (12 per cent). The resultant metal has improved casting qualities and is exceptionally tough and hard. Analysis has shown that this recipe is very consistent across the country, though the design of tools varies regionally. This might suggest that the metal was exported from a single centre somewhere in north Wales and was subsequently made up by smiths working as far away as Holland (Voorhout hoard: Butler 1963, 51–2; Northover 1982, 54), though we are still a long way from fully understanding the mechanics of these distributions.

In Middle Bronze Age II this northern industry begins to decline. Products are made with a lower tin content and using a different copper ore, perhaps now from mid-Wales; the tool and weapon industries seem to diverge (Northover 1982, 54; 1984). The everyday palstave continues to be locally made but the more prestigious weapons may have been imported from Ireland (using Northover's O metal). Eventually, by the end of the Middle Bronze Age, the individuality of the Welsh bronzesmiths is eclipsed and a metal mix (P) of ultimately French origin becomes dominant.

Artefacts

Early Bronze Age Metalwork

The dichotomy between the earliest metal industries in Britain and Ireland has already been mentioned. In the east metal goods first appear as status symbols in graves; in the west the context and products are different and suggest local production of, predominantly, tools rather than weapons. There are no copper grave-goods of English type in Wales: the earliest metal objects are flat axes. Six of these have been found, predominantly in north Wales. The most important find of this period is the hoard of three axes from Moel Arthur in Flintshire (Forde Johnston 1964) (**Fig. 3.7**), which is related in both metal content and shape to the Irish industry and indicates fairly clearly the direction from which the impetus came.

Knowledge of alloys and the establishment of a standard bronze (90 per cent copper, 10 per cent tin) is less easy to trace but analysis has shown that the new metal is widely used by 2,200 cal BC (Metal Assemblage III – such terms and the use of named 'traditions' relate to classificatory schemes charting the development of the industry (Fig. 2; Needham *et al.* 1989)). The alloy was standardised more rapidly in Britain and Ireland than on the continent. Production areas increase during this period and a major new centre can be recognised in Scotland making bronze flat axes, simple daggers and personal ornaments (the Migdale Marnoch tradition (Britton 1964)). Production is largely a feature of the Highland Zone, though recycling may conceal manufacture in non-metalliferous areas (Needham *et al.* 1989). The flat axe is the mainstay of all the industries of this period, whether Irish, Scottish, Welsh or English. The shape and proportion of the blades vary but hard and fast distinctions are difficult to establish. The Migdale axe itself has a broad butt and relatively narrow blade; the Irish Killaha axe is almost triangular with a very broad blade. The Welsh axes, exemplified by the hoard of four from Brithdir, Glamorgan (Needham 1979b) (**Fig. 3.7**), and the stone mould from Betws y Coed, Caernarfonshire (Williams 1924), are similar to the Irish ones but have a more angular outline which may prove distinctive. Despite the presence of decoration, often an indicator of Irish origin, it is difficult to positively identify many Irish imports at this time and the growing independence of the Welsh industry is shown by the increasing use of local ores.

The earliest copper axes were a simple block of metal cast in an open mould with the blade thinned and sharpened by subsequent hammering and annealing. They would have been set into their handles in the same way as a stone axe. This system must have proved unsatisfactory, for axes with a thinned butt soon appear (for instance the two types are associated in the Moel Arthur hoard (**Fig. 3.7**)). These are designed to fit into a split or 'knee' haft where the pointed butt slides between the two fingers of the haft and is bound tightly with a leather thong. However, even this system had its disadvantages: it could shift from side to side and it might cut back into the handle when used. We can witness the eventual solution of these two problems through the development of the axes of Metal Assemblages IV and V (Needham *et al.* 1989) and the gradual evolution of the true palstave, almost certainly the invention of north Welsh smiths.

No 'developed' flat axe has been found in a significant context in Wales but there are several chance finds of the type. They are characterised by a central thickening or median bevel to alleviate the problem of splitting the haft and by hammered flanges, the sides raised slightly to grip the handle and reduce movement. Axes at this stage may show one or other of these features, or occasionally both (Needham *et al.* 1989, Fig. 1).

Axes are the most common metal goods of the period but they are not the only products. Halberds, a puzzling weapon used, perhaps ceremonially, in Ireland, the adjacent areas of Britain and in northern Europe but not in southern England or France, occur in association with bronze axes of Metal Assemblages III and IV but are themselves made of copper. This use of what was by then an archaic metal suggests that they were perhaps symbolic rather than real weapons, despite their great size and weight. Ten or eleven halberds have been found in Wales; most of them belong to the common Carn or Cotton types (Harbison

(Opposite) *Fig. 3.7. Early Bronze Age hoards from Wales: copper axes from Moel Arthur, Flints. (after Forde Johnston 1964); bronze flat axes from Brithdir, Glam., Newport, Mon. and halberds and dagger from Castell Coch, Glam. (after Needham* et al. *1985); Ebnal hoard, Shropshire (outlines = lost objects) (After Burgess and Cowen 1972). Scale 1:4.*

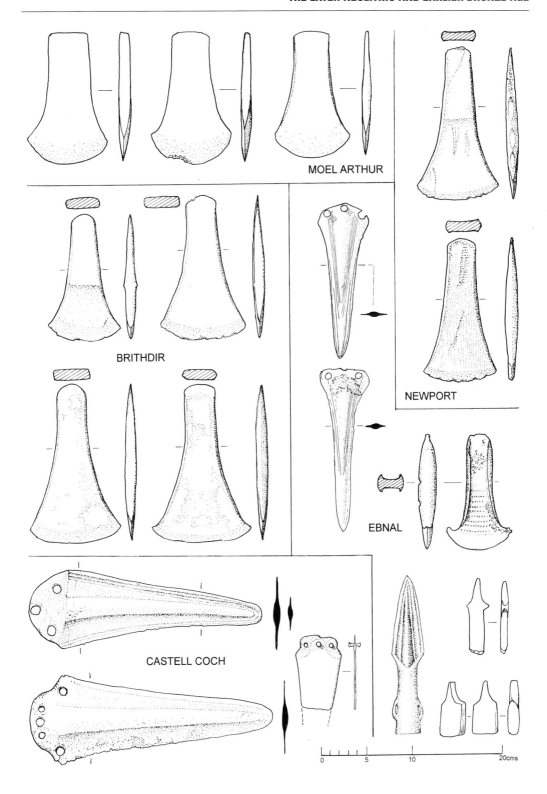

MOEL ARTHUR

BRITHDIR

NEWPORT

EBNAL

CASTELL COCH

1969) but some, like that from Pontrhydygroes, Cardiganshire (Savory 1980b, Fig. 29) have an odd, splayed midrib which indicates local design. A hoard found near Castell Coch, Glamorgan (Needham *et al.*1985), exemplifies the common types (**Fig. 3.7**).

A broken rivetted dagger was also included in the Castell Coch hoard. Like the halberds it was made of copper although typologically it belongs to a group of bronze daggers. Daggers are more commonly found in graves than in hoards, but even there they are relatively rare in Wales. Where a blade accompanies a burial it is more often a knife than a dagger. They are all attached to their handles by rivets, normally three in number, and the blades are flat. None would have been a very effective weapon, but the mere possession of a metal blade might have been deterrent enough.

Personal ornaments, mainly bracelets and armlets, are among the products of the Migdale tradition in Scotland. In Wales they are not common but the lost armlets from Pen y Bonc and pyre-damaged pieces from Llanddyfnan, both in the rich island of Anglesey, may have been comparable (Lynch 1991, 158, 175). A more impressive piece of jewellery of this period is the gold *lunula* from Bryncir, Caernarfonshire (J.J. Taylor 1980, Plate 15; Northover 1995, 519). Like so many of these beaten gold neck ornaments it was found in the nineteenth century in a peat bog. They never occur with burials, although jet necklaces, assumed to be their equivalents, frequently do. Presumably, therefore, they were not private property like other finery, and their final deposition is thought to be an act of collective renunciation or supplication. The majority of these ornaments have been found in Ireland but they occur in all the Irish Sea lands; details of manufacture, such as the pricked decoration on the Bryncir example, distinguish these 'provincial' pieces from the Irish series (J.J. Taylor 1980, 25–44).

The most spectacular gold item from Wales is the famous Mold Cape found in 1833 around the skeleton of a young man buried beneath a round barrow on the banks of the River Alyn at Mold (Ellis Davies 1949, 256–63; Powell 1953). This short cape, a seamless garment beaten over a block, is covered with an embossed design of round and lentoid 'beads' hanging over the neck and shoulders. Holes around the neck and lower edge show that it had been stitched to a leather lining but it cannot be considered a military garment for its design would have restricted movement of the arms. The embossed decoration might suggest a Late Bronze Age date but the context of burial, the presence of amber beads and the composition of the gold indicate an earlier date, contemporary with the Acton Park Complex (Northover 1995, 520).

The Migdale Marnoch industry and its counterparts in Wales demonstrated great skill within an inevitably limited technology, for they used only the open mould. The introduction of the double mould, which facilitated the production of three-dimensional and socketed castings, belongs to the next stage of industrial history, the Arreton Down Tradition, named after a hoard from the Isle of Wight (Britton 1964). For the first time the weight of evidence lies in the south of England and it is likely that the new technology was learnt from Germany.

The mainstay of the industry is still the axehead but weapons now become more important, with the spearhead appearing for the first time. All the products are clearly made in double moulds: the axes have substantial cast flanges, the daggers have stout midribs and many of the spearheads are socketed. The characteristic narrow axes with sharply recurved blades are found all over the south of England but are rare in Wales except for the notable hoard of eight from Menai Bridge, Anglesey (Lynch 1991, 218–20). The daggers and, to a lesser extent the spearheads, are grave finds and are particularly characteristic of the later Wessex graves (Gerloff 1975). Such weapons are very rare in Wales but one important hoard from the Marches demands discussion because it may hold the key to the relationship between the English Arreton Down tradition and the contemporary Irish Inch Island-Derryniggin industry.

This hoard, found at Ebnal in Shropshire, contained two daggers, an axe, an end-looped socketed spearhead, a trunnion chisel and an odd punch or other tool, now lost (Burgess & Cowen 1972) (**Fig. 3.7**). The spearhead is the most significant object: the looped variety is unusual in England where a tanged blade, or a socketed one secured by a peg, is the preferred type (Needham 1979a). In Ireland, by contrast, the looped version is common, but the discovery of a stone mould for these spears in Anglesey (Lynch 1991, 222–4) and a faulty casting at Bala (Savory 1966b) suggest that they were also made in Wales, so the Ebnal example is unlikely to be an import. This raises the possibility that Welsh bronzesmiths transmitted the new styles and casting technology to Ireland – a case of the pupil becoming the teacher. The chronology of the two industries is not sufficiently precise to prove this relationship but, in view of the vitality of Welsh metalworking in the following phase, it is a persuasive view (Burgess 1980a, 259).

Middle Bronze Age Metalwork

For the most part the Middle Bronze Age industries built upon the foundations laid in the Early Bronze Age but in North Wales in particular there were new developments which were of national significance. These new developments centred upon the design of an effective axehead – the palstave – whose ledge stop and high flanges overcame both the major problems of hafting. In addition, the smiths of the Acton Park Tradition, working with local raw materials, devised a metal-mix of exceptional quality (see p. 99).

During this experimental phase, which is difficult to date precisely but spans the centuries around 1,500 cal BC, various types of flanged axes were produced (Schmidt & Burgess 1981, 119–25). In northern England, Scotland and Ireland these rather unsatisfactory types persist for a long time. On the continent, in southern England and in Wales these 'proto-palstaves' are rare because they are rapidly replaced by the more effective 'true palstave'. This development can be documented in the hoard evidence from northern France and Germany where flanged axes and palstaves are often associated. In Britain this is rare but north Wales has two hoards belonging to this crucial period.

The first of these is from Moelfre Uchaf, Betws yn Rhos, Denbighshire, where a bar-stop axe, six unusual 'proto-palstaves' and a piece of thin metal were found beside a large boulder (Ellis Davies 1937) (**Fig. 3.8**). All these axes have very thin blades and look extremely experimental – not to say useless! The flanges of the 'proto-palstaves' curve inwards to grip the end of the handle but there is no bar or ledge stop. This stopping device is not used again but an echo of it may perhaps be seen in the shield moulding below the ledge stop on the true palstaves of Acton Park type. The bronze used at Moelfre Uchaf has a consistently high tin value but the lead content from axe to axe is variable – clearly the metal, too, is experimental.

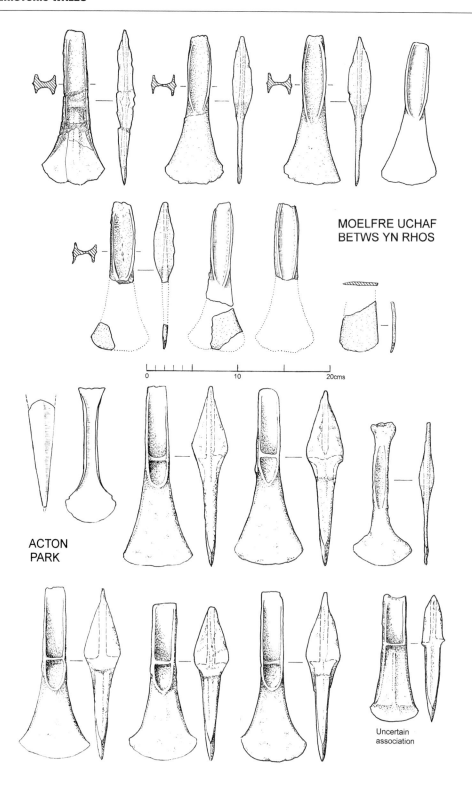

MOELFRE UCHAF
BETWS YN RHOS

0   10   20cms

ACTON
PARK

Uncertain
association

The second hoard, from Acton Park, Wrexham, contains fully developed palstaves together with two unfinished thin-bladed tools of uncertain use and part of a blade, perhaps a Group II dirk (Barnwell 1875) (**Fig. 3.8**). This hoard – which consistently uses the 'M' metal with a high tin level and about 3 per cent lead (Northover 1980, 231) – represents the confident, established stage of north Welsh metalworking, using advanced designs and tough metal. The Acton Park palstave may be characterised as large, with a narrow body and broad blade, a prominent, usually raised, shield moulding below the stop and high flanges, often angular in outline.

Such palstaves are common in north Wales and may be found in many parts of England but more importantly they occur in some significant German and French hoards (Butler 1963, 51–2; Schmidt & Burgess 1981, 119–25). In the hoards from Ilsmoor, Ruhlow, Voorhout and St Brélade, the Welsh palstaves can be recognised not only by shape but also by distinctive metallurgy (Northover 1982, 54–9), an indication of the leading role that this school of bronzesmiths played in the establishment of the tool which was to prove the mainstay of working life throughout the European Middle Bronze Age.

Doubt has been cast upon the authenticity of the single-rib palstave in the Acton Park hoard (Ehrenburg 1982) but an association of shield-pattern and single-rib palstaves at Coed Llan, Llanfyllin, confirms that the two types are contemporary (Wynn Williams 1877; Davies 1958). Their distribution, however, is slightly different, the single-rib type being more common in the east of Wales and the southern Marches (Burgess 1964). The development of such regional types increases in later centuries.

Weapons are not well represented among the products of the Acton Park industry but simple dirks, like that in the Wrexham hoard, may have been adopted from continental smiths with whom they were in contact. The dagger, the weapon of the Early Bronze Age, becomes elongated into a dirk or rapier in the Middle Bronze Age (Burgess & Gerloff 1981). The spearhead forms, too, are developments of the earlier types.

The ascendency of the Acton Park smiths may not have lasted very long. By the fourteenth century cal BC their distinctive metal was no longer widely used and the broad unlooped shield-pattern palstave had been superceded by a variety of lighter tools, often with a trident-pattern on the face. The large hoards of palstaves from Gloddaeth near Llandudno and Cemmaes in Montgomeryshire are typical of this phase (Ellis Davies 1941; Savory 1980b, no. 263) (**Fig. 3.9**). These types may occur with or without a loop on the side, but the loop eventually becomes standard. An interesting hoard comprising a looped trident-pattern palstave and two bronze palstave moulds, one looped, the other unlooped, comes from Deansfield, Bangor (Way 1856, 127–31) (**Fig. 3.9**). It epitomises the moment of change and also shows production continuing in north Wales, even though originality and initiative had been lost.

In the south-west of England this phase of the Middle Bronze Age is known as the Ornament Horizon (Smith 1959) because of the new fashion for neck ornaments, bracelets and pins evidenced in the smiths' workshop hoards and on the farms of their customers. The English torcs and bracelets are often of bronze like those of northern Europe, but in

(Opposite) *Fig. 3.8. Early palstave hoards: Moelfre Uchaf, Betws yn Rhos and Acton Park, Wrexham, both Denbighshire. Linear shaded pieces lost. (Acton Park after Burgess 1980). Scale 1:4.*

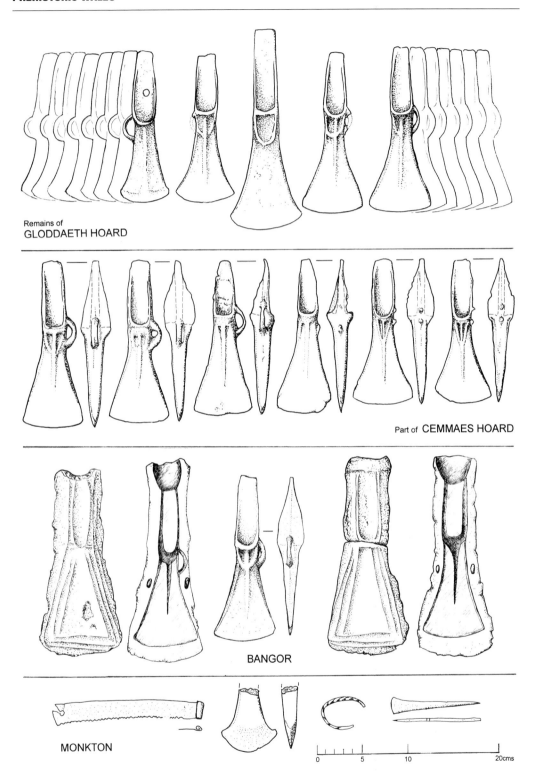

Remains of
GLODDAETH HOARD

Part of CEMMAES HOARD

BANGOR

MONKTON

0   5   10   20cms

Ireland and the west the fashions were translated into gold. Apart from the stimulation of goldworking, the impact of this tradition on Wales, as on Ireland, was very slight. Despite its strength just across the Bristol Channel, only the chisel, saw and twisted rod from Monkton, Pembrokeshire, reflect this tradition (Savory 1980b, no. 265) (**Fig. 3.9**).

Like the *lunulae* before them, the gold ornaments of the Middle Bronze Age are found in large numbers in Ireland and many must have been made there (Eogan 1994). However, the concentration of finds in west Wales, Brecon and Radnorshire suggests that local gold sources may have come into use (Northover 1995, 523). This is especially likely in relation to the cuff bracelets from Capel Isaf, Llandeilo (Savory 1977; Green *et al.* 1983). They are of Breton rather than Irish inspiration and their metal composition and simple hook closure link them to the lightly twisted ribbon torcs from Heyope, Radnorshire (Savory 1958), forming a convincing local group probably slightly earlier in date than the more widespread flanged torcs (Northover 1995, 522).

These latter ornaments are heavier bars of twisted gold, normally cruciform in section, with large hooked fastenings. The lengths vary and since none has been found in a grave or in association with a body it is difficult to know how they were worn. In Ireland the bar torcs may be either necklace-sized or long enough to be worn as a belt. In Britain they are nearly always belt-sized but have been coiled up to make an armlet or bracelet. In this form the long hooked terminals are inconvenient and useless and they may be bent back or even cut off. This modification would suggest that they were imported in their Irish form but used differently here. However, three torcs in the Llanwrthwl (Breconshire) hoard (**Pl. 13**), which may be of local manufacture, also had long terminals, one of which has been cut off in each case. The Llanwrthwl hoard is the largest Welsh find of such ornaments (Savory 1958). Four were found together beneath a heap of stones; all were about 1 metre long and coiled three or four times into armlets. One is made from a cruciform-sectioned bar (two strips hammer-welded together then prised apart and uniformly twisted to maximise the light and shade effect); two others are made from thin, twisted, square-sectioned wire, and the fourth from an untwisted circular rod. A similar group of three has been found recently at Tiers Cross near Milford Haven (Aldhouse-Green & Northover 1996a); two were of circular wire over a metre in length but tightly coiled into bracelet form with the terminals straightened; the third (approximately the same length) was a cruciform-sectioned one of 'Tara' type.

Seven other bar torcs, all of the long 'Tara' type, have been found in Wales, one of them coiled into an armlet, the others apparently not, though details of their discovery are vague (Eogan 1994, 129). These valuable ornaments have never been found in graves and the single finds may have been votive offerings, part of a religious tradition which was becoming increasingly important during the later part of the Bronze Age. The fact that the Llanwrthwl torcs were found under a marked cairn suggest that they, by contrast, were

(Opposite) *Fig. 3.9. Middle Bronze Age hoards: Gloddaeth, Caerns. – only 5 remain from a large hoard (drawn from a photograph); Cemmaes, Mont. originally at least 19 pieces (after Savory 1980b); Bangor, Caerns. two bronze moulds and a palstave (after Griffiths); Monkton, Pembs., saw, broken palstave, twisted rod and chisel (after Savory 1980b). Scale 1:4.*

hidden for safety with the intention of recovery and should be viewed as an economic rather than a religious phenomenon.

The number of weapons in Wales increases towards the end of the Middle Bronze Age and they begin to be found not in graves but in hoards in rather ambiguous circumstances. Like the goldwork, they might, with equal validity, be considered votive offerings or caches (Bradley 1990). It is also at this time that a metallurgical distinction between tools and weapons begins to emerge, suggesting a specialist weapon industry (Northover 1980, 234; 1984). Two notable hoards of this period are those from Cwm Moch, Maentwrog, and from Beddgelert (Burgess & Gerloff 1981, 114, 105–12). The former consists of three Group IV rapiers and a basal-looped spearhead from under a rock near a trans-montane route (**Fig. 3.10**). The latter was found in 1688 and is reported as consisting of about fifty rapiers found 'in a rock' near Sygun at the end of Llyn Gwynant. Only seven have survived from this, the largest hoard of these weapons from Britain. They are of various types and some must have been old when they were buried.

The weapons from these north Welsh hoards belong to British traditions, but in south Wales new weapons of continental type appear, heralding a major change in style of fighting and in industrial organisation. The fact that these changes are broadly contemporary with the period of economic stress generated by climatic deterioration raises unresolved questions about wider ranging social and political disruptions. A study of the metalwork of the Penard Phase, named after a hoard from near Swansea, reveals the growing influence of western France upon the industrial history of southern Britain (Burgess 1968a, 4–9). The problem is to know whether this influence was due to commerce or to a closer military and political contact. Wrecked boats filled with French tools and weapons, such as those at Salcombe and Dover (Muckleroy 1981) suggest the former; the introduction of influential new weapons might suggest the latter.

The Penard hoard is not large but it contains significant pieces that point the way to developments in later centuries (Burgess & Colquhoun 1988) (**Fig. 3.10**). There are three swords: two have broad tangs and leaf-shaped blades (Ballintober swords) indicative of a new style of use, slashing rather than thrusting; the other has lost its tang but has a more old-fashioned straight blade (Rosnoën type). These swords are related to the French Rixheim and Rosnoën types whose broad tangs provided a better handle attachment than the rivetted or notched rapier butt. The other significant new weapon at Penard is the pegged spearhead. From now on in the south all spears are attached by pegs and the proliferation of types in the Late Bronze Age shows that spearmen became an important fighting force. The metal arrowhead and the strange socketed axe were types which did not find favour in Britain.

Another Welsh hoard, that from Ffynhonnau in Breconshire, belongs to a slightly later stage of the same new industry (Burgess 1968b, Fig. 5) (**Fig. 3.10**). It contains a mixture of local material, a broken Cutts rapier and two palstaves, and some new pieces: a curved hunting knife of Urnfield type and two pointed spear ferrules (metal sheathing for the end of the spear shaft). These two significant hoards and the single Ballintober sword from Oystermouth (Green 1985b, 283) are in south Wales but generally this material is rare in Wales, the main impact of the changes being felt in the Thames Valley, at this time an area of expanding population and increasing wealth and importance.

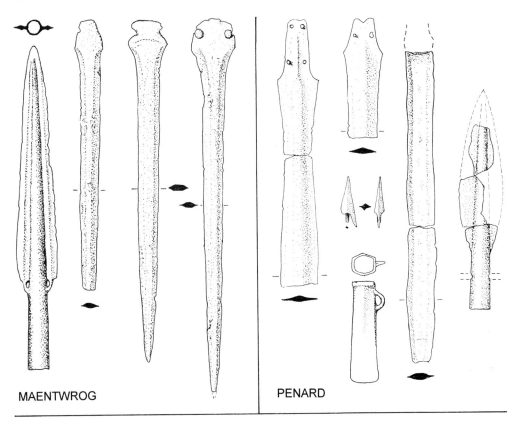

MAENTWROG

PENARD

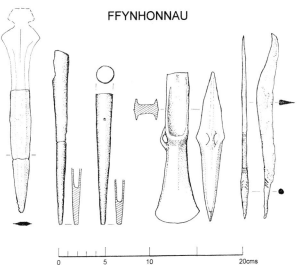

FFYNHONNAU

Fig. 3.10. Weapon hoards: Cwm Moch, Maentwrog; Penard, near Swansea and Ffynhonnau, Brecs. (after Burgess and Gerloff 1981). Scale 1:4.

The radical transformation of the industry which was begun during the Penard Phase is underlined by the findings of analysis which show that a new metal (P) was used containing less arsenic and nickel (Northover 1980, 234). This new metal was used in France and all over southern Britain, demonstrating the closeness of cross-Channel links which remained such a feature of the succeeding Late Bronze Age industries.

Stone Tools

Stone tools have a high survival rate but many are found without archaeological contexts so that precise dating is difficult. The 'trade' in polished axeheads appears to reach its zenith in the Late Neolithic (p. 56). Graig Lwyd stone from Penmaenmawr continued to be exploited in the Late Neolithic, as did the Preseli bluestone, Group XIII, used for standard felling axes and for battle axes and axe-hammers, the former with undisputed Bronze Age credentials. The striking silhouette of the outcrops, Carn Meini on Preseli, may have invested this stone with a special value which led to its use for parade weapons as well as for expensive buildings in distant Wessex (Lynch 1975b). Despite its name, though, it is not especially blue nor attractive as a polished stone, whereas many other battle axes and mace-heads are obviously made of rocks chosen for interest of colour or texture.

An exceptionally fine series of elegant ovoid mace-heads comes from north-east Wales (Roe 1968), including the splendidly decorated flint example from Maesmor near Corwen. None has an archaeological context but they reflect the increasing importance of this part of the country and its close links with the north of England where such mace-heads in various materials are common. It is interesting that in Yorkshire these objects occur in single graves and are judged to reflect the growing importance of the individual leader (Clarke *et al.* 1985, 65), whereas in north Wales they are absent from graves and may play a different role in a region where social stratification was less marked. The picrite from Cwm Mawr, Hyssington, is an unusually heavy rock which was favoured for axe-hammers (Shotton, Chitty & Seaby 1951). Its wide market suggests a specialised (but unidentified) use which demanded weight. There were very probably several small centres in Wales for the production of battle axes. They would not warrant the term 'factory' but would merit study.

Flint axes were imported into Wales from an early date but it is possible that their dominance of the south-east may be connected with the growing contact of that area with southern England in the Late Neolithic (Darvill 1989) (**Fig. 2.4**). There is no chalk in Wales; flint can only be found on the beaches and it is of poor quality. Such pebbles were certainly used in the Mesolithic and perhaps later, but in the Late Neolithic and Bronze Age better material became available. The discovery of a hoard of thirty-eight large flakes and an unfinished polished knife on the moors above Penmachno, Caernarfonshire (Ellis Davies 1939) suggests that such flint was formally traded (**Pl. 6**). The rectangular polished edge knife dates the hoard, for in the Late Neolithic there is a noticeable change in flintworking style: certain new forms of knives and of arrowheads become popular, together with the frequent use of edge polish (Piggott 1954, 358–9).

The import of high-quality flint, either from Yorkshire or from southern England, continues in the Early Bronze Age. In the Brenig cemetery on Hiraethog Bronze Age and

Mesolithic flakes could be distinguished simply by material, for all the demonstrably Bronze Age contexts yielded artefacts made from glossy dark flint quite unlike the pale flawed pebble material (Lynch 1993, 84, 187). It demonstrates the extent to which even quite impoverished communities might rely upon imported goods, although it should be noted that at Stackpole, perhaps because they were so close to the sea, the Bronze Age farmers still used pebble flint (Benson *et al.* 1990, 222).

The distinctiveness of Late Neolithic flintworking is not carried into the full Bronze Age (Pitts 1980). The most common undeniably Bronze Age tool is the flint knife, very often the plano-convex type with neat pressure flaking on the back but without a polished edge. These occur frequently in burials but are rare in other contexts. At Stackpole, the one large domestic assemblage from Wales, the Bronze Age tools are overwhelmingly (87 per cent) scrapers (Benson *et al.* 1990, 224).

Arrowheads which are made in several forms in the Late Neolithic – chisel, hollow-based and barbed and tanged (Green 1980) – occur on settlements and in burials (where a quiverful may be found), but also on remote moorland where they must be the forgotten detritus of distant hunting expeditions. A particularly notable collection has come from the margins of Llyn Bugeilyn on Plynlumon (Savory 1969b). Interestingly metal arrowheads were never adopted in Britain: the small bronze spear or javelin seems to take their place as a hunting weapon in the Middle Bronze Age.

Personal Decoration

Some idea of fashions in personal decoration may be gained from a study of beads, buttons, pins and bracelets which survived the burning of the corpse or were carefully placed with their owners' bones. By and large these decorations reflect a taste shared with the rest of the country (Shepherd 1985).

In the Late Neolithic jet from Yorkshire begins to appear in Wales, notably in north Wales which has close ties with that region and appears to have been richer than the south. The earliest pieces are a pair of belt sliders from a grave inside Gop Cave (Dawkins 1902, McInnes 1968, 144), and the commoner V-bored jet buttons. The button, ring and beads from Ysgwennant, possibly decorating a hanging purse, show that these buttons were not always used to fasten clothing (Day 1972). The disc necklace from Llong, Flintshire, is a common Beaker type, but unusually long (Lynch & Chambre 1984); the one from Pen y Bonc on Anglesey, which may have been accompanied by bronze armlets, belongs to a later, more showy, series whose best exemplars are found in the north (Lynch 1991, 157).

Glossy black beads of various materials were universally popular. A programme of analysis (Sheridan & Davis 1998) has shown that Whitby jet was indeed used on many occasions but that local substitutes were often found. In the south of England shale was used, while the fine ribbed beads from Bedd Branwen and Capel Eithin in Anglesey were made from an unusual type of lignite which may be local; there is also an anthracite bead from Breconshire.

Beads of more exotic materials must have been imported from further afield. Amber and faience were particularly prized by the wealthy chieftains of Wessex, and people in other parts of the country probably obtained them from there. There are only three occurrences of early amber in Wales (Beck & Shennan 1991, 192–4): one with the outstanding gold cape in what must be a priestly burial from Mold; one in Anglesey at the cemetery mound, Bedd Branwen; and one with a burial from Glamorgan. Faience is equally rare and also concentrated in the north. A pair of the normal segmented beads come from Llangwm, Denbighshire (Ellis Davies 1929, 275–81), a fragment of one from Tandderwen, Denbigh (Brassil 1991b, 76), and a more unusual spacer bead from Brynford near Holywell (Ellis Davies 1949, 43–9). This bead is a unique type, perhaps a product of the Scottish industry which imitated the Egyptian imports (Clarke *et al.* 1985, 216–20).

The Scottish bronze industry was a notable producer of personal ornaments and may be the source of the lost armlets from Pen y Bonc and the narrow bracelet from Llanddyfnan, both in Anglesey (Lynch 1991, 158, 175), an island which had many northern contacts. The bone and metal pins found in several cremation burials may also be considered objects of decoration, perhaps fixing hair or clothing, for one of the Anglesey examples was very soft – a mixture of copper and lead – and quite unsuitable for use as an awl (Lynch 1991, 199). Most of them are very simple, but three, again from the north, at Llanddyfnan, Cefn Goleu in Flintshire and Bryn Crûg near Caernarfon, were more elaborate and fashionable (Lynch 1991, 176; Bevan-Evans & Hayes 1955, 119; Stanley & Way 1868, 261).

Later Neolithic Pottery

The small but growing quantity of later Neolithic pottery from Wales is very fragmentary yet it is possible to recognise styles of decoration popular in other parts of Britain at this time (Gibson 1995a). So far no particular Welsh facies of these styles within the Peterborough Ware family has emerged, though a liking for bird bone decoration may be observed (Savory 1980a, 223) A recent programme of radiocarbon dating has failed to confirm any chronological sequence within the three main types – Ebbsfleet, Mortlake and Fengate wares – whose dates overlap within the Mid-Late Neolithic (3,400–2,500 cal BC (Gibson & Kinnes 1997)). It is worth noting that, despite the close links in the earlier period, the later Irish styles such as Goodlands and Moylough bowls cannot be recognised here. Contacts now seem to lie to the east.

The lightly impressed Ebbsfleet Ware has been found at Gwernvale (Britnell & Savory 1984) and in more problematic undecorated form at Capel Garmon (Lynch 1969, Fig. 57) and Four Crosses (Warrilow *et al.* 1986, 71). The more heavily decorated Mortlake and Fengate styles are commoner, occurring at thirty-three sites, in Anglesey, along the north and south coasts and in the Marches. It also occurs in what seem to be domestic pits at Llanilar near Aberystwyth indicating that the style eventually reached all parts of Wales (Gibson 1995a, 37).

Grooved Ware has only recently been confidently recognised in Wales. Less common than Peterborough Ware, it nevertheless occurs in the same areas, notably the Marches, with finds from Trelystan, Sarn y Bryn Caled and Walton, and Anglesey where sherds have

(Opposite) *Fig. 3.11. Peterborough pottery from Wales: 1 Ebbsfleet Ware; 3,4,5,9 Mortlake Ware; 2,6,7,8 Fengate Ware. 1 The Breiddin; 2 Ogmore; 3 Four Crosses; 4,5 Bryn yr Hen Bobl; 6 Castell Bryn Gwyn; 7 Walton; 8 Bryn Derwen; 9 Sarn y Bryn Caled. Sources: Musson 1991; Gibson 1994; 1995; 1999a; Warrilow et al. 1986; Lynch 1991.*

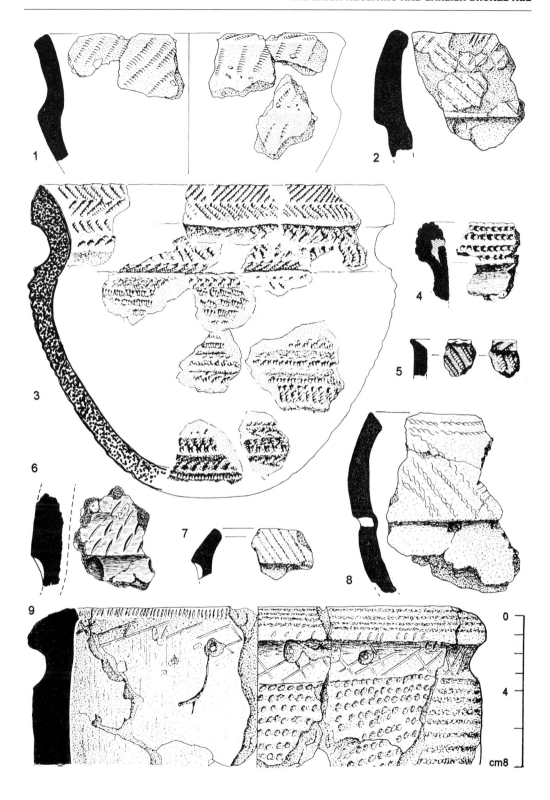

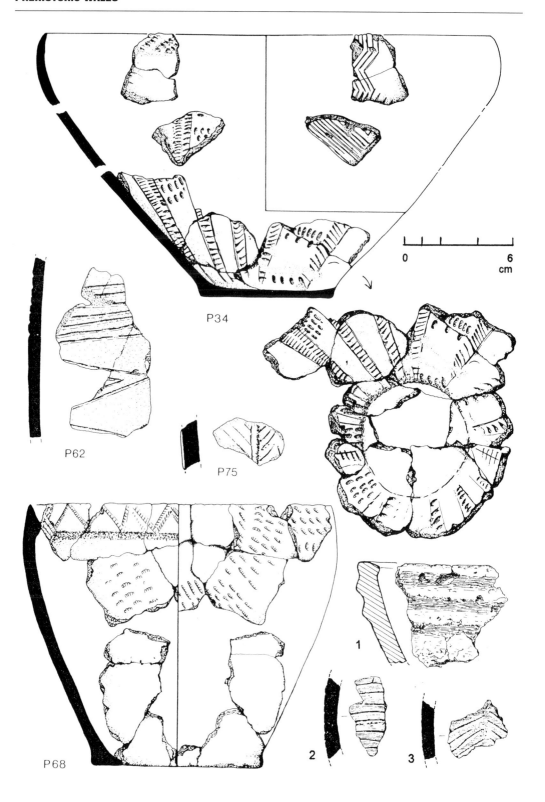

P34

P62

P75

P68

1

2

3

0   6
cm

been found at Lligwy tomb, Trefignath and Capel Eithin. At Capel Eithin shallow flared bowls with corrugated and applied decoration can be linked to the Woodlands sub-style (Lynch 1991, 342–3; Longworth in White & Smith 1999, 76). The large group (some sixty-eight vessels) from Walton, Radnorshire, belongs to the Durrington sub-style and includes large cordoned jars and smaller flared bowls with internal decoration (Gibson 1999a, 81–97). Dates from Walton and from Trelystan fall within the British range for the style, 2,800–2,400 cal BC.

In many parts of Britain Beaker pottery is seen as the hallmark of social and religious change, but in Wales early Beaker sherds are found in the old tombs, apparently used as part of traditional ceremonies. Eventually religious customs did change in the west, but even in eastern Wales where change was much earlier, the new burials occurred with native British styles, not the exotic Beaker.

Peterborough, Grooved Ware and Beaker pottery, though seldom intimately intermixed, occur in broadly the same kinds of settlement contexts in Wales dating to the centuries between 3,400 and 2,400 cal BC (Gibson 1995a; Gibson & Kinnes 1997). Beaker is definitely the latest style and continued to be used for domestic purposes until about 1,700 cal BC (Lynch 1993, 157–8). The settlements where it is found reflect a new pattern of land use (p. 87) but it is not clear whether this results from economic or social change (see **Fig. 3.2**).

The normal context for Beaker pottery in Britain as a whole is the single inhumation grave. In Wales these are relatively rare and the Beakers in them belong, for the most part, to styles which are judged to be late. Analysis of the forty or so sufficiently complete Beakers from Wales (according to the typological system outlined by Lanting and Van der Waals in 1972) reveals that none belongs to the earliest, Step 1, and very few to Steps 2–4. The later stages, Steps 5, 6 and 7, are relatively well represented. They are all of the tall, long-necked type with broader zones of more complex decoration. Pots of the final Step 7 sometimes revert to the 'bell' profile, but the decoration is no longer horizontally organised and a protruding foot becomes typical. The majority of these later pots accompany single inhumations, sometimes beneath small barrows or cairns, and several of them have characteristic grave-goods such as flint daggers or jet beads.

A programme of radiocarbon dating of human bone associated with Beakers has been carried out to test the validity of the various typological schemes (Kinnes *et al.* 1991). These schemes, though differing in detail and in interpretation, have been in broad agreement that the 'bell' shape, which occurs on the continent, is early and that the exclusively British long-necked types are later. Unfortunately the 121 dates obtained do not conform to this long-established pattern. They confirm that the style was current between 2,500 and 1,600 cal BC with maximum popularity around 2,200 to 2,000 cal BC but, like the Peterborough dating programme, can provide no typological coherence. Consequently the most popular of the typological sequences has been used here because it does provide a framework for the pottery and the associated goods that may have some approximation to a glimpsed historical reality.

(Opposite) *Fig. 3.12. Grooved Ware from Wales: P34 (internal and external decoration), P62, P75, P68 from Upper Ninepence, Walton, Rads. (from Gibson 1999a); 1 Capel Eithin, Ang.; 2–3 Lligwy, Ang. (from Lynch 1991).*

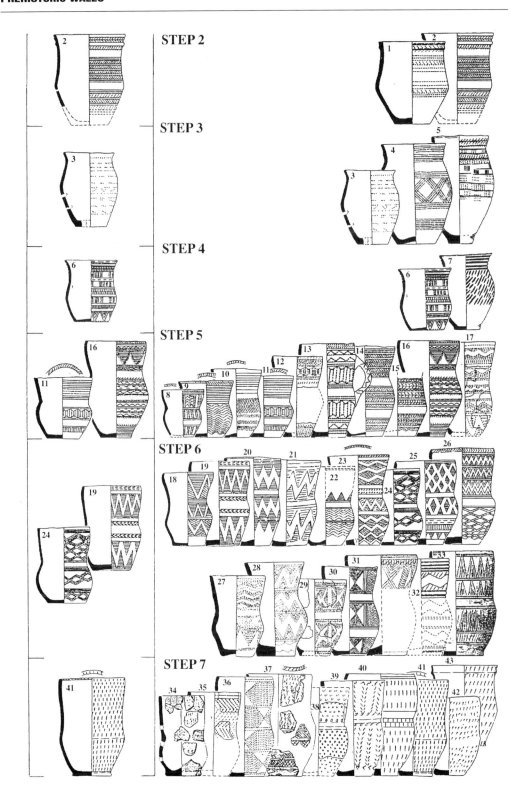

STEP 2

STEP 3

STEP 4

STEP 5

STEP 6

STEP 7

Earlier Bronze Age Pottery

Cremation became the standard system of burial in the full Early Bronze Age and pottery was used in funeral ceremonies in a variety of ways. Initially the bag of cremated bones was accompanied, as the unburnt body had been, by an 'accessory vessel', a pot presumably holding an offering of food or drink. Later the bones themselves were placed in a large pot and occasionally an accessory vessel stood beside it. Another optional adjunct is a small cup. The role of these 'pigmy cups' in the ceremonies is obscure, but they were eventually buried inside the urn on top of the bones. Sometimes, especially in South Wales, they are the only pot to accompany the bones.

There are two important styles of pottery used in these funerary contexts, Food Vessels and Collared Urns (Savory 1957; Longworth 1984). Both are believed to derive from native Late Neolithic styles, especially Peterborough Ware, but their early stages of development are centred in different regions. The Food Vessel series would seem to originate in northern England, especially Yorkshire, where they often accompany inhumations and consistently appear in earlier stratigraphic positions than Collared Urns (Burgess 1980b, 84–98). The early focus of Collared Urns, which never occur with inhumations, is more difficult to pinpoint, but was probably in the south or the Midlands (Longworth 1984). Eventually the urn was adopted everywhere, even in Scotland and Ireland where it was used alongside native pottery.

About 290 pots have survived in a reasonably intact state from Bronze Age burials in Wales. There are too many to describe in detail, but some generalisations may be attempted. A distinction should be made between those pots which accompany a burial and those which contain the bones. Apart from the Beakers already mentioned only two pots, both 'Beaker/Food Vessel Hybrids' were associated with inhumations. Others of this class, which has been augmented by recent excavations in Glamorgan and the Severn Valley, accompany cremations but do not contain them. As far as our information goes, the same is true of the Bowls (also known as Bowl Food Vessels). There are too few (only six) for dogmatic typology but most are richly textured and intricately decorated (**Fig. 3.14**, no. 3). They come mainly from the west and may have an Irish background.

Small Vase Food Vessels are also accessory vessels rather than containers (see **Fig. 3.17**, no. 8). They come in two main shapes, an upright vase with everted sloping rim and a more globular version. Many are richly decorated, often with 'false relief' patterns, but

(Opposite) *Fig. 3.13. All Welsh Beakers sorted according to Lanting and Van der Waals (1972) scheme. Pots on left typify the Step. (Drawings are mainly from D.L. Clarke,* Beaker Pottery of Great Britain and Ireland, *CUP 1970). Scale 1:8. 1 Sutton, Glam; 2 Penderyn, Brecs; 3 Ludchurch, Pembs; 4 Penarth, Caerns; 5 Llancaiach, Glam; 6 Llansilin, Denbs; 7 Ty Llwyd, Glam; 8 Caerhun, Caerns; 9 Aberbechan, Mont; 10 Moel Hebog, Caerns; 11 Bodtegir, Denbs; 12 Pant y Saer, Ang; 13 Cwm Du, Brecs; 14 Brymbo, Denbs; 15 Ty Du, Brecs; 16 Llithfaen, Caerns; 17 Porth Dafarch, Ang; 18 St Fagans, Glam; 19 & 20 Merthyr Mawr Warren, Glam; 21 Llandegai, Caerns; 22 Hendre'r Gelli, Glam; 23 Llanelltyd, Mer; 24 & 25 Ysgwennant, Denbs; 26, Llannon, Carm; 27 Llandaf, Glam; 28 Cwm Car, Brecs; 29 Llanbabo, Ang; 30 Llanharry, Glam; 31 Penarth, Caerns; 32 Cyffig, Carm; 33 Tan Dderwen, Denbs; 34 Welsh St Donats 3, Glam; 35 Darowen, Mont; 36 Rhosbeirio, Ang; 37 Tan Dderwen, Denbs; 38 Ystradfellte, Brecs; 39 Pentraeth, Ang; 40 Tremadoc, Caerns; 41 Plas Heaton, Denbs; 42 Llandegai, Caerns; 43 Talbenny, Pembs.*

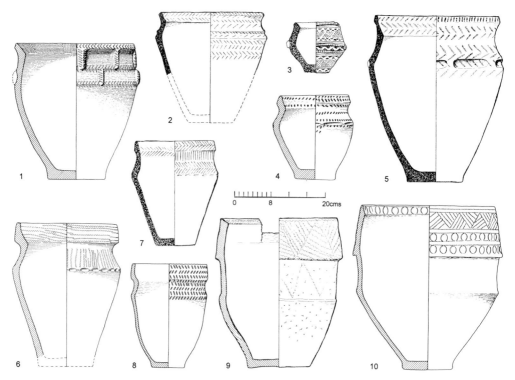

Fig. 3.14. Food Vessels and Urns from Wales. 1–2 Food Vessel Urns: Brynford, Flints.; Llangwyllog, Angl.; 3 Bowl: Manorbier, Pembs.; 4–5 Urns/FVs: Holt, Wrexham, Merddyn Gwyn, Angl.; 6–8 'Early' Collared Urns: Rhiw, Caerns., Bedd Branwen, Angl., Llanychaer, Pembs., 9 'Middle' Collared Urn, Brenig 44, Denbs.; 10 'Late' Collared Urn, Llangynidr, Brecs. (From Savory 1980b; Lynch 1991 and 1993). Scale 1:8.

others are completely plain. About eighteen have been found, predominantly in north and mid-Wales, emphasising a link with northern England.

The Vase Food Vessel shape occurs in a larger version (taller than 20 centimetres) – the Food Vessel Urn – which regularly contains cremated bone (see **Fig. 3.14**, no. 2). They are elegantly proportioned pots with a high shoulder, often grooved, and an everted rim. The decoration, which regularly appears on the inner slope of the rim and on the neck and shoulder, is rather unimaginative – invariably a small-scale herringbone pattern made by incision or various cord impressions. Continuous horizontal line schemes are rare. Occasionally, as at Brynford (**Fig 3.14**, no. 1) ribs were added; more heavily encrusted styles, occurring mainly in south-west Wales and perhaps resulting from Irish influence, should also be allocated to this group.

Attempts have been made to explain the persistent distinction between Collared Urns and Food Vessels in chronological, ethnic or class terms but none of these explanations is entirely satisfactory. In primary areas such as Yorkshire there is a fairly convincing stratification which might support a chronological distinction, but it does not apply in Wales where shared and exchanged decorative traits make disentanglement impossible.

This intermeshing of the two styles is epitomised by a group of pots – from Llanmadoc, Glamorgan; Holt near Wrexham; Trelystan 22, Montgomeryshire; Merddyn Gwyn and Llanddyfnan, Anglesey – which have been variously described as Food Vessels or as Collared Urns (**Fig. 3.14**, nos 4 and 5; **Fig. 3.17**, no. 7). Conversely, well-defined Food Vessels and Collared Urns are regularly found together in cemetery mounds (see p. 126). Though the detailed chronology of these sites may be open to debate it must be assumed that they are the product of unified communities, so a sharp ethnic devide between the users of the two styles would seem to be ruled out. At Llanddyfnan and at Treiorwerth, Anglesey, Cordoned Urns (**Fig. 3.17**, nos 4–6) are added to the stylistic mix and at the ceremonial circle on Moel Goedog near Harlech the Food Vessel Urn and the Collared Urns shared technological details which suggested that they had been made by the same potters (Jenkins in Lynch 1984b, 46).

The conclusion must therefore be that, at a time when faience was fashionable (contemporary with the later Wessex graves in the south of England), communities in Wales, especially those in the north, were prepared to make and use Food Vessels and Collared Urns indiscriminately. Some of their products were obvious hybrids while others retained the original distinctions. By that time the Food Vessel, which had appeared as an accessory to unurned cremations, may have had a long history behind it, whereas the Collared Urn, never used in that way, may have been a newer style, although it, too, is believed to have Late Neolithic roots. Were there more ancestral Peterborough Ware in north Wales, it would be tempting to suggest that the style emerged here at this time, the hybrid Urn/Food Vessels like those from Merddyn Gwyn being seminal.

The Collared Urn eventually became the dominant form of container for burnt bones. There are almost twice as many Urns as Food Vessels, but to say 'became' begs the question of sequential development which has remained very difficult to demonstrate. A typological sequence can be recognised and individual pots can be allocated to Early, Middle or Late groups, but associated goods do not confirm their chronological validity. For instance, almost identical small bone pommels have been found with a Food Vessel Urn, a hybrid Urn/Food Vessel, and Collared Urns of Early and Middle groups. A broader selection of Wessex II associations would link the Pigmy Cup with this range of contemporary pottery, and stratigraphic evidence from Treiorwerth and Llanddyfnan would add the Cordoned Urn as well. Radiocarbon dates are unhelpful. Some twenty-four pots of various kinds from Wales have been directly dated. The results range from 2,000–1,400 cal BC, a span comparable to that from Britain as a whole (Longworth 1984, 79–80), but it is perhaps symbolic that both ends of this range should come from one site, Capel Eithin in Anglesey, and should be applicable to very similar Early Collared Urns (Lynch 1991, 394)!

Despite the problems, it is perhaps worth reviewing the typological distinctions (Longworth 1984, 19–35; Burgess 1986). The Early group share decorative schemes with the Food Vessel Urns: small-scale patterns, dominated by herringbone, either incised or cord-impressed. However, horizontal line schemes are fairly common and the chief distinction is in the treatment of the relatively narrow collar with its concave internal moulding (probably to accommodate a wooden lid). This is not seen on true Food Vessels. A line of indentations (VSG) is common around the shoulder.

The Middle group have deeper collars with a less sharply defined internal moulding. Larger scale decoration is dominant and the VSG is rare. The Late group are of rather different proportions, often being as broad as they are tall, with a very narrow base. Virtually no internal moulding is present and the deep collar is defined rather by an external overhang. The top of the rim is often sloped and internal decoration is confined to this slope. It is also rare to find decoration below the collar, but the collars themselves are decorated with more elaborate patterns, quite often a two-tier scheme.

Whereas the Middle and Early groups share associations with the same relatively closely datable goods, the Late urns seldom contain associated objects, or only those, such as awls and small bronze knives, which have a long currency. The eyed bone pin may be a more exclusive association, but it, too, can be dated to Wessex II elsewhere so there is no reason to suggest that 'Late' urns do not overlap with the others for most of their currency.

The use of a 'pigmy cup' in funeral ceremonies was adopted in Wales, as in most parts of Britain, at a time when Collared Urns were being used. No direct association between one of these cups and a Food Vessel has been recorded from Wales, though they have been found at several cemetery sites where Food Vessels occur alongside the Urns. They are found chiefly with the 'later' series of Urns, especially in south Wales where there are also several instances of the pigmy cup alone accompanying the burial (for example, Sutton Phase 4, **Fig. 3.15**). Some of these are quite rich, like the one from Breach Farm, Glamorgan (Grimes 1939) which is contemporary with the earlier Wessex graves. This early use of the pigmy cup alone may explain the rarity of Food Vessels and Early Urns in the south.

The fifty or so pigmy cups from Wales are much less standardised than the larger pots (Savory 1958–60). Some are bi-conical, some globular, some are miniature versions of larger urns; several are exceptionally well made and carefully decorated, others are very tiny and crudely moulded.

Eighteen Welsh urns may be classified as Cordoned Urns, straight-sided jars with one or two bands of decoration defined not by undulation of the pot wall but by an applied cordon (see **Fig. 3.17**, nos 4–6). They come in two sizes, medium and large but the latter are admittedly difficult to distinguish from the Late Collared Urns. The type is common in Ireland and Scotland and their presence in Wales is likely to reflect influence from Irish Sea traffic. Interestingly their association with bronze razors in Ireland and Scotland is maintained in Wales, with examples at Fan y Big, Breconshire (Briggs *et al.* 1990) and Llanddyfnan, Anglesey (Lynch 1991, 173–5) (**Fig. 3.17**, nos 6 and 6a).

The extent of Irish influence on Welsh Bronze Age pottery is not perhaps as great as might be expected. The Early Bronze Age is a period when contacts seem to have waned (Lynch 1989). A few Bowls and some decorative traits in the south west and Anglesey suggest the influence of Irish styles, but the predominant forms are mainstream British.

Among burial urns, only the small one from Six Wells 271 in the Vale of Glamorgan (Fox 1941) can be ascribed to the Trevisker tradition of Devon and Cornwall. Its uniqueness highlights the strange isolation of south-west England at this time, although some later domestic pottery is claimed to show influences from that direction (see p. 202).

All the pottery discussed so far has come from burials and many believe that these styles were made exclusively for funerary use. However, excavations at Stackpole Warren and

Atlantic Trading Estate, Barry, have produced sherds which are clearly from Collared Urns indistinguishable from those used in graves (Benson *et al.* 1990; Sell 1998) and several of those in graves were damaged in antiquity and appear second-hand, so there is little reason to doubt that they represent the normal domestic storage jar.

Analysis of the clays and stone fillers used in the manufacture of this pottery in Anglesey and north Wales has suggested that it is a professional product and even rather mundane pots might be imported from some distance (Williams & Jenkins 1976; Jenkins in Lynch 1993, 196). This conclusion remains controversial, for the pots are not exceptionally well made and would be difficult to transport, but a pottery trade, proven in the Iron Age, might help to explain the great uniformity of the Urn and Food Vessel series.

This trade would seem to have been a victim of the economic collapse at the end of the Middle Bronze Age, for succeeding pottery is both rare and distressingly crude and unimaginative. The shapes are universally simple – straight-sided jars with plain rims; decoration is virtually absent except for occasional rough lines and fingernail marks. The fabric is normally coarse with much stone grit; where analysed it has been shown to be mainly locally derived (Wardle 1987; Benson *et al.* 1990, 219–22). This pottery occurs on domestic sites such as Stackpole Warren and Glanfeinion (**Fig. 3.5**) and at early hillforts (Musson 1991, 118–23) (see p. 150); occasionally it is associated with burials (see p. 212).

BURIAL MONUMENTS

Human burials provide one of the most important records from the prehistoric past, important not only for the tangible remains of bones and artefacts, evidence of health and disease, technology and trade, but more crucially, though more problematically, of social attitudes and religious thinking. Burials, moreover, provide the only self-conscious record that early man has left. Not surprisingly, therefore, they have been the subject of very intense study and a good deal of speculation.

The critical difference between the burial traditions of the earlier Neolithic and those that became dominant in the Bronze Age is the loss of anonymity through the adoption of individual rather than communal graves and the provision of grave-goods through which we can glimpse something of the personal circumstances of the deceased. The structure of the burial monuments changed to reflect the new values. Bronze Age monuments are simpler, were not specifically designed for re-entry (though many were re-used) and were universally circular in plan, reflecting the architecture of other contemporary religious structures. Though their apparent simplicity might suggest that they were built quite rapidly, excavation often shows that the process was still a long one, with several stages of funerary ritual which we cannot hope to fully understand. We should not forget that we cannot even be sure that every generation of leaders, let alone the whole population, would be afforded formal burial (Lynch 1993, 149). Dynamics of burial may reflect the perceived relationship between the living and their gods as much as the need to honour the dead.

The impulse behind the changes which overtook Britain during the Late Neolithic has been much debated. The huge communal tombs were abandoned in the south of England long before they were closed in Wales, if we may judge from the Late Neolithic pottery inside the Welsh ones. In Yorkshire large round mounds in which recognisable individuals were buried with their personal belongings are believed to mark the beginning of the new burial traditions. In many parts of the country the old certainties had broken down and the situation had become fluid. In Wales it is in the east, especially the Severn Valley, perhaps an area with little previous settlement, where these changes are most visible at an early date.

At Four Crosses near Welshpool a vast burial pit at the centre of what seemed to be a normal Early Bronze Age barrow, re-used on many occasions, contained three individual inhumations, one with a strange undecorated pot. Radiocarbon dates suggest that they were buried between 3,200 and 3,100 cal BC (Warrilow *et al.* 1986, 64). At Trelystan, only a few kilometres away, the sequence of burial activity begins with another single inhumation of much the same date (Britnell 1982, 136).

But despite this early appearance of individual burial in central Wales the system did not become widely established until a good deal later. The earliest Beaker pottery in Wales comes from megalithic tombs, still in use in the west. Of the thirty-nine burials accompanied by this universally fashionable pottery only a few, from the south, belong to its earlier stages (**Fig. 3.13**). It was not until the long-necked Beaker had become popular that the practice spread to the north and west. However, not all these burials are the expected single inhumations: several are cremations and some are multiple, with more than one body in the grave. Both these variations are harbingers of things to come in Wales.

The practice of single inhumation was slow to be adopted in Wales because of the strength of the megalithic tradition and, if one may judge from the paucity of graves (perhaps a fallible guide when so many are unexcavated) it was short-lived. The return to cremation seems to have been effected by 2,000 cal BC and it remains the norm throughout the rest of the Bronze Age. The impetus for this change is unknown. It is not accompanied by any conspicuous new introductions to suggest an upheaval of politics or population. The not infrequent discovery of unburnt and burnt bones in the same grave, as at Tandderwen, Denbighshire (Brassil 1991b, 83) and the occasional use of unnecessarily large graves for the burial of a small bag of 'ashes' suggests that the changeover was gradual and without rancour.

Though one may recognise older attitudes re-emerging in many parts of Wales in the Early Bronze Age (Lynch 1980), the Late Neolithic does seem to have been a genuine watershed. It is interesting that, except in Anglesey and Breconshire, no burial sites run through from the Neolithic to the Bronze Age, but several barrows show a sequence of re-use going back to a 'founding father' accompanied by a Beaker, the distinctive symbol of these 'new men' – whether they were truly strangers or perhaps local leaders adopting new strategies.

Monuments showing a sequence of burials, using both inhumation and cremation and favouring a variety of styles of pottery, occur in all parts of the country. The sequence must be demonstrated by evidence of enlargement or disturbance of the mound. Good examples are Merddyn Gwyn in Anglesey, where an inhumation with a late Beaker is central to a small round cairn enlarged when a cremation in a Food Vessel Urn and

(Opposite) *Fig. 3.15. Sutton 268'. Development and grave goods. 1. Child + Beaker under minimal cairn; 2. Inhumed man displaces child, cairn enlarged; 3. Cremations C–F covered by earth mound; 4. Cremation A + cup inserted, covered by enlarged walled mound; 5. Cremations B and X added. Adapted from Fox 1943.*

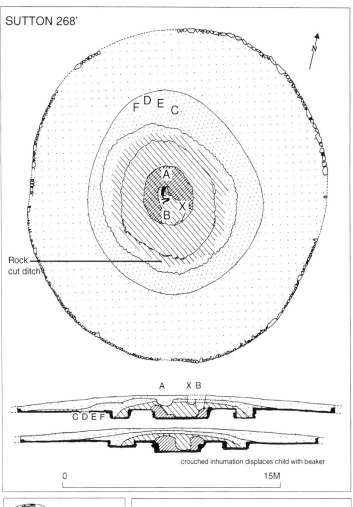

SUTTON 268'

F D E C

Rock cut ditch

A

B X

A X B

C D E F

crouched inhumation displaces child with beaker

0   15M

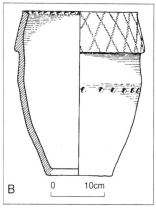

B   0   10cm

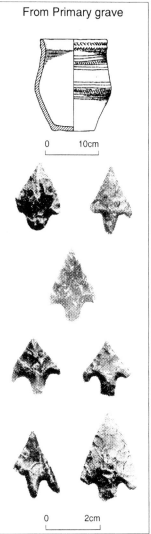

From Primary grave

0   10cm

0   2cm

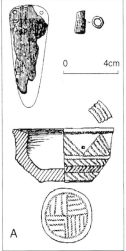

A   0   4cm

0   4cm

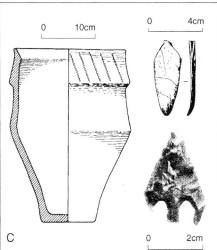

0   10cm

0   4cm

C   0   2cm

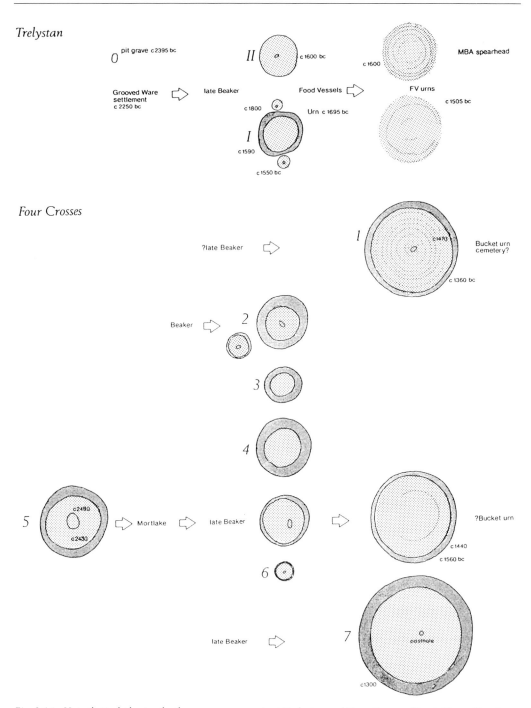

Fig. 3.16. *Hypothetical phasing for funerary monuments at Trelystan and Four Crosses, Mont. (From Warrilow et al. 1986). Note that dates quoted are in radiocarbon years bc, not cal BC.*

(Opposite) *Fig. 3.17. Plan and section of Cemetery Mound at Llanddyfnan, Anglesey, with selection of pottery and grave goods. 8 (Vase Food Vessel) is accessory to burial 7 (Food Vessel Urn); 4, 5 and 6 are Cordoned Urns (from Lynch 1991).*

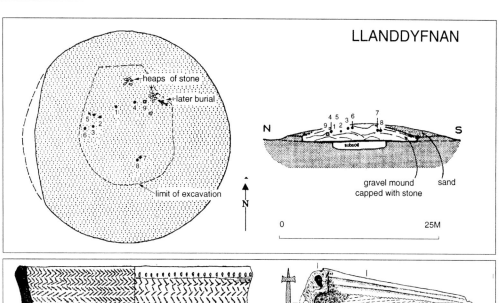

LLANDDYFNAN

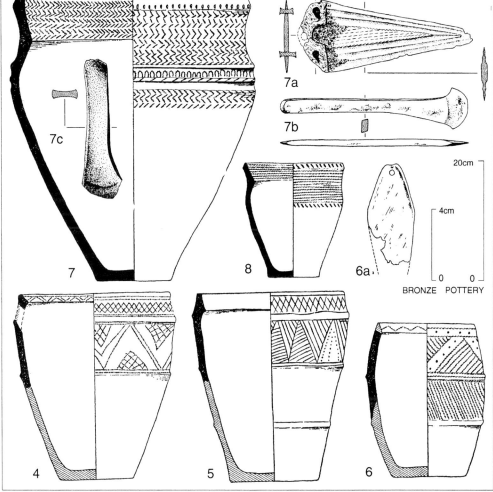

accompanied by a Bowl was placed just outside the original kerb. Two cremations in Collared Urns were later dug into the top of the enlarged mound (Hughes 1908). Similar sequences are recorded at Talbenny, Pembrokeshire (Fox 1942) and Sutton, Glamorgan (Fox 1943), though Food Vessels are not used for the cremations (**Fig. 3.15**). In Montgomeryshire, at the cemeteries of Trelystan and Four Crosses, a sequence of change, enlargement and multiplication of monuments continues from the very early inhumations through to a period in the early second millennium cal BC when the use of a single mound as a cemetery became a more common practice (Warrilow *et al.* 1986, 80–5) (**Fig. 3.16**).

The cemetery mound, in which up to a dozen or two dozen burials may be placed in the same barrow or cairn, is a phenomenon which is particularly characteristic of the north and west of Britain and of Ireland. It is recognisable by the absence of a central, primary grave and the presence of a group of burials scattered within the mound without apparent distinction. Ideally it should be possible to deduce that they were buried as a group, rather than individually, but the evidence is seldom that satisfactory.

In Ireland and Scotland these cemeteries often contain inhumation burials, or a mixture of inhumations and cremations. In Wales there are very few cemetery mounds with grouped inhumations – only a few on the south coast (Savory 1972). Moreover developments such as those at Four Crosses, Trelystan, Fridd y Carreg Wen (Williams 1921) and Merddyn Gwyn, where it is only at the final stage of enlargement that grouped burials are placed in the mound, suggest that this system of burial is adopted at a later date in Wales than in some other parts of the Highland Zone. In the south of England, where social stratification is most marked, the exclusive monument is much more common and survives in some parts, through to the fourteenth century cal BC.

By contrast, in most parts of Wales cemetery mounds had become the standard burial monuments by 2,000 cal BC, as may be judged by both radiocarbon dates and styles of pottery and grave-goods chosen. The facts that many different types of pottery were in contemporary use and that radiocarbon dates cannot confidently separate events less than two centuries apart make it difficult to establish the length of time that any cemetery might have been in use. Some may have been short-lived (Lynch 1971) (**Fig. 3.17**); others may have been used for up to 900 years, still receiving bone in the eleventh century cal BC. It may be significant that the sites which have produced these late dates, Capel Eithin in Anglesey (Lynch 1991, 351–6) and Bromfield in Shropshire (Stanford 1982), are both flat cemeteries without a mound to draw archaeological attention to their presence.

The distribution of surviving cairns and barrows in Wales (**Fig. 3.1**), being predominantly upland, enshrines one important truth – the opening of these virgin lands to settlement and exploitation – but it also conceals the continued occupation of the lowlands where subsequent agriculture has obliterated whole cemeteries like Tandderwen near Denbigh (Brassil 1991). On Lleyn air photography is only now beginning to fill out the Bronze Age map. In the south the Glamorgan ridges and the Brecon Beacons were newly colonised, but the rich lands of the Vale, which had been well occupied during the Neolithic, continued to support a wealthy population.

Anglesey and Pembrokeshire, which had been densely populated by builders of megalithic tombs, appear comparatively deserted in the Bronze Age. In both areas the cemetery mound is common, perhaps the dominant monument, and smaller mounds do not proliferate. It can be argued that these cemeteries appear where Neolithic collective traditions had been strongest. In virgin territories like Hiraethog, the single burial monument is present in greater numbers (Lynch 1993, 144–9). The vast majority of cairns remain unexcavated or have been robbed without record, so it is impossible to quantify this distinction accurately but it seems reasonable to suggest that pioneers may have adopted the new ethos with more enthusiasm.

In the absence of contemporary settlement it is difficult to discuss the rationale of the precise location of monuments. In some districts, such as Barbrook near Sheffield, the strict separation of farmland and cemetery can be recognised (Hart 1981). In Wales there are concentrations of burial and ceremonial monuments, such as those on Penmaenmawr in Caernarfonshire (Griffiths 1960) and Glandy Cross in Carmarthenshire (Ward et al. 1987), but the complementary settlement has not been found. In terms of landscape, however, it is possible to show that many cairns have been placed for dramatic effect, often on ridge crests or on the saddle of hills close to well-travelled paths (Lynch 1975b; 1984b). Excavation at some of these prominent monuments has shown that they do not always cover burials and it must be recognised that some mounds and tall stones may have marked territories or boundaries or served as political memorials of some kind (Lynch 1993, 44–6). As in the Neolithic, cairns may have carried a message for the living as well as the dead.

Almost without exception Bronze Age monuments are circular but there are many variations on this plan. Those which have a solid mound or platform of stone or earth may be distinguished from those which are annular; the former normally cover burials, the latter are ceremonial and provide evidence of non-funerary rituals. Externally the variations lie in the treatment of the kerb and the profile of the mound. These variations survive most clearly in the stone monuments and several distinctive and fairly standardised designs may be recognised (Lynch 1979; 1980).

The standard cairn, undoubtedly the most common type, is a simple heap of stone – some up to 20 metres across and 2 metres high – usually retained within a ring of substantial boulders often now buried within the collapse of loose stone (Pl. 19). What have been called cairn circles have an intermediate ring of spaced stones projecting through the mass of cairn material. Bryn Cader Faner in Merioneth (Pl. 15; Fig. 3.20) is undoubtedly the most dramatic of these. None has been excavated. Kerb circles have a contiguous or very close-set ring of stones surrounding a level space, often appearing empty but actually filled with a thin spread of stone (Pl. 14). Excavation at Cefn Caer Euni I (Lynch 1986b) and the exposed cist in Carn Llechart (RCAHMW 1976, no. 66) indicate their burial use. The platform cairn, deliberately designed as a low drum, may be more problematic in that disturbance can easily render it unrecognisable, but excavations at Brenig demonstrated the validity of the type and their primary burial use (Lynch 1993, 113–16). The choice of one of these specialised designs may imply some unusual factor in the persons buried, but this is impossible to demonstrate convincingly.

All these variants seem to be broadly contemporary, built during the second half of the third millennium cal BC. Only the exceptionally small kerb cairns (no more than 3–4 metres across but ringed by disproportionately large kerbstones) appear to be consistently later, belonging to the thirteenth century cal BC when traditions of formal burial were on the wane (Lynch 1993, 99–101).

Earthen mounds in Wales are normally built of turves and do not require the ditches which provide design distinctions in southern English barrows (**Pl. 17**). These turf mounds often cover elaborate settings of wooden stakes or rings of stone (cairn rings) indicative of prolonged preparatory rituals (Lynch 1993, 80–4). Only excavation can reveal these buried features, so the extent of the tradition cannot be mapped. The stone variants, on the other hand, can be identified by fieldwork (Lynch 1972b). Rather surprisingly few regional preferences emerge. All the standard types can be found in the stone-using parts of Wales; only the southern walled cairns like Sutton, Glamorgan, with their particular use of the pigmy cup, could claim to be regionally distinctive (Grimes 1938; Fox 1943; Savory 1969a) (**Fig. 3.15**).

Burial Rituals

When an unburnt body is laid in the grave it is easy to recognise those objects which were an incidental part of clothing and those that were placed for the use of the deceased in the after-life, to ease the journey or to maintain status in a new world envisioned in terms of the old. When cremation is adopted these distinctions become a little blurred. Some of the personal goods are burned and therefore must have adorned the corpse on the pyre; others are not and represent chosen offerings.

The position of the pyre in relation to the final burial place is variable. In some cases burnt earth and wooden structures beneath the mound suggest that it was close, but the evidence is not consistent. Sometimes the burnt bone was carefully collected and washed before it was placed in a container, a bag, a box or a large jar; sometimes collection was rather perfunctory and the bone is mixed with charcoal and soil from the pyre. Burial may be in a hole, in a stone box or cist or simply placed on the surface. Sometimes care is taken to protect the container from breakage (occasionally a double urn is used); sometimes there seems little concern.

An accessory vessel, normally a smaller pot placed beside or close to the cremation urn, is a frequent adjunct, as it was in inhumation graves. Most are found empty and the original content, perhaps food or drink, is unknown but the discovery of infant earbones within several north Welsh examples hints at less comforting funerary rites (Lynch 1971, 57). The presence of pigmy cups also suggests some formal and complex rituals surrounding the funeral itself, as does the frequent discovery of areas of burning and pits filled with charcoal. These features, sometimes scattered randomly, sometimes concentrated at points around the circumference which were subsequently emphasised by the construction of small annexes (Gibson 1993), are reminiscent of those found at ceremonial sites and serve to highlight the link between the two.

RELIGIOUS MONUMENTS

During the earlier Neolithic the religious activity of the community seems to have been concentrated at one point: the great family tomb which, in the west, fulfilled a number of roles, spiritual and perhaps political (if the two can be meaningfully separated in prehistory). Additionally, in southern England, the little-understood causeway camps are thought to have had a public role which may have operated at a broader level, engaging more than an immediate family group. This trend towards wider networks, divorced from the dominance of ancestors, may lie behind the widespread adoption of the henge monument, an even less well-understood phenomenon, but one which fulfills the ideal of a central gathering place, with a formal and regular plan (a circular bank and ditch enclosure with single or double entrance) but without a primary connection with human burial. It has been suggested that this movement away from the dominance of the family tomb may reflect a change in the perception of the spiritual powers controlling man's life, away from the ancestor group towards the idea of more individualised 'gods' (Parker Pearson 1999).

It is not clear where these changes first developed. If the causeway camp has any ancestral role it should be in the south; but Yorkshire, where individual graves with personal goods are early and where there are a lot of impressive henges, may hold the priority of religious change, while others have claimed that the intense religious climate of the Orkneys may have nurtured these developments. As far as Wales is concerned, henges seem to spring from introduced ideas, for they occur in areas exposed to eastern contact. If the situation at Bryn Celli Ddu in Anglesey (**Fig. 2.14**), where a small henge monument with bank, internal ditch and ring of stones, was subsequently obliterated beneath the mound of a fine new but anachronistic Passage Grave (O'Kelly 1969) is correctly interpreted, their construction caused some resentment among the local establishment – at least in Anglesey (Lynch 1991, 94–5).

With the old traditions still strong in the north-west, the new monuments and attitudes are likely to have come from further south and east. Air photographs and targeted excavation in the Walton Basin, Radnorshire, have revealed an impressive concentration of enclosures and other large-scale religious/public monuments in a significant border region (Gibson 1999). The huge Hindwell II enclosure there belongs to a series of large palisaded sites built in Britain and Ireland between 3,000 and 2,500 cal BC; it is the largest known, built around 2,500 cal BC with 1,530 posts standing 6 metres high. Buildings and activities within the enclosure remain unknown but it is close to other large-scale religious monuments, including a 'pit enclosure' with an entrance avenue similar to that at Meldon Bridge in Scotland. Together they form a ritual landscape of monumental proportions with implications for population, resources and power.

Such concentrations of monuments, too large to be the product of single family endeavour, become a feature of many regions of Britain in the later Neolithic and are interpreted as evidence for the growth of more overt and centralised power structures (Barrett 1994). They normally occur on flat land (usually valley floor) sites which may have been nodal points in long-distance communications. Because the monuments are judged to be essentially ceremonial or political, artefacts are rare and dating is reliant on radiocarbon. On this basis it has been claimed that these 'sanctuaries' had a long development and that the earliest components may be the *cursus* monuments, mysterious embanked avenues of varying width and length, but always strictly parallel (Gibson 1994, 188–90). Some of these focus on or incorporate pre-existing long barrows (Whittle *et al.* 1992) but their own claim to date to the Early Neolithic is based on radiocarbon alone, a not entirely satisfactory foundation. The regularity of their association with henge monuments would incline one to view them as essentially contemporary.

The most conspicuous components of these riverine sanctuaries are the circular henges, open-air sites defined by a bank and ditch, the ditch being almost invariably on the inside

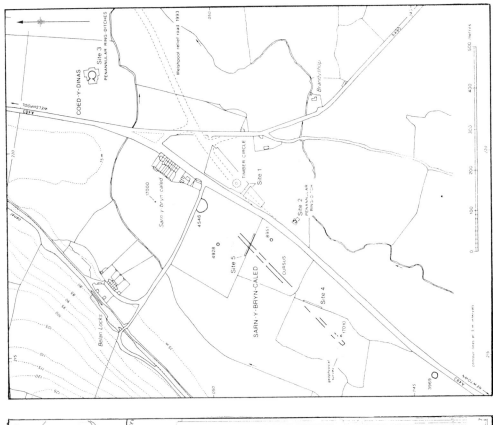

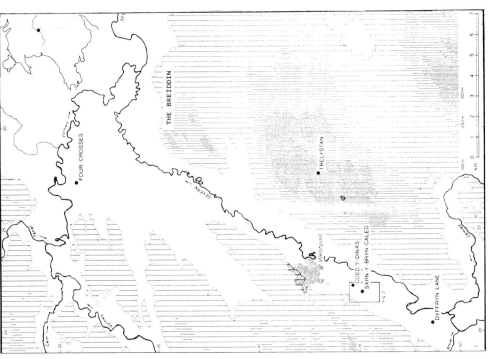

Fig. 3.18. Topographical setting and plan of monument complex at Sarn y Bryn Caled (from Gibson 1995).

of the bank – a non-defensive arrangement. The interior may contain a ring of upright stones or posts, but often nothing is found. They may have one or two causeway entrances (Class I and Class II) with some evidence that the latter form is slightly later.

Smaller embanked circles, free-standing timber rings and ring-ditches which had surrounded Bronze Age barrows may also be found in the vicinity, indicating that development and enlargement is certainly occurring and that, whatever their date of foundation, the importance of these religious centres continued well into the Bronze Age.

Because of their valley-floor location most of these sites have been recognised by aerial photography so their full distribution is unknown. At present the known distribution is eastern and coastal, echoing that of decorated pottery (see **Fig. 3.2**).

The very large monuments in the Walton Basin include two *cursus* but no classic henge; continued interest in the Bronze Age is evidenced by several barrows and an unusual 'Four Stone' circle (Gibson 1999a; Burl 1988). Further north, in the Severn Valley near Welshpool, just the area where new burial systems appear early, air photography and excavation have revealed two major sanctuaries, both probably with a long history. A complex henge at Dyffryn Lane, Berriew, itself the focus of a number of Bronze Age barrows (Gibson 1995b), would seem to form one end of a linear arrangement of monuments perhaps related to the striking profile of the Breiddin erupting from the floor of the valley. The centre of the group seems to be south of Welshpool at Sarn y Bryn Caled, where a *cursus* runs along the valley with small timber monuments beside it. Excavation of one of these (Gibson 1994) has shown that it was a double circle of tall wooden uprights (probably lintelled) with a cremation burial in the centre (**Fig. 3.20**). Four fine arrowheads arguably within the body before cremation suggest a sacrificial victim (Gibson 1992). This circle is Early Bronze Age in date but a neighbouring ring with wooden portal was earlier, built in the Late Neolithic; the *cursus* is claimed to be earlier still. Another crop-mark clearly indicating a circle of large posts marks another concentration of ceremonial and burial monuments on the floor of the Tanat Valley at Meusydd (St Joseph 1980).

Elsewhere in Wales the evidence is less consistent and is derived from untested aerial photography. Of eleven putative *cursus* monuments only three – Walton, Sarn y Bryn Caled and Llandegai – are confirmed (Gibson 1999b), while the intriguing circles on flat land at Bryncrug near Tywyn (Merioneth) and near Bala (Crew & Musson 1996, 12–13) might be settlement enclosures rather than henges. Either way, they expose our ignorance of earthwork monuments which lie on good agricultural land and demonstrate the returns which may come from examining air photographs.

Air photographs revealed the existence of a large sanctuary at Llandegai near Bangor which was excavated in 1966 (Houlder 1968; 1976). Here, on the site of an Early Neolithic house, there were two large henge monuments, one with a single entrance, and containing evidence for a significant link with the axe trade, the other with two entrances and producing enigmatic deposits of stone and Beaker pottery. Between them was the western end of a *cursus* which ran across the gravel ridge towards the Ogwen Valley and a small *hengiform* monument of unknown purpose. Unlike the situation in Anglesey, this mainland sanctuary seems to have been allowed to develop unhindered, for Bronze Age burials later clustered around it.

Fig. 3.19. View of Stone Circle at Gors Fawr, Pembs., looking west. The monument is set within an amphitheatre of hills overlooked by Carn Meini, the source of the Stonehenge bluestones. (Photo: copyright Mick Sharp).

Aerial photography in the Vale of Glamorgan and surviving earthworks in west Wales indicate that henges (or monuments akin to them) also penetrated the south of Wales, along the coastal corridor (Williams 1986, 12). None has been excavated on a scale large enough to illuminate date or function (Williams 1984).

The upland stone circles share several features with henges: consistent circularity, a design open to the sky, an absence of primary burial (though cremations may be added later), siting within a group of monuments (often a pair of circles, marker stones, outliers, alignments and attendant cairns), and frequent location at significant points on lines of communication. The earlier henges are normally in river valleys, the stone circles near cross-ridge paths. In both cases the siting may suggest use by more than one community coming together at a boundary. The upland stone circles are indicative of the shift in population; there is only one surviving in a lowland setting but their vulnerability to agriculture and the existence of wooden alternatives should not be forgotten. This may explain their virtual absence from Anglesey, the Lleyn Peninsula and the Vale of Glamorgan and their rarity in Pembrokeshire and eastern Wales. Stone circles are not especially common; some eighty are known (Grimes 1963 and later discoveries) but it is notable that they tend to cluster. Not only do they frequently occur in pairs, but certain regions – such as Mynydd Myddfai below Carmarthen Fan, the Kerry Hills running into Shropshire, and north Caernarfonshire – contain what must be significant concentrations. Unfortunately our ignorance of the precise role of these monuments makes it difficult to find an explanation for this.

The structure of the stone circle has been subject to a great deal of metrical and astronomical analysis (Thom *et al.* 1980) which is not susceptible of proof. The striking location of many of these sites, commanding wide views to distant horizons, encourages belief in some kind of calendrical significance based on the movement of heavenly bodies, but this is by no means certain and the old concerns of death and rebirth may have remained central. Only one Welsh stone circle, in the sense of an open ring of upright stones, has been excavated (Dunning 1943) but nothing was found to indicate its purpose. It stood on Mynydd Epynt, Breconshire, close to a ring cairn eventually used for burial (Lynch 1972b, 72–3). Other stone circles, such as the larger one on Mynydd Bach Trecastell (Grimes 1963, 135–6) and one at Clocaenog in Denbighshire (Ellis Davies 1929, 102), contain a central mound which is likely to cover a burial, perhaps added late in the history of the monument.

The other circular monuments which may be considered essentially ceremonial – embanked stone circles and ring cairns – show a consistent link with the burial of the dead, but also reveal evidence for other rituals which would seem to be more important, if one may judge from their primacy and repeated performance. Structurally the difference between these circular monuments and the stone circles is the presence of an enclosing ring of cairn material. In the embanked stone circles, like Druid's Circle on Penmaenmawr, the uprights stand on the inner edge of a substantial bank of stone (Griffiths 1960). The Druid's Circle and Meini Gwyr, Pembrokeshire (Ward *et al.* 1987), are large monuments with tall stones, much more impressive than the stone circles which in Wales have low, thin stones. They have entrances through the bank and at Druids' Circle excavation revealed a group of cremations in the centre, predominantly of children. A small cairn against the inner edge of the circle may have covered ceremonial deposits but was not fully excavated.

Smaller monuments with slighter but still conspicuous stones on the inside of the stone bank do not normally have an entrance. These have been called complex ring cairns to distinguish them from the simple, walled ring cairns without spaced uprights (**Pl. 16**), but the distinction may not be very meaningful (Lynch 1979). There is a graduated variance in design and use between the ceremonial stone circle with its open ring of stones and the solid burial cairn which so frequently covers some annular feature in wood or stone. Several ring cairns, architecturally the centre of this spectrum, have been excavated and the results clearly demonstrate the link.

Excavations at the ring cairns near Druid's Circle, Penmaenmawr (Griffiths 1960), in the Brenig cemetery (Lynch 1993, 117–34), on the slopes of Moel Goedog near Harlech (Lynch 1984b) and near Great Carn on Gower (Ward 1988) illustrate both the variety of design and the range of ritual activity which may be expected.

Moel Goedog (**Fig. 3.20**) had a ring of uprights about a metre high on the inner edge of the ring of cairn material; at Penmaenmawr the vertical element was not emphasised but

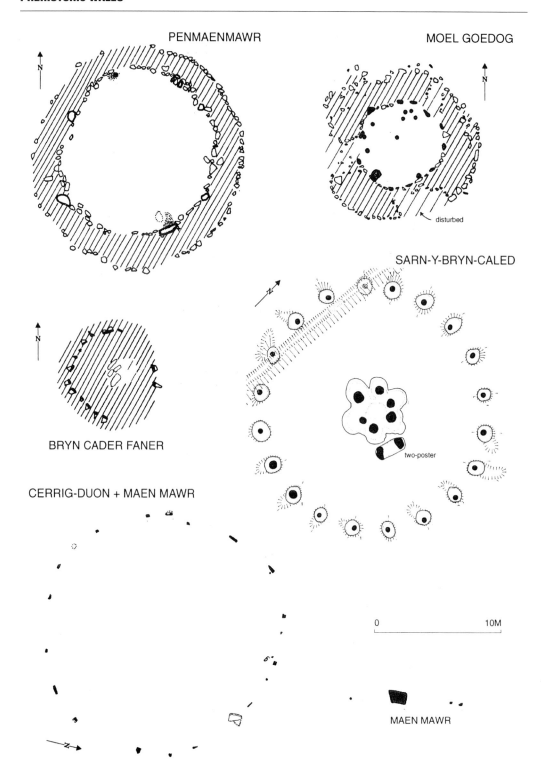

PENMAENMAWR

MOEL GOEDOG

disturbed

SARN-Y-BRYN-CALED

BRYN CADER FANER

two-poster

CERRIG-DUON + MAEN MAWR

0   10M

MAEN MAWR

there were larger stones at regular intervals around the ring; at Brenig the large ring was simply a walled enclosure about half a metre high but certain points on the circumference developed a special significance; on Gower the ring cairns had opposed entrances, like some of the ancestral henges. The provision of one or two entrances at even quite small monuments is much commoner in the south than in the north, though there are no other regional specialisations.

At Penmaenmawr 278 (**Fig. 3.20**) and Brenig the range of deposits was relatively limited but at the latter site the stratigraphy and the sequence of radiocarbon dates is instructive. Both sites contained pits dug against the inner edge of the ring and filled with charcoal or burnt earth. At Penmaenmawr burnt earth was in a small urn; at Brenig pure charcoal had been poured into the holes and capped by a stone. The earliest pit had been dug out again at a later date and more charcoal was buried. The relationship of the pits to the development of a sloping bank against the edge of the ring showed that this ritual had been repeated throughout the history of the site, which radiocarbon suggested might have been 500 or 600 years long. During that period three burials had been made within the ring, one in the centre and the others in a pit at the side. These belonged to the later phases of the monument and suggest a change in the emphasis of its use (Lynch 1993). The same conclusion could be drawn from the results at Moel Goedog where the only 'standard' burial belongs to a late stage in its history and the burial of charcoal continued through its 200-year history (Lynch 1984b). At this site, however, there was a primary deposit: a large pot containing a mixture of earth and cremated bone, in token quantity, only a few grammes in all. Another token deposit of bone in a shallow pit was permeated with soil from a lowland site, suggesting that the bone had been removed from a cairn elsewhere and reburied within the circle. Very similar evidence came from Great Carn Ring Cairn I on Gower (Ward 1988, 163) and at Trelystan it could be shown that one of the small cairns buried beneath the extension of Barrow II had been robbed in the Bronze Age (Britnell 1982, 153), the bone perhaps removed for just such a ceremonial use.

These monuments demonstrate that a variety of rituals were performed within the ring cairns, rituals that involved the burial of charcoal perhaps symbolic of the funeral pyre, though not actually the remains of the pyre itself because the wood is mixed, not oak, the preferred material for a pyre. The link with burial is none the less real for in the north of England and in Scotland the pyre itself is formally covered, while Welsh ring cairns frequently contain secondary burials. These monuments may occur in 'sanctuaries' among predominantly ceremonial monuments, as at Penmaenmawr, or within cemeteries, like Brenig, where they are the only non-burial monument (Lynch 1993, 143, 146). Moreover on some occasions it can be argued that they have been converted into a more traditional burial monument. At Letterston in Pembrokeshire a small cemetery contains a large turf mound which covers a delapidated embanked stone circle, the delapidation of the quartz surface of the central space indicating the two-period nature of the monument (Savory 1962–4).

(Opposite) *Fig. 3.20. Plans of circles and ring cairns. Ring cairns: Penmaenmawr Circle 278 (Caerns); Moel Goedog, Circle 1 (Mer). Cairn Circle: Bryn Cader Faner (Mer) (from Lynch 1993). Timber Circle: Sarn-y-Bryn-Caled, Mont (from Gibson 1994). Stone Circle and Outlier: Cerrig-Duon, Brecs. (from Grimes 1963).*

Fig. 3.21. Stackpole, Pembs. The Devil's Quoit during excavation showing platform of small upright stones with the Iron Age burial pit in the foreground. (Photo: courtesy of Cambria Archaeology)

Another, standing beside the stone circle on Mynydd Epynt, seems to have been a simple ring cairn with a central token burial which had also become delapidated before being converted to a mound by the addition of a turf covering (Dunning 1943; Lynch 1972b, 72–3).

The single standing stones which survive in many parts of Wales are generally considered to be components of the ritual landscape of the Late Neolithic and earlier Bronze Age, but without excavation the antiquity of many of the smaller examples cannot be guaranteed. They are common in south-west Wales (Williams 1988a) and in Anglesey (Wilson 1983), areas where cairns and barrows are comparatively rare, but their complete removal is so easy that the original distribution cannot be reconstructed with confidence. In the uplands it has been noted that the individual stones often stand close to trans-montane trackways and it has been suggested that they were way-markers (Bowen & Gresham 1967, 56–63) but it may be that they were memorials set at points where passers-by could see them (**Pl. 18**).

A tall stone is often a component of 'sanctuaries' and Stone Circle complexes, such as Cerrig Duon (**Fig. 3.20**), Nant Tawr, Gors Fawr (**Fig. 3.19**), where, being visible from afar, they may have had both a practical and a symbolic role. These complexes often also include alignments and avenues of upright stones of various sizes (Grimes 1963; Burl 1993). Some are composed of very small and apparently insignificant stones; others which are more substantial occasionally occur alone, at some distance from other monuments. None of these stones within a 'sanctuary' has been excavated so we cannot say anything about their role there and even if we had information, it is unlikely that we could correctly interpret it.

Recent excavations at lowland sites in south-west Wales (Williams 1988a) have revealed an unexpected complexity of platforms, pits and other structures around the stone, indicating that they attracted a good deal of ceremonial activity. The Devil's Quoit, erected over the site of the demolished Bronze Age house at Stackpole, is one of the clearest of these sites (Benson et al. 1990, 189–96). The tall stone stood at the west end of a large approximately rectangular platform of 3,000 pitched stones; aligned with it was a pit in which a post was later erected (**Fig. 3.21**). The far end of the platform was marked by an arc of stakes. There was a cremation of Bronze Age date buried within the platform and central to the stake arc there was an inhumation grave. Radiocarbon dates suggested that this burial had been made when the stone was at least a thousand years old. Other sites such at Gogerddan near Aberystwyth (Murphy 1992) were also the subject of renewed interest in the Iron Age.

This return to the old religious sites in the last centuries BC is a very fascinating phenomenon because in the intervening centuries the tradition of formal burial within built structures seems to have declined and the religious interests of the communities turned instead to natural sanctuaries, lakes and rivers and perhaps the sacred trees which are mentioned by classical writers but which are likely to elude archaeology (Bradley 1990). The discovery of finery like the Bryncir *lunula* (p. 102) in peat bogs and the fairly frequent location of ceremonial monuments near the source of rivers gives a hint that this concern with water was not entirely new in the Late Bronze Age, but a changed emphasis in religous practice is certainly another of the major transformations that characterise the centuries of economic and social crisis at the end of the Middle Bronze Age.

SOCIETY

It is difficult to clothe the bones of prehistory in flesh and blood, to provide people with a picture of society to which they can relate. The traditional concerns of history – the identification of peoples and the role of individual leaders, the interplay of personalities – elude us. The sources for social reconstruction are burial systems, grave-goods, artefacts and settlement and for Bronze Age Wales much of this evidence is scanty. The preference for individual burial in the Bronze Age is believed to reflect the growth of chiefdoms and the rise of powerful leaders. Dependence on new materials of restricted availability led to the growing importance of specialist crafts and exchange networks which enabled important individuals to exert more control and to maintain this control by more visible display. Thus, it is believed, an increasingly stratified society emerged from the family-dominated, ostensibly egalitarian, farming society of the Neolithic.

In Wales the phase of individual burial is short and the preference for cemetery mounds where no single person is given priority of place, despite clear differences in personal wealth, would suggest that family membership remained the basis of local power. This social situation is most obvious in the west. At the end of the Iron Age Roman writers identify at least five distinct tribes within Wales, so we should not expect total uniformity at earlier periods. In the Severn Valley, for instance, new ideas appear early and may have taken deeper root. It is notable that daggers appear more frequently in graves there and in later centuries weapon hoards are common. This might suggest that the Marcher area had more in common with the classic chiefdoms of Wessex than did other parts of Wales. The paucity of weapons in Welsh Early Bronze Age graves, where the true dagger, as distinct from the small personal knife, is rare, is in tune with the preference for cemetery mounds. The warrior does not appear as the admired ideal and it is fitting that the most spectacular symbol of power from Wales, the gold cape from Mold, was a priestly garment which could not have been worn by a fighting man.

Although the social character of Wales was perhaps more conservative than that of many parts of Britain, the country was not isolated. The presence of exotic beads of amber, faience and jet demonstrates that even quite remote communities could obtain luxuries from a distance and that fashions in clothes, as far as we can reconstruct them, changed in step with those elsewhere. At the beginning of the period the use of buttons suggests leather garments, perhaps quite neatly tailored, like those worn by the recently discovered man from the Alpine glacier, while the appearance of pins around 2,000 cal BC indicates a preference for woven cloaks and tunics like those from contemporary Denmark, and perhaps not unlike the modern kilt and plaid (Glob 1974).

The appearance of some Whitby jet in north Wales from the Late Neolithic onwards is evidence of contact with the north of England, maintained throughout the period. In this case the contact was not simply a matter of remote commercial exchange: the similarities in burial customs and monuments indicates that the connections across the southern Pennines ran deep and extended into many areas of social and religious life. In the earlier Neolithic the broad range of cultural contacts lay with Ireland; in the Bronze Age Yorkshire and the Peak District became the important partners. Although the standard of nineteenth-century excavation there does not permit certainty, it could be argued that communal burial persisted and eventually dominated, as it did in Wales, suggesting a shared social ethos. Religious compatibility is shown by the number of ring cairns and other variant circles in both regions, though the emphasis of their use may differ (Lynch 1993, 140).

The absence of a full settlement record prevents much discussion of the economic basis of life at this time. Houses are undoubtedly smaller than in the earlier period which may indicate either a move away from the extended family or simply a functional change. The use of land at higher altitude may suggest greater reliance on pastoral farming by some of the population, but arable agriculture was by no means abandoned, as the first formally defined fields at Stackpole show. In certain areas mineral resources were actively exploited. It is interesting that the local population does not seem to have gained conspicuous wealth; at Llandudno nothing has been found to compare with the rich cemeteries beside the Austrian salt mines. Perhaps the Mold Cape is the only tangible evidence of the wealth that must have accrued to north Wales during that period of industrial dominance.

The invisibility of earlier Bronze Age settlement must indicate that the farms or hamlets were undefended. This is in line with the rest of the country, whether or not warrior chiefdoms had developed. It is only at the end of the period, perhaps after a considerable increase in population as well as the deterioration of climate, that protective walls and weapons become necessary.

FOUR

THE LATE BRONZE AGE AND IRON AGE

Jeffrey L. Davies and Frances Lynch

INTRODUCTION

The watershed between the quiet peasant prosperity of the Middle Bronze Age and the troubled times of the Late Bronze Age is one which has been much discussed, the extent and depth of its traumas alternately maximised and minimised. In Wales, with its naturally damp climate and extensive uplands, the effects of deteriorating weather and agricultural misuse may be expected to have had a serious effect on settlement and this is indeed recognisable in many areas. Moreover patterns of exchange appear to be disrupted, with changed configurations in the later period. Material hardship seems also to have affected religious practice, with the building of barrows and stone circles coming to an end, though in the lowlands the placing of simple cremation burials in existing monuments remained more common than previously thought.

The most conspicuous change in the archaeological record for this period is the new visibility of settlements, now enclosed and in many cases seriously defended. Such settlements imply a new anxiety in society, a fear of attack and a need to consolidate friendly groupings, attitudes also reflected in the increasing importance of weapons. The fact that many of these weapons are of foreign design may hint at external factors in this 'crisis' but internal tensions are perhaps explanation enough. North-east Wales provides good evidence for the development of defence in the Late Bronze Age but the palisades and ramparts were often allowed to decay, suggesting periods of relaxation and the possibility that these defences may have been as much for display and civil control as for warfare.

The record of metalwork reflects the same fluctuations. The Penard and Wilburton traditions emphasise weapons of continental derivation but the amount of metal in circulation is relatively low. In the Ewart Park period (ninth–eighth centuries cal BC) there was a great deal of bronze around, the Irish trade had picked up and local tool-making workshops were flourishing. The introduction of the new metal, iron, seems to have been gradual but its impact may have been seriously disruptive for, after a period when bronze – both military finery and scrap – was 'dumped' in large quantities, there is a famine of metal of any kind which lasted throughout the Early Iron Age (seventh to c. fourth centuries cal BC). The role of international politics through this period has been the subject of much debate but it is now thought unlikely that any large-scale settlement by new people occurred at this time, although continental affairs undoubtedly influenced events in this country.

The break in religious practice, often considered an indicator of new populations, occurred at the beginning of the Late Bronze Age, but it is less a rupture than a shifting of emphasis. The role of burial seems to have diminished while the practice of offerings (arguably present since the Early Bronze Age) increased, to reach a crescendo in the ninth and eighth centuries cal BC. These offerings of wealth to the gods of water are epitomised by the deposits in Llyn Fawr in south Wales and by those from Llyn Cerrig Bach, Anglesey, an Iron Age shrine which demonstrates that the practice continued, though at a lesser pace, to the end of the period. Such links with the past are also to be seen in the later Iron Age practice of burial close to much older monuments. By and large Iron Age burials are rare and this contrast with the earlier Bronze Age was considered evidence for extensive change but the return to older sites calls this in question.

The Middle Iron Age, a period of consolidation, saw the development of complex exchange networks. Some of these networks operated on a Europe-wide basis, bringing beautiful diplomatic gifts and a familiarity with fashions in art and decoration that could be emulated by local craftsmen; others were regional, carrying commodities such as pottery and salt to distant parts perhaps within kinship linkages. For at this time the settlement record suggests that different parts of Wales were emerging with rather different social and political structures (reflected in the size and numbers of fortified sites or farmsteads) which foreshadowed the tribal politics recorded by the Romans some three or four hundred years later.

The Britain that the Romans invaded in the mid-first century AD was one with competing tribal groups at varying levels of political sophistication. In the south east named dynasties and a money economy can be recognised; in Wales such developments impinge only on the south-eastern border but industry was increasing, with new sources of copper being worked and iron being made from local bog ores. Communities gained even quite basic domestic goods through widespread exchange, and agriculture was prospering. The last centuries BC saw an improvement in climate that led to an expansion of farming such that the pollen evidence for the first time suggests that the landscape in fertile regions such as Anglesey was essentially 'open' and extensively worked. Wales was poised to step on to the stage of history.

CLIMATE AND VEGETATION

The close of the second and the beginning of the first millennium BC experienced one of the most widely accepted climatic changes of the Postglacial, the onset of the Sub-Atlantic phase, characterised by higher rainfall and much lower summer temperatures; deterioration became progressively more marked between 1,000 and 500 BC. Climatic change is also recorded in estuarine regions, such as that of the Severn where the deposition of marine clays records successive phases of marine transgression, interspersed by regression phases when peat growth occurred. Some areas were inundated about 1,200 cal BC; others between 900 and 400 cal BC (Rippon 1996, 14–24; Bell & Neumann 1997, 99–100). It is, in turn, arguable that this climatic deterioration is the most crucial factor in bringing about major changes in landscape and settlement pattern throughout the British Isles and determined many of the characteristic features of the millennium. These changes may have included a fall in population in the Later Bronze Age and subsequent recovery during the Iron Age. Wales, in company with the other western and northern parts of the British Isles, was severely affected, palaeoenvironmental evidence indicating far-reaching changes in land-use, ranging from the abandonment of much of the uplands and coastal regions for permanent settlement until about 500 cal BC or later.

In Wales the most widespread evidence for climatic change comes from peat bogs, many of which show a renewed and rapid peat growth (recurrence horizon) because of increased rainfall. Though these bogs had shown earlier phases of peat growth (Caseldine 1990, 46), they were not as extensive or as long-lasting as those of our period. Radiocarbon dates indicate the onset of climatic deterioration as early as *c.* 1,250 cal BC in the more maritime western parts of the British Isles though most dates tend to cluster between the eighth and fifth centuries cal BC. Radiocarbon dates for recurrence horizons at Llanllwch (Carmarthenshire) and Tregaron Bog (Cardiganshire) in the Middle Bronze Age and Later Bronze Age (Caseldine 1990, 55–6) are fairly representative, while hydrological changes possibly due to increased run-off are dated to the Late Bronze Age/earliest Iron Age at Waun Fignen Felen (Breconshire), Pwll Nant-Ddu (Radnorshire) and elsewhere. A slowing of peat growth and a lack of recurrence horizons indicate a period of climatic amelioration, with a return to relatively dry conditions, from *c.* 400 cal BC, which was to characterise the climate until the fifth century AD (Turner 1981). In some areas of the British Isles blanket bog began to form over abandoned field systems, extensive leaching and podsolisation led to a loss of soil fertility and tree cover failed to regenerate, leading to the extension of the moorlands which characterise so much of the Welsh uplands today.

Though the impact of climatic change is undoubted it may be noted that soil degeneration and blanket bog formation can be affected, and indeed triggered by non-climatic factors, of which the most important is human activities in clearing woodland coupled with the practice of poor husbandry. Earlier prehistoric clearances seem to have been mostly small, localized and temporary and the more remote parts of Wales remained heavily wooded. However, from the Late Bronze Age clearance or loss of woodland through changed environmental conditions, as represented in mire pollen records, was extensive with dated examples of this period at Cefn Graeanog (Caernarfonshire), Tregaron (Cardiganshire), Dinas (Pembrokeshire) and Waun Fignen-Felen (Breconshire). This probably corresponds to a period of climatic and demographic recovery when land shortages, whether for cultivation or grazing was a reality. The environs of Tregaron Bog were cleared *c.* 400 cal BC as a result of pastoral activity, and a similar explanation may be offered for the extensive burning of woodland on the lower slopes of the Ystwyth Valley and the Ystwyth Forest (Cardiganshire) plateau in the third and second centuries cal BC (Turner 1970). Early clearances in the vicinity of the farmsteads at Moel y Gerddi and Erw Wen in Merioneth (Kelly 1988, 140–2) had already been effected by the time they were founded. Thereafter clearances continued down to the late Roman period, effecting a marked and permanent reduction in the tree cover, coupled with a significant spread of grasses and heaths. Sometimes clearances were followed by regeneration, as at Coed Taf and Waun Fignen-Felen (both Breconshire). Certainly there is no need to assume a dramatic decline of woodland in all upland areas. For example, the iron-working settlement at Crawcwellt West, for which there is a magnetic chronology of between 700 and 300 cal BC, seems to have placed no great demand on local woodland for charcoal production (Crew 1998). Indeed the clearance of the surrounding landscape of sessile oak and alder, creating the predominantly open, moorland landscape, only occurred between 87 cal BC and AD 54 cal AD, thus corresponding to archaeological evidence for the latest stages in the history of the iron-working settlement (Chambers & Lageard 1993).

That lowland clearances were also a regular feature of the Iron Age is demonstrated by the evidence from mire pollen spectra from the vicinity of settlements as at Bryn Eryr on Anglesey (Longley 1998, 253) and Cefn Graeanog in Caernarfonshire (Fasham *et al.* 1998, 52–62, 160–2) in north Wales and Harding's Down in Glamorgan (Hogg 1973, 68) and Penycoed in Carmarthenshire (Murphy 1985, 108–9) in the south. In some cases landscapes were already open, or certainly lacking in timber for building in their later phases, as demonstrated at Erw Wen and Moel y Gerddi by the change from wooden to stone buildings. These landscapes also frequently reveal evidence for arable cultivation following clearance, as, for example, at Cefn Graeanog (Fasham *et al.* 1998, 82).

Important data pertaining to environmental change is also recorded in the Gwent Levels of south-eastern Wales. Middle Bronze Age occupation on the drying peat ended around 1,200 cal BC when large areas of the Levels began to be inundated by the sea. In fact there are two distinct episodes of marine transgression, a process which is also recorded on the Somerset Levels, between 1,220–900 and 800–470 cal BC (Rippon 1996, 20–4; Bell & Neumann 1997). The most likely explanation for this phenomenon is a relative rise in sea-level or increased storminess, both factors being most likely related to the climatic deterioration which occurred from the close of the second millennium. Though it was a gradual process, eventually the whole of the Levels was inundated, except for some of the back-fen areas, and there are no clearly dated structures of the period 900–500 cal BC in the Levels unless the Upton Track at Magor (dated 770–390 cal BC) is included. There was, however, opportunistic settlement in the Levels in the Middle Iron Age as evidenced by the laying down of trackways and the construction of timber buildings at Goldcliff and Redwick (see pp. 170, 177). Even so, during the relatively short occupation of the Goldcliff buildings there were occasional marine floods and the site was eventually sealed by marine alluvium (Bell & Neumann 1997, 108). Evidence of Later Iron Age activity is scarce, though at Magor Pill settlement on the marine alluvium is dated to around the first century BC (Rippon 1996, 24).

Once climatic amelioration had re-established itself, differences in aspect, rainfall, temperature and soils were to play an important role in governing differences in settlement pattern, settlement type, economy and population density in the various regions of Wales.

POPULATION

The probability of a decline in population from the end of the Middle Bronze Age through the Late Bronze Age, followed by a recovery from the middle of the first millennium, has already been mentioned. It will be further suggested that variations in the size of Iron Age settlements may be related to the potential productivity of the areas concerned, the sheer size and number of hillforts in areas such as the Marches suggesting a high population density. Moreover there are other indicators of a substantial increase in population in the latter half of the millennium. For example, it has been suggested that some upland reoccupation, with settlements such as those at Moel y Gerddi and Crawcwellt West, may have occurred in a phase of expansion from lower altitudes through a combination of a more equitable climate and increased population pressure (Chambers & Price 1988). Similarly, the remarkable expansion of unfortified settlements in regions such as south-west Wales in the second and first century cal BC could also be construed as evidence for a population increase. Indeed it has been argued that there is no reason why, at optimum, the population at the beginning of the first century AD could not have approximated to that of the high medieval period (Burgess 1985, 200).

No realistic assessment of this population is possible, despite attempts to extrapolate estimates of hillfort populations as an approximation of regional population densities (Guilbert 1981b). Stanford (1974), for example, utilising data from Herefordshire hillforts, suggested a population of around 33,000 for that county as against late eleventh and late fourteenth century AD populations of 20,500 and 25,800 persons respectively. This was predicated upon a population density of 200 persons per hectare at Croft Ambrey. However, such attempts are fraught with danger, not least of which is the questionable assertion that four-post structures at Croft Ambrey were houses and evenly distributed across the interior: he also makes no allowance for non-hillfort settlement in the region. Hogg (1960) and Alcock (1965) attempted similar analyses for the hillforts of north-west Wales, but postulated densities of no more than 30–50 persons per hectare. These compare more favourably with the estimated population densities for Danebury and Hod Hill (Cunliffe 1991, 365). If the 120 round-houses at Braich y Dinas (Caernarfonshire) and the 220 platforms at Moel Trigarn (Pembrokeshire) (**Pl. 19**) represent house-emplacements, then it indicates that communities numbering at least hundreds existed in some of the Welsh regions, but such estimates only go some way towards addressing regional population densities in respect of cooperative effort. Real figures are beyond our grasp, aerial photography having demonstrated the fallacy of interpreting settlement density solely on the basis of the hillfort evidence.

It is a reasonable assumption that this population was largely indigenous, subject to natural increase and not augmentation by periodic immigration. However, it was only some forty years ago that the population of much of the British Isles in the first millennium BC was regarded as the product of a protracted phase of immigration by peoples of continental origin who were considered to have introduced not only a new language, or new linguistic dialects, but also a new range of material culture described as 'Celtic'. A furious debate has recently raged among scholars as to whether the term Celtic has any validity, not least in an archaeological sense, and whether it should be applied to the ancient inhabitants of the British Isles at all (Collis 1996; Sims-Williams 1998; James 1999). A term originally used in an ethnic sense by Classical writers describing a large group of barbarian communities in north-western Europe has been used in different and conflicting ways by linguists, archaeologists, historians and art-historians. At a linguistic level we cannot deny that Wales was fully integrated into this Celtic-speaking zone by the time that Roman sources provide us with place- and tribal names in the first century AD – for example, the River Stuctia or the tribe of the Ordovices. But Sims-Williams (1998, 19–21) warns that great care is needed in interpreting the presence or absence of such Celtic names, nor can we determine for how long such a linguistic situation might have existed. To complicate the issue, we know of Celtic speakers who were not labelled Celts. The Britons are a classic instance (Pytheas, in Dinan 1911, 64).

Linguists formerly interpreted the presence of Celtic speakers as the product of large-scale colonisation, and sought archaeological confirmation of such an event (or events). The spread of Hallstatt, and particularly La Tene material culture – the continental manifestation of Celticity – to Britain, despite its diluted and insular form, was originally read as clear evidence of such settlement. Presently, however, there is either overt hostility to the whole concept of a link between an archaeological culture and the ancient Celts, especially where an ethnic interpretation is assumed (Collis 1996), or at best a healthy scepticism about matching changes in prehistoric material culture with hypothetical ethnic movements (Sims-Williams 1998).

The cultural base of Welsh communities in the first millennium BC – much akin to that of southern Britain as a whole – can only be loosely described as Celtic, and this has its origins not in folk-settlement from the continent, involving land-taking and displacement of those in power, but in a protracted phase of social and economic change and interaction affecting communities whose roots lay firmly within the region. We need not invoke a 'coming of the Celts' as such to Wales. While later prehistoric societies were occasionally prone to migration and displacement, or on a much more frequent but smaller scale the unwelcome attention of war-bands intent upon winning spoils, slaves and renown, there is no unequivocal evidence for the inward movement of such groups in the Welsh archaeological record of the first millennium BC. To deny the possibility of movement, both of groups and individuals, however, would be flying in the face of early historical evidence. Tacitus' record of the appearance of Caratacus' war-band among the Silures and the Ordovices, and his description of an Anglesey thickly populated with refugees, sounds a caveat, though the circumstances – the period of the Roman conquest – may have been special. Later still the expulsion of the Desi to south-west Wales in the post-Roman period and the dynastic struggles involving families with Hiberno-Norse links in eleventh century AD north-west Wales illustrate the role of external forces in reshaping the ethnic as well as the political framework. If war, expulsion or land-taking by adventurers played some part in shaping the regionalism evident in the socio-economic geography of Wales in the first millennium BC, other factors such as the breaking down of isolation through marriage links and gift-exchange cementing political alliances would have been no less important in adding novelty to the hitherto rather unexceptional cultural base of communities long resident in their respective territories.

SETTLEMENT

One of the most notable features of the archaeology of England, Scotland and Wales in the first millennium BC is the re-emergence and proliferation of settlements. These may be broadly defined as overtly defended, lightly enclosed or open. In Wales this settlement pattern is largely confined to the better quality soils of the lowlands or upland fringes, the true uplands being largely forsaken. The apparent dominance of defended enclosures, particularly those with formidable defences, has produced a one-sided picture since in most areas much more ubiquitous open, fenced or weakly embanked enclosures are either unrecognisable (unless special circumstances of preservation prevail) or have fallen victim to cultivation. Although aerial reconnaissance has been responsible for addressing the imbalance between fortified and unfortified settlement in some areas, such as the Marches, in others, as recent work on the Severn Levels has demonstrated, settlement density, stability and even morphology is unpredictable, tantalising and only recoverable in exceptional circumstances.

Prior to this phase of population recovery, growth and settlement expansion, Wales, in common with the British Isles as a whole, suffered an environmental crisis of the greatest magnitude as a result of climatic deterioration beginning about 1250, accelerating after 850 and reaching its coolest and wettest about 650 cal BC (Lamb 1981; Harding 1982). This drastically changed climate was particularly inimical to settlement in the more exposed western, central and northern uplands where a combination of climatic and anthropogenic factors led to leaching, podsolisation and extensive peat formation, but even lowland areas were not immune as is indicated by evidence for large-scale marine transgression in the region of the lower Severn Valley between c. 1,220–900 and 800–500 cal BC (Barber & Coope 1987). A massive loss of exploitable land and a dramatic curtailment of agricultural potential is envisaged throughout Wales, precipitating a protracted crisis which can only have led to an economic recession and certainly a bar to population growth if not an outright demographic decline.

One response to the crisis would have been a retreat from the uplands and a realignment of settlement in favour of more sheltered locations. However, not all the upland was abandoned, to judge by the pollen sequences from the Brenig Valley (Lynch 1993, 167). More significant is the wholesale failure of many Bronze Age settlements – even those in lowlands – to survive the turn of the second millennium BC. The evidence is stark and geographically wide-ranging. On the Severn Levels none of the earlier Bronze Age sites such as Redwick, Cold Harbour and Chapel Tump 1 survived the second millennium. Chapel Tump 2 could belong to the ninth–seventh centuries BC, but this must be regarded as doubtful. Apart from the Upton Track at Magor, dated 770–390 cal BC, there are no structures of the period 900–500 cal BC on the Levels, and most settlements were abandoned several hundred years earlier. It could well be argued that such wetland sites are untypical and dangerously exposed to climatic change anyway, but the evidence suggests that many dry-land settlements were also abandoned. Evidence for continuity of settlement from the Late Bronze Age into the Early Iron Age should be capable of rigorous testing, but presently no site on the dry margin of the Levels is beyond suspicion. For example, both Late Bronze Age and Early Iron Age pottery underlie the boundary banks of the later Iron Age farm at Thornwell Farm, Chepstow (Hughes 1996), but continuity remains unproven. Again on drier ground at Caldicot Castle Lake (Nayling & Caseldine 1997) the presence of a Wilburton sword chape in association with animal bones and a timber structure interpreted as a bridge, with associated dendrochronological dates of 990/989 BC, suggests activity within the late eleventh and earlier tenth centuries BC, possibly in a ritual context.

Further west the coastal settlement of timber buildings and fields at Stackpole in Pembrokeshire (Benson et al. 1990) (see pp. 87–9, 169) was apparently abandoned to sanding in the eighth century cal BC, though its earlier Bronze Age occupation suggests that its low-lying, south-western location was initially favourable to continued occupation. But it is inland that the evidence is most telling. Several defended settlements in the Llawhaden (Pembrokeshire) group – Woodside, Holgan and Pilcornswell (Williams &

Mytum 1998) – have shown evidence of Middle Bronze Age activity in pre-enclosure deposits, but there seems to be no connection whatsoever between this activity and sites which belong to the latter part of the first millennium BC. Unequivocal evidence of Later Bronze Age activity is lacking, despite intriguing evidence for what seems to be an early palisaded enclosure, with associated plough-marks, to the west of Drim Camp, an enclosed farmstead of the second and first centuries BC. An associated date of 762–398 cal BC for this palisaded phase could span the Late Bronze Age/Earliest Iron Age, but the date range is too wide to be valuable. A closely comparable suite of dates, derived from a series of timber structures beneath the Broadway enclosure (Williams & Mytum 1998), argues for initial settlement at the Late Bronze/Iron Age transition; but of settlement continuity from *c.* 1200 to 500 BC in this intensively investigated group of sites there is no sign. The issue of continuity or lack of continuity is an archaeological problem which may have fresh light thrown upon it in the future. Presently the evidence suggests that there was a long-lived settlement hiatus in west Wales in the first third of the first millennium BC, eloquent testimony to the impact of the sub-Atlantic climate.

One response to the challenges posed by climatic deterioration, and manifest throughout Britain, was conflict leading to a growing investment in physical security for groups of families through the construction of fortified settlements: hillforts. These monuments are among the most enduring features of the Welsh landscape and were to be latterly invested with all kinds of heroic associations from Caratacus to Vortigern. While they do represent a prominent feature of the late prehistoric landscape it is clear that in some cases, as in the Llawhaden area of Pembrokeshire, they represent only a short-lived – if sometimes recurring – element within the overall pattern of settlement, which for most of Wales was dominated by settlements of non-fortified character.

HILLFORTS

Hillforts encompass a wide morphological spectrum though a basic distinction can be made between sites which enclose more than a hectare, are clearly sited with a view to defence on hilltops and promontories, and possess substantial, or indeed formidable defences, and those sites which are generally smaller, more weakly sited and whose defences are insubstantial. Two types of settlement which have been previously included in the hillfort category – defended enclosures of the 'ringfort' type, such as Woodside and Dan y Coed (Pembrokeshire), and multiple-enclosure sites such as Y Bwlwarcau (RCAHMW 1976, I.2, 57–61) and Harding's Down (RCAHMW 1976, I.2, 51–3) – have been excluded from this discussion. Ringforts, classic examples of which are to be found in the south west, though scattered examples may be found from Glamorgan to the upper Severn, are often weakly sited, enclose less than half a hectare, with interiors containing five or six round-houses and with substantial univallate defences, are best categorised as defended farmsteads. Multiple-enclosure sites, with a propensity for sloping ground in upland locations and with very slight outer banks and ditches, are more suited to the requirements of small, pastoral communities. Both are considered in the section on Non-Hillfort Settlement (pp. 169–70).

Hillforts have been traditionally studied, classified and even dated on the basis of their siting, morphology and type of defence. Such classificatory schemes are fraught with peril

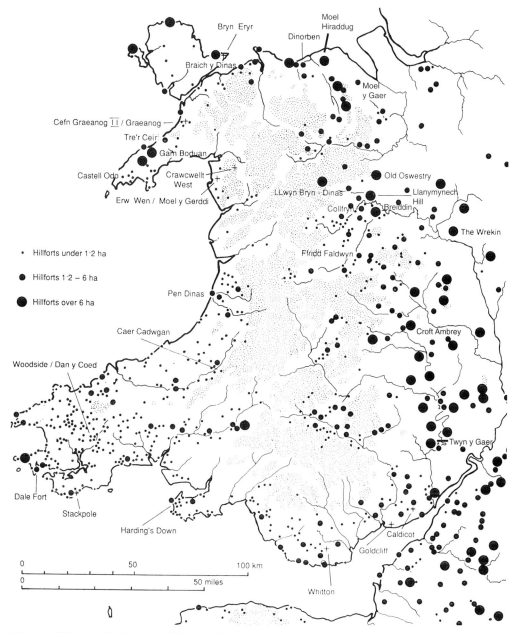

Fig. 4.1. Wales and the Marches: hill-forts and other sites mentioned in the text.

although some useful deductions can be drawn from such an approach, as long as it is unbiased and makes maximum use of the available excavated data. A brief overview is thus offered here.

The distribution of hillforts, particularly in relation to size, is uneven. Large and strongly defended hillforts are much more common in the central and northern Marches and along the north Wales seaboard, for example, Llanymynech Hill (57 hectares), Pen y Cloddiau (20.8), Moel Fenlli (8.4) and Moel Hiraddug (23). Further west their numbers and overall size diminish, though some relatively large examples still occur in Lleyn, for example Garn Fadrun (10.9 hectares) and Garn Boduan (11.2), while in Glamorgan and Monmouth there is a liberal sprinkling of forts enclosing more than 3 hectares. In the far south west they tend to become very numerous but very small indeed, with the majority enclosing little more than 1.5 hectares. Regional clusters are also known, as in the middle reaches of the Usk (RCAHMW 1986) and the upper Severn Valley, where sites of widely differing sizes occur (Spurgeon 1972). A fundamental difference between the large and small forts has long been recognised (Hogg 1972). The former point to the existence of sizeable communities involved in their building, if not their permanent occupation, the latter being plausibly the residence of a family or extended family group.

Contour forts, crowning prominent hilltops and with defences outwardly of dumped upcast from an external or internal ditch, are extremely common, encompass a wide size range and were built throughout the Iron Age. Many of those with closely spaced multivallate circuits are seemingly final modifications – often enlargements – of earlier defensive circuits, as at Cefncarnedd (Montgomeryshire) (**Pl. 22**), and belong to the Middle and Later phases of the Iron Age.

Promontory forts (**Pl. 21**), with defences built between inland stream valleys or on the margin of coastal cliffs as in south-west Wales, Glamorgan and Anglesey, are ubiquitous, ranging in size from tiny, univallate forts such as the Knave (Glamorganshire) to 3 hectare, multivallate sites such as The Bulwarks, Porthkerry (Glamorganshire). The apparently large size of some sites, such as the 20 hectare Wooltack Point (Pembrokeshire), is simply dictated by the need to draw the defences across a particularly narrow point on a headland, but this is certainly not the case with the south Glamorganshire forts which were manifestly designed to enclose substantial areas and were large-scale community projects (though many are now much reduced by coastal erosion).

Some sites are not readily classifiable in topographical terms. Two examples will suffice. The oval earthwork enclosing 0.9 hectares at Bryn Maen Caerau, Cardiganshire (Williams 1987), occupies a low knoll in the Teifi Valley and apparently replaced a palisade for which a date of 2520 ± 70 BP (CAR-1070) = 600–400 cal BC is available. While it clearly has defensive potential, the siting is nevertheless odd. The badly degraded univallate enclosure on level ground immediately north of the village at Caersws (Montgomeryshire) in the upper Severn Valley is even more peculiar. Its bank and ditch appear to be interrupted, and it is at least three times bigger (4.8 hectares) than any comparable enclosure on the valley floor but waterlogged samples from its ditch have produced a radiocarbon date of 520–190 cal BC (Jones 1993) which, though wide, indicates an Iron Age horizon.

The majority of hillforts are defended by revetted banks and ditches, multivallate sites with close-set defences generally matching univallate sites in terms of numbers and overall distribution in most areas, though there are local variations (**Fig. 4.1**). For example, forts defended by drystone walls have a wide distribution but are particularly common in the northern and western peninsulas. Though the majority of walled forts, such as Carn Goch (Carmarthenshire), are basically univallate, others such as Carn Ingli and Gaer Fawr (both

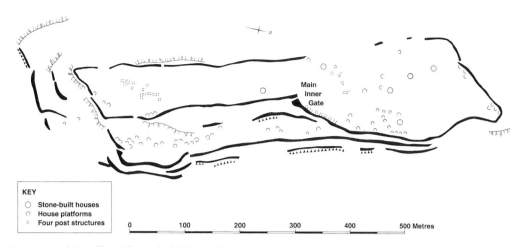

KEY
○ Stone-built houses
○ House platforms
∷ Four post structures

Fig. 4.2. Moel Hiraddug, Flints.: the hillfort defences and internal structures in simplified form. (Source: Brassil et al. 1981–2.)

in Pembrokeshire) have distinctive multiple enclosure plans, while sites such as Braich y Dinas (Caernarfonshire) share similar characteristics but probably evolved from successive phases of enlargement. Walled forts tend to have a multiplicity of posterns in addition to the main gates, as at Tre'r Ceiri (RCAHMW 1960, 101–3) while sites in the north west and particularly the south west are unique in the possession of *chevaux-de-frise* outside the walls. This defensive measure, comprising belts of angular stones set upright, is well known in northern and western Iberia and spread to the western coastal regions of Britain and Ireland. Good examples exist at Pen-y-Gaer, Llanbedr-y-Cennin (RCAHMW 1956, 100–1, Fig. 100), where it is found outside the western and southern defences, and at Caer Euni (Pembrokeshire). That the defensive measure may formerly have been more extensive, and also early, is indicated by its discovery beneath the added outer bank at Castell Henllys, also in Pembrokeshire (Mytum 1999). None of these walled forts shows traces of integral timbers in the defences, though walls may overlie composite defences of earth and wood, as at The Breiddin. Some of these walled forts were probably built early in the Iron Age, with banks and ditches being added later, as at Moel Hiraddug in Flintshire (Brassil *et al.* 1982) (**Fig. 4.2**). However, at The Breiddin a radiocarbon date of 2200 ± 90 BP (QL-1080) = 394–177 cal BC for the rampart – effectively a drystone wall – indicates that it could not have been built before the Middle Iron Age (Musson 1991). Another characteristic of these sites, particularly in the north west, is an interior filled with numerous traces of drystone round-houses, as, for example, at Garn Boduan, the destroyed Braich y Dinas (RCAHMW 1956, 85–6) and the well-known Tre'r Ceiri. Others, such as Moel Trigarn in Pembrokeshire (**Pl. 19**), show clear traces of very numerous elliptical emplacements for timber buildings, said to number more than 200 (Baring Gould *et al.* 1900), though at Dinorben many similar platforms proved to be quarries (Gardner & Savory 1964). Elsewhere, as at The Breiddin and Moel Hiraddug, internal buildings – timber round-houses and four-post structures – may only be revealed through the excavation of level areas in the interior, though at the latter traces of stone round-houses together with platforms for both stone and timber round-houses were already visible (**Fig. 4.2**).

The Late Bronze Age/Early Iron Age Transition: the earliest hillforts, *c.* 800–550 cal BC

It has already been suggested that the Late Bronze Age crisis precipitated unrest, conflict and major changes in social organisation, reflected in a recurring investment in the physical security of groups of families and their chattels by the construction of fortified villages. Though there is some evidence to suggest that this phenomenon has a wider regional compass in Wales, it is the northern and central Marches which appear to show the clearest primary evidence for this trend. This apparent eastern origin may be explicable by the fact that this interface between upland and lowland habitually supported a larger population, but one which in turn suffered proportionately greater stress because of the reduction of agricultural yields and an increasing reliance upon pastoralism, which would have multiplied the sources of conflict through cattle raiding. It is notable that weapons proliferate here in the Late Bronze Age.

These early Welsh hillforts seemingly belong to a much wider British horizon of earliest hillfort building (Cunliffe 1991) and tend to have slighter defences than their successors. The Breiddin hillfort (Musson 1991), occupying the north-western ridge of the volcanic outcrop of the Breiddin Hills, enclosed a very large area – possibly as much as 28 hectares – but had only a relatively slight timber-reinforced rampart, recalling comparable sites such as Winklebury I in Wessex (Cunliffe 1991, 346–8). Occupation deposits produced evidence of timber buildings and four-post structures (normally interpreted as store-buildings), late Bronze Age pottery and tools, weapons and items of personal adornment indicating that some of the inhabitants of what was manifestly a permanently occupied site were persons of high status. Radiocarbon dates suggest occupation from the close of the ninth century, well into the eighth or seventh centuries cal BC, when the site was burnt and then abandoned for perhaps half a millennium.

The defences of the eighth century cal BC univallate fort of Llwyn Bryn-dinas, commanding a stretch of the fertile Tanat Valley, and encompassing a more modest 2.4 hectares, were more impressive, comprising a stone revetted earthwork (Musson *et al.* 1992) (**Pl. 33**). However, the most commonly occurring defence around large communal settlements in the Late Bronze Age/Early Iron Age interface appears to be the palisade. Traces of these stout fences are frequently found beneath forts with stone and earthwork defences in England and the pattern is repeated in Wales. Early palisades were recognised in the Marches at Old Oswestry (Varley 1948) and Ffridd Faldwyn (O'Neil 1942; Guilbert 1981a). Since then their primacy in defensive contexts has been demonstrated time and again. A single palisade encircled the 3 hectare hilltop settlement of timber round-houses at Moel y Gaer, Flintshire (**Fig. 4.4**), for which a date in the eighth or seventh century cal BC is suggested (Guilbert 1976). At Dinorben a succession of palisades preceded the construction of a timber-laced rampart, dated 2450 ± 60 BP (CAR 122) = 770–400 cal BC (Gardner & Savory 1964; Guilbert 1979b; 1980). Though not specifically dated, these palisades are most likely related to a crop of ninth–seventh century cal BC radiocarbon dates from early deposits in the interior of the fort (Savory 1971a; Guilbert 1979b).

Pl. 19 Moel Trigarn, Pembs. Three Bronze Age cairns lie within the stone walls of the hillfort. Numerous 'hut platforms' can be seen below and to the left of the cairns. (Copyright, Dyfed Archaeological Trust)

Pl. 20 Castell Henllys, Pembs. Three reconstructed timber 'roundhouses', in their original positions within the hillfort. (Photo C.R. Musson. Copyright J.L. Davies)

Pl. 21 Caerau, Aberpwll, Pembs. Two promontory forts above the cliffs of the north Pembrokeshire coast. (Copyright, Dyfed Archaeological Trust)

Left: Pl. 22 Cefncarnedd, Mont. Multi-phase ridge-top hillfort with steep slopes on the right, removing the need for embanked defences along this side. (Copyright, Clwyd-Powys Archaeological Trust, 90-C-303).

Below: Pl. 23 Y Bwlwarcau, Glam. A fine example of a 'south-western type' of concentric-enclosure. (Copyright, Glamorgan-Gwent Archaeological Trust)

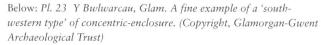

Pl. 24 Collfyn, Mont. The eastern half of the Iron Age/Romano-British settlement under excavation. (Copyright, Clwyd-Powys Archaeological Trust, Collfryn 82)

Pl. 25 Skomer Island, Pembs. The banks of prehistoric fields overlain at the top right by the straighter banks of the island's post-medieval settlement. (Copyright, Dyfed Archaeological Trust)

(Above left) *Pl. 26 Varchoel Lane, Mont. A complex sub-rectangular enclosure of probable Iron Age/Romano-British date. The small ring-ditch on the left, outside the enclosure, probably belongs to a Bronze Age round barrow rather than to an Iron Age roundhouse. (Copyright, Clwyd-Powys Archaeological Trust, 84-C-177)*

(Left) *Pl. 27 Llys Farm, Mont. The triple ditches of a sub-rectangular enclosure of probable late prehistoric date overlain by the single ditch and palisade-slot of a later, perhaps Dark Age, enclosure. (Copyright, Clwyd-Powys Archaeological Trust, 84-C-189)*

Pl. 28 Imaginative reconstruction of rituals of offering at Llyn Fawr. The wheeled vehicle is based on continental finds and rock engravings. This view does not show the awesome setting of the lake. (By permission of the National Museum of Wales)

Pl. 29 View of Llyn Cerrig Bach, Anglesey, source of the famous Iron Age votive deposit. (Photo copyright Mick Sharp)

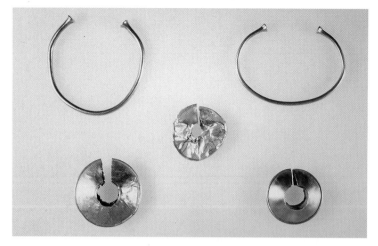

Pl. 30 Gold ornaments from Gaerwen, Anglesey. The two lock rings and two bracelets are part of the original find, now in the British Museum; the crushed lock ring was found during excavations at Capel Eithin, Gaerwen, in 1981. (Photo © Copyright The British Museum)

Pl. 31 The 'Snowdon Bowl', the handle of a Late Iron Age spun bowl decorated with red glass inlay. (Photo Douglas Madge, UWB)

Pl. 32 The 'Trawsfynydd Tankard', a large stave-built wooden tankard covered with bronze sheet and with a single cast handle. (Photo by permission of Liverpool Museum)

Pl. 33 Stone head from Hendy, Anglesey. The find circumstances of this carving are unknown but it is stylistically similar to Iron Age examples. It epitomises the difficulty of dating such carvings. It is now in Oriel Ynys Môn. (Photo copyright Mick Sharp)

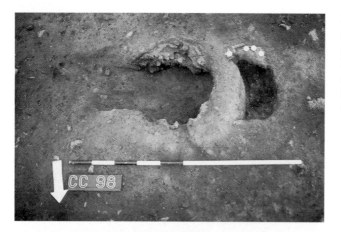

Pl. 34 (a & b) Furnaces from Crawcwellt, an iron-producing site in Merioneth. A shows two furnaces, one built into the base of the other. Note the thickness of the clay wall around the vitrified lining. B shows a similar furnace with broken arch through which the slag would be removed. (Photos copyright Peter Crew)

Pl. 35 Llwyn Bryn-dinas, Mont. A hillfort commanding magnificent views of the Tanat Valley. The earliest defences date from the Late Bronze Age/Early Iron Age transition but the site was reoccupied later when a workshop was built against the back of the rampart (see p. 211). (Copyright Clwyd-Powys Archaeological Trust 83-C-526)

Beyond the Marches and north-eastern Wales several other sites can now claim a very early origin on the grounds that they produce either the necessary radiocarbon dates, or a defensive sequence commencing with palisades. The promontory fort at Dale (Pembrokeshire) has produced dates which fall into the later ninth/earlier eighth century cal BC from an intermediate stage in a complicated defensive sequence, beginning with palisades of two phases and ending with two phases of rampart (Benson & Williams 1987). The small but strongly positioned univallate coastal fort at Pendinas Lochtyn in south Cardiganshire produced a single ninth-century cal BC date in association with timber structures in its interior, but the relationship with the defences is unknown (Scott & Murphy 1992). Palisaded defences are also known at two other south-western forts, Caer Bayvil (James 1987) and Castell Henllys. Finally in north-west Wales the palisaded enclosure at Castell Odo (Caernarfonshire) is associated with what are now recognised as later Bronze Age ceramics (Alcock 1960) (see p. 199).

These hilltop sites – certainly the large forts in the Marches – represent a dramatic and fundamental reappraisal of the needs of local communities. There has been much speculation as to the whys and wherefores of their origins and function. Cunliffe (1991) has argued that their equivalents in England were not intensively occupied by virtue of the sparsity of internal structures, houses in particular. He regards activities within them as short-lived and essentially serving the needs of specific social groups. The evidence from The Breiddin at least suggests otherwise. Indeed, there is little to distinguish the nature of the Late Bronze Age occupation from that of the second phase of occupation in the third or second century cal BC. However their origins and socio-economic functions are to be explained it would seem that forts such as The Breiddin and Llwyn Bryn-dinas were abandoned within a Later Bronze Age context, which suggests that the causal factors at least were either transient or spasmodic. Nevertheless they seem to have been the harbinger of a need on the part of many communities to combine their efforts – whether or not under coercion is unknown – with a view to protecting themselves and their chattels, thereby giving rise to the hierarchy of settlements that is one of the hallmarks of the second half of the first millennium BC. Whether the genesis of early hillfort building in the Marches reflects the ability of communities to accumulate agricultural surpluses in a more favoured climatic zone, coupled with control of resources and the presence of a dominant warrior aristocracy, as the Late Bronze Age metalwork might suggest, is uncertain, though this has been a favoured explanation.

Once established, the essential components of Later Bronze Age settlement, particularly that settlement hierarchy in which defended sites played an important part, coupled with a shift to lowland settings, or at least to the lowland/upland interface, were to continue for centuries thereafter. However, broad economic strategies had to be modified to cope with climatic changes, particularly the more favourable conditions prevailing in the drier areas of the east in comparison with that of the wetter but warmer west. A tendency for many of these fortified community settlements to be abandoned after a relatively short life (very probable at The Breiddin and Llwyn Bryn-dinas, and possible at Moel y Gaer where, despite the evidence for the replacement of several round-houses, occupation may not have outlasted a generation) suggests that social stress may have been transient. This is a recurrent pattern which is demonstrable at several other classic Iron Age hillforts.

Hillforts of the Early Iron Age, *c.* 550–400 cal BC

The trend towards the establishment of fortified community settlements led to a remarkable burst of renewed hillfort building all over southern Britain between the sixth and fifth centuries cal BC. This proliferation is seemingly well attested in the earliest phases of hillforts in the Marches such as Croft Ambrey, Midsummer Hill and Old Oswestry, though the dating evidence is poor. Hillforts became rapidly established further afield, evidenced by sites such as Moel y Gaer (Rhosesmor), Moel Hiraddug, Dinorben and Ffridd Faldwyn, and thence north and south-west beyond the Cambrian range. Though the sequence of development is tolerably clear in some parts of Wales, in others the lack of excavation and sound chronological indicators cloud the issue.

The sites which were chosen for hillforts in this period tend to be strong, naturally defensive positions, such as promontories or spurs. There is also evidence to suggest that many were re-established on older sites which had been palisaded; examples include Ffridd Faldwyn (Guilbert 1981a), Dinorben (Gardner & Savory 1964; Guilbert 1979b; 1980), Dale Fort (Benson & Williams 1987), and probably Llanstephan (Guilbert 1974) and Castell Henllys (Mytum 1999). Pre-rampart occupation is also attested at several forts in the south west, for example Coygan Camp (Wainwright 1967), Merlin's Hill (Williams *et al.* 1988), Pembrey Mountain (Williams 1981) and the Broadway enclosure (Williams & Mytum 1998), where it is dated to the eighth–fifth centuries cal BC.

These early forts are frequently of modest size. The first phase at Ffridd Faldwyn only enclosed 1.2 hectares and the earliest fort at the west end of the ridge at Cefncarnedd some 1.5 hectares (Spurgeon 1972). Dinorben with 2.4 and Moel y Gaer with 2.7 hectares enclosed are among the largest, though a site such as Moel Hiraddug may have enclosed 8 hectares or more (Brassil *et al.* 1982). The defences are invariably univallate, though they can take widely different forms. Ramparts of timber-framed 'box' type – common in the early hillforts of southern England (Cunliffe 1991, 316–20) – are also found in Wales. At Ffridd Faldwyn the rampart and single ditch which succeeded the palisades incorporated timbers in its structure, and became partly vitrified (O'Neil 1942). At Dinorben the single rampart and ditch, dated to the fifth–fourth centuries cal BC, was certainly timber-framed (Guilbert 1980) as was the rampart enclosing the 2.7 hectare 'planted' settlement at Moel y Gaer which Cunliffe regards as a specific type in which the main anchor timbers for the front face were widely spaced and the tail of the rampart revetted with close spaced verticals (1991, 318–19; Fig. 14.3). This has radiocarbon dates which overlap with those of the palisaded phase, and continue to the fourth–third centuries cal BC (Guilbert 1980).

In south-west Wales the evidence suggests comparable types of defences. For example, the early rampart at Dale Fort incorporated timbers (Benson & Williams 1987) as did that at Llanstephan (Guilbert 1974); both seem to be associated with sixth/fifth-century cal BC radiocarbon dates. At Castell Henllys a small early bank was built up against a revetment of close-set timbers, the whole being later buried within a large stone-revetted rampart which also seems to have incorporated timber-lacing, since it showed evidence of intense burning. By way of contrast the rampart at Broadway seems to have been of simple dump type (Williams & Mytum 1998, 65–6). Some walled forts such as Moel Hiraddug and Twyn y Gaer (Monmouthshire) are probably early, to judge by radiocarbon dates from one of the gates at the former (p. 154) and the stratigraphic sequence, coupled with radiocarbon dates, from the latter (Probert 1976). A sixth/fifth-century cal BC date is also possible for the construction of the stone rampart at Caer Cadwgan (Austin *et al.* 1984–8).

In north-west Wales stone-walled forts are numerous. Garn Boduan and Tre'r Ceiri are among the best-known examples. There are hints that the defences of some walled forts were modified by the addition of banks and ditches, although the only clearly demonstrable case is that of Dinas Dinorwic (RCAHMW 1960, 175–6). Unfortunately there are scarcely any radiocarbon dates for these north-western stone-walled sites, or those with apparently added banks and ditches, the exception being the tiny walled fort at Bryn y Castell (Merioneth) where the late dates suggest that the tradition was long-lived in this rock-dominant landscape (Crew 1984). Despite a broad generic resemblance there is no need to assume a cultural link between stone-walled forts in north-west and north-east Wales.

Where evidence is available for their morphology the gates of the great majority of these early forts are simple gaps in the ramparts. This is well demonstrated at the main inner gate and the north-west gate to the primary walled fort at Moel Hiraddug in Flintshire, though both are in effect situated at the end of a passageway (Houlder 1961b, Fig. 6; Guilbert 1979a). There are exceptions, however. At Castell Henllys the early gate was most complex and unusual in so far as it comprised a long passageway, revetted in stone, ending in a large timber tower from which the gates were hung. To its rear were two pairs of shallow, semi-circular 'guard-chambers' (Mytum 1999). Gates equipped with timber guard-chambers were apparently coming into vogue in the fifth century, if not earlier (Cunliffe 1991, 337). That these were being built in stone in Wales is indicated by the blocking of the simple portal which comprised the main inner gate at Moel Hiraddug (**Fig.**

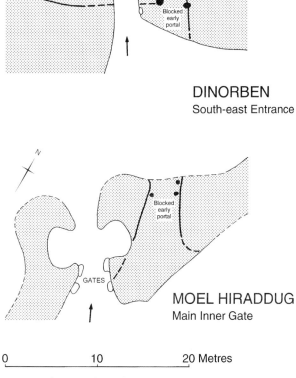

DINORBEN
South-east Entrance

MOEL HIRADDUG
Main Inner Gate

0   10   20 Metres

Fig. 4.3. Schematic plans of early gateways and guard-chambers at Dinorben, Denbs., and Moel Hiraddug. (Source: Guilbert 1979a.)

4.3) sometime between the earlier sixth and later fifth century cal BC (CAR-372, 373, 374). Its replacement, to one side, appears to have been a gate initially provided with a single sub-rectangular chamber in the east terminal of the rampart, until that was replaced by two curvilinear or C-shaped chambers immediately to the rear of the gates (Guilbert 1979a). A similar blocking and replacement with a pair of rectilinear chambers was evidenced at Dinorben (Guilbert 1979a). Sometimes the gates and guard-chambers are placed at the ends of long corridor entrances, as at Pen y Corddyn, but there is no evidence to indicate whether there is a chronological difference between the two types. It is possible that they are broadly contemporary and represent a type that was fashionable in the Marches and north-east Wales, and remained in use for a long time thereafter. There is no evidence that this type of gate exists elsewhere in Wales. Although the primary gate at Castell Henllys has two pairs of recesses they are quite unlike those discussed above. Following the destruction of this gate it was replaced by a four-post gate-tower with a pair of shallow recesses to its rear, until these too were given up, the gateway thereafter becoming a simple, narrow stone-revetted passageway.

Although the small coastal promontory forts which abound in south-west Wales frequently show evidence of later Iron Age and Romano-British occupation and have therefore often been considered to be relatively late, recent evidence from Porth y Rhaw (Pembrokeshire) (Crane 1998) suggests that such views need to be modified. The interior of this badly eroded site was packed with timber round-houses clearly of several phases. However, it is dates (2470 ± 70 BP (Swan-101) = 806–478 cal BC and 2430 ± 60 BP (Beta-124342) = 780–385 cal BC) from early features associated with the primary rampart which, coupled with the early dates from Dale Fort, suggest that at least some of these sites originate either in the later Bronze Age/Early Iron Age transition or within the Early Iron Age.

The Middle Iron Age, 400–150 cal BC

In central southern England the middle phases of the Iron Age saw a diminution in the number of hillforts, an increasing tendency for the remaining forts to to be defended by dump ramparts, with more elaborate gateways and the provision of extensive outworks, and a preference for multivallation (Cunliffe 1991). Some evolved into what Cunliffe has termed 'developed hillforts'. These are medium to large in size (generally about 5 to 12 hectares) and often show clear signs of having been enlarged. They were apparently intensively occupied by sizeable communities, with their internal arrangement being maintained over a considerable timespan. Cunliffe has suggested that such sites were important in the social structure of the times and embody the crystallisation of territories and the centralisation of power vested in an elite.

Many Welsh hillforts show signs of similar defensive evolution and enlargement in this period. Cefncarnedd (Montgomeryshire), dominating the upland bowl focused upon Caersws in the upper Severn Valley, saw the replacement of the 1.5 hectare univallate hillfort by a multivallate fort of 3.2 hectares which encompasssed the whole ridge (**Pl. 22**). The addition of annexes increased its size to 6 hectares. Ffridd Faldwyn was apparently enlarged from 1.2 to 4 hectares, the defences of the new fort being multivallate. Finally, on the west coast Pen Dinas, Aberystwyth, was progressively enlarged from a univallate fort of 1.6 hectares to a part-multivallate fort of 3.8 hectares, the latest phase of which, on the basis of ceramic evidence, cannot be earlier than the second century cal BC (Forde *et al.* 1963). Some show clear evidence of occupation by large communities, for example Garn Boduan and Braich y Dinas in the north-west and The Breiddin in the central Marches. However, none of these can be directly compared with sites such as Danebury (Hampshire) and Maiden Castle (Dorset), if only because they have received so little internal investigation. Moreover, instead of contraction in numbers the evidence from Wales suggests the reverse – an expansion of the hillfort phenomenon.

In the Marches and north-east Wales, however, there are some hillforts which do invite comparison with those of south-central England, at least in terms of size and indications of enlargement. After long abandonment Llwyn Bryn-dinas and The Breiddin were reoccupied. At the former the refurbishment of the rampart took place in the fourth–third century and again in the second–first century cal BC. At the latter a stone wall was built after 2200 ± 90 BP (QL-1080) = 394–177 cal BC. This enclosed a massive 28 hectares. Where building was possible the interior proved to be packed with timber round-houses and four-post structures, the latter often replacing houses (Musson 1991). By far the largest hillfort in the Marches, however, is Llanymynech Hill, impressively situated on the fringe of the Shropshire plain, and possibly enclosing as much as 57 hectares – making it one of the largest hillforts in Britain. Small-scale excavations indicate that its defences were certainly in existence by the late second century cal BC (Musson & Northover 1989). If its interior, which contained a small copper mine, was as densely built up as those of other Marcher hillforts such as Croft Ambrey, Midsummer Hill or The Breiddin, then we have to postulate the existence, in this region at least, of settlements which probably functioned as hilltop villages or townships, and by implication as centres of power.

At the northern extremity of the Marches hillfort belt Moel Hiraddug, already a large fort at 10.5 hectares, saw the addition of both wall and bank defences with ditches to augment the defences on the east, and to extend its perimeter by a series of outworks on the south, enlarging the site by a further 1.35 hectares (**Fig. 4.2**). Changes to the arrangement of guard-chambers at the main inner gate (**Fig. 4.3**) probably belong to this period. Many hillforts show phases of reconstruction and modification to their defences at this time. Moel y Gaer (Rhosesmor) was reoccupied in the fourth/early third century cal BC, a short-lived settlement of 2.7 hectares being defended by a timber-laced rampart and outer embanked palisade. The interior showed some evidence for zoning in the placement of round-houses and four-post structures (Guilbert 1976) (**Fig. 4.4**). The defences of the enlarged fort at Ffridd Faldwyn were similarly refurbished at a time when Malvernian ceramics were reaching the site. At Dinorben the defences were ultimately to take the form of dump ramparts and become multivallate.

Dump ramparts represent the most common type of defence in the Middle/Later Iron Age, but is an exceedingly simple form and there is evidence that some forts, such as the Broadway enclosure in south-west Wales, dating from about 500 cal BC (Williams & Mytum 1998), may have been so defended from the very beginning. Multivallate defences frequently replace, or are added to, those at sites which were hitherto univallate and had defences of wall or timber-framed 'box' type. There are problems in ascertaining their chronology, which seems to be very broad. The bivallate forts at Holgan and Pilcornswell, belonging to the fourth and third centuries cal BC (Williams & Mytum 1998) are pretty typical, and it is probable that the great majority of Welsh forts which possessed multivallate dump ramparts acquired them from the Middle phases of the Iron Age onwards. Also associated with such defences are deeply inturned entrances, those at Twyn y Gaer (Monmouthshire) (Probert 1976) being formed through the addition of successive elements to the inturned rampart terminals.

In south-west Wales forts of over 2.5 hectares enclosed are rare. Merlin's Hill (Carmarthenshire), one of the largest forts in the region, and initially a univallate enclosure of 1 hectare, was enlarged to 3.8 hectares sometime after 2310 ± 60 BP (CAR-958) = 490–350 cal BC, the ramparts being of dumped construction, and provided with an elaborate entrance (Williams *et al.* 1988). At Pen Dinas, Aberystwyth, the site was successively enlarged, the southern summit being provided with two stone-revetted ramparts on the landward side, and with an inturned entrance on the south. Phase IV, the final enlargement in a complex sequence, took place when Malvernian pottery was reaching the site, sometime between the third and first centuries BC (Forde *et al.* 1963). Most of the evidence from this western region concerns the development of small hillforts of the Castell Henllys or Holgan-Pilcornswell type (Williams & Mytum 1998). Some rose, some fell. Castell Henllys, for instance, though by this stage bivallate, was apparently no longer the prestigious well-defended site that it once had been.

In the south-east we have a region which abounds with medium-sized sites of 2–5 hectares enclosed; most are contour or coastal promontory forts showing considerable complexity in their defences. There are classic examples of multivallation, as at The Bulwarks, Porthkerry, an apparent frequency of dump ramparts and much care lavished on the protection of the gates, as at Caer Dynnaf, Llanblethian (Glamorganshire) and Pen y Crug (Breconshire). The problem here is of a singular lack of modern excavation and reliable dating evidence. Only rarely has it been possible to show sequences such as the addition of an annexe at Twyn y Gaer (Probert 1976), probably in the third century cal BC, or the replacement of a univallate, stone-walled enclosure of about 1.8 hectares with a simple gate by the impressive 4.2 hectare hillfort of Castle Ditches, Llancarfan (Hogg 1976). Even so, it is undated.

This is certainly a period which saw the appearance of minor forts (see p. 167), such as Collfryn in the upper Severn Valley, probably founded in the third century cal BC. Initially, it had widely spaced defences, recalling the multiple-enclosure forts of parts of upland Glamorgan and the south-west, though the defences are more massive. Their equivalents in south-western England have been dated to the Middle Iron Age and later (Cunliffe 1991, 252–6). Harding's Down West Fort (Glamorganshire) seems, on the basis of associated pottery, to be of a still later period (Hogg 1973).

The Late Iron Age, 150 cal BC to the Roman Conquest

This phase of hillfort usage is the least well understood. In the Marches and north-east Wales they certainly continued to be occupied into the first century BC judging by evidence from Moel Hiraddug and The Breiddin. Decorated shield fitments, conventionally dated to the second–first centuries cal BC (Hemp 1928; Savory 1976c, 30–2; Brassil *et al.* 1982) from the former suggest some activity, while at the latter radiocarbon dates suggest occupation certainly into the second century cal BC, if not later, and two decorated beads indicate that this could be be extended into the first century AD (**Figs 4.22, 1**, and **4.23, 21**). At Dinorben, too, occupation certainly continued, radiocarbon dates suggesting that Bank 2 was not built before the second–first centuries cal BC (Guilbert 1979b).

In south-east Wales numerous hillforts produce evidence of occupation in this period, solely on the basis of ceramic evidence. Llanmelin (Nash-Williams 1933b), Sudbrook (Nash-Williams 1939) and Caer Dynnaf (Davies 1967) are good examples. They produce pottery either in the Lydney/Llanmelin tradition, or South-Western Decorated Wares of Peacock's Glastonbury style 3 (p. 202) or plain late Iron Age wares which continue into the mid-first century AD (Jarrett & Wrathmell 1981) (**Fig. 4.25**). The large multivallate coastal promontory forts of the Vale of Glamorgan were also probably occupied in this period. The Bulwarks (Porthkerry), for instance, produced plain wares together with early Romano-British pottery (Davies 1973b). What is uncertain, though, is whether the occurrence of the latter on sites such as The Bulwarks, Llanmelin, Caer Dynnaf and Castle Ditches (Llancarfan) necessarily indicates continuity of occupation from the later Iron Age through the conquest. What little evidence is available for the chronology of the numerous small cliff-top forts of the Gower Peninsula, such as The Knave, or its inland equivalent Bishopston Valley, suggests occupation at the time when South-Western Decorated Wares were reaching the south Wales coast.

In south-west Wales the evidence clearly indicates the abandonment of hillforts – some of which may have had attenuated or spasmodic occupation sequences in any case – and their replacement between the second century cal BC and first century AD by strongly defended but very small ringforts (p. 169), normally enclosing less than 0.4 hectares (Williams 1988b). However, this process is not invariable and small hillforts such as Castell Henllys and Woodbarn Rath (Vyner 1986) seem to have remained in use, with occupation at the former seemingly continuing into the Romano-British period, though not within the defended area (Mytum 1999). Radiocarbon dates from Porth y Rhaw (Pembrokeshire) (Crane 1998) indicate that this coastal promontory fort continued to be occupied to the second century cal BC at least, and the frequency of Romano-British occupation within these cliff-top sites suggests that they remained an important element in the overall settlement pattern throughout the later Iron Age and beyond.

Hillfort Function

By virtue of their dramatic survival as impressive monuments of a past age hillforts have attracted considerable scholarly attention. The energy vested in their building, the maintenance of their defences and internal structures, sometimes their very size and complexity have given rise to numerous models of hillfort function within specific regions (Collis 1981). Some of these models are not mutually exclusive, but the application of a model drawn up for one region should not be applied wholesale. Potential socio-economic territories or even boundaries between social groupings have been drawn up for some regions (Cunliffe 1991), though opinion has been tempered of late. It is most unlikely that all hillforts functioned in the same way on either a temporal or spatial basis, even within well-defined geographical zones. The evidence has to be considered carefully, even on a site by site basis.

Hillforts were manifestly socially, if not economically, significant. Mytum (1996) has recently reiterated that the size and complexity of the defences and gates of the larger hillforts may be interpreted as investing them with monumental and symbolic functions. This is an interpretation which may be applied to even a modest fort such as Castell Henllys – at least in its earlier phases – when the gateways were complex, and a belt of *chevaux de frise* gave additional protection to the main approach. Thereafter, this element of monumentality was dispensed with and only a simple and poorly maintained access route was used. Elaborate outworks and banks of increasing size similarly protected the northern approach to the small, but very strongly situated Cardiganshire hillfort of Pen y Bannau (Davies & Hogg 1994, 269; Plate 1a), the remainder of the circuit being univallate and quite unsubstantial. It would be wrong, however, to assume that strong ramparts were merely 'boasting platforms'. There are clear indications that the period in which they were built was a violent one, even if warfare was spasmodic, small-scale and to some extent ritualised. A sling-stone dump within a round-house overlooking the approach to the later gate passage of the main inner gate at Moel Hiraddug (Davies 1969) indicates preparations for defence, while at Castell Henllys a massive sling-stone dump, coupled with evidence for the burning of the gates and a portion of the timber-laced rampart testifies to the threat and reality of assault. The early fort at Ffridd Faldwyn also showed evidence of burning and the vitrifaction of its timber-laced rampart (O'Neil 1942). The intensity of occupation on sites occupying the most exposed or uncongenial positions, such as The Breiddin, indicates that their builders were prepared to sacrifice convenience for security, sometimes for long periods. In some instances it is possible to suggest that communities were temporarily prepared to forsake low-lying settlements for exposed hilltops, as, for example, at Moel y Gaer (Flintshire) where the Phase 2 settlement of stake-walled round-houses and serried rows of four-post structures was short-lived, the occupation being of such short duration that timbers from the four-posters could be removed for re-use elsewhere (Guilbert 1975). Indeed, it is tempting to suggest that the three phases of occupation on the hilltop, each separated by centuries of disuse, can be related to a sub-regional cycle of unrest or open warfare (Davies 1995, 676, Fig. 35.3), a pattern that might be inferred for other areas as well.

Detailed analysis of the internal arrangement is vital to the investigation of hillfort usage. By and large Welsh hillforts show a fairly standard suite of structures: round-houses in stone and timber, and a range of rectilinear post-built structures – mainly four-posters, ranging from 2 to 3.5 metres across. The timber round-houses (**Pl. 20**) normally range from 7 to 11 metres in diameter, though the majority at The Breiddin were smaller at 5 to 7 metres. They are frequently found to have been built of stakes driven into the soil or contained within narrow wall-gullies, sometimes accompanied by drains, which in some cases may be internal and capped with slabs. The walls are assumed to have consisted of horizontally woven wattles, daubed with clay. Some houses have internal rings of roof-supports, and occasionally internal or more commonly projecting porches; occasionally there are two opposed doorways. More or less centrally placed hearths are commonly encountered, while pits and settings of stakes represent internal structures set on floors of beaten earth or clay. More rarely there is evidence for rectangular buildings which lack earth-fast elements, being set on sleeper-beams, such as the Phase 3 buildings at Moel y

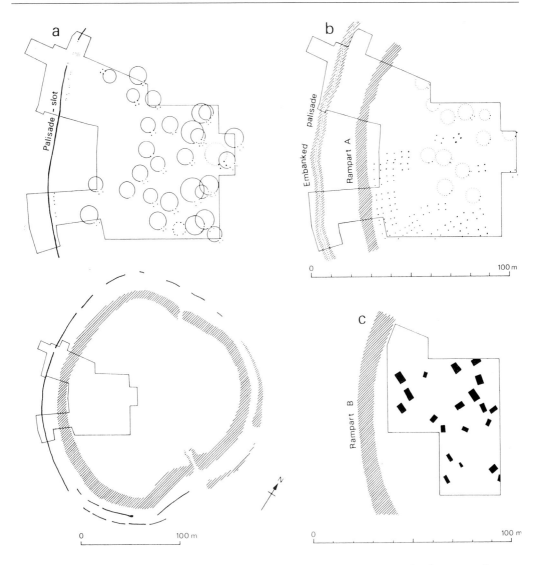

Fig. 4.4. Moel y Gaer, Flints.: the western defences and internal structures: (a) Phase 1; (b) Phase 2; (c) Phase 3. (Sources: Guilbert 1976; 1982.)

Gaer (**Fig. 4.4**). In rock-dominant areas round-houses are frequently stone-built, and so survive above ground and their relationships with one another and with other stuctures can be examined, sometimes without recourse to excavation. Their walls are invariably low and probably served largely as bases for the rafters. Though mostly circular or ovoid, some seem to have been specially modified to serve special functions, such as the snail-like buildings at Bryn y Castell and probably Garn Boduan, plausibly linked with metalworking (Crew 1984). Some hillforts, such as Moel Trigarn (Pembrokeshire), show evidence of hundreds of semi-circular building platforms for timber structures, which may not all have been houses (**Pl. 19**). At others, for instance Moel Hiraddug (**Fig. 4.2**) there was a mix of stone and timber round-houses, the stone buildings in some forts probably replacing those of timber because of a local shortage of wood. Four- (sometimes five and even six) post rectangular structures are common, though none has yet been encountered within hillforts in the north-west. They are, however, known at certain unfortified settlements such as Bryn Eryr (Longley 1998) and Llandegai (Caerns.) (Houlder 1967). These very substantial post-settings are normally interpreted as elements of raised structures for the storage of grain or other agricultural products, though Stanford (1974) has suggested that larger four-post structures within Marcher hillforts were dwellings.

Though excavation may reveal timber round-houses with associated four-post structures in a seemingly random arrangement, sometimes with houses being replaced by four-posters, or vice versa, as at The Breiddin (Musson 1991, 184), many hillforts show evidence for the zoning of structures, and are thus comparable to their English counterparts (Cunliffe 1991, 352–3). Zoning normally takes the form of a clear distinction between areas designated for the building of round-houses and of four-post structures; simple segregation of function between different areas which can be perpetuated over long periods. An intriguing example exists at Moel Hiraddug (**Fig. 4.2**), where a group of at least eight four-post structures was excavated on the surviving northern portion of the ridge, complementing at least a similar number that were built as a peripheral range to the lee of the inner rampart on the east (Davies 1971). Additionally, a further fifteen four-posters and one five-post structure have been identified in the southern extremity of the ridge (Brassil *et al.* 1982, Fig. 2). With one exception in the northern group which was overlaid by a stone round-house, these buildings were all clearly separated from round-houses, the peripheral range recalling a similar arrangement at Moel y Gaer or Walesland Rath in Pembrokeshire (Wainwright 1971). There was a little evidence to suggest that the four-posters at Moel Hiraddug had been replaced *in situ*, though there were also some overlaps. There was some evidence for zoning at The Breiddin, too, though the craggy interior prohibited the development of extensive zoned areas.

Moel y Gaer (Flintshire) exhibits the best example of zoning in Wales, with a clear distinction between areas reserved for the construction of stake-walled round-houses in the central portion of the site, and rows of four-posters, up to eight deep, being built to the rear of the southern rampart (**Fig. 4.4**). The arrangement of four-posters in a peripheral manner is also known at Dinorben and Ffridd Faldwyn. In the interiors of Marches hillforts at Croft Ambrey, Midsummer Hill and Credenhill only large four-posters have been identified. This has led to the belief that these larger examples were dwellings (Stanford 1974), but the excavations were limited and it is probable that the four-posters were merely elements of zoned interiors. What is also of interest is the fact that these Herefordshire sites show clear evidence for the recurrent rebuilding of their four-post structures, and thereby the maintenance of the planned layout over a long period. This implies that, like Danebury or Maiden Castle, they must have remained socially and economically important for a long time. The Phase 2 settlement at Moel y Gaer, by way of contrast, is of significance not only because of the excellent evidence for zoning, but also because it has the distinction of being a short-lived planted settlement, not an organic growth like its precursor.

Zoning is also a feature of much smaller defended settlements such as the south-western ringforts. For example, at Woodside, Drim and Walesland Rath the layout included a peripheral zone of four-posters, though at Woodside this seems to be the product of a long phase of development which initially saw the functional division of the interior into a northern portion reserved for round-houses and a south-western for four-posters, the southern portion apparently remaining empty, and perhaps reserved for animal penning (**Figs 4.5** and **4.6**). At Walesland Rath the peripheral four-posters are interpreted as only pertinent to an early phase, while at Dan y Coed the four-posters post-date a succession of round-houses. Clearly, even at sites where the whole internal arrangement has been recovered, it would be dangerous to assume a formal, zoned plan from the beginning, without making due allowance for the development of that structural arrangement over time.

Many hillforts seem to have a significant role to play within the society and economy of the period, but these roles may have been very different from place to place and from time to time. The very different chronologies and sometimes spasmodic occupations of some sites within their respective regions – as exhibited in the Llawhaden sequence, with small hillforts being replaced by ringforts from the second century cal BC – is an indication of this. Socio-economic differences arising from topography and geomorphology undoubtedly explain the startling contrasts between the hillforts of the Marches and their northern outliers on the one hand and those of south-west Wales on the other. For example, the distribution pattern of the larger hillforts of the Clwydian range – Pen y

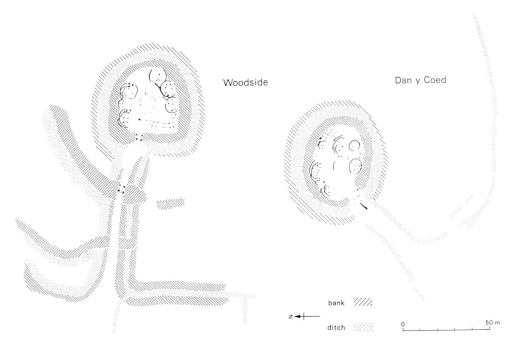

Fig. 4.5. Woodside and Dan y Coed 'ringforts', Pembs. (Source: Williams 1988.)

Cloddiau, Moel Hiraddug and Moel Fenlli – each overlooking a stretch of fertile vale, suggests that they could have functioned not only as refuges for valley-dwellers in times of stress, but also as the social, political and possibly even religious foci of these communities. Whether they acted as nodal points from which the agricultural resources of a rich river valley could be organised by an elite and integrated with those of a pastoral community on the heights of the Clwydian range is uncertain (Alcock 1965). Certainly, it would be dangerous to assume a redistributive function to these forts, with a residential elite in control, without the necessary proof.

That elites can be associated with some Welsh hillforts is indicated by high-status metalwork from Moel Hiraddug (Brassil *et al.* 1982) (**Fig. 4.20**) and Pen-coed-foel (Savory 1976b, 62), but their presence could be transient, and in any event the rarity and restricted range of material from later prehistoric sites in Wales makes such value judgements tentative in the extreme.

NON-HILLFORT SETTLEMENT

Though overshadowed by the hillforts the dominant settlement in later prehistoric times was the lightly enclosed or open farmstead, which must have shared a close, if sometimes spasmodic, relationship with their more impressive counterparts. The present-day distribution of many of these sites is largely a function of survival, since even those defined by earthworks are prone to obliteration by modern agriculture. Those delimited by fences or otherwise essentially open in character (for example, those discovered in the Gwent Levels) are particularly difficult to recognise unless they were rebuilt in stone or there are exceptional circumstances leading to their preservation. Settlements built of drystone – the most obvious – have a propensity to survive in rock-dominant marginal landscapes, though these can frequently be shown to be replacements for farmsteads built of wood, reflecting the exhaustion of local sources of building timber. The great majority of farm buildings in the Welsh regions, however, continued to be built of perishable materials.

While the distribution of defensible enclosures in some areas is fairly representative of their original density, aerial photography has played a key role in enhancing this pattern and in the discovery of very large numbers of sites of the non-defensive variety, appearing largely as crop-marks (**Figs 4.7, 4.10, 4.11**). More significantly this technique has fundamentally changed the settlement pattern in those areas – such as the central Marches – where defended sites were hitherto the sole representative of the settlement history of the region, but it is equally true of areas such as the Vale of Glamorgan where the density of new sites discovered in an area hitherto largely devoid of crop-mark evidence has caused some surprise (Driver 1995). Quite simply, aerial photography has produced crucial evidence concerning the character and spatial relationships of a great variety of non-defensive settlement, from the huts and fields of the north west to the ditched and fenced enclosures of the south west and east of Wales. For the first time well-populated landscapes appear and the bulk of the population can be seen not as hillfort-dwellers but as the occupants of small, lightly enclosed farmsteads.

North-west Wales is the only region where stone-built settlements have survived in substantial numbers, though a thin scatter of huts and enclosures can be found further afield from the Denbigh Moors in the north (Musson 1994, 105), the Breconshire/

Glamorgan uplands in the south (RCAHMW 1976; 1997) to the marginal landscapes and islands of the south west. Unfortunately, outside the north west their chronology is less secure. Here they have been intensively studied (RCAHMW 1956; 1960; 1964; Bowen & Gresham 1967; Smith 1974; 1977; Kelly 1988; 1991; Fasham *et al.* 1998), but it is only within the past decade or so that excavations have resolved some of the pressing problems associated with them. The present distribution of some thousand examples of stone round-house settlements is entirely relict, most lowland examples having been destroyed by agricultural operations. The great majority of settlements surviving above 200 metres comprise single houses: the remaining sites fall into the category of enclosed/nucleated settlements, 60 per cent of which survive below 200 metres. Present evidence suggests a high probability of a functional/economic – rather than than a chronological – distinction between the two types, for reasons cited below. One possibility is that they represent complementary elements of the late prehistoric agricultural regime.

The Royal Commission classified these settlements into four main types: Class I comprises upland huts; Class II huts and associated enclosures; Class III concentric enclosures; and Class IV enclosed homesteads, frequently associated with rectilinear field or irregular enclosure systems. Class II had been tentatively assigned to the Middle Bronze Age on the basis of comparable settlements in northern and south-western England, but recent work at Crawcwellt West (Crew 1989, 91) has demonstrated that this hypothesis, based entirely upon morphological comparisons, is unsustainable (see p. 92). Here, a 4 hectare settlement, initially of timber, then of stone round-houses and low enclosure walls and much concerned with the production of iron from the local bog ore, was occupied certainly from about 700 to 300 BC on the basis of magnetic dates (Crew 1998 and pers. comm.) The majority of Class II settlements, and probably many of Class I (see the Graeanog Ridge below), must therefore be of about the same date.

By virtue of excavations at two sites, Erw Wen and Moel y Gerddi (Kelly 1988), the Class III concentric enclosures can also be shown to belong to the second half of the first millennium BC (**Fig. 4.6**). At the former, a timber round-house and concentric palisaded enclosure was translated into stone, the whole sequence belonging to the eighth–fifth centuries cal BC. Moel y Gerddi shows a similar sequence, though apparently within the fourth–second centuries cal BC (see also pp. 93, 174).

The chronology and evolution of the Class IV enclosed homesteads can now be placed on a firmer footing, due in part to the excavation of a closely related group of prehistoric/Romano-British farms on the Graeanog Ridge in Caernarfonshire (Kelly 1991; Fasham *et al.* 1998). This demonstrated what was already evident from much earlier excavations: that the earliest stone phases of these settlements – often attributed to the Romano-British period – were not only demonstrably late prehistoric, but probably also succeeded timber phases. Although no evidence of a timber settlement was recovered at Graeanog or Cefn Graeanog II there was evidence to indicate agricultural activity (certainly a field system at the latter) on the ridge on the basis of radiocarbon dates of 410–215 cal BC. Indeed there is a high probability that the primary settlements were built of timber because the earliest farms at Graeanog and Cefn Graeanog II comprised simple, stone round-houses, dated *c.* 175 cal BC–cal AD 75 and *c.* 200–150 cal BC respectively. Their building seems to coincide with a change in building material, as well as a shift in

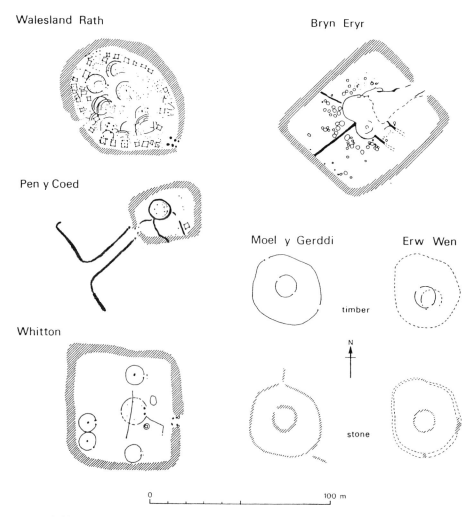

Fig. 4.6. Non-hillfort settlements: Walesland Rath, Pembs. (Source: Wainwright 1971); Bryn Eryr, Ang. (Source: Longley 1998); Pen y coed, Carms. (Source: Murphy 1985); Whitton, Glam. (Source: Jarrett & Wrathmell 1981); Moel y Gerddi and Erw Wen, Mer. (Source: Kelly 1988.)

settlement; perhaps the division of an existing landholding. It is also noteworthy that some of these settlements had a short occupation, for example at Cefn Graeanog II where forest regeneration followed a relatively brief phase of farming.

The trend appears to be for the initial phases of farmstead building in the region to be in timber, followed by the gradual replacement of timber buildings and fences with those of stone within the later first millennium BC. In some areas, where supplies of timber had always been inadequate – as in elevated coastal positions such as Ty Mawr, Anglesey (Smith 1987) – settlements may have had their house walls and enclosures built of stone from the very beginning. Where timber was still plentiful, settlements were still being built in this fashion as late as the early Romano-British period if the evidence fron Cefn Graeanog (Hogg 1969) is reliable. Another long-lasting and common building material in the region was clay, as exemplified by a group of three round-houses at Pant, Bryncroes (Ward 1993) and the solitary house at Bush Farm (Longley *et al.* 1998).

Though the evidence is small, it is clear that other types of farmstead existed in north-west Wales, particularly in the low-lying regions. A pair of timber round-houses – one a truly imposing building 14.7 metres in diameter (contrast with the stone round-house of 9 metres in internal diameter at Graeanog), and the largest prehistoric house known in north Wales – with associated four-post and two-post structures, built within Henge A at Llandegai (Houlder 1967) might be regarded as a piece of opportunistic building, the bank and ditch providing a ready-made enclosure. Bryn Eryr (Longley 1998) is an excavated example of another class of settlement, of which some half-dozen are known, all in Anglesey and thus probably linked to the agricultural potential of the island. Occupation seems to have begun in the Early/Middle Iron Age with a solitary, clay-walled round-house associated with an irregular, palisaded enclosure. Thereafter a smaller round-house was added and both were surrounded by a bank and ditch of rectangular plan, with a single entrance. Two six- or nine-post structures, probably granaries, also lay within the 0.3 hectare enclosure (**Fig. 4.6**). Radiocarbon dates indicate that it had been built by the third century cal BC. This is a type of late prehistoric farmstead commonly found elsewhere in England and Wales, for example Knock Rath (Pembrokeshire) and Whitton (Glamorganshire) (**Fig. 4.6**), but which appears only rarely in north-west Wales. In terms of status they probably represent the middle ground of the regional settlement hierarchy.

East of the Conwy evidence for non-hillfort settlement exists in a variety of forms, but more particularly as valley-floor and hill-slope enclosures revealed through aerial reconnaissance, particularly in the Clwyd and Tanat Valleys (Manley 1990; 1991). These have not been tested by excavation but to judge by evidence from similar sites in the central Marches their origins too probably lie within the later first millennium BC. Chance discoveries at Rhuddlan (Quinnell & Blockley 1994) and Prestatyn (Blockley 1989) – the latter the site of a second–first century BC timber round-house – show that unenclosed settlements must also have been widespread, particularly on the better soils of the coastal strip and the valley bottoms. Even more tantalising is evidence from the uplands, such as the timber round-houses discovered at Ty Tan y Foel, Cerrig y Drudion (Brassil 1992), close to the find-spot of the famous bronze bowl (see p. 189), and Nant y Griafolen, Brenig (Lynch 1993, 159–61) where a solitary timber round-house was associated with Malvernian pottery of the fourth–first century cal BC. Clearly, the uplands supported open settlements, but their relationship to the enclosed sites is unknown, nor can we determine whether they were occupied on a permanent or seasonal basis.

It is in the central borderland of England and Wales that dramatic evidence – largely the product of aerial photography – has necessitated a thorough reappraisal of the nature of settlement in a region dominated by large and impressive hillforts. Not only are there more than twice as many crop-mark sites as earthworks (**Fig. 4.7**), but by virtue of the fact that the great majority of these enclosures occupy hill-side and valley-bottom locations, they rectify what was otherwise a gross imbalance not only in the distribution but also in the topography of late prehistoric settlement. In so far as the valley-bottom sites are

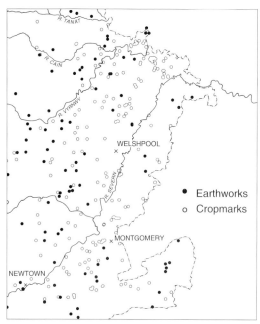

Earthworks

o Cropmarks

Fig. 4.8. Gors Wen, near Whitland, Pembs.
Rectilinear enclosure with 'antenna' ditches forming
an approaching drove-way. The modern farm
provides a scale. (Copyright T.A. James).

Fig. 4.7. Enclosures of probable Iron Age/Romano-
British date in the north-central borderland of Wales.
To the east of the national boundary sites show a similar
pattern. (Source: Clwyd-Powys Archaeological Trust.)

Fig. 4.9. Blaentwrog II,
near Lladygwydd,
Carms. Rectilinear
enclosure of Iron
Age/Romano-British
date. (Copyright, Dyfed
Archaeological Trust).

concerned, defensibility was not a consideration: of the others about 40 per cent lie in positions where defence may have been a factor. In terms of size they range from 0.1 to 2 hectares, though the majority enclose less than half a hectare. It is important to bear in mind that these crop-mark sites are essentially an index of modern (or at least recent) arable, and that a large number of ploughed-out settlements will remain undetected until either modern pasture reverts to arable or suitable conditions exist for the detection of others. Hence, there is an inbuilt bias in the distribution of crop-marks, although they do reflect, as is the case of multi-period crop-marks in the Walton Basin (Gibson 1999a), itself a pocket of fertile lowland thrust into hill-country, the propensity of man to settle in the most pedologically well-endowed areas.

Whimster (1989) classified these enclosures into curvilinear, rectilinear and hybrid types, which were in turn sub-divided into fourteen groups in all. Whether these morphological differences represent differences in date, function or cultural preferences is unclear. The curvilinear types are more prevalent in the western Marches, while the rectilinear ones tend to be overwhelmingly eastern and to favour lowland locations. For example, the recent surveys of the Wroxeter region in Shropshire indicate that 56 per cent of the enclosures were rectilinear, compared with only 25 per cent in the county of Montgomeryshire. Although many of the rectilinear types were originally considered to be of Romano-British date, it is gratifying to note that what little excavation has been undertaken suggests that, like those at Sharpstones Hill Sites A and E (Barker *et al.* 1991) in Shropshire, they originate within the Middle Iron Age. For example, at Hindwell I enclosure (**Fig. 4.13e**) in the Walton Basin in Radnorshire a trapezoidal, univallate enclosure with a single entrance close to a corner produced pottery of saucepan-pot tradition (**Fig. 4.25**, no. 3), of fourth/second-century cal BC date in the upper fill of its re-cut ditch, confirming a Middle Iron Age date for the site (Gibson 1999a). Evidence as to the socio-economic role of the smaller, predominantly univallate enclosures is presently lacking. No internal structures, other than a few post-holes, were revealed in the small area investigated at Hindwell I and aerial photography rarely shows internal structures. An exception here are ring-ditches – possibly timber houses – at Park Cottage near Caersws (Silvester & Britnell 1993). However, the interpretation of the majority of these sites as farmsteads would not be unreasonable in the light of evidence from across the border. Where enclosures lie in adjacent positions then they may either point to a sequence of occupation or to an inter-relationship comparable to that advocated for sites in the Llawhaden area of Pembrokeshire (pp. 172, 219).

Multiple-ditched enclosures such as those in a hill-slope position at Collfryn (Britnell 1989) (**Pl. 24**) and on the valley floor at Arddleen (Britnell & Musson 1984) are common in the region, their defences being often multi-period and the interiors reflecting a complex history. Some are even overtly defensively sited, and the term small hillfort would not be entirely inappropriate in some cases. These sites surely represent something quite different from our farmstead enclosures. Musson (1991) has tentatively suggested that they belong to a higher rung of the socio-economic ladder as 'pioneering' settlements, sometimes succeeded by sites of less overtly defensible type.

South-west Wales exhibits a great diversity in non-hillfort settlement. These range from stone-built huts and enclosures, such as those on Bernard's Well Mountain and more

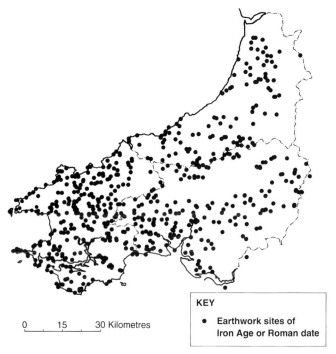

0   15   30 Kilometres

KEY

●   **Earthwork sites of
Iron Age or Roman date**

*Fig. 4.10. Distribution of earthwork sites of probable Iron Age/Romano-British date in south-west Wales.
(Source: Dyfed Archaeological Trust.)*

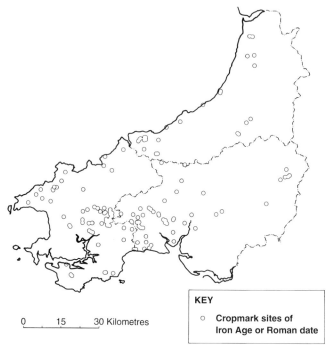

0   15   30 Kilometres

KEY

○   **Cropmark sites of
Iron Age or Roman date**

*Fig. 4.11. Distribution of cropmark sites of same likely date in the same region. (Source: Dyfed Archaeological
Trust.)*

impressively on Skomer (Evans 1990), to the well-defended ringforts (**Fig. 3.4; Pl. 25**). The huts and enclosures are sparsely distributed features of the far western littoral, and though a first-millennium chronology has been suggested for them it remains unproven. Evidence that open settlements of this type were formerly more common is indicated by timber buildings, burnt mounds and associated field systems of a permanent (but occasionally besanded) coastal settlement of the third century cal BC and later at Stackpole (Benson *et al.* 1990). That early Iron Age settlements of open, or more likely fenced, character also existed inland is indicated by timber structures of the eighth–fifth centuries cal BC in a pre-rampart context at the Broadway enclosure (Williams & Mytum 1998, 10), and a possible palisaded enclosure of 762–398 cal BC west of the enclosed farmstead at Drim (Williams & Mytum 1998, 12).

These sites apart, settlements, whether represented by earthwork or crop-mark evidence, range widely from weakly sited banjo-type and concentric antenna enclosures – both analogous to the ringforts – to a variety of univallate enclosures of sub-circular or rectilinear form. These are relatively prolific on the better quality soils of south Pembrokeshire and south Carmarthenshire and also on the sands and gravels of the lower Teifi Valley in Cardiganshire where crop-mark formation has been significant (Davies & Hogg 1994, 227) (**Figs 4.10, 4.11**). Few of these have been tested by excavation, but those which were, proved to belong to the later Iron Age. The rectilinear embanked and ditched farmstead enclosure at Penycoed, Carmarthenshire (Murphy 1985), is a good example (**Fig. 4.6**). Founded within the third century cal BC–early first century AD it comprised a single timber round-house, a series of fenced yards and a solitary four-poster within a small enclosure approached by a 50 metre long ditched and embanked 'droveway'.

An analogous type of settlement is the concentric antenna enclosure, a class of site that has been recorded only by aerial photography on better quality land, largely between Carmarthen and Haverfordwest (James 1990) (**Fig. 4.8**). These sites comprise a well-defined, ovoid, ditched inner enclosure, ranging from 45 to 85 metres in diameter, with an entrance gap linked to a much larger outer enclosure by a pair of ditches. In terms of size the inner and outer enclosures have a ratio of about 1:3, and the outer enclosure is sometimes defined by a palisade rather than a ditch. This type of site has obvious affinities to sites such as Bodringallt (Pembrokeshire), with its palisaded outer enclosure, and which has produced a second-century cal BC date (Williams & Mytum 1998, 72–3). Small, univallate rectilinear enclosures – some with sharp angles, others with a curvilinear side – are also well known in this region. The most intensively excavated examples are Merryborough Camp (Crossley 1964) and Knock Rath (Crossley 1965; 1979); both contain numerous timber round-houses and though presently lacking secure dating evidence they probably belong to the Middle to Later phases of the Iron Age. These have comparitors at Bryn Eryr, Hindwell I and Whitton (**Figs 4.6; 4.13**) and probably represent middle-ranking sites within the regional settlement spectrum.

At the apex of the non-hillfort settlement pyramid of this south-westerly region are sites such as Woodside and Dan y Coed which have been interpreted as defended high-status farms (Williams & Mytum 1998) (**Fig. 4.5**). Though very small in internal area, and morphologically analogous to farms such as Penycoed (**Fig. 4.6**) and the concentric antenna enclosures, their more substantial ramparts and ditches, four-post timber gate-towers (including a second interrupting the approach at Woodside), numerous round-houses, and developed storage function, sets them apart. These settlements – and we must include other sites such as Walesland Rath (Wainwright 1971) (**Fig. 4.6**) in this broad category – were being built in the second and first centuries cal BC, and many continued in occupation into the Roman period. The fact that some at least of these sites seem to be consumers rather than producers of agricultural produce suggests that they were elite residences and the focus of local power.

This explosion in data concerning the character and distribution of non-hillfort settlement is also graphically attested in south-east Wales. Evidence for open coastal settlements has long been known as the result of the periodic discovery of Iron Age material in sanded environments, such as at Merthyr Mawr Warren in Glamorganshire (Savory 1976b). Here the evidence suggests recurrent occupation, interrupted by episodes of besanding, and involving metalworking and possibly burial from the fourth century BC onwards to judge by the number of La Tene I brooches from the locality.

However, as far as coastal settlement is concerned it is the exciting evidence from the peat shelves of the Gwent Levels that commands attention. After a phase when this wetland was apparently not built upon, the construction of the Upton Track at Magor (770–390 cal BC) (Bell & Neumann 1997, 98), followed by evidence of settlement in the form of Middle–Later Iron Age pottery at Magor Pill (Whittle 1989) demonstrate renewed interest in a drier landscape. At Goldcliff no fewer than thirteen trackways – one dendrochronologically dated to 336–318 BC – allowed passage through this zone and connected settlements such as the remarkably preserved group of seven rectangular buildings for which fourth-century BC dendrochronological dates are available. Building 1 is the best preserved (**Fig. 4.12**). Built of roundwood and diagonal wattles, it measured 8.4 x 5.6 metres and possessed rounded corners, axial posts supporting the roof and roundwood flooring. Plank divisions suggest that its interior was divided up into animal stalls and there were large numbers of cattle hoofprints in the vicinity of Buildings 6 and 8. They are a hitherto unknown type of 'domestic' architecture in a British context (Bell & Neumann 1997, 104), but they contained no hearths and showed no sign of domestic activity. Cumulatively this suggests that these settlements are opportunistic, and represent a highly specialised wetland way of life in marked contrast to those of the third century cal BC at Glastonbury and Meare across the estuary.

Away from the wetlands the fertile soils of the the Vale of Glamorgan and the plain of Monmouth appear to have supported a large population dwelling in a great variety of enclosed settlements. As elsewhere, some, such as Mynydd Bychan (Glamorganshire) with a very small but strongly defended perimeter, and showing occupation in the second century cal BC–first century AD (Savory 1954; 1955), invite comparisons with the south-western ringforts. Other small but multivallate sites, perhaps of similar high social status, are being increasingly recognised through aerial photography, though the majority – for example Kenson Wood, Glamorganshire (**Fig. 4.13**), are enclosed by much slighter banks and ditches or fences (Driver 1995). Markedly rectilinear settlements such as Whitton and Cae Summerhouse contrast with those of curvilinear form, and where excavated have been shown to belong to the second or first centuries cal BC and later, with occupation in many instances continuing into the Romano-British period. The rectilinear, embanked and

Fig. 4.12. Rectangular Building 6 at Goldcliff, Gwent Levels. Oak planks from this building are dendrochronologically dated 273 and 271 BC. Scale 2m. (Photo: L. Boulton; Copyright: M. Bell)

ditched 0.3 hectare univallate enclosure at Whitton (Jarrett & Wrathmell 1981), apparently not established before the first quarter of the first century AD, contained between one and three timber round-houses and had a strong tower over the gate. It may be reasonably interpreted as a high-status farm (**Fig. 4.6**). Cae Summerhouse, morphologically similar but now seen to be concentric (Musson 1994, 29), and apparently with an open phase pre-dating the construction of the inner bank and ditch, also seems to have functioned as a farmstead though there is little evidence as to its internal arrangement in a pre-Roman context (Davies 1973a).

Few sites outside the Vale of Glamorgan have been tested by excavation. At Thornwell Farm near Chepstow, Late Iron Age pottery sealed beneath stone enclosure walls suggests that these were not built until very late in the prehistoric sequence, otherwise the settlement morphology is difficult to define (Hughes 1996). Similar uncertainties exist in the case of another settlement, associated with penultimate Iron Age ceramics, a La Tène III fibula and a Dobunnic coin of *c.* AD 20–30, which underlay a Romano-British agricultural settlement at Caldicot (Robinson 1988). These indicate a tendency for numerous Romano-British agricultural settlements in this region either to have been founded within the later Iron Age or to have an earlier site close by. Good examples of such exist at Llandough, where a palisade and gully on differing alignments appear to be associated with a timber round-house, and where South-Western Decorated and penultimate Iron Age pottery underlie a Romano-British villa; and also at Biglis where some structural evidence and similar ceramic range underlies another presumed villa. These instances could be multiplied many times over. Recent work, for example on a rectangular enclosure at Church Farm, Caldicot (Insole 1997) has only served to strengthen this long-recognised trend (Davies 1980).

The density attained by these late Iron Age settlements in lowland Glamorgan and Monmouthshire and the tendency for many to cluster, for example in the Waycock Valley (Driver 1995), suggest a substantive change in the settlement pattern of this rich low-lying region from the later second century BC onwards: quite simply, there is a proliferation of sites. However, it is clear that as in south-west and north-west Wales these sites need not be strictly contemporary, or for that matter all late. The late prehistoric settlement pattern in the Llawhaden district of Pembrokeshire also shows a clear pattern of successive but generally short-lived settlements, beginning with open or palisaded sites in the earliest Iron Age, followed by small bivallate forts in the Middle Iron Age and ending with the ringforts of the Late Iron Age (Williams & Mytum 1998, 140–4). Other types of non-hillfort settlement in this region – bar the stone round-hut settlements – are also late, a trend which is demonstrable for a large proportion of the farmsteads of ditched and embanked type in the other Welsh regions. Future research in these regions is also likely to reveal a pattern of settlement shift over time, even if the majority of the smaller enclosed settlements prove to date to after 200 cal BC, demonstrating a considerable expansion of settlement zones and of the population at large, possibly coupled with socio-political changes. A major challenge is also likely to be posed as far as the recognition of hitherto poorly represented Early and Middle Iron Age undefended settlements is concerned, together with an examination of the relationship, if any, that existed between overtly defensible and undefended settlements over the span of the second half of the first millennium BC.

SUBSISTENCE

Though climatic deterioration accentuated the bioclimatic diversity of the principality in the first millennium BC, it was soils, aspect and social status as well as precipitation and hours of sunshine that determined subsistence strategies. The resurgence of agrarian systems and their relative success can be measured by the capacity to support an ever-growing population, demonstrable by an increase in settlement density, even a recolonisation of landscapes which had been abandoned late in the second millennium, and the production of surpluses both for exchange and the sustenance of an elite. Mixed agriculture was obviously the norm, though the relative proportion of cereal cultivation to animal husbandry was clearly variable and there is the complicating factor of its assessment at what are considered to be 'consumer' rather than 'producer' settlements. Soil quality will obviously have rendered cereal cultivation more successful in some areas than in others, hence the distinction which has been drawn within a micro-region such as south-west Wales between the largely pastoral northern and eastern uplands and the truly mixed economy of the southern and western lowlands (Williams 1988b). This distinction is probably broadly correct, though the relative quantities of cereal evidence from lowland settlements such as Woodside and Dan y Coed, as opposed to their upland comparitors, Caer Cadwgan and Castell Henllys, does not empirically demonstrate the case.

Evidence for field systems of this period is patchy, though elements survive in several parts of Wales. The most impressive are those small, squarish relict fields, defined either by low stone walls or earthen banks and lynchets, formerly extensive but increasingly vulnerable to destruction by upland improvement schemes, on the northern and western flanks of the Snowdonia massif (RCAHMW 1956; 1960; 1964; Bowen & Gresham 1967; Crew & Musson 1996, 20–5). These appear in blocks of up to 10 hectares and are associated with a variety of stone (and probably earlier timber) settlements. At Cefn Graeanog II a lynchet and an agricultural soil pre-dating the building of a stone round-house have been dated to 2305 ± 40 BP (CAR-70) = 410–215 cal BC (Fasham *et al.* 1998, 9). In west Wales similar fields probably connected with arable use survive on Pembrey Mountain (Williams 1981) and Stackpole (Benson *et al.* 1990), with fragments elsewhere along the south Carmarthenshire and Pembrokeshire littoral; the most impressive examples are found on Skomer (**Pl. 25**) where substantial blocks of fields defined by low stone walls, or earth banks faced with drystone, grading into lynchets, survive all along the island's coastline. Here the evidence for cultivation is conclusive, though the occupation, associated with circular, stone-built houses, may have been short (Evans 1990). In the more intensively cultivated landscapes of the Welsh borders rare examples of rectilinear fields formerly survived in the vicinity of the settlement at Collfryn, while possible field systems are also associated with several lowland settlement enclosures where boundary ditches, visible as crop-marks, share a similar alignment with the enclosures, for example at Lower House, Llandysilio (Silvester & Britnell 1993). Pit alignments, such as those at Four Crosses, represent another facet of land division, but hitherto have proved difficult to date.

Evidence for plough-marks is another clear index of arable. Such are known in the sandy soil at Stackpole, while pre-rampart instances occur at two other south-western sites, Woodbarn Rath (Vyner 1986) and Drim (Williams & Mytum 1998). Not surprisingly evidence for the plough, and tools connected with arable, is thin. A rare example of a wooden ard-tip was found in the ditch at Walesland Rath (Wainwright 1971) but the scarcity of pre-Roman examples of reaping-hooks and sickles probably reflects the propensity to recycle metal rather than any absolute rarity. By way of contrast grain-processing equipment, querns and mortars – the latter being a standard piece of equipment on settlements in north-west Wales – are very common, even on settlements where environmental and other data suggests little evidence for arable, such as the farmstead at Penycoed (Murphy 1985). At Cae Summerhouse and Twyn y Gaer saddle-querns were being superseded by those of the beehive variety in late Iron Age contexts (Davies 1973a; Probert 1976).

The data pertaining to the varieties of crops grown in late prehistoric Wales indicates that the pattern is entirely consistent with evidence from contemporary settlements in other parts of southern Britain (Caseldine 1990, 75–7; Cunliffe 1991, 372–3). Cereals in the form of wheat and barley were pre-eminent, with spelt gaining clear ascendancy over emmer. The latter is considered a contaminant of the spelt crop at Woodside and Dan y Coed in the south-west, though it seems to have been the main crop at Ty Mawr (Smith

1987, 34) and equal to spelt at Bryn Eryr on Anglesey (Longley 1998, 260). Emmer was also apparently the main crop grown in the vicinity of The Breiddin and around Collfryn. Barley, of the hulled or six-rowed variety, was widely cultivated, with the exception of areas of high acidity and poor drainage. There is a major problem in assessing the frequency or absence of particular types of cereals insofar as there is inbuilt bias in the survival of some types in sampling contexts, leading to an under-representation of those crops (Fasham *et al.* 1998, 48). For instance, evidence for the cultivation of oats and rye is very small, though there is some at Penycoed; as yet there is no evidence for legumes in a Welsh context.

It is considered that crops were most likely stored in the ear in above-ground granaries of the four-, five- or six-post variety, which are ubiquitous in settlement contexts throughout Wales, the exception being the hut-group settlements of the north-west. Curiously, these post-built structures, averaging some 2–2.5 metres square for the smallest, were clearly present at other settlements in this region, for example Bryn Eryr and Llandegai (Houlder 1967), so different storage arrangements presumably prevailed. A stone-supported granary is suggested at Ty Mawr (Smith 1987, 23). It is highly probable that the nature of the commodity stored in these structures – if storage was indeed their prime function – could have varied over time and from site to site.

It was a long-held view that the dictates of topography, soils and climate would have led to the dominance of pastoralism in the subsistence strategies of late prehistoric communities in Wales (Fox 1932). While recent research has tempered this view by demonstrating the widespread incidence of arable even at high altitudes, the low density of cereal remains at many sites suggests that the economy – even in those areas where cereal cultivation is held to have had a more significant role – was still basically pastoral. High-altitude cereal-growing, such as that at Erw Wen is judged atypical and unsuited to the terrain so may have been a response to unusual pressures (Kelly 1988, 141). To complicate matters some settlements such as Woodside, though producing evidence of cereals, may have been primarily consumers rather than producers of grain, the emphasis being upon stock-raising. The result is that in most cases the character of the environmental evidence, combined with a dearth of assemblages of animal remains, particularly from sites in the west, makes it extremely difficult to assess the relative importance of arable to pastoralism.

In the absence of the remains of domesticated animals the role of pastoralism may be judged by the presence of specific features arguably designed for the control of livestock. In north-west Wales the stone-built concentric circles, such as Llwyn-du Bach (Bersu & Griffiths 1949) where one or two round-houses lie within a 26 metre diameter enclosure whose entrance is flanked by walls forming a droveway that curves round to form a roughly concentric outer enclosure of around 60 metres in diameter, are clearly corrals. The timber enclosures at Erw Wen and Moel y Gerddi are manifestly the same thing (Kelly 1988, Fig. 28). These northern examples are dwarfed by the much larger concentric antenna enclosures of south-west Wales, a region where aerial photography has played a key role in the recognition of numerous settlement outworks. These sites (**Fig. 4.13h, i**) consistently show a continuous ditch – or sometimes a palisade – linking the inner and outer enclosures (James 1990), the latter of very large size and clearly related to the management of livestock.

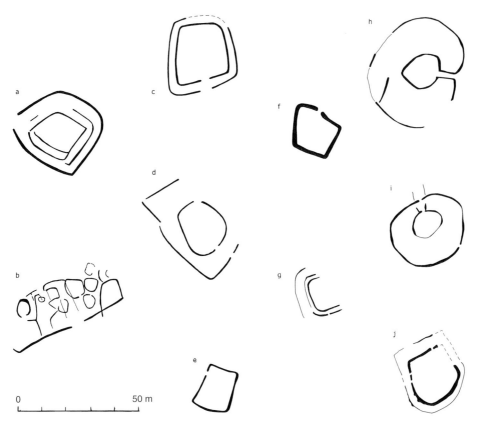

Fig. 4.13. Non-defensive enclosures as represented by cropmarks: (a) Varchoel Lane. Mont. (Copyright, RCAHME) (See Pl. 26); (b) Nr. New Hall, Llandrinio, Mont. (Copyright, RCAHMW); (c) Great Cloddiau, Kerry, Mont. (Copyright, RCAHME); (d) Henfron, Mont. (Copyright, RCAHME); (e) Hindwell I, Rads. (Copyright, Clwyd-Powys Archaeological Trust); (f) Ffynnoncyff, Ferwig, Cards. (Copyright, RCAHMW); (g) Kenson Wood, Glam. (Copyright, RCAHMW); (h) Henllan Farm II, Whitland, Pembs. (Copyright, RCAHMW); (i) Cawrence, Llechryd, Cards. (Copyright, RCAHMW); (j) Ffynnon, Tremain, Cards. (Copyright, RCAHMW). Scale 1:12500.

In south-west Wales there is a remarkable frequency of settlements which are either equipped with annexes, such as Scollock Rath, or more typically have an elongated embanked and ditched approach comparable to the 'banjo' enclosures of Wessex, which have been interpreted as an aid to the control of moving herds (Cunliffe 1991, 22–3). At the small farmstead of Penycoed the approach is some 50 metres long and terminates in ditches which begin to curve around, perhaps to an outer, concentric enclosure. The same feature is evidenced in a more elaborate form at Woodside and Dan y Coed, with an earlier fenced approach at the latter (**Fig. 4.5**). Also of some interest is the fact that there were no four-post structures in the early phases of Dan y Coed; only round-houses are evidenced, the large area free of structures being plausibly used for animal penning.

Multiple-ditched enclosures (**Pls 26** and **27**) are also common in eastern mid-Wales and the Welsh border, though no examples of the long drovewayed and concentric antenna types of settlement are known. One site, apparently unique, at New Hall, Llandrinio (**Fig. 4.13b**), consists of a group of seven ditched, ovoid enclosures, two showing entrances in close proximity to one another, and apparently defined on the west by a boundary ditch with a wide entrance gap. A stock-management role is manifest but the chronology remains unknown.

In south-eastern Wales evidence of pastoralism is largely restricted to the larger settlements such as Gaer Fawr and Y Bwlwarcau (RCAHMW 1976, Figs 30 and 33) with their concentric form and relatively slight earthworks and droveways. However, at the pre-Roman farm at Whitton (Jarrett & Wrathmell 1981) (**Fig. 4.6**) the large amounts of yardage and the presence of fence-lines, coupled with the absence of evidence for cereal cultivation prior to the conquest, suggests an overwhelmingly pastoral economy.

At the smaller end of the settlement spectrum are those examples of isolated stone-built huts and hut-groups associated with small enclosures which are to be found variously from the uplands of north-west Wales to those of Breconshire (RCAHMW 1997, 210–70) and Pembrokeshire, for example Bernard's Well Mountain (**Fig. 3.4**). These are undoubtedly pastoral settlements.

The communities who built many of the hillforts are also deemed to have considered the needs of livestock; indeed, a strong pastoral element in their economy has been advocated (Savory 1976a, Fig. 13; 1980c, 301, Fig. 6). Classic instances are those sites which either have an excessively wide interspace between the ramparts, such as Caerau, Henllan (Williams 1945), or have less well-defended pendant annexes, as at Moel Trigarn or Cefncarnedd (**Pls 19 and 22**). That annexes could also have existed in less durable form is graphically demonstrated at Twyn y Gaer where no fewer than eight successive fence alignments of an annexe were recorded prior to its translation into earthwork (Probert 1976).

Any assessment of the relative importance of differing animal species in the economy is fraught with difficulty because of the scarcity of large, well-dated bone assemblages. Occasionally the evidence is such that it does not even require bone survival, as at Goldcliff West in the Gwent Levels (Bell & Neumann 1997, 103), where the rectangular buildings not only lack hearths but are surrounded by the impressions of cattle hoofprints, indicating that seasonal grazing was an important factor in the local economy. Over much of Wales, however, such graphic evidence is irrecoverable and acid soils are inimical to the preservation of bone. When bone does survive, as at Bryn Eryr (Longley 1998), it is often a poor sample, in this instance merely indicating that cattle and sheep were being reared. Settlements on calcareous soils provide better assemblages which invite inter-site and regional comparisons. Cattle were overwhelmingly dominant at Coygan Camp (Wainwright 1967) and broadly equal in number to sheep at Dinorben (Gardner & Savory 1964) and Collfryn (Britnell 1989). By way of contrast at the very Late Iron Age settlements in south Wales, at Cae Summerhouse and Thornwell Farm, Chepstow (Hughes 1996), sheep/goat were of considerable economic significance, echoing a discernible trend in the Late Iron Age economy of southern England.

Even settlements which produce few or no animal remains testify to the significance of sheep. Spindle-whorls are a ubiquitous domestic item at the great majority of sites, while loom-weights, known at Prestatyn, The Breiddin, Castle Ditches, Llancarfan, and Biglis, attest to the production of woollen cloth.

Pigs were also relatively common and their frequency at Coygan Camp may indicate recurrent feasting. Domestic fowl were also kept, while additional protein was obtained through the hunting of a variety of game, fishing and the gathering of shellfish. Indeed recent interest in the archaeology of coastal habitats has led to the recognition of fish-traps at several sites in the Gwent Levels. At Cold Harbour Pill and Rumney Great Wharf (Rippon 1996) they are set into palaeochannels, and comprise either circular groups of posts around which wattles had been woven or double lines of posts set at right angles to the channel. Though their dating is uncertain they probably belong to the first millennium BC.

TRANSPORT AND COMMUNICATIONS

Long-established ridgeways of late Neolithic and Early Bronze Age date continued to be important through-routes on higher ground, but the more permanent and dense settlement pattern of the first millennium BC, coupled with enforced changes brought about by the increasing wetness of the climate from the later second, undoubtedly instituted far-reaching changes in transport and communication systems. Trackways, sometimes embanked, and often deeply worn by the passage of animals, are a familiar feature of the approaches to many settlements in the south-west and the Marches, such as Dan y Coed, Pembrokeshire (**Fig. 4.5**) and Varchoel Lane, Montgomeryshire (**Pl. 26**). These relics are indicative of what must have been an extensive network which formerly traversed the landscape of the later first millennium, particularly in those areas where soil quality encouraged dense settlement.

Where marshy areas had to be crossed or where opportunistic settlement sprang up in wetlands then artificial trackways had to be constructed. The known examples are restricted to the area of a former great raised bog which extended from the eastern outskirts of Cardiff to the vicinity of the Second Severn Crossing. At Goldcliff (Bell & Neumann 1997, 102–3) there is evidence for no fewer than thirteen trackways. These are a far cry from the long and massive corduroy road, designed for the passage of wheeled vehicles, at Corlea in Ireland (Raftery 1994, 98), and are more in keeping with the much earlier Sweet Track in Somerset. The Goldcliff trackways vary in scale and construction, ranging from simple brushwood bundles thrown into palaeochannels running between timber buildings, to more substantial tracks of corduroy timbers, sometimes pegged with roundwood, to a kind of cradle supporting brushwood and some planking. A dendochronological date of 336–318 BC, coupled with a range of radiocarbon dates (Bell & Neumann 1997, 98), suggest that these trackways are intimately connected with the exploitation of this wet environment in the fourth century cal BC, though the Upton Track at Magor may be earlier.

Estuaries and river valleys attracted prehistoric settlement not only because of associated fertile lowland but also because of the ease of communication by boat. In this respect the Welsh side of the Severn Estuary has provided rare evidence of later prehistoric water transport. This takes the form of planks from two sewn boats of Middle Bronze Age date from Caldicot Castle Lake and Goldcliff. The Caldicot craft, at 3439 ± 19 BP (UB-3472) = 1874–1689 cal BC the oldest yet found, was built of oak planks fastened together with yew stitching and with caulking of moss. It was narrow and relatively long but lacked a significant keel or stem (McGrail in Nayling & Caseldine 1997, 210–14). The Goldcliff boat (Bell & Neumann 1997, 105), re-used as an element of a trackway and dating to after 1017 BC on the basis of dendrochronology, was smaller but produced evidence of raised cleats. Both were probably propelled and steered by paddles. They can be compared with similar sewn-plank boats from Brigg and North Ferriby on the Humber, and as such belong to a widespread boat-building tradition in northern Europe spanning the period from around 1,500 to 800 cal BC. There is little doubt that such vessels were commonly used along the Severn Estuary and the rivers flowing into it, and were were also easily capable of making voyages across it, to judge by the widespread distribution of bronzes such as the South Welsh type of socketed axe, and of pottery of presumed West Country origin on several coastal Middle Bronze Age and Iron Age settlements in south-east Wales.

No craft belonging to the classic Iron Age is represented in the rich anaerobic archaeological deposits of the Severn Levels, though boats undoubtedly continued to be used as a common means of transport. To judge by the third century AD Barlands Farm boat (Nayling *et al.* 1994), which was bigger and equipped with a mast step clearly designed for sailing, there had been considerable advances not only in boat/shipbuilding techniques but also in propulsion by the Romano-British period. McGrail, however, suggests that such vessels stem from an earlier non-Roman tradition which was certainly manifest in Atlantic/northern English Channel waters towards the close of the first millennium BC. If bigger, estuarine (if not sea-going) vessels were indeed being built by Welsh communities by the time of the Roman conquest, then it could explain the presence of two early Roman fortlets on the north Devon coast at Old Burrow and Martinhoe (Fox & Ravenhill 1966) designed to ward off sea-borne raids by the then still unconquered Silures.

The body of evidence available for the study of land transport burgeons from the middle of the first millennium BC. It essentially takes two forms: first, evidence for the growing importance of the horse as a riding and a traction animal; secondly, evidence for wheeled transport. As a simple draught animal the humble ox was never replaced in a domestic or economic context. Doubtless the sled or cart continued to be drawn by the trained ox, as did the ard. But there is growing pan-European evidence for an enhanced status given to the horse – a semi-sacred animal – in a ceremonial and then overtly military capacity. The mounted warrior undoubtedly enjoyed high-status as did his chariot-driven equivalent.

The earliest evidence for the horse as a status-enhancing animal lies in the later Bronze Age/Earliest Iron Age transition and takes the form of bronze horse-harness and jangles of ninth-century cal BC date, and ultimately of French Urnfield origin, found at Parc-y-meirch, near the foot of the crags on which the early promontory fort of Dinorben, Denbighshire, was situated (see p. 182). Some two hundred years later bronze cheek-pieces from a horse-bit, decorative bronze discs (*phalerae*) and other items found at Llyn Fawr (**Fig. 4.16**) relate to harness of the type then fashionable in Hallstatt C contexts in eastern France and Belgium. However, with a few exceptions, such as the decorated linch-pin from Collfryn, Montgomeryshire (Britnell 1989, 26), it is only at the close of first millennium BC and the beginning of the first millennium AD that the evidence becomes more plentiful. With the exception of the chariot fittings from the Llyn Cerrig Bach deposit, including asymmetrical bits that are probably exclusive to chariot ponies and iron tyres that betoken the existence of expert wheelwrights who could shrink tyres on to wooden felloes, the evidence largely consists of linch-pins and terrets through which the reins passed from the driver's hands over the yoke of the vehicle and to the bits of the draught-ponies. Some of the latter – such as the large terret from the Lesser Garth hoard, Glamorganshire, or the terret, terminal rings for a three-link bridle-bit and strap ornament in the Seven Sisters hoard, Glamorganshire (Davies & Spratling 1976) (**Fig. 4.22**) and the comparable Chepstow strap ornament – may be richly decorated with coloured glass inlay, and in the case of the terminal rings surely relate to the practice of chariotry among the Silures at a date not far removed from the Roman invasion. Apart from these gaudy and presumably expensive items, the simple iron linch-pin with a broad, semi-circular head, from the Lesser Garth hoard (Savory 1966a, 33–4), is probably more representative of utilitarian vehicle fitments on carts and wagons whose passage across the landscape would require at least some investment in the upkeep of trackways.

ARTEFACTS

Introduction: Metalwork Contexts

Before discussing the metalwork itself we should consider the context of deposition of metal objects, particularly of the larger and increasingly common hoards of the Late Bronze Age. A hoard may be defined as a group of objects found together under circumstances suggesting deliberate deposition at one time, hidden perhaps in the hope of recovery, or simply abandoned or renounced as an act of sacrifice or propitiation. A guide to the motives of such deposition may lie in the content of the hoard and its location. Varied objects of value hidden beneath some marker are normally interpreted as 'personal hoards', the private property of an individual. The razor, beads and harness from Llangwyllog, Anglesey, may be an example (Lynch 1991, 242). Multiple copies of tools, such as the socketed axes, several from the same mould, from St Mellons, Glamorganshire, may be recognised as the stock in trade of a merchant (Stanton 1984b). Large quantities of broken implements, often cut up into small pieces for remelting, have been categorised as scrap hoards. The large hoard from Guilsfield, Montgomeryshire, which contains many broken pieces as well as an unsuccessful spearhead casting, is a well-known Welsh example (Davies 1967) (**Fig. 4.14**).

Such explanations are utilitarian and rational and in many cases must be true. However, a surprisingly large number of metalwork hoards, especially those containing weapons or other specialised equipment, are found in bogs and other wet locations. These have been interpreted as offerings to deities (Bradley 1990). The votive interpretation is reinforced by the difficulty of retrieving objects thrown into water, by the deliberate damage or decommissioning of the weapons and by the often exclusively military or high-status/high-value nature of the material (**Pl. 28**).

The practice of wetland deposition is certainly at its peak in the Late Bronze Age, when hoards such as Broadward and Pant y Maen, containing swords and specialised spearheads (Burgess, Coombs & Davies 1972), and Parc-y-Meirch with fine harness and horse bones (Sheppard 1941) are good examples. It continues, however, into the Iron Age with the famous Llyn Fawr deposit from an upland lake in Glamorgan, dating from the beginning of the period (**Pl. 28**; **Fig. 4.16**), and the collections of parade gear from Llyn Cerrig Bach, Anglesey, and Tal y Llyn, Merioneth (**Fig. 4.21**), from the end, when there was a renaissance in ritual activity.

Hoards are important in chronological argument because the objects in them should be closely contemporary. Where hoards can be confidently identified as merchants' stock or personal belongings this is self-evident. Scrap hoards, however, are likely to contain obsolete pieces while votive hoards, where the shrine probably received offerings over a long period, are much less secure bases for chronology.

In the Later Bronze Age the custom of placing personal belongings with the dead was in decline. Relatively few objects are found in graves of the period, which themselves are rare (Burgess 1976). Graves are equally rare in the Iron Age but there are some important pieces, notably the Cerrig y Drudion bowl (Ellis Davies 1929, 85–9) (**Fig. 4.17**), and some small personal ornaments from burials (Murphy 1992). To these contexts may be added a few significant settlements where tools, personal ornaments and even broken weapons have been found. For the Late Bronze Age the most important finds are those from The Breiddin, where a socketed axe, a socketed knife and hammer, several pins and half a bronze bracelet, and fragments of a spearhead and two swords have come from well-stratified contexts (Musson 1991, 132–8).

Hillforts like The Breiddin and Twyn y Gaer (Probert 1976) and prosperous farmsteads like Collfryn (Britnell 1989) have also produced evidence for Iron Age equipment but, considering the scale and length of occupation, the quantity and range of material is usually disappointing because iron was so assiduously recycled (Crew 1995, 276). The recent publication of The Breiddin provides a convenient summary of a typical range of such equipment (Musson 1991, 138–72).

Late Bronze Age Metalwork

The history of the Late Bronze Age industries of Wales may be divided into two strands: weapons and tools. Weapons become increasingly common, reflect introduced styles and attitudes and may be the products of a separate group of smiths using distinctive raw materials and technology (Northover 1982; 1984). The tools on the other hand reflect a growing regionalism in which local preferences in products and design are dominant. The widespread use of the Ewart Park sword, for instance, contrasts with the limited distribution of the South Welsh socketed axe.

The dichotomy between weapons and tools is seen most clearly in Late Bronze Age I when weapons belonging to the Wilburton Complex first appear in Wales, notably in the Marches and the Severn Valley (Savory 1958). A new programme of radiocarbon dating on wooden spear or tool handles shows that this new tradition begins in the mid-eleventh century cal BC (Needham *et al.* 1997). This industry, which is centred in the south-east of

(Opposite) *Fig. 4.14. Selection of bronze tools and weapons from the Guilsfield hoard, Mont. (after Savory 1980b). 1,6 lunate-opening spears; 2,5,7 hollow-bladed spears; 3,4 complex-sectioned spears (note decoration on 4); 8, 9, 11 late palstaves; 10 socketed axe; 12, 13 spear ferrules; 14, 16–19 tongue chapes; 15 rectangular chape; 20 hilt and blade of 'Wilburton' sword; 21, 22 socketed gouges; 23, 24, ingots; 25 faulty spear casting; 26 casting jet. Scale 1:4.*

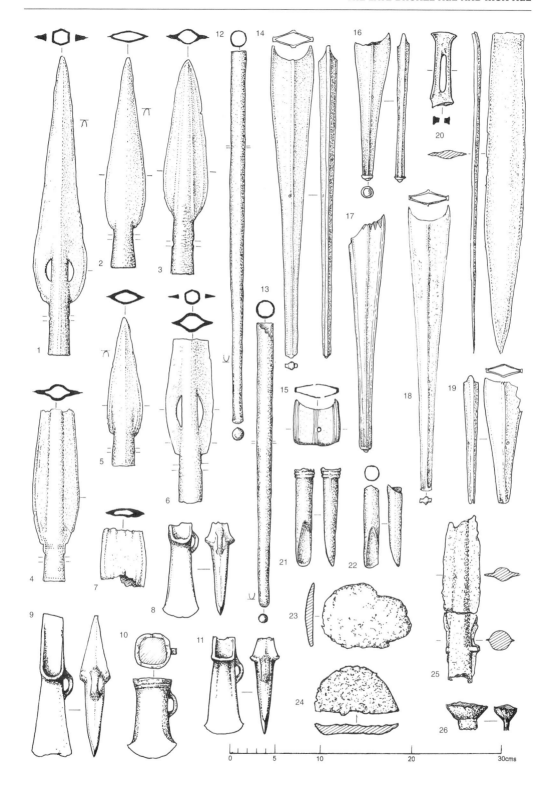

England, uses copper ore imported from central Europe and adds a very high percentage of lead to the mix, probably to facilitate their characteristically thin castings (Northover 1982, 59–63). This technology suggests a more easterly European connection than the Atlantic contacts of the Penard phase but the most conspicuous products are still weapons, especially spearheads found in very large numbers and great variety alongside broad, markedly leaf-shaped swords (Burgess 1968a).

The Welsh hoard which best reflects this period is the large assemblage of scrap found outside Gaer Fawr hillfort at Guilsfield in the Severn Valley (Davies 1967). Among the 120 pieces are broad sword blades, tongue chapes (scabbard covers), straight spear ferrules and many spearheads, including distinctive hollow-bladed and lunate-opening types. Alongside these weapons are examples of the local tools, with gouges and light narrow-bladed palstaves predominating. This metalwork is obviously being made at Guilsfield and there are several other hoards from the Marches containing similar equipment – Willow Moor, Bishops Castle, Broadward (Burgess, Coombs & Davies 1972, 240–3) – but in the rest of Wales this material is rare. Only at the very end of its currency does it reach the west, when swords and spears were thrown into the bog at Pant y Maen near Newcastle Emlyn (Griffiths 1957).

The succeeding industrial phase, Ewart Park, covering the ninth and eighth centuries cal BC, sees a realignment of the metal trade towards the Atlantic regions where its eponymous sword type – the Carp's Tongue sword – is most frequently found (Burgess 1968a; Northover 1982, 65–7). In Wales weapons, especially spears, seem to become less important and local industries, most clearly defined at this time, concentrate on making tools. Another traditional contact reawakened at this time is trade with Ireland which seemingly had languished during the Middle Bronze Age.

Four regional industries may be recognised in Wales, those in the north west and the south east being the most sharply defined (Burgess 1980a, 271–3). In the north west the Great Orme tradition is characterised by a strong preference for palstaves, many of them, like those from Llangefni and in the hoard from Bodwrog, Anglesey, being exceptionally massive (Lynch 1991, 366–8). The handle of a gouge from the Bodwrog hoard has a radiocarbon date of 2,720 ± 45 BP (OxA-4652) = 990–800 cal BC (Needham *et al.* 1997, 72). Weapons are relatively common but the Great Orme hoard itself exemplifies the other ingredient: the goldwork and other trade goods passing between Ireland and northern Europe (Savory 1958, 56).

The majority of these fine pieces come from Anglesey: gold bracelets and 'lock-rings' from Gaerwen (**Pl. 30**) and Beaumaris; Baltic amber beads, then fashionable in Ireland, from the personal hoard from Llangwyllog and among the metalworker's stock at Ty Mawr, Holyhead (Lynch 1991, 239–49). Finds from further east, such as the harness hoard from Parc-y-Meirch, Dinorben (Sheppard 1941), and the gold decorated shale boat/bowl from Caergwrle (Green 1985a), belong to this same traffic, bringing exotic objects from both east and west. However, finds of strap-like bracelets in bronze and gold (**Fig. 4.23**), together with a small gold ingot in two instances (Green 1983; Aldhouse-Green & Northover 1996b), demonstrate that there is a notable non-Irish element in the goldwork, which may be local (Eogan 1994, 84–5; *contra* Northover 1995, 527).

South-west Wales has surprisingly little metalwork of this period and the industry in the north east is eclectic. The customers, who included those living at The Breiddin, where the charred handle of a characteristic ribbed axe gave a radiocarbon date of 2,704 ± 50 BP (BM 798) = 940–800 cal BC (Musson 1991, 137), normally preferred socketed axes to palstaves but the styles chosen are heterogeneous (Ehrenburg 1989). A hoard found at Gwernymynydd near Mold (Grenter 1989), containing palstaves, socketed axes and a bronze mould for a socketed axe, epitomises this variety.

In the south east, by contrast, it is the uniformity of the socketed axes made and used there which defines the territory. The South Welsh axe is a very distinctive though rather shoddy product, one of several regional types of ribbed axe. It is characterised by its high-set loop and lack of a true collar, the three (often converging) ribs springing from directly below the rough cornice-like lip (**Fig. 4.16**). These axes occur plentifully in several hoards from Monmouthshire and Glamorgan, often as multiple copies from the same mould (Stanton 1984b). The largest single group, however, comes from Stogursey, Somerset (Needham 1981) where the type may have originated, for the Cornish Gwithian axes, which are very similar but longer and more slender, seem to be rather earlier (Schmidt & Burgess 1981, 173–5).

The distribution of the type within Wales is heavily concentrated in the south east and it has been suggested that it may reflect a tribal territory (Savory 1958, 49; Burgess 1980a, 249). Recent finds, however, have extended the distribution northwards to the Severn Valley and westwards to Ysbytty Ystwyth, Myddfai and Pembrokeshire, but the predominance of the south east is maintained (Briggs & Williams 1997).

The popularity of the South Welsh axe did not survive much beyond 800 cal BC when the next industrial phase, associated with the appearance of new weapons and a renewed eastern metallurgical link begins (Northover 1982, 67). As with the earlier Wilburton swords and spears it is possible that this continentally derived Hallstatt C material reflects social and political changes which were of greater significance than the more easily recorded industrial reorientation. Alongside the specifically Hallstatt swords, harness and razors – all masculine attributes which might hint at raiders – there are some distinctive tools such as large rib-and-pellet axes and socketed sickles like those in the Cardiff and Llyn Fawr hoards (Nash Williams 1933a; Fox 1939) (**Fig. 4.16**). Apart from these two hoards, finds from this period are rare; they include a bronze Gundlingen sword from Brogyntyn near Oswestry, dress pins from Moel Hiraddug and Ffridd Faldwyn, and a razor from Dinorben (Savory 1976a, 20–1). It is interesting that many of these objects come from early hillforts.

The Llyn Fawr hoard has given its name to the period because of the fine Hallstatt sword, made of iron, which was found in the lake (**Fig. 4.16**). This is one of the earliest identifiable appearances of the new metal in Britain and it marks a horizon of great importance. Two other iron objects, a spear and a socketed sickle, were also found. They indicate a substantial use of the new malleable but never molten metal. However, the adoption of designs better suited to cast bronze shows that iron-working was not yet fully understood (Avery 1993, 101). The Llyn Fawr hoard, however, is not an ideal chronological marker because it must be a votive deposit and may represent offerings made over a long period.

Two bronze cauldrons which were obviously old when they were placed in Llyn Fawr must have been made long before 800 cal BC, the generally accepted date for the arrival of

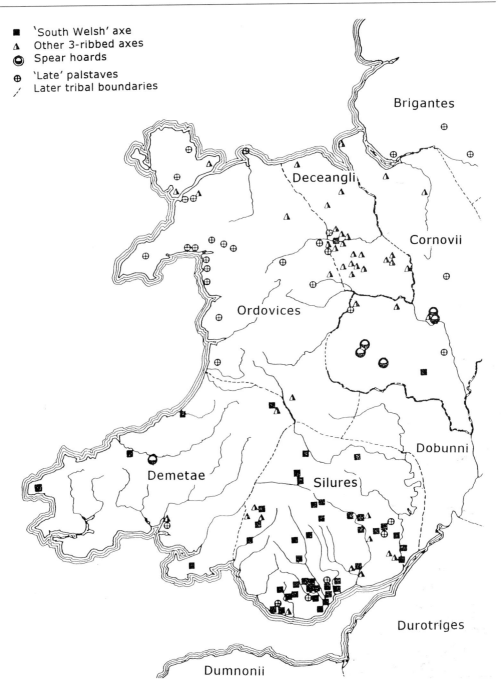

■ 'South Welsh' axe
△ Other 3-ribbed axes
◉ Spear hoards
⊕ 'Late' palstaves
⟋ Later tribal boundaries

Brigantes

Deceangli

Cornovii

Ordovices

Demetae

Silures

Dobunni

Dumnonii

Durotriges

Fig. 4.15. Map of Late Bronze Age metalwork and later tribal areas in Wales. From Burgess 1980. More recent discoveries maintain this pattern.

(Opposite) *Fig. 4.16. Llantwit Major, Glam: spears, late palstave, South Welsh and other socketed axes, sickle. Cyncoed, Glam: late palstave and South Welsh axe. Llyn Fawr, Glam., part of votive deposit from the lake: Rib-and-pellet axes, Hallstatt razor and horse harness, socketed gouges, iron spearhead, socketed sickles (2 bronze, 1 iron), iron Hallstat sword (not found on same occasion as the rest). (After Savory 1980b and* Archaeologia *vol 71). Scale 1:4.*

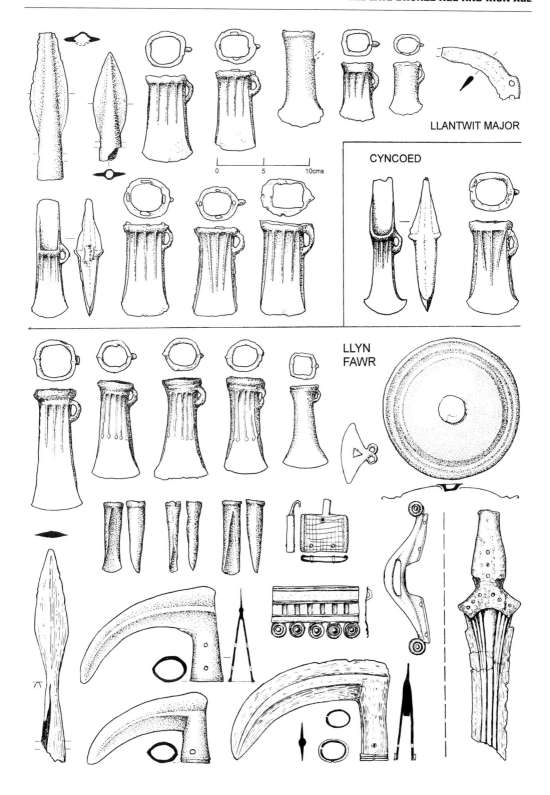

LLANTWIT MAJOR

CYNCOED

LLYN
FAWR

Fig. 4.17. The 'Arthog Bucket', a 'Kurd bucket' judged to be an imported piece. (Photo: by permission of the National Museum of Wales)

(Below) *Fig. 4.18. One of the two cauldrons from Llyn Fawr votive deposit. (Photo: by permission of the National Museum of Wales)*

Hallstatt C material. Cauldrons made from rivetted sheets of bronze belong to a class of ceremonial equipment related to feasting and hospitality, central to the cohesion of the chief and his warband. Wales has produced one of the earliest British examples of the impressive metal containers from which this tradition sprang. This is the Arthog bucket from Merioneth, a deceptively simple piece which is a *tour de force* of skilful shaping (Hawkes & Smith 1957; Briggs 1987). The strap handles and separate base plates suggest it was an import from central Europe; it was an influential piece in the development of the native series which combined the bucket shape with the handle system preferred for cauldrons. Scrap from these cauldrons, usually the substantial cast handles, begins to appear in hoards of Wilburton type (*c*. 1,100 cal BC) (Burgess 1979b; Needham *et al*. 1997) and the cauldrons themselves have often been found in Irish bogs or British rivers where they are difficult to date. Those from Llyn Fawr are the only Welsh examples, and their apparent association with rib-and-pellet axes (Schmidt & Burgess 1981, 244–6) and the like suggests the type was long-lived, as does a new radiocarbon date from Broom, Warwickshire (Needham *et al*. 1997, 98).

Three bronze shields, one from a bog near Harlech, one from the slopes of Moel Siabod, Snowdonia, and the third from Rhyd y Gors near Aberystwyth, belong to this same tradition of aristocratic equipment offered to the gods. They are far too thin to give any protection in battle and must be parade pieces. Twenty-nine other examples have been found in similar votive circumstances across Britain (Coles 1962; Needham 1979c). A recent excavation find of a Yetholm-type shield very like the Harlech one, from South Cadbury, Somerset, reinforces the idea that these fine pieces were deliberately sacrificed (Coles *et al*. 1999).

The arrival of iron must have seriously disrupted and changed the economics of the metal industry which was arguably already in trouble, for metal of any kind is exceptionally rare for the first three or four centuries of the Iron Age (Northover 1984). The new metal, iron, has a different origin and a different technology; the ores have a different distribution (in Wales bog ores may have been exploited) and the methods of smelting and final implement manufacture demand different skills: prehistoric iron cannot be cast in moulds but must be hammered and welded to shape. The means by which this new knowledge and skill was spread is still obscure (Alexander 1981) but the apprenticeship of a blacksmith is a long one. Bronze, however, did not become valueless overnight. Throughout the Iron Age it remained the medium of decoration and display, but everyday life, charted through the chance discovery of tools and domestic equipment, is no longer so well illuminated, for iron must have been regularly recycled and moreover does not survive well in the ground. In the Iron Age, in contrast to the Bronze Age, chance finds of axes, for instance, are exceptionally rare, though the tool must have been equally common in use.

Fine Metalwork: Background and Context

In the late fifth and early fourth centuries cal BC the distinctive art style known as La Tène developed in the region north of the Alps – a fusion of three traditional styles with a background in Late Bronze Age and Hallstatt art, exotic and fabulous Scythian forms and the proto-classicism of Etruscan metalwork imported from south of the Alps (Megaw &

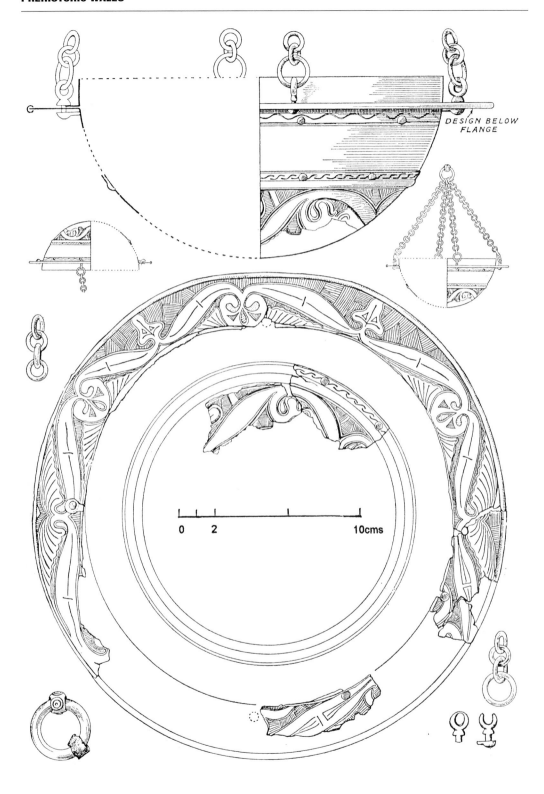

DESIGN BELOW
FLANGE

0   2   10cms

Megaw 1989). This La Tène style became the emblem of Iron Age elites all over Europe, where regional sub-styles developed through the stimulus of imported exemplars, possibly arriving as gifts between chiefs.

In Wales the bronze hanging bowl or jar cover from a grave at Cerrig y Drudion, Denbighshire (**Fig. 4.19**), is an example of such an early piece, normally reckoned to be an import probably of early third-century cal BC date (Stead 1982). Its rim is decorated in the rather stiff Waldalgeshiem Style – the earliest widespread form of this art. Other early pieces from Wales are small personal ornaments, 'safety pin' brooches with a humped bow from Moel Hiraddug, Flintshire, and Merthyr Mawr Warren in Glamorgan, and bracelets from Coygan Camp, Carmarthenshire (Brassil *et al.* 1982; Savory 1976b, 105, 106) (**Fig. 4.23, 18**). More significant is the mould from Worm's Head, Gower, used for making knobbed beads in French early La Tène style which has been claimed as evidence for the adoption of the new style by local craftsmen (Savory 1974).

Iron Age bronzework is almost exclusively of aristocratic type and reflects an image of heroic chiefs who rode in chariots armed with glistening equipment and rewarded their followers with generous and elegant hospitality. Surprisingly little of this fine material is from settlement sites; most comes instead from votive sites. The hillforts, assumed to be the residences of the chiefs, have produced little. Shield fittings from the ditch at Moel Hiraddug and torcs from Pen coed foel, Cardiganshire and Tre'r Ceiri, Caernarfonshire, are relevant, but little is known of their contexts within the forts (Ellis Davies 1949, 100–6; Savory 1976b, 61; Hughes 1907). A few pieces, such as the enamelled terret from Lesser Garth (Savory 1966a), come from near caves – perhaps domestic, perhaps workshops – and some fragments have been found at farm settlements, such as the decorated linch-pin from Collfryn, Montgomeryshire (Britnell 1989).

Iron Age Weapons and Decorative Metalwork

High-status Iron Age metalwork from Wales consists mainly of decorative items made of bronze. In contrast to the Late Bronze Age, Iron Age weapons are surprisingly rare. Only at Llyn Cerrig Bach (see p. 214) is there any quantity of functional iron weaponry: swords, daggers and spears. Among the swords, which are perforce much simpler in design than bronze ones, are narrow blades dating from perhaps the third–second centuries cal BC and broader ones of probable first century AD date, a good indication of the longevity of this shrine. Part of a simple iron dagger was found at The Breiddin (Musson 1991, 144) but other hillforts and settlement sites have produced few weapons.

More widespread is parade gear, especially the fittings from long oval shields, and the accoutrements of horses and chariots. These come from a variety of contexts, including votive deposits, caves and settlements. This variety would suggest a genuine use in the real world but it remains difficult to imagine an effective chariot charge over the rocky terrain of Anglesey, despite the evidence for twenty-two chariot wheels among the Llyn Cerrig Bach deposit.

(Opposite) *Fig. 4.19. Cerrig y Drudion bowl (from* Antiquaries Journal *1926). Scale 1:2, alternative reconstructions at a smaller scale.*

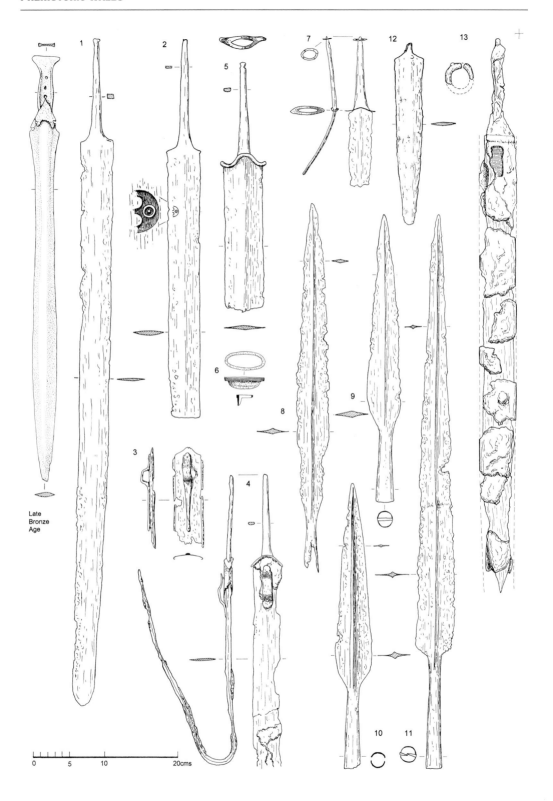

Late
Bronze
Age

0   5   10   20cms

The known British parade shields have decorative bronze covers to the hand grip ('shield boss') and pelta-shaped sheets of decorated bronze nailed on either side. Llyn Cerrig Bach, Moel Hiraddug and Tal y Llyn included other thin embossed plaques which may also have been attached to shields, or perhaps to the superstructure of a chariot (Savory, 1976c) (**Figs 4.21; 4.22**).

Harness for either driven or ridden horses is represented by three-link and single-piece bits from Llyn Cerrig Bach, Chepstow, Hengwm (Merioneth) and among the late hoard – probably Silurian loot – from Seven Sisters, Glamorgan (Fox 1946; Trett 1988; Bowen & Gresham 1967, 175; Davies & Spratling 1976). The Seven Sisters hoard of native harness and Roman military fittings belongs to the final years of conflict with Rome and includes several enamelled or glass-inlaid pieces (**Fig. 4.20**). The strap link from Chepstow and the exceptionally fine terret from Lesser Garth are other examples of enamelling used on impressive horse gear (Savory 1966a).

The social hierarchy of chiefs and followers was cemented by the distribution of favours and hospitality; consequently equipment for feasting looms large in the archaeological record: in graves in some regions and among votive offerings. The early bowl or jar cover from Cerrig y Drudion and the late enamelled one found on the slopes of Snowdon (Savory 1976b, 43, 62) may be seen in this light, as also the large bronze-covered wooden tankard from Trawsfynydd and the decorative iron firedog from Capel Garmon, both single finds from bogs (Savory 1968) (**Fig. 4.19; Pls 31** and **32; Fig. 4.27**). The handle from Porth Dafarch, Anglesey, and the rim binding from the hillfort on Penmaenmawr show that such tankards might have been in use in establishments of differing social status (Corcoran 1952; Webster 1975); just as the bronze mirror from Llechwedd du is evidence of wealth and sophistication in Merioneth (Bowen & Gresham 1967, 174).

Expressions of corporate rather than personal wealth in iron may be recognised at Llyn Cerrig Bach where two slave-gang chains, themselves of considerable value, hint at the source of much of this wealth. The four currency bars or trade iron from the same deposit are the only bars yet found in Wales, despite evidence for iron-making in the region. In the south of England several hoards of such bars in later hillforts reflect the communities' wealth in high-quality raw materials and the increasing availability of iron towards the end of the period (Crew 1994). At Llyn Cerrig Bach blacksmiths' tools were also offered along with several fragments of bar iron, an indication of the high status of this essential craft and the perceived value of the material (**Fig. 4.26**).

The decoration on the various fine bronzes may be used as an indication of date and also as a clue to the vigour of local workshops and the direction of their contacts and inspiration. However, such discussions are beset with difficulty because of the lack of firmly dated archaeological contexts and the essential subjectivity of stylistic debate.

(Opposite) *Fig. 4.20. Iron Age weapons. Late Bronze Age sword (Ewart Park type) for comparison of length. 1–4 narrow swords and scabbards. Armourer's mark on 2; 5–6 wider sword and scabbard fitting; 7 dagger; 8–11 spearheads (1–11 are all from Llyn Cerrig Bach, Anglesey); 12 dagger from The Breiddin, Mont; 13 sword in scabbard from burial at Gelliniog Wen, Anglesey. (From Lynch 1991 and Musson 1991). Scale 1:5.*

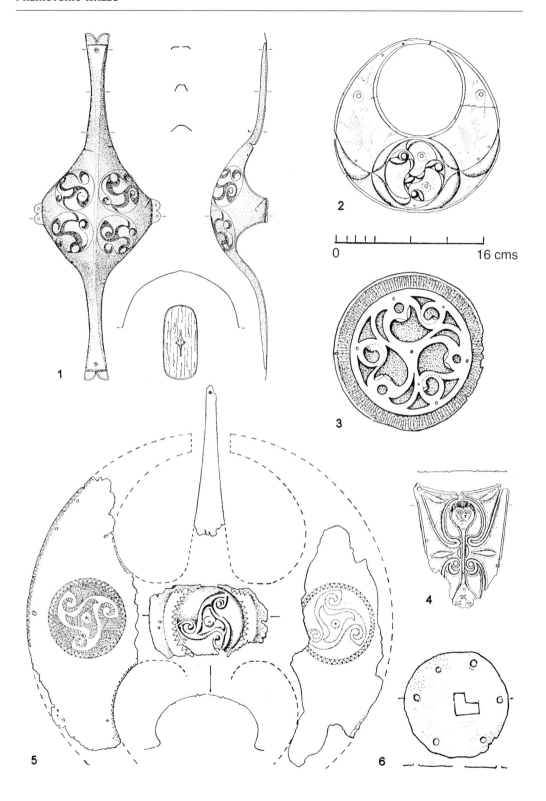

0   16 cms

Serious discussion of the Welsh La Tène material began in 1943 with the discovery of the Llyn Cerrig Bach deposit, the foundation of Sir Cyril Fox's wide-ranging study of British art, *Pattern and Purpose* (1958) in which he placed the Anglesey pieces at the beginning of the confident 'insular' style, but argued that they were made elsewhere, probably in southern England. Later discoveries led Dr Savory to re-examine this premise and to argue for an early and independent school of Welsh metalworking, producing fine parade shields decorated with elegant triskeles, using a characteristic 'rocked tracer infill' to define engraved patterns (Savory 1965; 1968; 1971b, 64–75; 1976b, 28–37; 1976c). This view has not won universal acceptance, largely because of the very uncertain date of the crucial Tal y Llyn hoard – a mixed votive deposit which contains material certainly of Roman origin (**Fig. 4.21**).

More recent surveys of British Iron Age art (Stead 1985; Megaw & Megaw 1989) vary in their view of the point at which British art branches out from continental exemplars but are in broad agreement in acknowledging the precocious position of the Cerrig y Drudion fragments at about 300 cal BC, and follow Fox in his view of the key position of the Llyn Cerrig Bach pieces which they date to about 100 cal BC, a later horizon than some other scholars would favour. Megaw places Tal y Llyn firmly in the first century AD because of the use of brass and of compasses in the layout, pointing out that the triskele motif and basketry backgrounds are a long-lived fashion (Megaw & Megaw 1989, 226; Dungworth 1996, 409–10). Stylistic dating and the chronology of votive hoards are both so fraught with difficulty that Stead declines to mention Tal y Llyn at all. While most writers agree that the introduction of red glass inlay occurs in the mid-first century AD there is some dispute about which of the Late Celtic pieces truly belong to a pre-Roman horizon in Wales.

The question of regional schools of metalwork, much discussed by both Fox and Savory, has receded from the debate, but on-going work on metal analysis of both copper alloy (Northover in Lynch 1991) and iron (Salter & Ehrenreich 1984) may soon revive this issue. Analysis of the copper in the Cerrig y Drudion bowl is consistent with a continental (Breton) origin and Fox's south-western links have been confirmed for some at least of the Llyn Cerrig Bach material, though locally made iron is also in evidence (Northover in Lynch 1991, 392–3).

The palmettes on the Cerrig y Drudion bowl have a rather laboured symmetry which betrays its origin in the continental Waldalgesheim style (**Fig. 4.19**). The piece comes from a long cist discovered without detailed record in 1924 (Ellis Davies 1929, 85–9). Recent excavations in the same field failed to locate the findspot but have revealed the remains of a prehistoric round-house (Brassil 1992) (see p. 165). The historical context of the bowl remains difficult to assess since its early date and exotic origin cause it to stand in perplexing isolation.

All the other fine pieces belong to the freer Insular style, dubbed Style V by Stead (1985, 21–3), and show the preference for balance over symmetry which finds its ideal expression

(Opposite) *Fig. 4.21. Earlier decorative material. 1, 2 shield boss and crescentic plaque from Llyn Cerrig Bach, Anglesey. 3–6 from Tal y Llyn, Merioneth. 3 openwork tinned plaque with bronze backing; 4 trapezoid plaque; 5 shield boss with pelta-shaped plaques 6 Roman lock plate (from Lynch 1991 and Savory 1980b). Scale 1:4.*

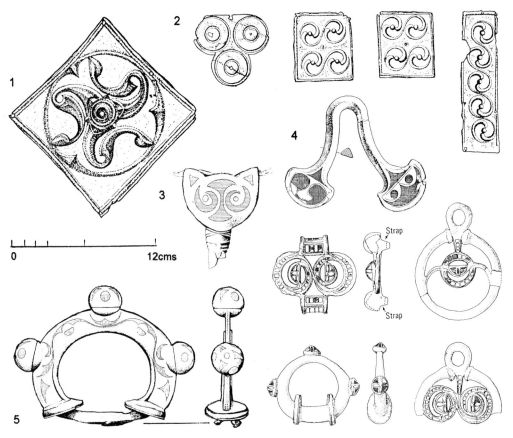

Fig. 4.22. Later decorative material. 1 Moel Hiraddug plaque, Flints; 2 stamped plaques from Llyn Cerrig Bach, Ang; 3 Red enamelled handle from a bowl from Snowdon; 4 enamelled (red and yellow glass) harness from Seven Sisters hoard, Glam. 5 Red enamelled terret from Lesser Garth, Pentyrch, Glam. (from Savory 1980b and Lynch 1991). Scale 1:3.

in the triskele. These three-legged patterns may be created by either repoussé-work or engraving and it is a characteristic of this style that several techniques may be used on the same piece – as on the Tal y Llyn shield fittings (**Fig. 4.21**). Hatching using a rocked tracer tool has been claimed as especially characteristic of a North Welsh school, but it is not an exclusive trait. The plump triskele on the crescentic plaque from Llyn Cerrig Bach, with its lobed ends like puffin heads and its sinuous 'trumpet voids', is generally quoted as the

(Opposite) *Fig. 4.23. Late Bronze Age and Iron Age personal ornaments. 1–8 Pins in bronze and iron: 1–3 The Breiddin, Mont; 4, 5, 7 Dinorben, Denbs; 6 Merthyr Mawr Warren, Glam; 8 Rhuddlan, Flints; 9–11 Late Bronze Age bracelets: 9 Llanarmon yn Iâl, Denbs (gold); 10 Ty Mawr hoard, Ang (bronze); 11 The Breiddin (bronze); 12–14 Early La Tène brooches: 12 Moel Hiraddug, Flints; 13–14 Merthyr Mawr Warren; 15–17 Late La Tène brooches: 15 Glyn, Ang; 16 Lligwy, Ang; 17 Sudbrook, Mon; 18 La Tène bracelet: Coygan Camp, Carm; 19 blue and white glass beads, Garn Boduan, Caerns; 20 Glass bangle, Crawcwellt, Mer; 21 bronze decorated bead, The Breiddin; 22 glass beads: Collfryn, Mont; Walesland Rath, Pembs and Abersoch, Caerns; 23 silver-gilt brooch, Carmarthen. (From Musson 1991, Lynch 1991, Savory 1976a, Britnell 1989 and Green 1983.) Scale 1:2.*

194

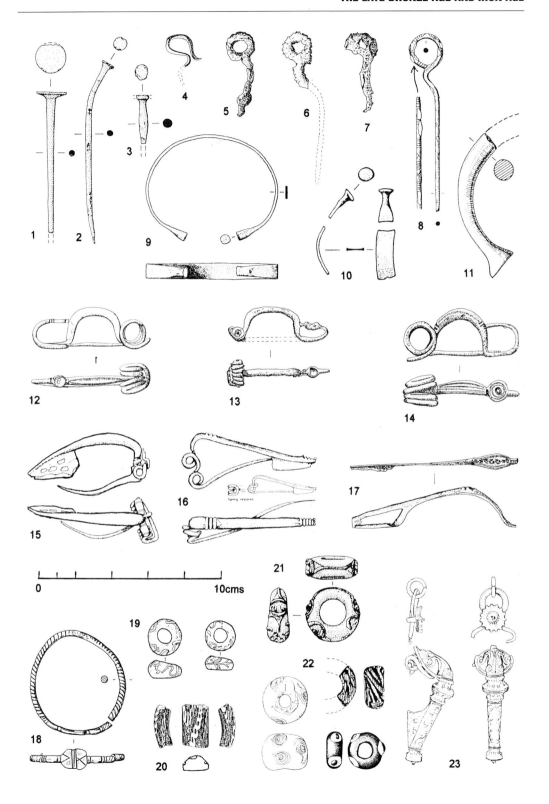

quintessence of this style which becomes more emaciated in later examples such as the Moel Hiraddug plaque (**Fig. 4.22**) and the well-known series of mirrors from graves in southern England which can be dated to about 50 cal BC–50 AD (Fox 1958).

The much-disputed Tal y Llyn hoard contains the metal fittings of two shields (one with a rather formal triskele, the other with a lyre pattern), two openwork discs with a looser triskele design created by compass work, and two trapezoid plaques with a fleshy leaf design between two opposed heads. These plaques are in a mix of zinc and copper – a true brass rather than bronze (Dungworth 1996, 409–10). Zinc occurs naturally in some Welsh copper (Musson *et al.* 1992) but its value in Tal y Llyn is higher and must be a deliberate alloy. Moreover the presence of a Roman lock-plate (Spratling 1966) indicates a first-century AD date for some of the pieces, though others could have been old when deposited. The faces on the Tal y Llyn plaques are unusually simple. More typical of the La Tène taste for the fantastic and teasing is the grotesque animal face on the fragment of harness from Chepstow (Trett 1988).

A clearer chronological horizon can be seen with the introduction of red champlevé enamel or glass inlay work in the mid-first century AD. This technique is derived from south-eastern England with which contacts were certainly increasing in the late Iron Age. It is possible that pieces such as the Snowdon bowl (**Fig. 4.22; Pl. 31**), with a cat face in red enamel on the handle and a spun body, may have been actually made in the south, but the enamelwork terret from Lesser Garth is believed to be of local manufacture (Savory 1966a). The Capel Garmon firedog, though the only Welsh example of a type far more common in southern England, cannot be an import because it is so much more baroque than any from the south or from northern France (Piggott 1971) (**Fig. 4.27**). Southern English artistic influence therefore was being absorbed by creative local craftsmen.

A further refinement of the enamelling technique reached south Wales during the period of Roman conquest – polychrome enamel with white, yellow and blue inlay as seen in the Seven Sisters hoard and on the Chepstow strap link (Davies & Spratling 1976; Savory 1976b, Plate V). This technique does not seem to have reached the north, but some of the latest pieces deposited in Llyn Cerrig Bach, the series of die-stamped scroll plaques (Fox 1946, 21), show the rather dull mechanical uniformity which contact with Rome was casting over the previously sparkling Iron Age decorative arts.

Personal Ornament

The metal collar or torc is believed to have denoted high rank in Iron Age society since several deities are shown with such neck rings. In the absence of rich graves it is not surprising that they are rare in Wales. In the nineteenth century a knobbed one was found at Clynnog, Caernarfonshire, and part of a flat decorated collar was ploughed up within the hillfort of Pen coed Foel, Cardiganshire (Savory 1976b, 56, 62). A later type, dating to the Roman period but reflecting older fashions, was found within the great fort at Tre'r Ceiri (Hughes 1907).

Amber was the fashionable material for beads in the Late Bronze Age but thereafter glass – rare and expensive throughout Britain, where only two manufacturing sites are known (Cunliffe 1991, 461) – was the preferred material. Beads have been found on a number of settlement sites where it is often difficult to know whether they belong to the

Iron Age or to the Roman period when such small personal luxuries became much more widely available. Blue glass beads with white trail ornament have been found at Walesland Rath, Sudbrook, Collfryn, Breiddin and Garn Boduan, all sites occupied both in the Iron Age and the Roman period (Guido 1978; Musson 1991, 158–60).

The most closely dated glass ornaments are the fragments of blue and green bangles from two iron-working sites in Merioneth, Bryn y Castell and Crawcwellt (Crew 1989). The nature of the white trailed decoration marvered flush with the body of the bangle distinguishes these from the more common Romano-British types, and the context at Bryn y Castell, where occupation of the hillfort ceased with the Roman conquest, confirms an Iron Age date, though the place of manufacture remains unknown. In the Late Bronze Age bracelets had usually been of gold.

Brooches of 'safety pin' design replaced the straight pin as a clothes fastener in the early La Tene period. Pins were worn at The Breiddin hillfort in the Late Bronze Age (Musson 1991, 135–6) but at Moel Hiraddug the 'humped' La Tène style brooch was preferred. By the first century AD brooches are rather more common and more streamlined (Stead 1985, 26). Finds from Anglesey and north Wales of La Tène III types fashionable in south-east England would seem to confirm Tacitus' statement about refugees from that region in the island (Lynch 1991, 380). Normally the brooches are of bronze or copper alloy, but may be of iron, like those from the Breiddin (Musson 1991, 142–4). The exceptionally fine 'trumpet' brooch in silver gilt from Carmarthen is believed to be of local manufacture, perhaps using gold from Dolaucothi. Like the Tre'r Ceiri beaded torc and decorated brooch, it suggests the continuation of Iron Age traditions of design into the Roman period (Boon & Savory 1975; Megaw & Megaw 1989, 230).

Domestic equipment and tools

Few of the artefacts which make up the characteristic Iron Age domestic assemblage are culturally or chronologically sensitive. The most common are stone objects, such as hammerstones, rubbing stones, mortars and querns (both saddle and rotary). Many facetted rubbing stones have such a regular shape that they must have had some specific use, perhaps skin dressing, but these tools have not yet received the detailed study that might unlock their information potential. The querns have received rather more study, for they may be made from specialised rocks (though Welsh distributions have not yet been traced). In the course of the period there is a major technological advance: the introduction of the more efficient rotary or 'beehive' quern, though the saddle quern with its elongated bun-shaped rubber continued to be used. The Iron Age date of this introduction is demonstrated at Twyn y Gaer, Monmouthshire (Probert 1976, 115–16) (see p. 173) and confirmed by the decoration of some rotary querns in north Wales with running spirals of La Tène inspiration (Griffiths 1951) but the source of the new technology remains uncertain.

Spindle-whorls, like querns some of the commonest chance finds, are another Iron Age artefact awaiting close study. These small flat stones weighted the bottom of a spindle and caused it to twist the thread as it was drawn out from the bunch of carded wool. Several examples are decorated (Savory 1967). This decoration is normally radial or circular and includes dot and circle motifs which may also be found on weaving combs, another tool

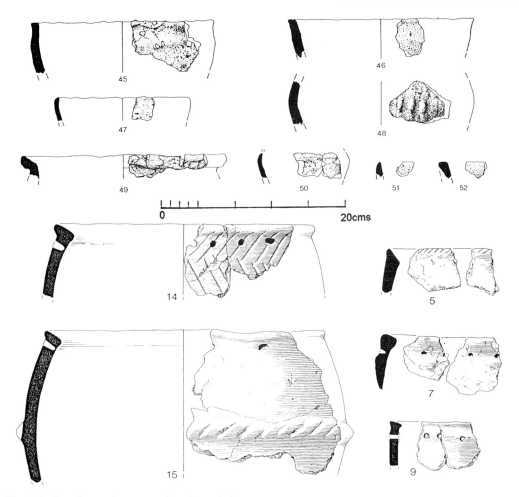

Fig. 4.24. Late Bronze Age pottery from beneath the rampart at The Breiddin (top) and from Rhuddlan (below). (From Musson 1991 and Quinnell & Blockley 1994). Scale 1:4.

probably used mainly by women. Spindle-whorls have been found in Iron Age contexts at The Breiddin, Crawcwellt, Castle Ditches and Biglis, Glamorgan, and at Prestatyn (Musson 1991, 156–8) but the vast majority are chance finds, lost while their owners were watching flocks or walking around the farm. The occasional baked clay loomweight like that from The Breiddin (Musson 1991, 158), is normally believed to be another indication of cloth production though this identification has recently been questioned (Poole in Cunliffe 1995, 285–6).

Craft and agricultural tools in iron are very rare; most must have been recycled (Crew 1995, 276). The limited range from the fairly extensive excavations at The Breiddin are indicative of the general paucity (Musson 1991, 141–7). Despite the belief that some bars of trade iron imitate iron ploughshares, wooden ones like that from Walesland Rath (Wainwright 1971) were probably far more common, alongside wooden spades, flails and rakes in age-old designs. The iron sickles and blacksmith's tongs from The Breiddin and Llyn Cerrig Bach, identical to modern ones, demonstrate the longevity of such utilitarian tools (**Fig. 4.26**).

The frequent discovery of flint blades on Iron Age and Romano-British sites might perhaps suggest residual finds but it is equally probable that this traditional material was still used for small tools, just as were bone and antler.

In the absence of pottery over much of Wales, wooden bowls or woven baskets must have been the most common containers. They seldom survive, but the rare examples from the pond on The Breiddin (Musson 1991, 161–72) (**Fig. 4.25**, nos 13, 15) and the ladle from Caldicot on the Gwent Levels (Nayling & Caseldine 1997, 207–8) are an indication of what must have existed everywhere. The bronze-covered wooden tankard from Trawsfynydd, built from finely cut concave staves with a neatly turned base, demonstrates the quality of woodworking which could be achieved (Fox 1958, 109) (**Pl. 32**).

Late Bronze Age and Iron Age Pottery

Pottery is relatively rare in Wales throughout this period. In the Late Bronze Age it is of poor quality but locally made. In the Early Iron Age it is difficult to identify any pottery anywhere, but in the Middle and Late Iron Age traded pottery becomes available in the Marches and south Wales, although there appears to be very little locally made material. Vessels of wood and leather must have been widely used instead (Earwood 1993).

Pottery of a general Later Bronze Age type is being increasingly recognised in Wales. It belongs to a broad family of which the Deverel Rimbury branch is the most familiar (Burgess 1980a, 131–44). It generally consists of bucket- or barrel-shaped vessels; decoration includes slashes and perforations beneath the rim and the fabric is normally coarse with large stone grits which may break the surface. Within this rather undistinctive group it is possible to recognise two sub-styles, one with incurved profiles and internally bevelled rims, the other more straight-walled, with flat rims and less decoration. The recently published assemblage from Rhuddlan (Quinnell & Blockley 1994, 132–8) may be considered characteristic of the first. It has been given a date range of 1,550–1,050 cal BC but this is not securely based. More firmly dated, to *c.* 900 cal BC, is the material from under the rampart at The Breiddin hillfort, Montgomeryshire (Musson 1991, 118–24), which is typical of the second group. The date of the pottery from the earliest phase of occupation at Castell Odo on the tip of Lleyn has been much disputed (Alcock 1960). Though it is rather better finished than the material discussed above it must belong to this general horizon, but as an outlier it is difficult to categorise dogmatically.

The currently known distribution in Wales is mainly eastern and from coastal areas in the north and south but a single cordoned sherd from Darren hillfort near Aberystwyth (Driver 1996) suggests that the real distribution may be wider. It is known from several hillforts in the Marches and from burial contexts in the same region. In the north it has been found at settlements and in burials. In the south it occurs in lowland Monmouthshire, there is a notable, dated assemblage from Pembrokeshire and it also occurs in caves and barrows in the Vale of Glamorgan, Gower and the Brecon Beacons.

The pottery occurs in domestic contexts both at open sites such as Stackpole Warren, the Gwent Levels, Glanfeinion (**Fig. 3.5**) and Rhuddlan (Benson *et al.* 1990; Allen 1996;

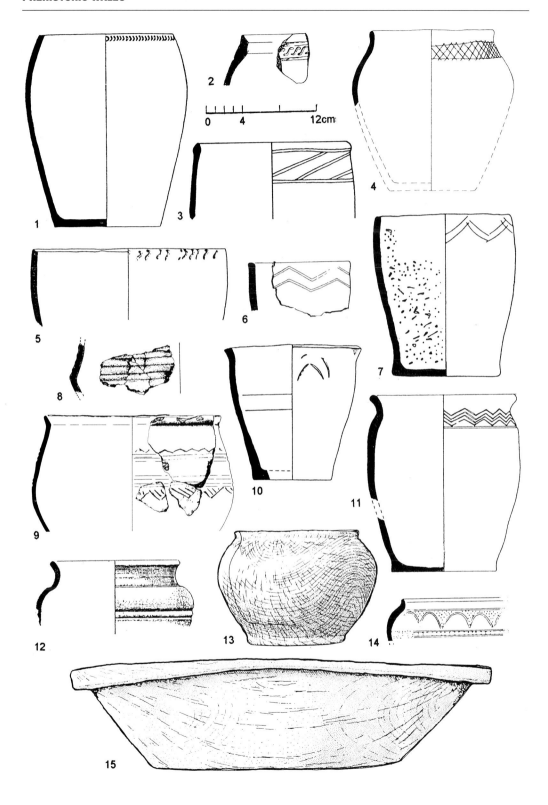

Britnell *et al.* 1997) and at other locations, such as Coygan Camp, Dale Fort, Coed y Cwmdda, and The Breiddin which were subsequently defended (Wainwright 1967; Benson & Williams 1987; Owen-John 1988). Its use continued at The Breiddin and other Marcher forts through the first centuries of defence. Despite its crudity it seems to have been the only pottery available, for it was used to contain cremated bone at several sites (see pp. 211–12).

The presence of pottery comparable to Deverel Rimbury jars and of Wilburton bronzework in the Severn Valley is an interesting conjunction but the fact that wherever this coarse pottery has been analysed it can be shown to be of local manufacture may be of more significance (Wardle 1987; Morris 1994, 374–6). The sophisticated pottery industries of the earlier Bronze Age may have been victims of the retrenchment of the so-called Late Bronze Age crisis period and local communities may have been forced back on their own resources until a new network of trade was established in the Middle Iron Age. However, sherds of flint-tempered pottery from Rumney Great Wharf on the Gwent Levels and the few fine Decorated sherds from Caldicot (**Fig. 4.25**, no. 9) hint at the survival of some longer distance contacts through this time in certain favoured regions (Allen 1996, 11; Nayling & Caseldine 1997, 243–5).

The date-span of this coarse pottery in Wales is not firmly established. A radiocarbon date of 1,400–1,170 cal BC for a crude burial urn from Pennant Melangell, Montgomeryshire (Britnell 1994, 84–5, 95), suggests a Middle Bronze Age beginning for the style, perhaps at that time available alongside better pottery. Other radiocarbon dates from The Breiddin, Glanfeinion and Stackpole show that it was certainly in use during the thirteenth and ninth centuries cal BC and this would seem to be its main *floruit*, but for how long it continued is uncertain. A range of dates is available from the Rumney Great Wharf sites, one of which suggests a Middle Iron Age survival (Allen 1996, 10). However, the style does not occur alongside the traded pottery in the Marches and no pottery of any kind was found at the seventh- and fourth-century cal BC concentric enclosures in Merioneth (Kelly 1988).

Pottery distributed from production centres in the Malvern Hills begins to appear in the Marches from about the fourth century cal BC. Rare haematite-coated sherds of Wessex origin from Old Oswestry (Hughes 1994, 69–70) hint at an earlier initiation of long-distance trade (**Fig. 4.25**, no. 8), but the use of commercially produced pottery is largely a feature of the Middle Iron Age (400–100 cal BC) and the more southerly Marcher region. It is found mainly in hillforts such as The Breiddin and Twyn y Gaer, but it also reached much smaller establishments like Enclosure 1 at Hindwell in the Walton Basin, Radnorshire, and the isolated house in the Brenig Valley (Morris 1994, 378; Gibson 1999a, 97–9; Lynch 1993, 159–61).

(Opposite) *Fig. 4.25. Iron Age pottery. 1–3 Malvernian A; 4 Limestone ware from Malvern region; 5 Malvernian Bi; 6–7, 10–11 Llanmelin Style; 8 Haematite Ware; 9 Decorated; 12 Wheel-thrown jar; 13, 15 Wooden bowls; 14 SW Decorated Style. 1 Pen Dinas, Cards.; 2, 5, Croft Ambrey, Heref.; 3 Hindwell, Walton; 4,13,15 The Breiddin, Mont.; 6,11 Llanmelin, Mon.; 7 Magor Pill, Mon.; 8 Old Oswestry; 9 Caldicot, Mon.; 10 Coygan Camp, Carm.; 12, Sudbrook, Mon.; 14 Castle Ditches, Llancarfan, Glam. (From Forde* et al. *1963, Peacock 1968, Musson 1991, Gibson 1999a, Whittle 1989, Savory 1976b, Nayling & Caseldine 1997 and Hogg 1976.) Scale 1:4.*

The earliest, most complex and most widespread of these imported potteries are the Malvernian Wares (Croft Ambrey–Bredon Hill style in Cunliffe's terminology) which can be identified both petrologically and stylistically (Peacock 1968). The use of different rock tempers (igneous rock (A); two different types of limestone (B1 and B2); crushed sandstone (C); and mudstone) has led to the identification of five different production centres within a few kilometres of the Malvern Hills. Each was producing broadly similar 'saucepan' pots with stamped and grooved decoration just below the rim, but type A is much neater and has more complex rims than types B or C. Their distributions also vary slightly, A being the most widespread, but all appear to be roughly contemporary. A coarse ware tempered with dolerite from the Clee Hills has, not unexpectedly, a more restricted distribution in the central Marches (Morris 1981).

The ceramic history of Monmouthshire and the south-eastern coast of Wales is different since pottery was used to a much greater extent there in the later centuries BC; it also demonstrates an increasing contact with regions across the Severn. Among the undistinguished coarse wares mentioned earlier there are pots with slightly more complex decoration, a flat expanded rim and projecting foot which have been dubbed 'Trevisker-related Ware', indicative of contact across the Bristol Channel where it can be found on similar coastal settlements such as Brean Down (Bell 1990; Allen 1996; Whittle 1989). The later history of the area shows that these contacts persisted, evidenced by fine Decorated sherds from Caldicot and the distribution of various limestone-tempered wares (Nayling & Caseldine 1997, 243–5; Spencer 1983).

The hillfort at Llanmelin, where three phases of development can be recognised, provides some stratigraphic context for two styles of this pottery (Savory 1976a, 38). The first, associated with the second phase at Llanmelin (the multiple ramparts and simple entrance), has been named from this site the Llanmelin–Lydney Style (Cunliffe 1991, Fig. A.18; Spencer 1983, Class B). The shapes are reminiscent of the earlier 'saucepan pots' and chevron and curvilinear ('eyebrow') ornament is sparsely applied. At Llanmelin this style is succeeded by South Western Decorated Wares of Group 3 of the Glastonbury Style originating in the Mendips but probably imitated in south Wales (Peacock 1969). This pottery is found more extensively on settlements in Monmouthshire and the Vale of Glamorgan, such as Biglis, Whitton and Llandough (Allen 1998; Robinson 1988, 33) and on the Gower peninsula, for example at the Knave promontory fort (Williams 1939). The currency of these styles is judged to lie from about 200 cal BC to AD 50.

In the final decades before and during the Roman conquest a local coarse ware (Spencer 1983, Class A) was produced and sparsely distributed as far as Dan y Coed and Woodside in the far south west, a region that was previously aceramic (Williams 1988b). A little wheel-thrown cordoned pottery of southern English type reached south Wales (**Fig. 4.25**, no. 12), where it has been found at Sudbrook Camp and further west in the late phases of Mynydd Bychan and perhaps even at Walesland Rath (Savory 1976b, 41–2).

In the Marches Malvernian Wares may have continued in use up to the Roman conquest when war and upheaval disrupted long-distance contacts and trade. Other regions of Wales beyond the reach of the Marcher networks, though in receipt of other more valuable imports, remained aceramic to the last.

Introduction

During this period of crisis and recovery the scale of exchange fluctuated. The crisis of the Late Bronze Age appears to have thrown communities back on their own resources with the markets, especially in everyday objects, being notably localised. By contrast, in the prosperous Middle and Late Iron Age what may be reckoned trade, as we might recognise it, expanded and styles with far distant antecedents became fashionable among the elite.

Late Bronze Age Trade

Earlier Bronze Age trade which is recognisable to us today is almost exclusively concerned with metal goods and with scrap. Individual site studies may suggest that other commodities such as pottery may have travelled some distance (Lynch 1993, 152; Wardle 1987), but the patterns are not sufficiently clear to warrant the term trade, even in the imprecise sense in which we can understand these mechanisms at this time.

The crisis at the close of the Middle Bronze Age is likely to have disrupted metal trading networks and it is not until the ninth century cal BC that new patterns emerge. In some areas, such as south-east Wales, where the local industry was strong and a 'tribal network' may have been developing, what is virtually a monopoly situation can be seen. In the north, once the centre of a strong local industry, small centres of manufacture may be recognised (Lynch 1991, 367) but they do not dominate the market and a wide variety of axe types may be found (Ehrenburg 1989). Perhaps this variety may be partly due to the revival of east–west contacts carrying luxury goods between Ireland and eastern England and beyond. The distribution of Irish gold bracelets and lock-rings and of north European amber beads and bronze harness decorations in Anglesey and along the north Wales coast is evidence of this route and the wealth of some local communities (Eogan 1994, 106).

The weapons industry within Wales is best exemplified by the Wilburton material from the central Marches. Specialised spearheads and sword fittings (though the swords themselves are rare) belong to a distinctive English industry with French connections using new sources of metal. Even though the Guilsfield hoard (**Fig. 4.14**) contains both tools and weapons the two industrial strands remain distinct for different metal mixes are used, indicating a sophisticated understanding of the qualities needed and contact with far-flung supply networks.

Some of these networks would have dealt in scrap metal, for in the Later Bronze Age there is a great increase in hoards of broken or deliberately cut-up castings, some of which are French pieces that are never seen in their pristine form in Britain. Long-distance exchange of scrap metal therefore fuelled the southern English metal industry and, to a certain extent, the Welsh one even though radiocarbon dates from the Great Orme indicate that mining still continued there. This cross-channel trade is confirmed by the discovery of wrecked cargoes at Dover, Salcombe and Freshwater West in Milford Haven, where axes, bronze ingots and two broken swords, one possibly a French Carp's Tongue type, have been found on the beach (Muckleroy 1981; DAT report 14393 *unpublished*).

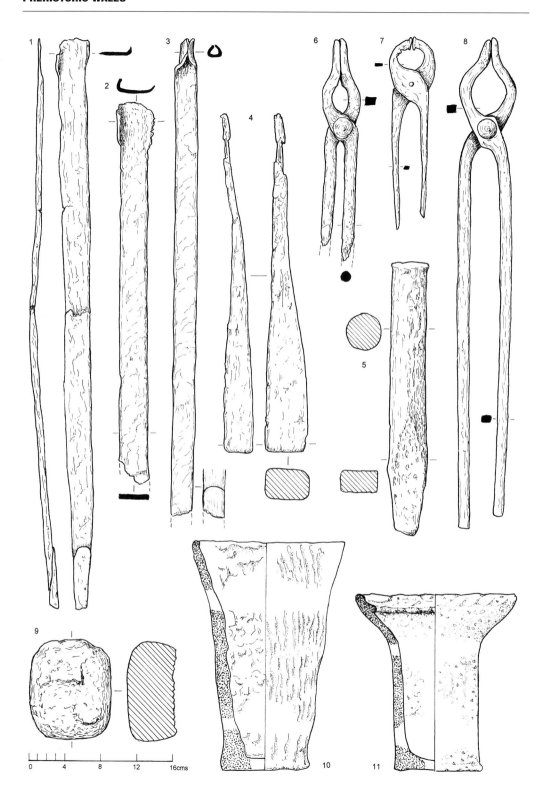

Iron Age Trade

Foreign contacts – socio-political or commercial – in the Iron Age continue to bring in individual pieces of fine metalwork, but the bulk trade in metal may have waned. Indeed it has been claimed that at the beginning of the period the metal market collapsed and there was a serious crisis in the industry which saw some decline in casting skills (Northover 1984, 130–1, 137). Iron is less amenable to the types of analysis that have proved rewarding in the study of copper alloys but the discovery of hoards of 'trade iron' in certain southern English hillforts demonstrates that equally extensive distribution networks may be expected, at least in the later half of the period (Hedges & Salter 1979; Ehrenreich 1985; Crew 1995).

Analysis of the Llyn Cerrig Bach deposit is instructive for this period. The bronzes show use of copper from Dartmoor, much used in south-west England up to 50 BC, and of copper with a high zinc content from Llanymynech, Montgomeryshire. Both are new ore sources in the context of the Welsh industry (Northover in Lynch 1991). The trade iron includes at least four currency bars with distinctive welded tips, including one plough-share type in high phosphorous iron which could be the product of north Welsh bog ores, and a Malvern bar of low phosphorous/high carbon iron which suggests a reciprocal trade in iron with different properties (Crew & Salter 1993).

Despite our inability to quantify the trade in Welsh metals we can demonstrate an expansion of trading in other commodities, notably pottery and salt. The Middle and Late Iron Age distribution of decorated pottery in south-east Wales and the Marches has already been described (pp. 201–2). Several production centres were located on the Malvern Hills, presumably because of the suitability of clays and tempers there. Their fluctuating fortunes and competing distributions suggest a professional commercial enterprise but initial access to the network may have been based upon tribal or kinship groups because the heartland of this pottery seems to correspond to what was, by the Roman period, Dobunnic territory. Another interesting aspect of this study is the proportion of local and traded pottery used (Morris 1994, 378). In the eastern sector and the Cotswolds consumers had access to traded wares and to locally produced jars; further west and north the professionally produced pottery is the only sort available – confirmation of the aceramic status of north and most of west Wales throughout the Iron Age.

The later limestone-tempered wares cannot be so precisely localised but their distribution in south Monmouthshire and coastal south Wales suggests that they may have been carried by shipping in the Bristol Channel (Spencer 1983). The two shores exhibit many similarities in the later prehistoric period, in contrast to their apparent isolation in the earlier Bronze Age, and it could be argued that an influx of new settlers may be partly

(Opposite) *Fig. 4.26. Trade iron and tools: 1, 2 'plough-share' bars; 3 spit bar (note welded tips on 1 & 3); 4 drawn bar; 9 billet; 5 chisel; 6–8 tongs. 1–3, 7, 8 Llyn Cerrig Bach, Ang; 4, 5 Lesser Garth, Pentyrch, Glam; 9 Ffestiniog, Merioneth; 6 The Breiddin. (After Lynch 1991, Crew and Salter 1993; Savory 1976a, Musson 1991.) Salter containers (VCP): 10 Droitwich type from Croft Ambrey; 11 Cheshire type from Collfryn (after Morris 1986). Scale 1:4.*

responsible for the increased contact at the end of the period, though shifts in political allegiance may produce the same effect.

Salt was, and is, an especially valuable commodity because it enables food to be preserved and stored over winter. The salt mines of Hallstatt underpin one of the richest communities of Iron Age Europe, though we cannot see the distribution of their product. In Britain the situation is reversed. The wealth of the producers is not visible, but the distribution of the cakes of salt can be documented through recognition of their coarse clay containers, broken and cast aside as the salt was used. These sherds – dubbed Very Coarse Pottery (VCP) – had been recognised on Iron Age sites for many years but it was some time before their role was understood (Gelling & Stanford 1965).

Two varieties are present, one a straight-sided cone, the other more vase-like with a widely flaring top (**Fig. 4.26**, nos 10 and 11). Analysis of the plentiful stone grit in the clay has shown that the two shapes come from different salt springs: the vase-shaped ones (Stony VCP) are from Cheshire and the conical ones from Droitwich in the West Midlands (Morris 1985). These first appear in the sixth and fifth centuries cal BC with market spheres which, during the third to first centuries cal BC, are divided at the Severn. By the fourth century cal BC production had increased at both centres but the Cheshire springs were gaining ground, or were distributed by a different, more open system, for some of their products may be found as far south as the Usk Valley, and west into Merioneth and Anglesey which they reached in the second century cal BC. The early distribution of Droitwich salt corresponds closely with that of Malvernian A pottery and reinforces the idea of a controlled tribal trading network (Morris 1994, 384–7).

The salt containers are found most frequently in hillforts such as Moel Hiraddug, Old Oswestry, Dinorben, Twyn y Gaer and Sudbrook, but are not restricted to these centres of social power and control for they have been found in equally large quantities at other settlements such as Collfryn, the enclosed hut group at Pant y Saer, Anglesey, and even the isolated house at Cerrig y Drudion (Brassil 1992).

If Midlands salt containers did not reach south-west Wales, was this because sea-salt of local origin was being used? If this was so, why did Cheshire salt reach the maritime parts of north-west Wales? Could it have been exchanged for another commodity, perhaps metal? (Davies 1995, 688) The study of the salt industry in Britain as a whole can illuminate a great number of the problems of understanding the physical and social mechanics of trade in prehistory but it also demonstrates how many significant factors still elude us as we try to distinguish functional from ritualised behaviour, chronology from status and come to terms with gaps in the evidence (Morris 1994).

One of the major questions is the extent to which trade was controlled. Could tribal leaders use their power to redistribute rare and valuable commodities as a means of ensuring the loyalty of followers? Analysis of imported materials has been used to argue that the larger forts may have been redistribution centres where tribal power and cohesion were reinforced in this way (Cunliffe 1983, 166–7; 1987, 30). It is possible to distinguish between open, down-the-line exchange systems and controlled distributions but obviously the same commodity may have a different role close to source and at distant sites, while social custom may invest objects with unexpected status.

The concentration of salt containers and Malvernian A pottery at Midsummer Hill in Herefordshire (Stanford 1981) has led to suggestions that this fort might be a major tribal redistribution centre, but positive proof is not forthcoming. However, it remains tempting to interpret in kinship terms such tight-knit and coincident distributions in the Marcher hillforts and the similar occurrence of Lydney–Llanmelin pottery further south (Davies 1995, 695). In contrast a sparse extended pattern, such as that of fine metalwork, may suggest diplomatic gifts.

The most graphic confirmation of such diplomatic gifts and contacts with distant lands is the discovery of the skull of a Barbary ape from North Africa in Early Iron Age levels at Navan Fort near Armagh (Waterman 1997, 122–5). In the iron-producing region of south-east Wales a scatter of second–first-century cal BC Gaulish coins (Boon 1980b) and a find of earlier Breton axes (so lead-rich as to be useless as tools and believed to be a form of currency (Cunliffe 1991, 420)) may hint at the metal trading mentioned by Strabo (III.5.11). The Graeco-Roman anchor of similar date from Porth Felen, Lleyn (Boon 1977), is another proof of these voyages which can easily explain the presence of fine pieces like the Arthog bucket, the Cerrig y Drudion bowl and the Iberian statuette from Aust (Fox 1958, xxiv), likely to be gifts to chieftains who could smooth the way for foreign merchants. One may imagine that such voyages were becoming more and more common during the later prehistoric period. By the first century BC Caesar describes a situation in which cross-Channel contact, both commercial and political, was intense; coastal archaeology is now revealing remains of the contemporary boats (see pp. 177–8).

In Late Iron Age England certain sites such as Hengistbury Head seem to become flourishing trading entrepots in what may be a truly commercial context (Cunliffe 1987). Such sites are recognised by a concentration of imported goods, by the growth of ancillary industries on the fringe of the port and by the use of currency of low denominations indicative of true exchange rather than hoarding. Exotic finds from Merthyr Mawr Warren on the coast of Glamorgan – three Marzabotto-type brooches, a Braubach style sherd and a Gaulish coin – are suggestive of some similar entrepot on the Ogmore Estuary (Savory 1990). However, the other features, notably the coin economy, are not present there.

Coins were never in regular use in Iron Age Wales but there are some significant finds. In south-east Wales the early Gaulish coins may indicate some foreign trading, perhaps for iron (Boon 1980b) and in the period 35 BC–AD 43 a tight distribution of Dobunnic silver coins in the same region suggests a genuine market use and possibly socio-political links between the Dobunni and the Silures. Elsewhere in Wales, especially in the north, only a very few gold coins of very varied origin are found, more suggestive of hoarding, perhaps by refugees from south-east England fleeing before the Romans (Boon 1988).

Industry

Bronze manufacturing industries everywhere expanded during the Late Bronze Age and their organisation became more distinct and formalised (see pp. 180–2). Technical studies indicate several specialist networks, weapon smiths, sheet-bronze workers and regionally based tool producers, existing to service an increasingly hierarchical society (Northover 1984). Radiocarbon dates show that the copper mines of north and mid-Wales, described

Fig. 4.27. Iron Age firedog from Capel Garmon, Denbighshire. (Photo: by permission of National Museum of Wales)

in the previous chapter, were still in production through the Late Bronze Age, despite the likelihood that galleries in the Great Orme may have reached depths at which flooding would have been a problem. However, the extensive use of foreign scrap metal in the Late Bronze Age may have been either a cause or a symptom of difficulties in the native mining industry, perhaps confirmed by the frequent changes in ore sources during the Late Bronze and Iron Ages (Northover 1984).

Northover (1995, 287–8) suggests that by the end of the seventh century cal BC copper and tin extraction had virtually ceased in Britain, and when metallurgical activity began to revive in the Middle Iron Age new and previously unused copper deposits were opened up. The best Welsh example is Llanymynech Hill, Montgomeryshire, where a hillfort was built over a copper mine producing distinctive zinc-rich ores which can be recognised in later Iron Age products such as the shield fitting from Moel Hiraddug and a horse bit from Llyn Cerrig Bach. It was also the ore being used at nearby Llwyn Bryn-dinas in the fourth century cal BC (Musson *et al.* 1992, 279).

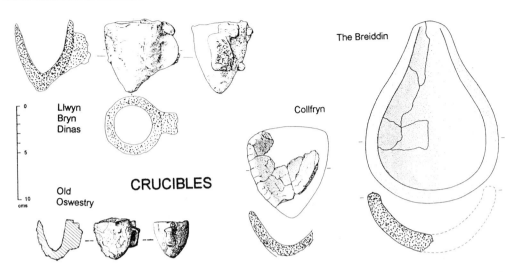

Fig. 4.28. Iron Age crucibles for working bronze. (From Musson 1991, Musson et al. 1992, Savory 1976a and Britnell 1989.) Scale 1:4.

Prehistoric exploitation of Welsh gold has not been demonstrated by fieldwork, but the significant south Welsh cluster of Middle Bronze Age gold artefacts, especially unusual bracelets (see p. 107), suggests that the gold resources of Dolaucothi may have been known and used. Indeed the apparent rapidity with which the Roman workings were established, immediately after the Flavian conquest (AD 73–7) suggests that they knew of a resource to be tapped there – knowledge that must have been based on native exploration (Jones & Maude 1991).

The process by which an understanding of the manufacture and use of iron spread through Europe and into Britain is poorly documented (Alexander 1981; Ehrenreich 1985). Very small pieces of iron appear in Late Bronze Age hoards in France and the designs of the earliest full-scale products, like the sickle from Llynfawr (**Fig. 4.16**), are more appropriate to bronze formed in a mould than to iron which must be hammered and welded into shape. All this suggests that the new metal was worked by traditional native craftsmen who only gradually learnt its potential and limitations. This new technology seems to have become established in Britain by about 800 cal BC (Needham *at al.* 1997, 98–9).

The process of smelting and smithing iron into a usable bar is a three-fold one, in the course of which up to 90 per cent of the original weight of material may be lost as slag and scale (Crew 1991a). The iron ore is loaded into a low shaft furnace and smelted to a bloom – a mass of iron and slag – which must be hammered to beat out the slag and compress the iron to a rectangular billet. Some iron may have been traded in this form but more often it was worked into a long thin bar. Such secondary smithing removes the final impurities and reveals the intrinsic quality of the iron: hard but springy, malleable but strong, and capable of being joined by welding and of being recycled many times.

There are several types of these bars, the drawing out being a guarantee of quality. In Britain the commonest forms are variants of the flat bar with worked ends, previously known as currency bars. In Wales the only surviving examples are those from the votive deposit at Llyn Cerrig Bach and one from Llanstephan, but other forms of trade iron are known from Lesser Garth, Pentyrch (a long pointed billet), and from the Forest of Dean (small, rounded, smithed blooms) and cuboid billets from the Festiniog area of Merioneth (Crew 1994 and pers. comm.) (**Fig. 4.26**).

Experiments have shown that the process of making iron is more difficult than was previously appreciated and is very dependant on temperature and timing, requiring the services of experienced smelters and blacksmiths. The resulting artefacts therefore must have had a value far higher than we – who regard iron as a purely utilitarian material – would now imagine. Experimental data (Crew 1991a) suggests that the process of collecting the raw materials and smelting and smithing it for the Capel Garmon firedog (**Fig. 4.27**) would have required some three to four man-years work. It is not surprising that so little was thrown away and that large iron artefacts such as firedogs, chains and anchors do not occur until production had expanded in the Late Iron Age.

Consequently the main evidence for iron production and use comes not from the artefacts but from the manufacturing debris, predominantly slag and smithing scale. Recent work in Merioneth has revealed a previously unsuspected local industry, using bog ores smelted and smithed at specialist sites (Crew 1991c). Two of these sites – Bryn y Castell, a small hillfort (Crew 1986), and Crawcwellt, an open settlement (Crew 1989; 1991b, 1998) – have been meticulously excavated and provide full evidence for the technology and its quantification.

Ironworking at these sites took place in large timber or stone buildings which might contain up to fifteen small furnaces. The bases of these furnaces are bowl-like, but experiments have shown that they must have been low shaft furnaces, each of which could have been used on a large number of occasions (Crew 1991a) (**Pl. 34**). The huts, too, were rebuilt on several occasions. At Bryn y Castell one stone-built workshop was reshaped, producing a snail-like form, to provide reduced illumination for smithing hearths against the opposite wall. Outside the door of these buildings large slag dumps had accumulated. These contain both slag and occasional lumps of ore indicative of smelting, and plano-convex hearth bases and smithing scale, the product of smithing billets and bars. Stone anvils are also present which would have been used at floor level.

Careful sampling and experimentation have enabled calculations of total production to be made. These indicate that, despite the impressive size of the dumps, the total production from these specialist sites was relatively small and they cannot have been supplying a large region (Salter & Ehrenreich 1984; Crew 1991c). This local industry flourished in Merioneth from about 300 cal BC to AD 60 when the Roman invasion seems to have brought it to an end. Even though they were not producing very large quantities of iron the rewards may have been high, for rare glass bangles have been found at both sites (**Fig. 4.23**). The establishments were broadly contemporary, although one was defended while the other was an open settlement – which raises intriguing questions of social context.

In contrast to the rarity of primary metal production, evidence for secondary metalworking, either bronze or iron or both, has been revealed by excavation at most settlements. The scale is normally small, no more than would be needed for self-sufficiency in minor tools and repairs. Again the evidence is from hearths and working debris rather than products and it comes from hillforts like Dinorben (Gardner & Savory 1964, 226–7), Old Oswestry (Hughes 1994), The Breiddin (Musson 1991, 147–9) and Llwyn Bryn-dinas (Musson *et al.* 1992), and lesser settlements like Collfryn, where several crucibles for bronze-working were found (Britnell 1989) and the small forts of the Llawhaden group (Williams & Mytum 1998). Clearly metalworking on this small scale was not restricted to any particular social group.

Llwyn Bryn-dinas (**Pl. 35**) provides a rare glimpse of a third-century cal BC workshop used for both bronze- and iron-working (Musson *et al.* 1992). A circular hut or shelter, perhaps 5 metres across, was tucked in under the lee of the ninth-century cal BC rampart. Seven small hearths were found, together with a spread of magnetic hammerscale indicating a forge; non-ferrous and ferrous slag, fragments of crucibles and furnace lining were scattered around the charcoal-strewn floor. Local copper was used, but probably not smelted on site. The workshop was short-lived and the scale of production limited but it is proof of the range of skills available within one relatively small Iron Age community.

The evidence for other more domestic crafts, such as spinning, weaving, leather and bone-working, may be found at all levels of society, although the incidence of spindle-whorls, loomweights and smoothing stones is not as common as might be expected. Another previously domestic craft, pottery, was highly localised in the central Marches and south-east Wales but was not a craft practised in north or west Wales (see pp. 197–202).

DEATH AND RELIGION

The rituals of death and burial were clearly central to the religious attitudes and practices of the Bronze Age. Funerary monuments are an important element of the cultural landscape and the bodies beneath them are laid to rest with complex ceremonies relating both to their past status in this world and to their expected role in the next. In the Late Bronze Age this tradition, like so many, appears to break down. Burial monuments and stone circles are no longer built and religious activity is focused instead at votive sites near rivers and lakes.

In both the Late Bronze Age and the Iron Age formal burial appears to have been largely abandoned but the advent of radiocarbon dating and the practice of more extensive excavation on settlement sites has demonstrated that, as always, the change has been exaggerated. Religious practice undoubtedly suffered a shift, but strands can be recognised that link the Earlier Bronze Age with the succeeding periods when traditions of burial, though more varied and less monumental than before, are not totally eclipsed.

Late Bronze Age Burials

Forty years ago cremations in Cordoned Urns and 'overhanging rim urns' were regularly ascribed to the Late Bronze Age. The revised dating of these urns created a gap in the burial record (Burgess 1974). However, though a decline in burial at this time is undoubtedly real, it is not complete, for radiocarbon dates have shown that some urned cremations were being buried in the thirteenth to seventh centuries cal BC. These bones are often in plain coarse jars (see pp. 199–201) and were usually buried in the top of pre-existing mounds where they were particularly vulnerable to plough damage. The poor pottery and the shattered condition of these burials has meant that in the past they were often disregarded.

Recent excavations in both north and south Wales have shown, through radiocarbon dating and pottery typology, that such burials were relatively common, especially at lowland sites. Barrows were re-used at Welsh St Donats in Glamorgan and at Four Crosses near Welshpool (Ehrenburg *et al.* 1982; Warrilow *et al.* 1986). Rarely, as at Llanllechid (Caernarfonshire) and Llanelian (Denbighshire) where only coarse pottery was found, a new monument was constructed (RCAHMW 1956, Fig. 15; Ellis Davies 1929, 204–5). Late burials also occur at flat cemeteries, such as Capel Eithin in Anglesey and Bromfield in Shropshire (Lynch 1991, 353; Stanford 1982), where the lack of markers must imply a continuous tradition of use. On the other hand at Plas Gogerddan and Stackpole a break, or redirection, of tradition must have occurred, for standing stones, which do not mark Earlier Bronze Age graves, attracted burials in the Late Bronze Age and Iron Age (Murphy 1992).

The implication of secondary use and the rarity of new monuments is that burial was becoming more low-key, a conclusion borne out by the lack of grave-goods. Only nine burials in Wales were accompanied by Later Bronze Age metalwork and all these are rather uncertain records (Burgess 1976). Moreover many late jars contain only token deposits, and often no bone, only charcoal or burnt grain as at Marlborough Grange in Glamorgan (Savory 1969a).

The decline of grave-goods and the increasing presence of votive deposits in the barrows has led some to suggest that the offering of fine possessions in bogs and rivers may have some connection with funerary offerings, especially since human bones may also be found in these same rivers (Bradley 1990, 112–14). Some such method of disposal might explain the real reduction in archaeologically visible burials in this period.

Iron Age Burial

Fifty years ago Iron Age burials were rare in many parts of Britain but the practice of more extensive excavation, especially within hillforts, has dramatically altered the situation (Whimster 1981). Their previous invisibility has been due to the undoubted move away from special burial monuments towards the performance of rituals within settlements, and towards diverse burial systems, many of which involved incomplete skeletons. Isolated human bones found in storage pits, previously interpreted as rubbish of a rather macabre kind, are now thought to relate to fertility rituals, also evidenced by the careful burial of animal skeletons in similar contexts (Cunliffe 1991, 505). Complete bodies under ramparts are probably sacrificial victims, for example, the young man beneath the bank at Maiden Castle who was undoubtedly buried alive (Wheeler 1943, Plate XLIV).

The human bones found on Middle Iron Age sites should not perhaps be considered 'normal' burials for their deposition is not standard and probably relates more to an active use in ritual within the settlement area (Cunliffe 1991, 507). In this the contrast with the Bronze Age is very marked. It is only in the Later Iron Age that more formal burial returns, although it is not a universal practice and seems always to be restricted to the upper echelons of society, for the accompanying grave-goods are often very fine (Collis 1973).

The record of Iron Age burial in Wales has been conveniently summarised by Murphy (1992). It shows that, as in England, several deposits of human bone have been found in or close to hillforts, often in the ditches. Unfortunately few are securely dated, but those from Coygan Camp, Mynydd Bychan and Llanmelin in south Wales probably belong to the Late Iron Age. Men, women and children are represented; some are carefully laid out, flexed or extended, while others seem to have been more casually treated. There are a few examples of cremation, as at Castell Bucket (Williams 1985), where radiocarbon assay is the only clue to date. Burials in the vicinity of the unenclosed Iron Age settlement on Merthyr Mawr Warren are not very securely dated (Murphy 1992, 34).

Perhaps the most interesting Iron Age burials are those associated with earlier religious sites. The most complex is that from Stackpole, Pembrokeshire, where an inhumation, carefully placed within an arc of posts, was added on the centre line of the platform of small upright stones surrounding a large standing stone known as the Devil's Quoit (**Fig. 3.21**; p. 137). Three small children were buried nearby (Benson *et al.* 1990, 228). A similar situation developed at Plas Gogerddan near Aberystwyth where a standing stone erected in the Middle Bronze Age became the focus for Late Bronze Age, Iron Age and even Early Medieval cremation and inhumation burials, one of them with two late La Tène bronze brooches (Murphy 1992).

It is difficult to know whether such sites represent a continuity of religious activity through at least a thousand years, or a revival of interest in abandoned sites with a recognisable ritual background. Soil developing around the Devil's Quoit suggested abandonment (Benson *et al.* 1990, 194, 196). The re-use of standing stones seems, on present evidence, to be a particular feature of south-west Wales (Williams 1988a) but even older sites, such as the Neolithic chambered tombs at Trefignath, Bryn yr Hen Bobl, Anglesey, and the cairn at Ystrad Hynod, near Llanidloes, also show renewed activity at this date, though its nature often remains unexplained (Lynch 1991, 86, 334; Murphy 1992, 35).

In the first century cal BC changes in religious thinking may have been quite widespread for it is from now on that more formal graves begin to appear outside settlements (Cunliffe 1991, 507–9). However, they remain rare in the archaeological record, perhaps because they are not marked by any covering monument. They may be dated by the return to the custom of placing personal ornaments with the body, like the brooches at Plas Gogerddan.

The best known of these rich graves is the earliest. The Cerrig y Drudion bowl (or lid) (Stead 1982; **Fig. 4.19**; pp. 189, 193) was found in an empty stone cist assumed to have held an inhumation (Ellis Davies 1929, 85–9) and may have been old when deposited, for the other graves, such as that at Gelliniog Wen, Anglesey, with a broad-bladed sword (Lynch 1991, 282) (**Fig. 4.20**, no. 13) and those with helmets, mirrors and 'spoons' belong to the first century AD. The records of these rich finds from south Wales – Ogmore, Llanwnda and Castell Nadolig, Penbryn – are all distressingly vague and have some elements of myth about them (Boon 1980a; Murphy 1992, 32–4). However, the 'spoons' from Castell Nadolig (Barnwell 1882, 214–15) do survive, though the two helmets from Ogmore, more securely linked to burials (Anon. 1872), do not.

Religious Sites and Artefacts

The physical separation of religious sites from burial monuments begins in the Late Neolithic (Lynch 1980). Henges and stone circles are normally assumed to be the settings for non-funerary ceremonies, although the distinction was not a sharp one. We can know little of these ceremonies and the mythologies and world-view behind them, but it may be significant, in the light of later developments, that several Early Bronze Age circles stand close to water and to the source of rivers.

In the Late Bronze Age the role of the circles and of the graves of the ancestors appears to decline, while ritual activity is transferred to rivers, bogs and springs where offerings of valuable metalwork seem to take the place of grave-goods and monument-building as an expression of community prestige and sacrifice. This custom of offering weapons, perhaps the spoils of war, and expensive equipment such as cauldrons which would have been the focus of the chief's hearth and hence of his role as provider for his people, reaches its apogee during the Late Bronze Age. The deposit from Llyn Fawr, Glamorgan, is the best example from Wales (Fox 1939), but many other hoards have been interpreted as similar votive offerings (see **Pl. 28**, pp. 179, 189).

It is believed that this tradition of sacrificing wealth, mostly in the form of weapons and the metal for their manufacture, may have a social as much as a religious role. Rivalry between chiefs may have been resolved by such sacrifices, as it was among the Canadian Indians by their potlatch ceremonies, and some have seen them as a mechanism for the maintenance of economic balance between groups with a developing tribal identity in a world of increasing competition (Bradley 1990, 137–9). Such socio-political aims would not, however, have been explicit; a religious impetus would undoubtedly have been the immediate spur for such actions.

The custom continues into the Iron Age but it may have been on the wane, for Iron Age deposits, at least in Britain, are rarer. They also contain a larger element of living sacrifice, of animals and even of humans (Fitzpatrick 1984). The element of secular display and economic competition may have been less; religious fervour may have been more. Although the practice continues and water remains significant, it is interesting that very few of the Late Bronze Age offering places were used in the Iron Age. At Llyn Fawr the entire lake was dug out yet nothing later than about 700 cal BC was found; at Llyn Cerrig Bach in Anglesey clearance was extensive but no Bronze Age material was found (Fox 1939; 1946).

Llyn Cerrig Bach is the best known of the Iron Age deposits in Britain (Fox 1946) (**Pl. 29**). Almost two hundred pieces of equipment, mainly weapons and elements of harness and chariots, were found in this small peat-filled basin when the nearby airfield was constructed in 1943. The presence of narrow-bladed swords, all rendered useless by bending (**Fig. 4.20**), suggests that offerings began here in the third century cal BC (or earlier to judge from radiocarbon dates from the animal bones (P. MacDonald pers. comm.)) and continued until the Roman invasion of the island in AD 60. This end date is based upon the presence of broad-bladed swords and fine ironwork such as the slave chains and upon the absence of enamel decoration which might have been expected here in the second half of the first century AD. The deposit is overwhelmingly military, with both functional and parade weapons, but also includes elements of secular wealth, trade iron and blacksmiths' tools of high value, together with animal bones. The origin of this fine equipment has been much debated: is it purely local or was it gathered from distant regions? In 1946 the latter view was preferred and it was suggested that this small lake must have been a shrine of immense importance to which offerings were sent from all over Britain and even, to a lesser extent, from Ireland. Since then the quality and quantity of Iron Age material found in north Wales has increased and the possibility that all the equipment could have been in use locally has gained ground (Savory 1973). It is probable that the parade gear from Tal y Llyn in Merioneth came originally from a similar votive deposit (Savory 1964). The Capel Garmon firedog and the Trawsfynydd tankard, both bog finds, must be part of the same tradition, but are single finds and not necessarily indicative of long-established shrines.

In Europe Iron Age offerings are often found in the ditches of formally defined sanctuaries, like the one at Gournay in northern France (Brunaux 1988). In southern France, under increasing Roman influence, stone temples were built with images of gods and their supplicants. In Britain such man-made centres of sacrifice and worship also begin to appear in the later part of the period (Woodward 1992). However, purely natural sites like Llyn Cerrig Bach remain important and some of the more famous later centres, such as the healing shrines at Bath and Lydney in Gloucestershire, develop around natural springs (Cunliffe 1971; Wheeler & Wheeler 1932). Caves, as entrances to the underworld, may also have been places of worship and sacrifice, but it is difficult to separate such use from normal 'domestic' occupation (Rutter 1948, 75; Savory 1966a).

The renewed interest in standing stones at this time has already been mentioned in relation to burials. The complexity of arrangements around the Devil's Quoit at Stackpole might well warrant its description as a shrine or sanctuary, as might the undated wooden structures leading up to the stones at St Ishmaels and Mynydd Llangyndeyrn and they could have been the focus of religious activities which have left no evidence (Williams 1988a; Ward 1983). Two small carved stones of phallic appearance from Trefollwyn, Anglesey, are reminiscent of decorated stones from Ireland and Brittany and, as the only known British examples of the kind, perhaps add to the island's standing as a religious centre (Edwards 1997).

Excavations within hillforts in southern England have occasionally revealed focal structures, interpreted as shrines since it is believed that control of religious ceremonial would have enhanced the power of those who ruled the forts (Cunliffe 1991, 512). No Welsh hillfort has produced convincing evidence of this kind, but Romano-British statuettes found at Llys Awel near the spring below Pen y Corddyn, Abergele, may be evidence of such a shrine (Manley *et al.* 1991, 126–7).

In south-east Wales, where Roman influence became strong, stone-built shrines were erected during the first centuries AD. Several are likely to have had Iron Age origins. In the territory of the Silures a circular stone temple of Romano-British type at Gwehelog near Usk appears to lie within a rectilinear precinct (Wilson 1991) and the famous shrine of Nodens at Lydney, Gloucestershire, also seems to have had pre-conquest origins, developing into a great healing centre by the third century AD (Wheeler & Wheeler 1932; Casey & Hoffman 1999).

Beneath the floor of the fourth-century AD temple at Caerwent, the tribal capital of the Silures, an almost life-size stone head had been buried, possibly for safety (Boon 1976).

Such representations of the gods or of head-hunting trophies were plentiful in antiquity because the head was thought to express the essence of the personality and, being stone, they are relatively common survivors. Some fifteen have been recorded from Wales (Megaw 1966; 1967; Ross 1992) but many more undoubtedly exist in walls and gardens which have not yet been drawn to archaeological attention (**Pl. 33**). Unfortunately it is often impossible to establish their date.

There are three approaches to the problem of dating such stone heads: context, attributes and style of carving. Context is the surest but is very rare. Sculptures from stratified deposits at Caerwent, Caerhun, Lydney, Carmarthen and Holt belong to the Roman period but reflect a native tradition (Megaw 1966; 1967; Brewer 1986). Unstratified finds from rivers or wells have suggestive but not provable contexts (Savory 1976b, 77; Jones 1984). Attributes – a torc around the neck, horns, multiple faces or incorporation on a pillar or statue-menhir – may be an indication of antiquity but on chance finds dating cannot be certain. Two statue-menhirs from south-west Wales (one from Laugharne topped with a head carved in the round, the other from Port Talbot with a bas-relief face) are reminiscent of a number of continental pillars and are likely to belong to the Iron Age (Megaw 1966). The third approach to dating – the style of carving – is the least secure, for many medieval and later heads may be equally 'primitive'. This applies also to the very much rarer wooden carvings, though in such a case radiocarbon dating may demonstrate antiquity.

Our knowledge of the pre-Roman pantheon is very slight. It is based upon inscriptions and sculpture, mainly from Roman Gaul where images and attributes may have become merged with those of the Roman gods; upon the commentary of Roman and Greek outsiders; and upon the legends and festivals preserved in medieval Irish and Welsh texts but filtered through a Christian understanding (M.J. Green 1986; Hutton 1991).

A broad division among the gods emerges from this study. Female gods seem to represent the land and are territorial; male gods represent and protect the tribe and are more mobile; in many legends they marry the goddess of the land. These gods are multi-functional and incorporate both good and evil attributes. The major influences on religious thought were the concerns of the agricultural year and the natural environment on which man depended. The gods therefore were seen as manifestations of these forces: the sky and the heavenly bodies who controlled the weather; the land, the sea and rivers which could give food, fertility and healing for man and beast. Animals occur frequently in Iron Age iconography, sometimes as attributes of certain gods or as tribal totems like the White Horse of Uffington, sometimes perhaps as powers in their own right (Green 1992).

In Europe, where the information is plentiful, it is possible to recognise regional preferences for particular representations and to suggest that some gods are local and others more universal, but in Britain and especially in Wales the evidence is so sparse that such an analysis would be unrewarding. It is possible to recognise sky gods, such as Taranis, rapidly assimilated to Jupiter, by their thunderbolts; sun gods, represented by the wheel; the horned god Cernunnos, who appears as lord of the animals; and the mother goddess, with a cornucopia and other symbols of fertility. Such concepts are extremely widespread and may be found all over the Indo-European world. It is possible that the chariot wheels at Llyn Cerrig Bach may indicate a connection with the sun god (Lynch 1991, 295n), while the universal mother goddess was venerated by the Silures in Romanised Caerwent (M.J. Green 1986). Healing shrines like those at the source of the Seine in Burgundy and at Lydney were normally under the protection of a more local deity. At Lydney inscriptions show that this was Nodens whose attribute was a dog, the healing quality of the dog's saliva being widely acknowledged from Anubis in ancient Egypt to St Roche (Wheeler & Wheeler 1932).

The hierarchy which sustained this religious structure is described for us by Posidonius (Tierney 1960; Koch & Carey 1995). The priesthood, recruited from among the sons of noblemen, was divided into three ranks: Druids, *vates* or diviners, and bards (Green 1997). The Druids were the chief priests and the repository of customary law and the rules of ritual practice. For this they had to undergo a long and meticulous training and their position as guardians of correct behaviour in both the secular and religious spheres gave them considerable power in tribal society. This power may have been increased by their cross-tribal mobility, for Caesar implies (*de Bello Gallico* VI, xiii, xiv) that they were a rallying point for national resistance. They themselves, however, are not recorded as fighters except on one notable occasion when they were present at the defence of Anglesey against Paulinus in AD 60 (Tacitus *Annals* XIV, xxx) This, and the unusual ferocity of the Roman attack upon the island's religious sites, led to the suggestion that Anglesey was a major Druidic stronghold. The rich and varied deposit at Llyn Cerrig Bach might lend support to such a theory but unfortunately archaeology cannot provide the necessary proof (Lynch 1991, 313).

SOCIAL STRUCTURE

Our knowledge of the politics of prehistoric peoples is always indirect, derived either from accounts written by strangers, from post-Roman Irish and, to a lesser extent, Welsh literature, or from fallible interpretation of burials, settlements and trading patterns. For Europe in the Iron Age two lines of evidence are present. Greek and Roman writers, notably Caesar, discuss their northern neighbours in some detail and the rich graves surrounding great fortresses tend to confirm the picture they paint (Cunliffe 1988). In Wales the evidence is much less clear but is susceptible to interpretation in the light of what we know about contemporary Europe.

The graves of Hallstatt Europe suggest a society of chiefs and warriors held together by bonds of personal loyalty cemented by the offering of favours and rewards (Renfrew & Shennan 1982). The graves of chiefs equipped with wine and drinking cups reveal that, at the upper levels of society, these rewards were very personal and centred around the feast where champions' deeds of bravery were recognised. The presence of imported wine also reveals that the power to hold loyalty might be dependent upon the power to control access to coveted prizes. Exotic objects or animals from distant places – like the Barbary ape which died at Navan in Ireland (Waterman 1997, 122–5) – are witness to the trading embassies which underpinned this power system. The relationship with the bulk of the farming population is less easy to define but a system of clientage and the offering of tribute in return for protection may be easily imagined. The degree of freedom within such a relationship may have varied through space and time.

Such personal systems of government are potentially unstable and in southern France more formal *civitates* were developing, with elective offices of state, akin to those of the Roman Republic (Nash 1978). Further north things remained more old-fashioned and chiefs and minor kings survived. Britain is one of the old-fashioned areas but the social structure had never been uniform and the degree of centralisation and the size of the relevant territories would have varied a good deal.

The idealised picture of a typical Celtic community has the kin-group as its basic unit, a number of which constituted a tribe, with a king at its head. In Ireland there was even a hierarchy of kings. Below the king were the nobles and the skilled men including priests, bards and craftsmen, and below these in turn were the various degrees of free men, then bondmen, in the service of their social superiors, and, finally, slaves.

The king and the nobles formed the warrior caste whose power and prestige depended upon martial prowess and the ability to attract and maintain retainers or clients. Warfare thus became endemic and is reflected in the creation of hillforts and other defensible sites which could be used for the storage of wealth or booty and the hosting of feasts for retainers, and the emphasis upon the possession and exchange of prestige goods, particularly arms and armour. Literary sources emphasise the deeds of heroes, ritualised individual combat between champions (featuring head-taking), and raiding. To this end hillforts and other defensible enclosures are deemed likely to have been high-status sites. Certainly they were functionally defensive and in some instances are known to have been attacked (Stanford 1972, 30). But the physical appearance of a site – involving multivallation and elaborate entrances – may have been as much for personal aggrandisement as for defence. This may be particularly applicable to the smaller sites whose defences are often out of all proportion to their size. Their ability to store agricultural produce – the number of four-post structures at some sites being much more than needed for their likely population – and protect livestock may also demonstrate the status and coercive power of their inhabitants.

It has been suggested that the larger hillforts, where these occur, may have functioned as territorial centres, symbolically if not always in a practical sense. Cunliffe (1991, 352–7, 533) firms up this opinion. He sees some of the larger Wessex hillforts assuming a role as central places, representing the social, economic and religious foci of specific groups from the Middle Iron Age onwards, with certain forts having attained pre-eminence at the expense of others, which were abandoned. This is a view which has not received general acceptance (Collis 1981). There is no evidence to suggest that such processes were ever at work in Wales, but had they been then it is in the plethora of Marcher hillforts that we might expect to find the tell-tale traces. Similarly, the view that all major hillforts housed a king and a proportion of his retainers, including craftsmen, while smaller hillforts and the more impressive defended enclosures were the residences of lesser nobles is again too simplistic, since it makes no allowance for changes within the socio-economic system over a span of half a millennium.

At a crude level variations in the size of hillforts across Wales must represent differences in population and social structure. Indeed the presence of large hillforts such as The Breiddin, strongly defended enclosures such as Collfryn, and small embanked farmsteads in the Marches probably represent a quite different social structure from that represented by the ringforts and embanked farmsteads of the south west. However, in a comparison of contemporary structures and artefact assemblages at The Breiddin and Collfryn, Musson (1991, 187–90) has warned of the danger of assuming that these two sites are in any way typical of their class, or that differences in round-house size, involvement in the salt and pottery trades, metalworking debris and so on can be easily interpreted on a socio-economic basis given the differences in the size of the excavated areas and the topography of the two sites.

It has been suggested that two basic socio-economic systems existed in Wales and the Marches: an eastern redistributive economy in those zones dominated by large hillforts, where agricultural surpluses were stored and exchanged, and political power was vested in dominant chiefs who exercised their authority from major hillforts; and a western clientage economy in a region where major hillforts were few, political power fragmented and vested in a large number of petty chiefs, and where a dichotomy existed between producer farms and consumer settlements (Cunliffe 1991, 394–8; Williams 1988b). The larger populations implied by the greater size of the Marches forts, though fragmented, were nevertheless likely to be more amenable to manipulation, since they seem to have shared common cultural traits indicated by common ceramic forms. A strongly knit alliance of clans might then be expected in the northern and southern Marches respectively.

The situation in south-west Wales appears to have been very different. Williams (1988b) has suggested two contrasting social systems in this area: a redistributive system, possibly based upon a surplus of animal products, in a zone of larger hillforts in the north and east of the region; and a clientage system in the inland south and west based upon a multiplicity of small enclosures, some of which were of higher status than others. The resulting social system overall would have been based upon small clans who rarely acted in concert. Although such broad social distinctions may have some validity, in particular the lack of suitable conditions for the creation of centralised tribal communities on the southern English model, there are uncertainties about the finer points, particularly the existence of a clientage system based upon archaeological interpretations of food-producing strategies (Williams & Mytum 1998, 142–4).

Evidence for social sub-division may possibly be reflected in the juxtaposition of sites, or the internal layout of settlements of otherwise similar type. The pairing of settlements, such as Woodside and Dan y Coed (Pembrokeshire) (**Fig. 4.5**) is a common phenomenon, particularly in western Britain, and is considered to be a product of the proliferation of settlements caused by the system of partible inheritance (Williams & Mytum 1998, 144; Cunliffe 1983, 87). At Drim in south-west Wales a single round-house sufficed for what was probably a single family, while at Woodside there are two groupings of three round-houses sufficient for two families. At the latter we may be observing either the expansion of a family group or a personal entourage possibly maintained under client relationships (Williams & Mytum 1998, 137). Comparable groupings are known elsewhere. For example, Smith's (1977) analysis of the enclosed homesteads in north-west Wales also suggested variable social groups, ranging from single and extended families to small nucleations. Whether these undefended settlements housed bondmen as well as lower-status freemen is a matter for conjecture. As for slaves, the only archaeological record of them is in the form of two splendidly preserved gang-chains, presumably for the fettering of prisoners of war, from Llyn Cerrig Bach, Anglesey (Fox 1946, 84–5).

BIBLIOGRAPHY

Alcock, L. 1960. 'Castell Odo. An embanked settlement on Mynydd Ystum, near Aberdaron, Caernarvonshire', *Archaeologia Cambrensis* 109, 78–135.

Alcock, L. 1965. 'Hillforts in Wales and the Marches', *Antiquity* 35, 184–95.

Aldhouse-Green, S.H.R. 1996. 'Hoyle's Mouth and Little Hoyle caves', *Archaeology in Wales* 36, 70–1.

Aldhouse-Green, S.H.R. 1997. 'The Paviland research project: the field assessment', *Archaeology in Wales* 37, 3–12.

Aldhouse-Green, S.H.R. 1998a. 'The archaeology of distance: perspectives from the Welsh palaeolithic', in Ashton *et al.* (eds), 1998, 137–45.

Aldhouse-Green, S.H.R. 1998b. 'An Upper Palaeolithic shouldered point and other lithics', in N.W. Jones, 1998, 'Excavations within the Medieval town at New Radnor, Powys, 1991–92', *Archaeological Journal* 155, 158–61.

Aldhouse-Green, S.H.R. (ed.). In press. *Paviland Cave and the 'Red Lady': a Definitive Report*, Bristol: Western Academic & Specialist Press.

Aldhouse-Green, S.H.R. & Housley, R.A. 1993. 'The Uskmouth mattock: a radiocarbon date', *Archaeologia Cambrensis* 142, 340.

Aldhouse-Green, S.H.R. & Northover, J.P. 1996a. 'The Discovery of Three Bronze Age Gold Torques in Pembrokeshire', *Archaeologia Cambrensis* 143, 37–45.

Aldhouse-Green, S.H.R. & Northover, J.P. 1996b. 'Recent finds of Late Bronze Age Gold from South Wales', *Antiquaries Journal* 76, 223–8.

Aldhouse-Green, S.H.R. & Pettitt, P.B. 1998. 'Paviland cave: contextualising the Red Lady', *Antiquity* 72, 756–72.

Aldhouse-Green, S.H.R., Scott, K., Schwarcz, H., Grün, R., Housley, R., Rae, A., Bevins, R. & Redknap, M. 1995. 'Coygan Cave, Laugharne, South Wales: A Mousterian site and hyaena den: a report on the University of Cambridge excavations', *Proceedings of the Prehistoric Society* 61, 37–79.

Aldhouse-Green, S.H.R., Stringer, C.B. & Pettitt, P. 1996. 'Holocene hominids at Pontnewydd and Cae Gronw', *Antiquity* 70, 444–7.

Aldhouse-Green, S.H.R., Whittle, A.W.R., Allen, J.R.L., Caseldine, A.E., Culver, S.J., Day, M.H., Lundquist, J. & Upton D. 1992. 'Prehistoric human footprints from the Severn Estuary at Uskmouth and Magor Pill, Gwent, Wales', *Archaeologia Cambrensis* 141, 14–55.

Alexander, J.A. 1981. 'The coming of iron-using to Britain', in H. Haefner (ed.) *Fruhes Eisen in Europa*, Schaffhausen.

Allen, D. 1993. 'Brenig 53: Mesolithic and Neolithic occupation area', in Lynch, 1993, 17–22.

Allen, J.R.L. 1996. 'Three later Bronze Age occupations at Rumney Great Wharf on the Wentlooge Level, Gwent', *Archaeology in the Severn Estuary: 1995* 6, 9–12.

Allen, J.R.L. 1998. 'Late Iron Age and earliest calcite-gritted ware from sites on the Severn Estuary Levels: Character and Distribution', *Studia Celtica* 32, 27–41.

Alley, R.D., Meese, D.A., Schumm, C.A., Gow, A.J., Taylor, K.C., Grootes, P.M., White, J.W.C., Ram., Waddington, E.D., Mayeski, P.A. & Zielinski, G.H. 1993. 'Abrupt increases in Greenland snow accumulation at the end of the Younger Dryas event', *Nature* 362, 527–9.

Allsworth-Jones, P. 1993. 'The Archaeology of Archaic and Early Modern Homo sapiens: an African perspective', *Cambridge Archaeological Journal* 3, 21–39.

Anon. 1872. Note in *Archaeologia* 43, 553–6, Plate 36.

ApSimon, A.1985/6. 'Chronological Contexts for Irish Megalithic Tombs', *Journal of Irish Archaeology* 3, 5–15.

Armstrong, K. 1993. *A History of God*, London: Heinemann.

van Arsdell, R.D. 1989. *The Celtic Coinage of Britain*, London: Spink.

Ashton, N.M., Healy, F. & Pettitt, P.B. (eds). 1998. *Stone Age Archaeology: essays in honour of John Wymer*, Oxford: Oxbow Monograph 102.

Atkinson, R.J.C. 1968. 'Old Mortality: some aspects of burial and population', in J. Coles & D. Simpson, 1968, 83–94.

Atkinson, R.J.C. 1972. 'Burial and Population in the British Bronze Age', in F.M. Lynch & C.B. Burgess, 1972, 107–16

Atkinson, T.C., Briffa, K.R. & Coope, G.R. 1987. 'Seasonal temperatures in Britain during the last 22,000 years, reconstructed using beetle remains', *Nature* 325, 587–92.

Austin, D., Bell, M. & Burnham, B.C. 1984–8. *The Caer Cadwgan Project. Interim Reports 1984–8*, Lampeter: St David's University College.

Avery, M. 1993. *Hillfort Defences of Southern Britain*, Oxford, British Archaeological Reports, British Series 231.

Barber, J. 1982. 'Arran', *Current Archaeology* 83, 358–63.

Barber, J. 1990. 'Variations on a theme', in V. Buckley, 1990, 98–101.

Barber, K.E. & Coope, G.R. 1987. 'Climatic history of the Severn Valley during the last 18,000 years', in K.G. Gregory, J. Lewin & J.B. Thornes (eds), 1987, *Palaeohydrology in Practice*, Chichester: Wiley, 201–15.

Barham, L., Priestly, P. & Targett, A. 1999. *In Search of Cheddar Man*, Stroud: Tempus.

Baring-Gould, S. 1903. 'The Exploration of Clegyr Voia', *Archaeologia Cambrensis* 6th series 3, 1–11.

Baring-Gould, S., Burnard, R. & Anderson, I.K. 1900. 'Exploration of Moel Trigarn', *Archaeologia Cambrensis* 54, 189–211.

Barker, C.T. 1992. *The Chambered Tombs of South West Wales* Oxford: Oxbow Monograph 14.

Barker, G. 1985. *Prehistoric Farming in Europe*, Cambridge: Cambridge University Press.

Barker, P.A., Haldon, R. & Jenks, W.E. 1991. 'Excavations on Sharpstones Hill near Shrewsbury, 1965–71', in M.O.H. Carver (ed.), 1991, 15–57.

Barnwell, E.L. 1875. 'The Rhosnesney Bronze Implements', *Archaeologia Cambrensis* 4th series 6, 70–3.

Barnwell, E.L. 1882. 'Articles supposed to be spoons', *Archaeologia Cambrensis* 36, 208–19.

Barrett, J.C. 1994. *Fragments from Antiquity: an archaeology of social life in Britain 2900–1200 BC*, Oxford: Basil Blackwell.

Barrett, J.C. & Kinnes I.A. 1988. *The Archaeology of Context in the Neolithic and Bronze Age: Recent Trends*, Sheffield: Sheffield University, Dept. of Archaeology and Prehistory.

Barton, N. 1997. *Stone Age Britain*. London: English Heritage.

Barton, R.N.E. 1989. 'Long blade technology in southern Britain', in C. Bonsall (ed.), 1989, *The Mesolithic in Europe. Papers presented at the third international symposium, Edinburgh 1985*, Edinburgh: John Donald, 264–72.

Barton, R.N.E. 1999. 'The Late Glacial or Late and Final Upper Palaeolithic colonization of Britain', in J. Hunter & I. Ralston (eds), 1999, 13–34.

Barton, R.N.E., Berridge, P.J., Walker, M.J.C. & Bevins, R.E. 1995. 'Persistant places in the Welsh Mesolithic: an example from the Black Mountain upland of South Wales', *Proceedings of the Prehistoric Society* 61, 81–116.

Barton, R.N.E., Price, C. & Proctor, C. 1997. 'Wye Valley Caves Project: recent investigations at King Arthur's Cave and Madawg rock shelter', in S.G. Lewis & D. Maddy (eds), 1997, 63–73.

Barton, R.N.E. & Roberts, A.J. 1996. 'Reviewing the British Late Upper Palaeolithic: new evidence for chronological patterning in the Lateglacial record', *Oxford Journal of Archaeology* 15, 245–65.

Barton, R.N.E., Roberts, A.J. & Roe, D. (eds). 1991. *The Late Glacial in North-West Europe: Human Adaptation and Environmental Change at the End of the Pleistocene*, London: Council for British Archaeology, Research Report 77.

Baynes, E.N. 1909. 'The Excavation of Two Barrows at Ty'n y Pwll, Llanddyfnan, Anglesey', *Archaeologia Cambrensis* 6th series 9, 312–32.

de Beaune, S.A. 1987. *Lampes et Godets au Paleolithique*, 23rd supplement to *Gallia Prehistoire*, Paris: CNRS.

de Beaune, S.A. & White, R. 1993. 'Ice Age Lamps', *Scientific American*, March 1993, 108–13.

Beck, C. & Shennan, S. 1991. *Amber in Prehistoric Britain* Oxford: Oxbow Monograph 8.

Bell, M. 1990. *Brean Down Excavations, 1983–1987*, English Heritage Archaeological Report no. 15.

Bell, M. 1992. 'Goldcliff', *Archaeology in Wales* 32, 61.

Bell, M. 1993. 'Intertidal archaeology at Goldcliff in the Severn Estuary', in J. Coles, V. Fenwick & G. Hutchinson (eds), 1993, *A Spirit of Enquiry: essays for Ted Wright*, Exeter: Wetland Archaeology Research Project, University of Exeter, 9–13.

Bell, M. & Neumann, H. 1997. 'Prehistoric intertidal archaeology and environments in the Severn Estuary, Wales', *World Archaeology* 29.1, 95–113.

Bell, M., Allen, J.R.L., Barton, R.N.E., Coard, R., Crowther, J., Cruise, G.M., Ingrem, C. and Macphail, R. 1999. 'The Goldcliff late Mesolithic site, 5,400–4,000 cal BC', in Bell, M., Caseldine, A. & Neumann, H. *Prehistoric Intertidal Archaeology in the Welsh Severn Estuary*, York: Council for British Archaeology, Research Report 120, 33–63.

Benedict, R. 1934. *Patterns of Culture*, Boston/New York: Houghton Miffin Co.

Benson, D. & Williams, G. 1987. 'Dale Fort', *Archaeology in Wales* 27, 43.

Benson, D.G., Evans, J.G., Williams, G.H., Darvill, T. & David, A. 1990. 'Excavations at Stackpole Warren, Dyfed', *Proceedings of the Prehistoric Society* 56, 179–245.

Berridge, P. 1994. 'Cornish axe factories: Fact or fiction?', in N. Ashton & A. David (eds), 1994, *Stories in Stone*, Oxford: Lithic Studies Occasional Paper 4, 45–56.

Bersu, G. & Griffiths, W.E. 1949. 'Concentric circles at Llwyn-du Bach, Penegroes, Caernarvonshire', *Archaeologia Cambrensis* 100 (2), 173–206.

Bevan-Evans, M. & Hayes, P. 1955. 'Report on the Cairn on Cefn Goleu near Moel Fammau', *Flintshire Historical Society Publications* 15, 112–37.

Binant, P. 1991a. *La Préhistoire du Mort*, Paris: Editions Errance.

Binant, P. 1991b. *Les Sépultures du Paléolithique*, Paris: Collection Archéologie Aujourd'hui, Editions Errance.

Blockley, K. 1989. *Prestatyn 1984–5 An Iron Age Farmstead and Romano-British Industrial Settlement in North Wales*, Oxford: British Archaeological Reports, British Series 210.

Boaz, N.T. & Almquist, A.J. 1999. *Essentials of Biological Anthropology*, New Jersey: Prentice Hall.

Boon, G.C. 1976. 'The Shrine of the Head, Caerwent', in G.C. Boon & J.M. Lewis, 1976, 163–76.

Boon, G.C. 1977. 'A Graeco-Roman anchor-stock from North Wales', *Antiquaries Journal* 57, 10–30.

Boon, G.C. 1980a. 'A neglected Late Celtic Mirror-Handle from Llanwnda near Fishguard', *Bulletin of the Board of Celtic Studies* 28, 743–4.

Boon, G.C. 1980b. 'A Gaulish coin from Merthyr Mawr Warren, Glamorganshire', *Bulletin of the Board of Celtic Studies* 29, 345.

Boon, G.C. 1988. 'British coins from Wales', in D.M. Robinson (ed.), 1988, 92.

Boon, G.C. & Savory, H.N. 1975. 'A silver trumpet brooch with relief decoration in parcel gilt from Carmarthen and a note on the development of the type', *Antiquaries Journal* 48, 100–3.

Boon, G.C. & Lewis, J.M. 1976. *Welsh Antiquity: Essays presented to Dr H.N. Savory*, Cardiff: National Museum of Wales.

Bostock, J.L. 1980. 'The History of the Vegetation of the Berwyn Mountains, North Wales, with emphasis on the Development of the Blanket Mire', unpub. PhD, University of Manchester.

Boujot, C. & Cassen, S. 1993. 'Neolithic funerary structures in the west of France', *Antiquity* 67, 477–91.

Bowen, E.G. & Gresham, C.A. 1967. *History of Merioneth. Volume I: From the earliest times to the Age of the Native Princes*, Dolgellau: The Merioneth Historical and Record Society.

Bradley, R.J. 1978. *The Prehistoric Settlement of Britain*, London: Routledge & Kegan Paul.

Bradley, R.J. 1990. *The passage of Arms: an Archaeological analysis of Prehistoric Hoards and Votive Deposits*, Cambridge: Cambridge University Press.

Bradley, R.J. & Edmonds, M. 1988. 'Fieldwork at Great Langdale, Cumbria 1985–1987: Preliminary Report', *Antiquaries Journal* 68, 181–209.

Bradley, R.J. & Edmonds, M. 1993. *Interpreting the Axe Trade*, Cambridge: Cambridge University Press.

Bradley, R.J. & Suthren, R. 1990. 'Petrographic analysis of hammerstones from the Neolithic quarries at Great Langdale', *Proceedings of the Prehistoric Society* 56, 117–22.

Brassil, K.S. 1991a. 'Mesolithic', in J. Manley *et al.* (eds), 1991, 47–54.

Brassil, K.S. 1991b. 'Prehistoric and Early Medieval Cemeteries at Tandderwen, near Denbigh, Clwyd', *Archaeological Journal* 148, 46–97.

Brassil, K.S. 1992. 'Ty Tan y Foel, Cerrig y Drudion', *Archaeology in Wales* 32, 58.

Brassil, K.S. 1993. 'Ty Tan y Foel, Cerrig y Drudion', *Archaeology in Wales* 33, 50.

Brassil, K.S., Guilbert, G.C., Livens, R.G., Stead, W.H. & Bevan-Evans, M. 1982. 'Rescue excavations at Moel Hiraddug between 1960 and 1980', *Journal of the Flintshire Historical Society* 30, 13–88.

Brewer, R.J. 1986. *Corpus Signorum Imperii Romani: Corpus of Sculpture of the Roman World. Great Britain* vol. 1. Fascicule 5. *Wales*, Oxford: British Academy.

Briggs, C.S. 1977. 'Stone axe "trade" or glacial erratics?', *Current Archaeology* 57, 303.

Briggs, C.S. 1987. 'Buckets and Cauldrons in the Late Bronze Age of NW Europe: A Review', *Actes de Colloque de Bronze de Lille* Supplement de la *Revue Archaeologique de Picardie*, 161–87.

Briggs, C.S., Britnell, W.J. & Gibson, A.M. 1990. 'Two Cordoned Urns from Fan y Big, Brecon Beacons, Powys', *Proceedings of the Prehistoric Society* 56, 173–8.

Briggs, C.S. & Williams, G. 1997. 'The Late Bronze Age Hoard from Allt Gelli Felen, Myddfai, Carmarthenshire, and other recent finds of South Welsh axes', *Archaeologia Cambrensis* 144, 37–51.

Brindley, A.L., Lanting, J.N. & Mook, G.W. 1990. 'The radiocarbon dating of Irish *fulachta fiadh* and their context', *Journal of Irish Archaeology* 5, 25–33.

Britnell, W.J. 1982. 'The excavation of two Round Barrows at Trelystan, Powys', *Proceedings of the Prehistoric Society* 48, 133–201.

Britnell, W.J. 1984. 'A barbed point from Porth-y-Waen, Llanyblodwel, Shropshire', *Proceedings of the Prehistoric Society* 50, 385–6.

Britnell, W.J. 1989. 'The Collfryn hillslope enclosure, Llansantffraid Deuddwr, Powys: excavations 1980–1982', *Proceedings of the Prehistoric Society* 55, 89–134.

Britnell, W.J. 1991. 'The Neolithic', in J.F. Manley *et al.*, 1991, 55–64.

Britnell W.J. 1994. 'Excavation and Recording at Pennant Melangell Church', *Montgomeryshire Collections* 82, 41–102.

Britnell, W.J. & Musson, C.R. 1984. 'Rescue excavations of a Romano-British double-ditched enclosure at Arddleen, Llandrinio, northern Powys', *Archaeologia Cambrensis* 133, 91–9.

Britnell, W.J. & Savory, H.N. 1984. *Gwernvale and Penywyrlod: Two Neolithic Long Cairns in the Black Mountains of Brecknock*, Cardiff: Cambrian Archaeological Monographs 2.

Britnell, W.J., Silvester, R.J., Gibson, A.M., Caseldine, A.E.; Hunter, K.L., Johnson, S., Hamilton-Dyer, S. & Vince, A. 1997. 'A Middle Bronze Age Round-House at Glanfeinion, near Llandinam, Powys', *Proceedings of the Prehistoric Society* 63, 179–97.

Britton, D. 1964. 'Traditions of metal-working in the Later Neolithic and Early Bronze Age of Britain: Part I', *Proceedings of the Prehistoric Society* 29, 258–325.

Brunaux, J.-L. 1988. *The Celtic Gauls: Gods, Rites and Sanctuaries*, trans. D. Nash, London: Seaby.

Buckland, W. 1823. *Reliquiae Diluvianae*, London: John Murray.

Buckley V. 1990. *Burnt Offerings: International Contributions to Burnt Mound Archaeology*, Dublin: Wordwell.

Burgess, C.B. 1964. 'A Palstave from Chepstow with some observations on the earliest palstaves in the British Isles', *Monmouthshire Antiquary* 1, pt 1, 117–24.

Burgess, C.B. 1968a. 'The Later Bronze Age in the British Isles and north-western France', *Archaeological Journal* 125, 1–45.

Burgess, C.B. 1968b. *Bronze Age Metalwork in Northern England*, Newcastle.

Burgess, C.B. 1974. 'The Bronze Age', in A.C. Renfrew (ed.), 1974, *British Prehistory*, London: Duckworth.

Burgess, C.B. 1976. 'Burials with metalwork of the later Bronze Age in Wales and beyond', in G.C. Boon & J.M. Lewis, 1976, 81–104.

Burgess, C.B. 1979a. 'The background of early metalworking in Ireland and Britain', in M. Ryan (ed.), 1979, 207–14.

Burgess, C.B. 1979b. 'A Find from Boynton, Suffolk, and the end of the Bronze Age in Britain and Ireland', in C.B. Burgess & D.G. Coombs (eds), 1979, *Bronze Age Hoards: Some Finds Old and New*, Oxford: British Archaeological Reports, British Series 67, 269–83.

Burgess, C.B. 1980a. 'The Bronze Age', in J.A. Taylor (ed.), 1980b, 243–86.

Burgess, C.B. 1980b. *The Age of Stonehenge*, London: Dent.

Burgess, C.B. 1985 'Population, climate and upland settlement', in D. Spratt & C.B. Burgess (eds), 1985, *Upland Settlement in Britain. The Second Millennium BC and after*, Oxford: British Archaeological Reports, British Series 104, 195–230.

Burgess, C.B. 1986. '"Urnes of no small variety": Collared Urns Reviewed', *Proceedings of the Prehistoric Society* 52, 339–51.

Burgess, C.B., Coombs, D.G. & Davies, D.G. 1972. 'The Broadward Complex and Barbed Spearheads', in F.M. Lynch & C.B. Burgess (eds), 1972, 211–83.

Burgess, C.B. & Cowen, J.D. 1972. 'The Ebnal Hoard and Early Bronze Age metal-working traditions in Ireland and Britain', in F.M. Lynch & C.B. Burgess (eds), 1972, 167–81.

Burgess, C.B. & Gerloff, S. 1981. *The Dirks and Rapiers of Great Britain and Ireland*, Praehistorisches Bronzfunde, IV.7, Munich, UISSP, C.H. Beck'sche Verlag.

Burgess, C.B. & Colquhoun, I. 1988. *The Swords of Britain*, Praehistorisches Bronzfunde, IV.5, Munich, UISSP, C.H. Beck'sche Verlag.

Burl, H.A.W. 1988. *Four Posters: Bronze Age Stone Circles of Western Europe*, Oxford: British Archaeological Reports, British Series 195.

Burl, H.A.W. 1993. *From Carnac to Callanish. The prehistoric Stone Rows and Avenues of Britain, Ireland and Brittany*, Newhaven: Yale University Press.

Burnham, B.C. & Davies, J.L. (eds). 1991. *Conquest, Co-existence and Change: Recent Work in Roman Wales*, *Trivium* 25, Lampeter: St David's University College.

Burton, J. 1984. 'Field research at the stone axe quarries of Western highlands and Simbu Provinces, Papua New Guinea', *Bulletin of the Indo-Pacific Prehistoric Association* 5, 83–92.

Butler, J.J. 1963. 'Bronze Age Connections across the North Sea', *Palaeohistoria* 9, Monograph. Groningen.

Campbell, J.B. 1977. *The Upper Palaeolithic of Britain*, 2 volumes, Oxford: Clarendon Press.

Campbell, S. & Bowen, D.Q. 1989. *Geological Conservation Review: Quaternary of Wales*, Peterborough: Nature Conservancy Council.

Cantrill, T.C. & Jones, O.T. 1911. 'Prehistoric Cooking Places in South Wales', *Archaeologia Cambrensis* 6th Series 11, 253–86.

Carver, M.O.H. (ed.). 1991. 'Prehistory in Lowland Shropshire', *Transactions of the Shropshire Archaeological and Historical Society* 67, 1–8.

Case, H.J. 1961. 'Irish Neolithic Pottery: Distribution and Sequence', *Proceedings of the Prehistoric Society* 27, 174–233.

Case, H.J. 1969. 'Neolithic Explanations', *Antiquity* 43, 176–86.

Case, H.J. & Whittle, A.W.R. 1982. *Settlement patterns in the Oxford region: excavations at the Abingdon causewayed enclosure and other sites*, London & Oxford: Council for British Archaeology Research Report 44.

Caseldine, A. 1990. *Environmental Archaeology in Wales*, Lampeter: Cadw and St David's University College, Lampeter.

Casey, P.J. & Hoffman, B. 1999. 'Excavations at the Roman Temple in Lydney Park, Gloucestershire in 1980 and 1981', *Antiquaries Journal* 79, 81–143.

Caulfield, S. 1983. 'The Neolithic settlement of N. Connaught', in T. Reeves-Smyth & F. Hamond, 1983, 195–216.

Chambers, F.M. 1982. 'Environmental history of Cefn Gwernffrwd, near Rhandirmwyn, Mid Wales', *New Phytologist* 92, 607–15.

Chambers, F.M., Kelly, R.S. & Price, S.-M. 1988. 'Development of the late prehistoric cultural landscape in upland Ardudwy, north-west Wales', in H.H. Birks, H.J.B. Birks, P.E. Kalund & D. Moe (eds), 1988, *The Cultural Landscape: Past, Present and Future*, Cambridge: Cambridge University Press, 333–48.

Chambers, F.M. & Price, S.-M. 1988. 'The environmental setting of Erw Wen and Moel-y-Gerddi: prehistoric enclosures in upland Ardudwy, north Wales', *Proceedings of the Prehistoric Society* 54, 93–100.

Chambers, F.M. & Lageard, J.G.A. 1993. 'Vegetational history and the environmental setting of Crawcwellt, Gwynedd', *Archaeology in Wales* 33, 23–5.

Champion, T.C., Gamble, C., Shennan, S. & Whittle, A. 1984. *Prehistoric Europe*, London: Academic Press.

Charters, S. & Evershed, R. *et al.* 1997. 'Simulation experiments for determining the use of ancient pottery vessels: the behaviour of epicuticular leaf wax during boiling of a leafy vegetable', *Journal of Archaeological Science* 24, 1–7.

Chitty, L.F. 1963. 'The Clun–Clee Ridgeway: a Prehistoric Trackway across South Shropshire', in I.Ll. Foster & L. Alcock (eds), 1963, 171–92.

Clark, J.G.D. 1938. 'Microlithic industries from tufa deposits at Prestatyn, Flintshire, and Blashenwell, Dorset', *Proceedings of the Prehistoric Society* 4, 330–4.

Clark, J.G.D. 1939. 'Further note on the tufa deposit at Prestatyn, Flintshire', *Proceedings of the Prehistoric Society* 5, 201–2.

Clark, J.G.D. 1966. 'The Invasion Hypothesis in British Archaeology', *Antiquity* 40, 172–89.

Clark, J.G.D. 1972. *Star Carr: a case study in Bioarchaeology*, USA: Addison-Wesley Modular Publications no. 10.

Clark, J.G.D. 1980. *Mesolithic Prelude*, Edinburgh: Edinburgh University Press.

Clarke, D.L. 1976. 'Mesolithic Europe: the economic basis', in G. Sieveking *et al.*, (eds), 1976, 449–82.

Clarke, D.V., Cowie, T.G. & Foxon, A. 1985. *Symbols of Power in the Age of Stonehenge*, London: HMSO.

Clayton, D. & Savory, H.N. 1990. 'The excavation of a Neolithic hut floor on Cefn Glas, Rhondda 1971–4', *Archaeologia Cambrensis* 139, 12–20.

Cleal, R.M.J., Walker, K.E. & Montague, R. 1995. *Stonehenge in its Landscape. Twentieth Century Excavations*, London: English Heritage.

Clough, T.H.McK. & Cummins, W.A. 1979. *Stone Axe Studies*, London: Council for British Archaeology, Research Report 23.

Clough, T.H.McK. & Cummins, W.A. 1988. *Stone Axe Studies II*, London: Council for British Archaeology, Research Report 67.

Cloutman, E. 1983. Studies of the Vegetational History of the Black Mountain Range, South Wales, unpub. PhD, University of Wales.

Coles, J.M. 1962. 'European Bronze Shields', *Proceedings of the Prehistoric Society* 28, 156–90.

Coles, J.M. & Simpson, D.D.A. 1968. *Studies in Ancient Europe: Essays presented to Stuart Piggott*, Leicester: Leicester University Press.

Coles, J.M. & Coles, B. 1986. *Sweet Track to Glastonbury*, London: Thames & Hudson.

Coles, J.M., Leach, P., Minnitt, S.C., Tabor, R. & Wilson, A.S. 1999. 'A Later Bronze Age shield from South Cadbury, Somerset, England', *Antiquity* 73, 33–48.

Colgrave, B. & Mynors, R.A.B. 1991. *Bede's Ecclesiastical History of the English People*, new edition, Oxford: Clarendon Press.

Collis, J. 1973. 'Burials with weapons in Iron Age Britain', *Germania* 51, 121–33.

Collis, J. 1981. 'A Theoretical study of hillforts', in G. Guilbert (ed.), 1981, *Hill Fort Studies*, 66–76.

Collis, J. 1985. 'Review of B. Cunliffe, *Danebury: An Iron Age Hillfort in Hampshire, Vol. I*', *Proceedings of the Prehistoric Society* 51, 348–9.

Collis, J. 1996. 'The Origin and Spread of the Celts', *Studia Celtica* 30, 17–34.

Conroy, G.C. 1997. *Reconstructing Human Origins: a Modern Synthesis*, London: W.W. Norton & Company.

Corcoran, J.X.W.P. 1952. 'Tankards and tankard handles of the British Early Iron Age', *Proceedings of the Prehistoric Society* 18, 85–102.

Corcoran, J.X.W.P. 1969. 'The Cotswold–Severn Group 1. Distribution, Morphology and Artifacts; 2. Discussion', in T.G.E. Powell *et al.*, 1969, 13–104.

Corcoran, J.X.W.P. 1972. 'Multiperiod Construction and the Origin of the Chambered Long Cairn in western Britain and Ireland', in F.M. Lynch & C.B. Burgess (eds), 1972, 31–64.

Craddock, P. 1979. 'Deliberate alloying in the Atlantic Bronze Age', in M. Ryan (ed.) 1979, 369–85.

Crampton, B. & Webley, D.P. 1966. 'A Section through the Mynydd Troed long barrow, Brecknock', *Bulletin of the Board of Celtic Studies* 22, 71–7.

Crane, P. 1998. 'Porth y Rhaw, Solva', *Archaeology in Wales* 38, 102–3.

Crew, P. 1984. 'Bryn y Castell', *Archaeology in Wales* 24, 37–43.

Crew, P. 1986. 'Bryn y Castell hillfort – a late prehistoric iron-working settlement in north west Wales', in B.G. Scott & H. Cleere (eds), 1986, *The Crafts of the Blacksmith*, Belfast, 91–100.

Crew, P. 1989. 'Crawcwellt West excavations, 1986–1989: a late prehistoric upland iron-working settlement', *Archaeology in Wales* 29, 11–16.

Crew, P. 1991a. 'The experimental production of prehistoric bar iron', *Historical Metallurgy* 25.1, 21–36.

Crew, P. 1991b. 'Crawcwellt West', *Archaeology in Wales* 31, 19.

Crew, P. 1991c. 'Late iron age and Roman iron production in north-west Wales', in B.C. Burnham & J.L. Davies (eds), 1991, 150–60.

Crew, P. 1994. 'Currency bars in Britain – typology and function', in M. Mangin (ed.), 1994, *La Siderurgie ancienne de l'est de la France dans son contexte Europeen*, Besançon: UISSP, 345–50.

Crew, P. 1995. 'Aspects of the Iron Supply', in B. Cunliffe, 1995, 276–84.

Crew, P. 1998. 'Excavations at Crawcwellt West, Merioneth, 1990–1998. A late prehistoric upland iron-working settlement', *Archaeology in Wales* 38, 22–35.

Crew, P. & Crew, S. 1990. *Early Mining in the British Isles*, Plas Tan y Bwlch Occasional Papers 1, Maentwrog: Snowdonia National Park.

Crew, P. & Musson, C.R. 1996. *Snowdonia from the Air*, Penrhyndeudraeth: Snowdonia National Park/RCAHMW.

Crew, P. & Salter, C. 1993. 'Currency Bars with welded tips', in A. Espelund (ed.), 1993, *Bloomery Ironmaking during 2000 years: In Honorem Ole Evenstad*, III, Trondheim: UISSP.

Crossley, D.W. 1964. 'Excavations at Merryborough Camp, Wiston, a Pembrokeshire protected enclosure, 1963', *Bulletin of the Board of Celtic Studies* 21, 105–18.

Crossley, D.W. 1965. 'Excavations at Knock Rath, Clarbeston, 1962', *Bulletin of the Board of Celtic Studies* 21, 264–75.

Crossley, D.W. 1979. 'Excavations at Knock Rath, Clarbeston, Pembrokeshire, 1963–7', *Bulletin of the Board of Celtic Studies* 28, 521–7.

Cummins, W.A. 1974. 'The Neolithic stone axe trade in Britain', *Antiquity* 48, 201–5.

Cummins, W.A. 1979. 'Neolithic stone axes: distribution and trade in England and Wales', in T. Clough & W. Cummins (eds), 1979, 5–12.

Cunliffe, B.W. 1971. *Roman Bath Discovered*, London: Routledge & Kegan Paul.

Cunliffe, B.W. 1983. *Danebury: Anatomy of an Iron Age Hillfort*, London: Batsford.

Cunliffe, B.W. 1987. *Hengistbury Head, Dorset. Vol.1: Prehistoric and Roman Settlement, 3500 BC–AD 500*, Oxford: OUCA Monograph 13.

Cunliffe, B.W. 1988. *Greeks, Romans and Barbarians: spheres of interaction*, London: Batsford.

Cunliffe, B.W. 1991 *Iron Age Communities in Britain. An account of England, Scotland and Wales from the Seventh Century BC until the Roman Conquest*, 3rd edn. London: Routledge.

Cunliffe, B.W. 1995. *Danebury: An Iron Age Hillfort in Hampshire. Volume 6: A Hillfort Community in Perspective*, York: Council for British Archaeology Research Report 102

Cunliffe, B. & Miles, D. 1984. *Aspects of the Iron Age in central southern Britain*, Oxford: Oxford University Committee for Archaeology Monograph 2.

Currant, A.P. 1984. 'The mammalian remains', in H.S. Green, 1984a, 171–80.

Currant, A. & Jacobi, R. 1997. 'Vertebrate faunas from the British Late Pleistocene and the chronology of human settlement', *Quaternary Newsletter* 82, 1–8.

Daniel, G.E. 1941. 'The Dual Nature of the Megalithic Colonisation of Prehistoric Europe', *Proceedings of the Prehistoric Society* 7, 1–49.

Darvill, T.C. 1982. *The Megalithic Chambered Tombs of the Cotswold–Severn Region*, Gloucester: Vorda.

Darvill, T.C. 1989. 'The Circulation of Neolithic stone and flint axes: a case study from Wales and the mid-west of England', *Proceedings of the Prehistoric Society* 55, 27–43.

Darvill, T.C. 1996. 'Neolithic buildings in England, Wales and the Isle of Man', in T.C. Darvill & J. Thomas (eds), 1996, 77–111.

Darvill, T.C. & Thomas, J. 1996. *Neolithic Houses in north-west Europe and beyond*, Oxford: Oxbow Monograph 57.

David, A. 1989. 'Some aspects of the human presence in West Wales during the Mesolithic', in C. Bonsall (ed.), 1989, *The Mesolithic in Europe*, Edinburgh: John Donald, 241–53.

David, A. 1990. 'Palaeolithic and Mesolithic Settlement in Wales with Special Reference to Dyfed', unpubl. PhD thesis, University of Lancaster.

David, A. 1991. 'Late Glacial residues from Wales: a selection', in N. Barton, A.J. Roberts & D.Roe (eds), 1991, *The Late Glacial in North-West Europe: Human Adaptation and Environmental Change at the End of the Pleistocene*, London: Council for British Archaeology, Research Report 77, 141–59.

David, A. & Williams, G. 1995. 'Stone axe manufacture: new evidence from the Preseli Hills, west Wales', *Proceedings of the Prehistoric Society* 61, 433–60.

Davidson, A. 1998. 'Nant Porth, Bangor', *Archaeology in Wales* 38, 96–8.

Davies, D.G. 1967. 'The Guilsfield Hoard: a Reconsideration', *Antiquaries Journal* 47, 95–108.

Davies, J.A. 1924. 'Fourth report on Aveline's Hole', *Proceedings of the University of Bristol Spelaeological Society* 2 (1922–5), 104–14.

Davies, J.D. 1958. 'Palstaves of Welsh Provenance in the Grosvenor Museum, Chester', *Bulletin of the Board of Celtic Studies* 18, 194.

Davies, J.L. 1969. 'Moel Hiraddug', *Archaeology in Wales* 9, 9–10.

Davies, J.L. 1971. 'Moel Hiraddug', *Archaeology in Wales* 11, 8–9.

Davies, J.L. 1973a. 'Cae Summerhouse, Tythegston', *Morgannwg* 17, 53–7.

Davies, J.L. 1973b. 'An excavation at the Bulwarks, Porthkerry, Glamorgan', *Archaeologia Cambrensis* 122, 85–98.

Davies, J.L. 1980. 'Aspects of Native Settlement in Roman Wales and the Marches', unpubl. PhD thesis, University of Wales, Cardiff.

Davies, J.L. 1995. 'The Early Celts in Wales', in M.J. Green (ed.), 1995, *The Celtic World*, London: Routledge, 671–700.

Davies, J.L. & Spratling, M. 1976. 'The Seven Sisters Hoard: a centenary study', in G.C. Boon & J.M. Lewis, 1976, 121–48.

Davies, J.L. & Hogg, A.H.A. 1994. 'The Iron Age', in J.L. Davies & D.P. Kirby (eds), 1994, *Cardiganshire County History. Volume 1. From the earliest times to the coming of the Normans*, Cardiff: University of Wales Press.

Davies, M. 1989. 'Recent advances in cave archaeology in southwest Wales', in T. Ford (ed.), 1989, 78–91.

Davies, O. 1937. 'Mining sites in Wales', *British Association Annual Report for 1937*, 229–41.

Davis, V.R. 1985. 'Implement petrology: the state of the art: some problems and possibilities', in A.P. Phillips (ed.), 1985, *The Archaeologist and the Laboratory*, York: Council for British Archaeology Research Report 58, 33–5.

Dawkins, W.B. 1874. *Cave Hunting*, London: Macmillan.

Dawkins, W.B. 1902. 'On the Cairn and Sepulchral Cave at Gop, near Prestatyn', *Archaeologia Cambrensis* 6th series 11, 161–81.

Day, W. 1972. 'The Excavation of a Bronze Age Burial Mound at Ysgwennant, Llansilin, Denbighshire', *Archaeologia Cambrensis* 121, 17–50.

Dennell, R. 1983. *European Economic Prehistory*, London: Academic Press.

Dennell, R. 1997. 'The world's oldest spears', *Nature* 385, 767–8.

De Valera, R. 1960. 'The Court Cairns of Ireland', *Proceedings of the Royal Irish Academy* 60 C, 9–140.

Dinan, W. 1911. *Monumenta Historia Celtica I: notices of the Celts in the writings of the Greek and Latin authors from the 10th century BC to the 5th century AD*, London: D. Nutt.

Dixon, P.W. 1988. 'Crickley Hill, 1969–1987', *Current Archaeology* 110, 73–8.

Dodd, A.H. 1972. *A Short History of Wales*, London: Batsford. (Reprinted 1990.)

Driver, T. 1995. 'New cropmark sites at Aberthaw, South Glamorgan', *Archaeology in Wales* 35, 3–9.

Driver, T. 1996. 'Darren Hillfort', *Archaeology in Wales* 36, 61.

Duarte, C., Maurício, J., Pettitt, P.B., Souto, P., Trinkaus, E., van der Plicht, H. & Zilhao, J. 1999. 'The early Upper Palaeolithic human skeleton from the Abrigo do Lagar Vehlo (Portugal) and modern human emergence in Iberia', *Proceedings of the National Academy of Sciences, USA* 96, 7604–9.

Dungworth, D. 1996. 'The production of copper alloys in Iron Age Britain', *Proceedings of the Prehistoric Society* 62, 399–422.

Dunning, G.C. 1943. 'A Stone Circle and Cairn on Mynydd Epynt', *Archaeologia Cambrensis* 97, 169–94.

Dutton, A. & Fasham, P.J. 1994. 'Prehistoric copper mining on the Great Orme, Llandudno, Gwynedd', *Proceedings of the Prehistoric Society* 60, 245–86.

Earwood, C. 1993. *Domestic Wooden Artefacts in Britain and Ireland from Neolithic to Viking times*, Exeter: University of Exeter Press.

Earwood, C. & Thomas, D. 1995. Note in *Archaeology in Wales* 35, 37–8.

Edmonds, M.R. 1995. *Stone Tools and Society: working stone in Neolithic and Bronze Age Britain*, London: Batsford.

Edwards, N, 1997. 'Two Carved Stone Pillars from Trefollwyn, Anglesey', *Archaeological Journal* 154, 108–17.

Ehrenburg, M. 1982. 'The contents of the Acton Park, Rhosnesney, Denbighshire, Hoard', *Bulletin of the Board of Celtic Studies* 30, 165–7.

Ehrenburg, M. 1989. 'The interpretation of regional variability in British and Irish Bronze Age metalwork', in H.-A. Nordstrom & A. Knape (eds), 1989, *Bronze Age Studies: Transactions of the British Scandinavian Colloquium in Stockholm May 10–11, 1985*, Stockholm: Statens Hist. Museum, 77–87.

Ehrenburg, M., Price, J. & Vale, V. 1982. 'The Excavation of two Bronze Age Round Barrows at Welsh St Donats, South Glamorgan', *Bulletin of the Board of Celtic Studies* 29, 776–842.

Ehrenreich, R.M. 1985. *Trade, Technology and the ironworking community in the Iron Age of southern Britain* Oxford: British Archaeological Reports, British Series 144.

Ellis Davies, 1929. *Prehistoric and Roman Remains of Denbighshire*, Cardiff: William Lewis.

Ellis Davies, 1937. 'A small hoard of flanged bronze celts from Betws yn Rhos, Denbighshire', *Archaeologia Cambrensis* 92, 335.

Ellis Davies, 1939. 'A Hoard of Large Flint Flakes from Penmachno, Caernarvonshire', *Archaeologia Cambrensis* 94, 106–7.

Ellis Davies, 1941. 'Gloddaeth Bronze Celts (palstaves), Caernarvonshire', *Archaeologia Cambrensis* 96, 205.

Ellis Davies, 1949. *Prehistoric and Roman Remains of Flintshire*, Cardiff: William Lewis.

Eogan, G. 1986. *Knowth and the Passage Tombs of Ireland*, London: Thames & Hudson.

Eogan, G., 1994. *The Accomplished Art. Gold and Goldworking in Britain and Ireland during the Bronze Age, c. 2300–650 BC*, Oxford: Oxbow Monograph 42.

Evans, J.G. 1990. 'An Archaeological Survey of Skomer, Dyfed', *Proceedings of the Prehistoric Society* 56, 247–67.

Fasham, P.J., Kelly, R.S., Mason, M.A. & White, R.B. 1998. *The Graeanog Ridge. The Evolution of a Farming Landscape and its Settlements in North-West Wales*, Aberystwyth: Cambrian Archaeological Monographs no. 6.

Fitzpatrick, A.P. 1984. 'The deposition of La Tène iron age metalwork in watery contexts in southern England', in B. Cunliffe & D. Miles, 1984, 178–91.

Flannery, T. 1994. *The Future Eaters*, Reed Books, Australia.

Fleming, A. 1976. 'Early Settlement and the Landscape in west Yorkshire', in G. de G. Sieveking, I.H. Longworth, & K.E. Wilson (eds), 1976, 359–73.

Fleming, A. 1989. *The Dartmoor Reaves: Investigating Prehistoric Land Divisions*, London: Batsford.

Ford, T. (ed.) 1989. *Limestones and Caves of Wales*, Cambridge: Cambridge University Press.

Forde, D.F., Griffiths, W.E., Hogg, A.H.A. & Houlder, C.H. 1963. 'Excavations at Pen Dinas, Aberystwyth', *Archaeologia Cambrensis* 112, 125–53.

Forde Johnston, J. 1957. 'Megalithic Art in the North-west of Britain: The Calderstones, Liverpool', *Proceedings of the Prehistoric Society* 23, 20–39.

Forde Johnston, J. 1964. 'A Hoard of Flat Axes from Moel Arthur', *Flintshire Historical Society Publications* 21, 99–100.

Foster, I.Ll. & Alcock, L. (eds) 1963. *Culture and Environment: Essays in Honour of Sir Cyril Fox*, London: Routledge & Kegan Paul.

Fox, A. & Ravenhill, W. 1966. 'Early Roman Outposts on the North Devon Coast: Old Burrow and Martinhoe', *Proceedings of the Devon Archaeological Exploration Society* 24, 3–39.

Fox, C. 1932. *The Personality of Britain*, Cardiff: National Museum of Wales.

Fox, C. 1939. 'A Second Cauldron and an Iron Sword from the Llyn Fawr Hoard, Rhigos, Glamorgan', *Antiquaries Journal* 19, 369–404.

Fox, C. 1941. 'A Datable Ritual Barrow in Glamorganshire', *Antiquity* 15, 142–61.

Fox, C. 1942. 'A Beaker Barrow, enlarged in the Middle Bronze Age at South Hill, Talbenny, Pembrokeshire', *Archaeological Journal* 99, 1–32.

Fox, C. 1943. 'A Bronze Age Barrow ("Sutton 268") in Llandow Parish, Glamorgan', *Archaeologia* 89, 89–126.

Fox, C. 1946. *A find of the Early Iron Age from Llyn Cerrig Bach, Anglesey* Cardiff: National Museum of Wales.

Fox, C. 1958. *Pattern and Purpose: a survey of early Celtic art in Britain*, Cardiff: National Museum of Wales.

Gamble, C., Mellars, P.A., Healy, F., Wymer, J., Aldhouse-Green, S., Ashton, N., Barton, N., Lawson, A. & Pettitt, P. 1999. *Research Frameworks for the Palaeolithic and Mesolithic of Britain and Ireland*, London: Prehistoric Society.

Gardner, W. & Savory, H.N. 1964. *Dinorben: a hillfort occupied in Early Iron Age and Roman Times*, Cardiff: National Museum of Wales.

Gelling, P. & Stanford, S.C. 1965. 'Dark Age pottery or Iron Age ovens?', *Transactions of the Birmingham & Warwickshire Archaeological Society* 82, 77–91.

Gerloff, S. 1975. *The Early Bronze Age Daggers in Great Britain and a reconsideration of the Wessex Culture*, Praehistorisches Bronzfunde, VI.2, Munich: UISSP, C.H. Beck'sche Verlag.

Gibson, A.M. 1992. 'The Timber Circle at Sarn-y-Bryn-Caled, Welshpool, Powys: ritual and sacrifice in Bronze Age mid-Wales', *Antiquity* 66, 84–92.

Gibson, A.M. 1993. 'The excavation of two cairns and associated features at Carneddau, Carno, Powys, 1989–90', *Archaeological Journal* 150, 1–45.

Gibson, A.M. 1994. 'Excavations at the Sarn y Bryn Caled Cursus Complex, Welshpool, Powys, and the timber circles of Britain and Ireland', *Proceedings of the Prehistoric Society* 60, 143–223.

Gibson, A.M. 1995a. 'First impressions: a review of Peterborough Ware in Wales', in I. Kinnes & G. Varndell (eds), 1995, *Unbaked Urns of Rudely Shape: Essays on British and Irish Pottery for Ian Longworth*, Oxford: Oxbow Monograph 55, 23–39.

Gibson, A.M. 1995b. 'The Carreg Beuno Prehistoric Landscape', *Montgomeryshire Collections* 83, 41–58.

Gibson, A.M. 1996. 'A Neolithic enclosure at Hindwell, Radnorshire, Powys', *Oxford Journal of Archaeology* 15.3, 341–7.

Gibson, A.M. 1999a. *The Walton Basin Project: Excavation and Survey in a Prehistoric Landscape 1993–7*, York: Council for British Archaeology Research Report 118.

Gibson, A.M. 1999b. 'The Cursus Monuments and possible Cursus Monuments of Wales', in A. Barclay & J. Harding, *Pathways and Ceremonies: the Cursus Monuments of Britain and Ireland*, Neolithic Studies Group Seminar Papers: 4. Oxford: Oxbow, 130–40.

Gibson, A.M. & Kinnes, I. 1997. 'On the urns of a dilemma. Radiocarbon and the Peterborough problem', *Oxford Journal of Archaeology* 16.1, 65–72.

Glob, P.V. 1974. *The Mound People: Danish Bronze Age Man Preserved*, London: Faber.

Gordon-Williams, J.P. 1926. 'The Nab Head chipping floor. 2', *Archaeologia Cambrensis* 81, 86–110.

Green, H.S. 1974. 'Early Bronze Age Burial, Territory and Population in Milton Keynes, Buckinghamshire, and the Great Ouse Valley', *Archaeological Journal* 131, 75–139.

Green, H.S. 1980. *The Flint Arrowheads of the British Isles*, 2 vols, Oxford: British Archaeological Reports, British Series, 75.

Green, H.S. 1981a. 'A palaeolithic flint handaxe from Rhosili, Gower', *Bulletin of the Board of Celtic Studies* 29, 337–9.

Green, H.S. 1981b. 'The first Welshman: excavations at Pontnewydd', *Antiquity* 55, 184–95.

Green, H.S. 1983. 'A Late Bronze Age Gold Hoard from Llanarmon yn Iâl, Clwyd', *Antiquaries Journal* 63, 384–7.

Green, H.S. 1984a. *Pontnewydd Cave*, Cardiff: National Museum of Wales.

Green, H.S. 1984b. 'The Old and Middle Stone Ages, 1: The Palaeolithic Period', in G. Williams (ed.), 1984, *Glamorgan County History. Vol. II: Early Glamorgan, Pre-History and Early History*, Cardiff: Glamorgan County History Trust Ltd, 11–33.

Green, H.S. 1985a. 'The Caergwrle Bowl, not oak but shale', *Antiquity* 59, 116–17.

Green, H.S. 1985b. 'Four Bronze Age Sword-finds from Wales', *Bulletin of the Board of Celtic Studies* 32, 283–7.

Green, H.S. 1986. 'Prestige and Aggression: the evidence of lithic studies', *Archaeology in Wales* 26, 10.

Green, H.S. 1987. 'The Disgwylfa Fawr Round Barrow, Ceredigion, Dyfed', *Archaeologia Cambrensis* 136, 43–50.

Green, H.S. 1988. 'Pontnewydd Cave: the selection of raw materials for artefact-manufacture and the question of natural damage', in R.J. MacRae & N. Maloney (eds), 1988, *Non-Flint Stone Tools and the Palaeolithic Occupation of Britain*, Oxford: British Archaeological Reports, British Series, 189.

Green, H.S. 1989a. 'The Stone Age cave archaeology of South Wales', in T. Ford (ed.), 1989, 70–8.

Green, H.S. 1989b. 'Some recent archaeological and faunal discoveries from the Severn Estuary Levels', *Bulletin of the Board of Celtic Studies* 36, 187–99.

Green, H.S., Guilbert, G. & Cowell, M. 1983. 'Two Gold Bracelets from Maesmelan Farm, Powys', *Bulletin of the Board of Celtic Studies* 30, 394–8.

Green, H.S. & Wainwright, G.J. 1991. 'Flintwork and polished stone axes', in C.R. Musson, 1991, 113–16.

Green, H.S. & Walker, E. l991. *Ice Age Hunters: Neanderthals and Early Modern Hunters in Wales*, Cardiff: National Museum of Wales.

Green, M.J. 1986. *The Gods of the Celts*, Gloucester: Sutton.

Green, M.J. 1992. *Animals in Celtic Life and Myth*, London: Routledge.

Green, M.J. 1997. *Exploring the World of the Druids*, London: Thames & Hudson.

Grenter, S. 1989. Note in *Archaeology in Wales* 29, 46.

Gresham, C.A. 1985. 'Notes on Two Anglesey Tombs', *Archaeologia Cambrensis* 134, 225–7.

Gresham, C.A. & Irvine, C.H. 1963. 'Prehistoric Routes across North Wales', *Antiquity* 37, 54–8.

Griffiths, W.E. 1950. 'Early Settlements in Caernarvonshire', *Archaeologia Cambrensis* 101, 38–71.

Griffiths, W.E. 1951. 'Decorated querns from North Wales', *Ulster Journal of Archaeology* 9, 49–61.

Griffiths, W.E. 1957. 'The Pant y Maen Bronze Hoard', *Bulletin of the Board of Celtic Studies* 17, 118–24.

Griffiths, W.E. 1960. 'The Excavation of Stone Circles near Penmaenmawr, North Wales', *Proceedings of the Prehistoric Society* 26, 303–39.

Grimes, W.F. 1938. 'A Barrow on Breach Farm, Glamorgan', *Proceedings of the Prehistoric Society* 4, 107–21.

Grimes, W.F. 1939. 'The Excavation of Ty Isaf Long Cairn, Brecknockshire', *Proceedings of the Prehistoric Society* 5, 119–42.

Grimes, W.F. 1960. *Excavations on Defence Sites 1939–45: I Neolithic–Bronze Age*, London: HMSO.

Grimes, W.F. 1963. 'The Stone Circles and Related Monuments of Wales', in I.Ll. Foster & L. Alcock (eds), 1963, 93–152.

Groenman van Waateringe, W. 1983. 'The early agricultural utilisation of the Irish landscape: the last word on the Elm Decline?', in T. Reeves-Smyth & F. Hamond, 1983, 217–32.

Grogan, E. & Eogan, G. 1987. 'Lough Gur Excavations by Sean P. O'Riordain: Further Neolithic and Beaker Habitations on Knockadoon', *Proceedings of the Royal Irish Academy* 87 C, 299–506.

Guenther, M.G. 1997. 'African foragers', in J.O. Vogel (ed.), 1997, *Encyclopedia of Precolonial Africa: Archaeology, History, Languages, Cultures and Environments*, London: Altamira Press, 179–84.

Guido, C.M. 1978. *The Glass Beads of the prehistoric and Roman periods in Britain and Ireland*, Society of Antiquaries Research Report 35.

Guilbert, G.C. 1974. 'Llanstephan Castle: 1973 Interim Report', *Carmarthenshire Antiquary* 10, 37–48.

Guilbert, G.C. 1975. 'Planned hillfort interiors', *Proceedings of the Prehistoric Society* 41, 203–21.

Guilbert, G.C. 1976. 'Moel y Gaer (Rhosesmor) 1972–1973: an area excavation in the interior', in D.W. Harding (ed.), 1976, *Hillforts: later prehistoric earthworks in Britain and Ireland*, London: Academic Press, 303–17.

Guilbert, G.C. 1979a. 'The guard-chamber gateways at Dinorben and Moel Hiraddug hill-forts, and the problem of dating the type in north Wales', *Bulletin of the Board of Celtic Studies* 28, 516–20.

Guilbert, G.C. 1979b. 'Dinorben 1977–8', *Current Archaeology* 65, 182–8.

Guilbert, G.C. 1980. 'Dinorben C14 dates', *Current Archaeology* 70, 336–8.

Guilbert, G.C. 1981a. 'Ffridd Faldwyn', *Archaeological Journal* 138, 20–2.

Guilbert, G.C. 1981b. 'Hill fort functions and populations: a sceptical viewpoint', in G.C. Guilbert (ed.), 1981, *Hill Fort Studies*, 104–19.

Hamilton, M. & Aldhouse-Green, S.H.R. 1998. 'Ogmore-by-sea', *Archaeology in Wales* 38, 113–15.

Harbison, P. 1969. *The Daggers and Halberds of the Early Bronze Age in Ireland*, Praehistorisches Bronzfunde VI.1, Munich: UISSP, C.H. Beck'sche Verlag.

Harding, A.F. 1982. *Climate Change in Later Prehistory*, Edinburgh: Edinburgh University Press.

Hart, C.R. 1981. *The North Derbyshire Archaeological Survey*, Chesterfield: North Derbyshire Archaeological Trust.

Hawkes, C.F.C. & Smith, M.E. 1957. 'On some Buckets and Cauldrons of the Bronze and Early Iron Age', *Antiquaries Journal* 37, 131–98.

Healey, E. & Green, H.S. 1984. 'The lithic industries', in W.J. Britnell & H.N. Savory, 1984, 113–35.

Hedges, J. 1987. *Tomb of the Eagles: a window on Stone Age tribal Britain*, London: Murray

Hedges, R.E.M. & Salter, C.J. 1979. 'Source determination of iron currency bars through the analysis of slag inclusions', *Archaeometry* 21.2, 161–75.

Hemp, W.J. 1928. 'A La Tène Shield from Moel Hiraddug, Flintshire', *Archaeologia Cambrensis* 83, 253–84.

Hemp, W.J. 1930. 'The Chambered Cairn of Bryn Celli Ddu', *Archaeologia* 80, 179–214.

Hemp, W.J. 1935. 'The Chambered Cairn known as Bryn yr Hen Bobl, near Plas Newydd, Anglesey', *Archaeologia* 85, 253–92.

Herne, A. 1988. 'A time and place for the Grimston Bowl', in J. Barrett & I. Kinnes (eds), 1988, 9–29.

Heyworth, A. & Kidson, C. 1982. 'Sea-level changes in southwest England and in Wales', *Proceedings of the Geologists Association* 93, 91–112.

Hibbert, F.A. 1993. 'The Vegetational History', in Lynch, 1993, 10–15.

Higgs, E.A. & Yealand, S. 1967. 'Appendix', in J.C. Harvey, R. Morgan & D.P. Webley, 1967, 'Tooth Cave, Ilston, Gower. An Early Bronze Age occupation', *Bulletin of the Board of Celtic Studies* 22, 277–85.

Hogg, A.H.A. 1960. 'Garn Boduan and Tre'r Ceiri', *Archaeological Journal* 117, 1–39.

Hogg, A.H.A. 1969. 'Cefn Graeanog: a native site of the Roman Period', *Transactions of the Caernarvonshire Historical Society* 30, 8–20.

Hogg, A.H.A. 1972. 'The Size-Distribution of Hill-forts in Wales and the Marches', in F.M. Lynch & C.B. Burgess (eds), 1972, 293–306.

Hogg, A.H.A. 1973. 'Excavations at Harding's Down West Fort, Gower', *Archaeologia Cambrensis* 122, 55–68.

Hogg, A.H.A. 1976. 'Castle Ditches, Llancarfan, Glamorgan', *Archaeologia Cambrensis* 125, 13–39.

Houlder, C.H. 1961a. 'The Excavation of a Neolithic Stone Implement Factory on Mynydd Rhiw in Caernarvonshire', *Proceedings of the Prehistoric Society* 27, 108–43.

Houlder, C.H. 1961b. 'Rescue excavations at Moel Hiraddug I – excavations in 1954–55', *Journal of the Flintshire Historical Society*, 19, 1–20.

Houlder, C.H. 1967. 'Llandegai', *Current Archaeology* 5, 116–19.

Houlder, C.H. 1968. 'The Henge Monuments at Llandegai', *Antiquity* 42, 216–21.

Houlder, C.H. 1976. 'Stone Axes and Henge Monuments', in G.C. Boon & J.M. Lewis (eds), 1976, 55–62.

Houlder, C.H. 1994. 'The Stone Age', in J.L. Davies & D. Kirby (eds), 1994, 107–23.

Hughes, G. 1994. 'Old Oswestry hillfort: Excavations by W.J. Varley 1939–40', *Archaeologia Cambrensis* 143, 46–91.

Hughes, G. 1996. *The Excavation of a Late Prehistoric and Romano-British Settlement at Thornwell Farm, Chepstow, Gwent, 1992*, Oxford: British Archaeological Reports, British Series 224.

Hughes, H H. 1907. 'Report on excavations carried out at Tre'r Ceiri in 1906', *Archaeologia Cambrensis* 61, 38–62.

Hughes, H.H. 1908. 'Merddyn Gwyn Barrow, Pentraeth', *Archaeologia Cambrensis* 62, 211–20.

Hunter, J. & Ralston, I. (eds) 1999. *The Archaeology of Britain*, London: Routledge.

Hutton, R. 1991. *The Pagan Religions of the Ancient British Isles: their Nature and Legacy*, Cambridge, Mass.: Basil Blackwell.

Insole, P. 1997. 'Church Farm, Caldicot', *Archaeology in Wales* 37, 72–4.

Jacobi, R.M. 1980. 'The early Holocene settlement of Wales', in J.A. Taylor (ed.), 1980b, 31–206.

Jacobi, R.M. 1987. 'Misanthropic miscellany: musings on British early Flandrian archaeology and other flights of fancy', in P. Rowley-Conwy, M. Zvelebil & H.P. Blankholm (eds), 1987, *Mesolithic Northwest Europe: Recent Trends*, Sheffield: University of Sheffield, 163–8.

James, H. 1987. 'Excavations at Caer, Bayvil, 1979', *Archaeologia Cambrensis* 136, 51–76.

James, S. 1999. *The Atlantic Celts. Ancient People or Modern Invention*, London: British Museum Press.

James, T. 1990. 'Concentric antenna enclosures – a new defended enclosure type in west Wales', *Proceedings of the Prehistoric Society* 56, 295–8.

Jarrett, M.G. & Mann, J.C. 1969. 'The Tribes of Wales', *Welsh History Review* 4, 161–71.

Jarrett, M.G. & Wrathmell, S. 1981. *Whitton: an Iron Age and Roman farmstead in south Glamorgan*, Cardiff: University of Wales Press.

Jelinek, J. 1992. 'New Upper Palaeolithic burials from Dolní Vestonice', in M. Toussaint (ed.), 1992, *Five Million Years, the Human Adventure*, Liège: Etudes et Recherches Archéologiques de l'Université de Liège no. 56, 207–28.

Jenkins, D.A. 1991. 'The environment: past and present', in J. Manley *et al.* (eds), 1991, 13–25.

Jenkins, D.A. 1995. 'Mynydd Parys Copper Mines', *Archaeology in Wales* 35, 35–7.

Johnson, N. & Rose, P. 1994. *Bodmin Moor: an Archaeological Survey*, vol. 1. London: English Heritage/RCAHME.

Jones, G.D.B. & Maude, K. 1991. 'Dolaucothi: the dating problem', in B.C. Burnham & J.L. Davies (eds), 1991, 169–71.

Jones, M. Vaughan 1984. 'A Celtic head from Llanallgo, Anglesey', *Archaeologia Cambrensis* 133, 154–5.

Jones, N. 1993. 'Caersws', *Archaeology in Wales* 33, 52–4.

Jones, P.R. 1980. 'Experimental implement manufacture and use: a case study from Olduvai Gorge, Tanzania', *Philosophical Transactions of the Royal Society of London* B 292, 189–95.

Jones, R., Benson-Evans, K. & Chambers, F.M. 1985. 'Human influence upon sedimentation in Llangorse Lake, Wales', *Earth Surface Proc. Landf.* 10, 227–35.

Jones, S. 1996. *In the Blood: God, Genes and Destiny*, London: HarperCollins.

Jope, E.M. 1952. 'The porcellanite axes of the north of Ireland: Tievebulliagh and Rathlin', *Ulster Journal of Archaeology* 15, 31–60.

Joussaume, R. 1988. *Dolmens for the Dead: megalith building throughout the world*, London.

Junker, L.L. 1996. 'Hunter-gatherer landscapes and lowland trade in the prehispanic Philippines', *World Archaeology* 27.3, 389–410.

Keiller, A. 1965. *Windmill Hill and Avebury*, Oxford: Clarendon Press.

Kelly, R.S. 1988. 'Two late prehistoric circular enclosures near Harlech, Gwynedd', *Proceedings of the Prehistoric Society* 54, 101–51.

Kelly, R.S. 1990. 'Meyllteyrn Uchaf', *Archaeology in Wales* 30, 43.

Kelly, R.S. 1991. 'Meyllteyrn Uchaf', *Archaeology in Wales* 31, 16.

Kelly, R.S. 1992a. 'Meyllteyrn Uchaf Double Ditched Enclosure', *Archaeology in Wales* 32, 58.

Kelly, R.S. 1992b. 'The Excavation of a Burnt Mound at Graeanog, Clynnog, Gwynedd, in 1983', *Archaeologia Cambrensis* 141, 74–96.

Kingdon, J. 1993. *Self-Made Man and his Undoing*, London: Simon & Schuster.

Kinnes, I.A. 1988. 'The Cattleship Potemkin: the First Neolithic in Britain', in J. Barrett & I. Kinnes (eds), 1988, 2–8.

Kinnes, I.A., Gibson, A.M., Ambers, J. & Bowman, S. 1991. 'Radiocarbon dating and British Beakers: the British Museum Programme', *Scottish Archaeological Review* 8, 35–68.

Klein, R. 1989. *The Human Career*, Chicago: University of Chicago Press.

Koch, J.T. & Carey, J. 1995. *The Celtic Heroic Age: Literary Sources for ancient Celtic Europe and Early Ireland and Wales*, Andover, Mass.: Celtic Studies Publications.

Lacaille, A.D. & Grimes, W.F. 1955. 'The prehistory of Caldey', *Archaeologia Cambrensis* 104, 85–165.

Lacaille, A.D. & Grimes, W.F. 1961. 'The Prehistory of Caldey: Part II', *Archaeologia Cambrensis* 110, 30–70.

Lamb, H.H. 1981. 'Climate from 1000 BC –AD 1100', in M. Jones & G.W. Dimbleby (eds), 1981, *The Environment of Man: the Iron Age to the Anglo-Saxon period*, Oxford: British Archaeological Reports, British Series 87, 53–65.

Lanting, J.N. & van der Waals, J.D. 1972. 'British Beakers as seen from the Continent', *Helinium* 12, 20–46.

Lascelles, D.B. 1995. 'Holocene Environmental and Pedogenic History of the Hiraethog Moors, Clwyd', unpubl. Ph.D. thesis, University of Wales, Bangor.

Legge, A.J. & Rowley-Conwy, P.A. 1988. *Star Carr Revisited*, London: University of London.

Leighton, D. 1997. *Mynydd Du and Fforest Fawr: the Evolution of an Upland Landscape in south Wales*, Aberystwyth: RCAHMW.

Lewis, A. 1990. 'Underground exploration of the Great Orme Copper Mines', in P. Crew & S. Crew, 1990, 5–10.

Lewis, J. 1991. 'Excavation of a Late Devensian and Early Flandrian site at Three Ways Wharf, Uxbridge, England: interim report', in Barton *et al.*, 1991, 246–55.

Lewis, J.M. 1974. 'Excavations at Rhos-y-Clegyrn prehistoric site, St Nicholas, Pembs.', *Archaeologia Cambrensis* 123, 13–42.

Lewis, S.G. & Maddy, D. (eds) 1997. *The Quaternary of the South Midlands and the Welsh Marches: Field Guide*, London: Quaternary Research Association.

Livens, R.G. 1970. 'A Fragment of Copper Ingot found at Parc Newydd, Llanbedrgoch', *Transactions of the Anglesey Antiquarian Society*, 247–53.

Longley, D. 1998. 'Bryn Eryr: An Enclosed Settlement of the Iron Age on Anglesey', *Proceedings of the Prehistoric Society* 64, 225–74.

Longley, D., Johnstone, N. & Evans, J. 1998. 'Excavations on two farms of the Romano-British period at Bryn Eryr and Bush Farm, Gwynedd', *Britannia* 29, 185–246.

Longworth, I.H. 1984. *Collared Urns of the Bronze Age in Great Britain and Ireland*, Cambridge.

Lynch, F.M. 1969. 'The Megalithic Tombs of North Wales' and 'The Contents of Excavated Tombs in North Wales', in T.G.E. Powell *et al.*, 1969, 107–74.

Lynch, F.M. 1971. 'Report on the Re-excavation of two Bronze Age Cairns in Anglesey: Bedd Branwen and Treiorwerth', *Archaeologia Cambrensis* 120, 11–83.

Lynch, F.M. 1972a. 'Portal Dolmens in the Nevern Valley', in F.M. Lynch & C.B. Burgess (eds), 1972, 67–84.

Lynch, F.M. 1972b. 'Ring Cairns and Related Monuments in Wales', *Scottish Archaeological Forum* 4, 61–80.

Lynch, F.M. 1975a. 'Excavations at Carreg Samson, Mathry, Pembrokeshire', *Archaeologia Cambrensis* 124, 15–35.

Lynch, F.M. 1975b. 'The Impact of Landscape on Prehistoric Man', in J.G. Evans, S. Limbrey & H. Cleere (eds), 1975, *The Effect of Man on the Landscape: Highland Zone*, London: Council for British Archaeology, Research Report 11, 124–6.

Lynch, F.M. 1976. 'Towards a Chronology of Megalithic Tombs in Wales', in G.C. Boon & J.M. Lewis (eds), 1976, 63–79.

Lynch, F.M. 1979. 'Ring Cairns: their design and purpose', *Ulster Journal of Archaeology* 42, 1–19.

Lynch, F.M. 1980. 'Bronze Age Monuments in Wales', in J.A. Taylor (ed.), 1980b, 233–41.

Lynch, F.M. 1984a. 'Discussion', on pottery in W.J. Britnell & H.N. Savory, 1984, 106–10.

Lynch, F.M. 1984b. 'Moel Goedog Circle I, A Complex Ring Cairn near Harlech', *Archaeologia Cambrensis* 133, 8–50.

Lynch, F.M. 1986a. 'Archaeology and the Physical Evidence for Man in Wales', in P.S. Harper & E.Sunderland (eds), 1986, *Genetic and Population Studies in Wales*, Cardiff: University of Wales Press, 15–30.

Lynch, F.M. 1986b. 'Excavation of a Kerb Circle and Ring Cairn on Cefn Caer Euni, Merioneth', *Archaeologia Cambrensis* 135, 81–120.

Lynch, F.M. 1989. 'Presidential Address. Wales and Ireland in Prehistory, a fluctuating Relationship', *Archaeologia Cambrensis* 138, 1–19.

Lynch, F.M. 1991. *Prehistoric Anglesey*, Llangefni: Anglesey Antiquarian Society, 2nd edn.

Lynch, F.M. 1993. *Excavations in the Brenig Valley: A Mesolithic and Bronze Age Landscape in North Wales*, Cardiff: Cambrian Archaeological Monographs 5.

Lynch, F.M. 1997. *Megalithic Tombs and Long Barrows in Britain*, Princes Risborough: Shire Books.

Lynch, F.M. & Burgess, C.B. 1972. *Prehistoric Man in Wales and the West: Essays in Honour of Lily F. Chitty*, Bath: Adams & Dart.

Lynch, F.M. & Chambre, J. 1984. 'Report on the excavation of a Bronze Age Barrow at Llong near Mold', *Flintshire Historical Society Publications* 31, 13–28.

Manchester, K. & Roberts, C. 1995. *The Archaeology of Disease*, Stroud: Cornell University Press, 2nd edn.

Manley, J.F. 1990. 'A Late Bronze Age Landscape on the Denbigh Moors, North east Wales', *Antiquity* 64, 514–26.

Manley, J. 1991. 'Small Settlements', in J. Manley *et al.* (eds), 1991, 97–115.

Manley, J. & Healey, E. 1982. 'Excavations at Hendre, Rhuddlan: the Mesolithic finds', *Archaeologia Cambrensis* 131, 18–48.

Manley, J.F., Grenter, S. & Gale, F. 1991. *The Archaeology of Clwyd*, Mold: Clwyd Archaeology Service.

Maylan, N. 1991. 'Thornwell Farm', *Archaeology in Wales* 31, 22.

McGrew, W.C. 1991. 'Chimpanzee material culture: what are its limits and why', in R.A. Foley (ed.), 1991, *The Origins of Human Behaviour*, London: Unwin Hyman, 13–24.

McInnes, I. 1968. 'Jet sliders in late Neolithic Britain', in J.M. Coles & D.D.A. Simpson (eds), 1968, 137–44.

Megaw, J.V.S. 1966. 'A Celtic cult head from Port Talbot, Glamorgan', *Archaeologia Cambrensis* 115, 94–8.

Megaw, J.V.S. 1967. 'A further note on Celtic cult heads in Wales', *Archaeologia Cambrensis* 116, 192–4.

Megaw, R. & Megaw, V. 1989. *Early Celtic Art from its beginnings to the Book of Kells*, London: Thames & Hudson.

Mellars, P.A. 1976a. 'Settlement patterns and industrial variability in the British Mesolithic', in G. Sieveking *et al.* (eds), 1976, 375–99.

Mellars, P.A. 1976b. 'Fire ecology, animal populations and man: a study of some ecological relationships in prehistory', *Proceedings of the Prehistoric Society* 42, 15–46.

Mercer, R.J. 1981. 'Excavations at Carn Brea, Illogan, Cornwall, 1970–3', *Cornish Archaeology* 20, monograph.

Mercer, R.J. 1990. *Causeway Enclosures*, Princes Risborough: Shire Books.

Mithen, S. & Lake, M. 1996. 'The southern Hebrides Mesolithic project', in T. Pollard & A. Morrison (eds), 1996, *The Early Prehistory of Scotland*, Edinburgh: Edinburgh University Press, 123–51.

Morris, E.L. 1981. 'Ceramic exchange in western Britain: a preliminary view', in H. Howard & E.L. Morris (eds), 1981, *Production and Distribution: a Ceramic Viewpoint*, Oxford: British Archaeological Reports, International Series 120, 67–81.

Morris, E.L. 1982. 'Iron age pottery from western Britain: another petrological study', in I Freestone, C. Johns & T. Potter (eds), 1982, *Current Research in Ceramics: thin section studies*, London: British Museum Occasional Paper 32, 15–27.

Morris, E.L. 1985. 'Prehistoric salt distributions: two case studies from western Britain', *Bulletin of the Board of Celtic Studies* 32, 336–79.

Morris, E.L. 1994. 'Production and Distribution of Pottery and Salt: a review', *Proceedings of the Prehistoric Society* 60, 371–94.

Muckle, P. & Williams, J.Ll. 1993. 'Graiglwyd axe factory excavation', *Archaeology in Wales* 33, 46–8.

Muckleroy, K. 1981. 'Middle Bronze Age Trade between Britain and Europe: a maritime perspective', *Proceedings of the Prehistoric Society* 47, 275–97.

Murphy, K. 1985. 'Excavations at Penycoed, Llangynog, Dyfed, 1983', *Carmarthenshire Antiquary* 21, 75–112.

Murphy, K. 1992. 'Plas Gogerddan, Dyfed: A Multi-period Burial and Ritual Site', *Archaeological Journal* 149, 1–38.

Musson, C.R. 1991. *The Breiddin Hillfort: a later prehistoric settlement in the Welsh Marches*, London: Council for British Archaeology, Research Report 76.

Musson, C.R. 1994. *Wales from the Air. Patterns of Past and Present*, Aberystwyth: RCAHMW.

Musson, C.R. & Northover, J.P. 1989. 'Llanymynech Hillfort, Powys and Shropshire: observations on construction work 1981', *Montgomeryshire Collections* 77, 15–26.

Musson C.R., Britnell, W.J., Northover, J.P. & Salter, C.J. 1992. 'Excavations and metal working at Llwyn Bryn-dinas hillfort, Llangedwyn, Clwyd', *Proceedings of the Prehistoric Society* 58, 265–84.

Mytum, H. 1996. 'Hillfort siting and monumentality: Castell Henllys and geographical information systems', *Archaeology in Wales* 36, 3–10.

Mytum, H. 1999. 'Castell Henllys', *Current Archaeology* 161, 164–72.

Nash, D. 1978. 'Territory and state formation in central Gaul', in D.Green, C. Hazelgrove & M. Spriggs (eds), 1978, *Social Organisation and Settlement*, Oxford: British Archaeological Reports, International Series 47, 455–75.

Nash-Williams, V.E. 1933a. 'A Late Bronze Age hoard from Cardiff', *Antiquaries Journal* 12, 299–300.

Nash-Williams, V.E. 1933b. 'An early Iron Age hill fort at Llanmelin, near Caerwent, Monmouthshire', *Archaeologia Cambrensis* 88, 232–315.

Nash-Williams, V.E. 1939. 'An early Iron Age coastal camp at Sudbrook, near the Severn tunnel, Monmouthshire', *Archaeologia Cambrensis* 94, 42–79.

Nayling, N., Maynard, D. & McGrail, S. 1994. 'Barlands Farm, Magor, Gwent: A Romano-British Boat Find', *Antiquity* 68, 596–603.

Nayling, N. & Caseldine, A. 1997. *Excavations at Caldicot, Gwent: Bronze Age Palaeochannels in the Lower Nedern Valley*, York: Council for British Archaeology, Research Report 108.

Needham, S.P. 1979a. 'A Pair of Early Bronxe Age Spearheads from Lightwater, Surrey', in C.B. Burgess & D. Coombs (eds), 1979, *Bronze Age Hoards: Some Finds Old and New*, Oxford: British Archaeological Reports, British Series 67, 1–40.

Needham, S.P. 1979b. 'The Extent of Foreign Influence on Early Bronze Age axe development in Southern England', in M. Ryan (ed.), 1979, 265–93.

Needham, S. 1979c. 'Two recent British shield finds and their continental parallels', *Proceedings of the Prehistoric Society* 45, 111–34.

Needham, S. 1981. *The Bulford–Helsbury Manufacturing Tradition*, London: British Museum Occasional Paper 13.

Needham, S.P., Lawson, A.J. & Green, H.S. 1985. 'A1–6 Early Bronze Age Hoards', London: British Museum, British Bronze Age Metalwork Associated Finds Series.

Needham, S.P., Lees, M.N., Hook, D.R. & Hughes, M.J. 1989. 'Developments in the Early Bronze Age metallurgy of Southern Britain', *World Archaeology* 20, 383–402.

Needham, S.P., Ramsey, C.B., Coombs, D., Cartwright, C. & Pettitt, P. 1997. 'An independent Chronology for British Bronze Age Metalwork: the Results of the Oxford Radiocarbon Accelerator Programme', *Archaeological Journal* 154, 55–107.

Newcomer, M.H. 1984. 'Flaking experiments with Pontnewydd raw materials', in H.S. Green, 1984a, 153–8.

Northover, J.P. 1980. 'Analysis of Welsh Bronze Age Metalwork', Appendix in H.N. Savory, 1980b, 229–43.

Northover, J.P. 1982. 'The Exploration of the long distance Movement of Bronze in Bronze and Early Iron Age Europe', *Bulletin of the University of London Institute of Archaeology* 19, 45–72.

Northover, J.P. 1984. 'Iron age bronze metallurgy in central southern England', in B. Cunliffe & D. Miles, 1984, 126–45.

Northover, J.P. 1995. 'Bronze Age Gold in Britain', in G. Morteani & J.P. Northover (eds), 1995, *Prehistoric Gold in Europe*, Dortrecht: NATO ASI Series, 515–31.

O'Kelly, M.J. 1954. 'Excavations and experiments in ancient Irish cooking-places', *Journal of the Royal Society of Antiquaries of Ireland* 84, 105–55.

O'Kelly, C. 1969. 'Bryn Celli Ddu, Anglesey: A Re-interpretation', *Archaeologia Cambrensis* 118, 17–48.

O'Neil, B.H.St.J. 1942. 'Excavations at Ffridd Faldwyn Camp, Montgomery, 1937–39', *Archaeologia Cambrensis* 97, 1–57.

O'Nuallain, S. 1972. 'A Neolithic House at Ballyglass, near Ballycastle, Co. Mayo', *Journal of the Royal Society of Antiquaries of Ireland* 102, 2–11.

O'Riordain, S.P. 1954. 'Lough Gur Excavations: Neolithic and Bronze Age houses on Knockadoon', *Proceedings of the Royal Irish Academy* 56 C, 297–459.

Owen-John, H. 1988. 'A hill-slope enclosure in Coed y Cymdda, near Wenvoe, south Glamorgan', *Archaeologia Cambrensis* 137, 43–98.

Parfitt, K. 1993. 'The Dover Boat', *Current Archaeology* 133, 4–8.

Parker, A.G. & Chambers, F.M. 1997. 'Late-Quaternary Palaeoecology of the Severn, Wye and Upper Thames', in S.G. Lewis & D. Maddy (eds), 1997, 31–48.

Parker Pearson, M. 1999. 'From ancestor cult to divine religion', *British Archaeology* no. 45, 10–11.

Peacock, D. 1968. 'A petrological study of certain iron age pottery from western England', *Proceedings of the Prehistoric Society* 34, 414–27.

Peacock, D. 1969. 'A contribution to the study of Glastonbury ware from south-western Britain', *Antiquaries Journal* 49, 41–69.

Peterson, D. & Goodall, J. 1993. *Visions of Caliban: on Chimpanzees and People*, New York: Houghton Mifflin.

Pétrequin, P., Arbogast, R.-M., Bourquin-Mignot, C., Lavier, C. & Viellet, A. 1998. 'Demographic growth, environmental changes and technical adaptations: responses of an agricultural community from the 32nd to the 30th centuries BC', *World Archaeology* 30.2, 181–92.

Pettitt, P.B. 1999. 'Disappearing from the world: an archaeological perspective on Neanderthal extinction', *Oxford Journal of Archaeology* 18, 217–40.

Piggott, S. 1954. *Neolithic Cultures of the British Isles*, Cambridge: Cambridge University Press, reprinted 1970.

Piggott, S. 1962. *The West Kennet Long Barrow: Excavations 1955–56*, London: Ministry of Works Archaeology Report 4.

Piggott, S. 1971. 'Firedogs in Iron Age Britain and beyond', in J. Boardman, M.A. Brown & T.G.E. Powell (eds), 1971, *The European Community in Later Prehistory: Studies in Honour of C.F.C. Hawkes*, London: Routledge & Kegan Paul, 243–70.

Pitts, M.W. 1980. *Later Stone Implements*, Princes Risborough: Shire Books.

Pitts, M.W. 1996. 'The Stone Axe in Neolithic Britain', *Proceedings of the Prehistoric Society* 62, 311–72.

Pitts, M.W. & Jacobi, R.M. 1979. 'Some aspects of change in flaked stone industries of the Mesolithic and Neolithic in southern England', *Journal of Archaeological Science* 6, 163–77.

Powell, T.G.E. 1953. 'The Gold Ornament from Mold, Flintshire, North Wales', *Proceedings of the Prehistoric Society* 19, 161–79.

Powell, T.G.E. 1973. 'Excavation of the Megalithic Chambered Cairn at Dyffryn Ardudwy, Merioneth, Wales', *Archaeologia* 104, 1–49.

Powell, T.G.E. & Daniel, G.E. 1956. *Barclodiad y Gawres*, Liverpool: Liverpool University Press.

Powell, T.G.E., Corcoran, J.X.W.P., Scott, J.G. & Lynch, F.M. 1969. *Megalithic Enquiries in the West of Britain*, Liverpool: Liverpool University Press.

Preece, R.C. (ed.) 1995. *Island Britain: a Quaternary Perspective*, London: Geological Society special publication no. 96.

Price, M.D.R. & Moore, P.D. 1984. 'Pollen dispersion in the hills of Wales: a pollen shed hypothesis', *Pollen et Spores* 26, 127–36.

Probert, A. 1976. 'Twyn y Gaer hillfort, Gwent: an interim assessment', in G.C. Boon & J.M. Lewis, 1976, 105–20.

Quinnell, H. & Blockley, M., with Berridge, P. 1994. *Excavations at Rhuddlan, Clwyd. 1969–73. Mesolithic to Mediaeval*, London: Council for British Archaeology, Research Report 95.

Radford, C.A.R. 1958. 'The Chambered Tomb at Broadsands, Paignton', *Proceedings of the Devon Archaeological Exploration Society* 5, 147–66.

Raftery, B. 1994. *Pagan Celtic Ireland. The Enigma of the Irish Iron Age*, London: Thames & Hudson.

RCAHMW. 1937. *An Inventory of the Ancient Monuments in Anglesey*, London: HMSO.

RCAHMW. 1956. *An Inventory of the Ancient Monuments in Caernarvonshire. Volume I: East*, London: HMSO.

RCAHMW. 1960. *An Inventory of the Ancient Monuments in Caernarvonshire. Volume II: Central*, London: HMSO.

RCAHMW. 1964. *An Inventory of the Ancient Monuments in Caernarvonshire Volume III: West*, London: HMSO.

RCAHMW. 1976. *An Inventory of the Ancient Monuments in Glamorgan. Volume I: Pre–Norman. Parts I–III*, Cardiff: HMSO.

RCAHMW. 1986. *An Inventory of the Ancient Monuments in Brecknock (Brycheiniog). The Prehistoric and Roman Monuments. Part II: Hill-forts and Roman Remains*, Cardiff: HMSO.

RCAHMW. 1997. *An Inventory of the Ancient Monuments in Brecknock (Brycheiniog). The Prehistoric and Roman Monuments Part I: Later Prehistoric Monuments and Unenclosed Settlements to 1000 AD*, Stroud: RCAHMW.

Reeves-Smyth, T. & Hamond, F. 1983. *Landscape Archaeology in Ireland*, Oxford: British Archaeology Reports, British Series 116.

Renfrew, A.C. 1973. 'Monuments, Mobilisation and Social Organisation in Neolithic Wessex', in C. Renfrew (ed.), 1973, *The Explanation of Culture Change: Models in Prehistory*, London, 539–58.

Renfrew, A.C. 1976. 'Megaliths, Territories and Populations', in de Laet, S.J. (ed.), 1976, *Acculturation and Continuity in Atlantic Europe mainly during the Neolithic Period and the Bronze Age*, Brugge: de Tempel, 198–220.

Renfrew, A.C. & Shennan, S.J. 1982. *Ranking Resource and Exchange: Aspects of the Archaeology of Early European Society*, Cambridge: Cambridge University Press.

Reynier, M.J. 1998. 'Early Mesolithic settlement in England and Wales: some preliminary observations', in Ashton *et al.* (eds), 1998, 174–84.

Richards, M. 1998. 'Bone stable isotope analysis: reconstructing the diet of humans', in A.W.R. Whittle & M. Wysocki, 1998, 165–6.

Richards, M., Smalley, K., Sykes, B. & Hedges, R. 1993. 'Archaeology and genetics: analysing DNA from skeletal remains', *World Archaeology* 25.1, 18–28.

Rightmire, G.P. 1997. 'Deep roots for the Neanderthals', *Nature* 389, 917–18.

Rippon, S. 1996. *Gwent Levels: the evolution of a wetland landscape*, York: Council for British Archaeology Research Report 105.

Ritchie, J.N.G. 1970. 'Excavation of the Chambered Cairn at Achnacreebeag', *Proceedings of the Society of Antiquaries of Scotland* 102, 31–55.

Rivet, A.L.F. & Smith, C. 1979. *The Place-Names of Roman Britain*, London.

Roberts, M.B., Stringer, C.B. & Parfitt, S.A. 1994. 'A hominid tibia from Middle Pleistocene sediments at Boxgrove, UK', *Nature* 369, 311–13.

Robinson, D.M.(ed.) 1988. *Biglis, Caldicot and Llandough: three late Iron Age and Romano-British sites in south-east Wales. Excavations 1977–79*, Oxford: British Archaeological Reports, British Series 188.

Roe, F.E.S. 1968. 'Stone mace-heads and the latest Neolithic cultures of the British Isles', in J.M. Coles & D.D.A. Simpson (eds), 1968, 145–72.

Ross, A. 1992. *Pagan Celtic Britain: Studies in iconography and tradition*, London: Routledge & Kegan Paul, revised edn.

Rutter, J.G. 1948. *Prehistoric Gower: The early Archaeology of west Glamorgan*, Swansea: Welsh Guides.

Ryan, M. (ed.) 1979. *The Origins of Metallurgy in Atlantic Europe: Proceedings of the Fifth Atlantic Colloquium, Dublin 1978*, Dublin: Irish Government Publications.

Sahlins, M. 1974. *Stone Age Economics*, London: Tavistock Publications.

Salter C.J. & Ehrenreich, R. 1984. 'Iron age metallurgy in central southern Britain', in B. Cunliffe & D. Miles, 1984, 146–61.

Sargent, H.C. 1923. 'The massive chert formation of north Flintshire', *Geological Magazine* 110, 168–83.

Savory, H.N. 1952. 'The Excavation of a Neolithic Dwelling and a Bronze Age Cairn at Mount Pleasant Farm, Nottage, Glam.', *Transactions of the Cardiff Naturalists Society* 81, 75–92.

Savory, H.N. 1954. 'The Excavation of an Early Iron Age fortified settlement on Mynydd Bychan, Llysworney (Glam.) 1949–50. Part 1', *Archaeologia Cambrensis* 103, 85–108.

Savory, H.N. 1955. 'The Excavation of an Early Iron Age fortified settlement on Mynydd Bychan, Llysworney (Glam.) 1949–50', *Archaeologia Cambrensis* 104, 14–51.

Savory, H.N. 1957. 'A Corpus of Welsh Bronze Age Pottery: Food Vessels', *Bulletin of the Board of Celtic Studies* 17, 196–233.

Savory, H.N. 1958. 'The Late Bronze Age in Wales: some new Discoveries and new Interpretations', *Archaeologia Cambrensis* 107, 3–63.

Savory, H.N. 1958–60. 'A Corpus of Welsh Bronze Age Pottery: Pigmy Cups', *Bulletin of the Board of Celtic Studies* 18, 89–118.

Savory, H.N. 1962–4. 'Excavations at a Third Round Barrow at Pen-dre, Letterston (Pembs.) 1961', *Bulletin of the Board of Celtic Studies* 20, 309–25.

Savory, H.N. 1964. 'The Tal y Llyn hoard', *Antiquity* 38, 18–31.

Savory, H.N. 1965. 'A new hoard of La Tene metalwork from Wales', *Celticum* 12, 163–206.

Savory, H.N. 1966a. 'A find of early iron age metalwork from the Lesser Garth, Pentyrch (Glam.)', *Archaeologia Cambrensis*115, 27–44.

Savory, H.N. 1966b. 'Bronze spearhead from Bala (Mer.)', *Bulletin of the Board of Celtic Studies* 21, 371–3.

Savory, H.N. 1967. 'Early Iron Age decorated spindle-whorls from north and mid-Wales', *Bulletin of the Board of Celtic Studies* 22, 207–8.

Savory, H.N. 1968. *Early Iron Age Art in Wales*, Cardiff: National Museum of Wales.

Savory, H.N. 1969a. 'The excavation of the Marlborough Grange Barrow, Llanblethian (Glam) 1967', *Archaeologia Cambrensis* 118, 49–72.

Savory, H.N. 1969b. 'Deposit of Bronze Age flint arrowheads on the Plynlimon Moorland', *Bulletin of the Board of Celtic Studies* 23, 291–4.

Savory, H.N. 1971a. 'A Welsh Late Bronze Age Hillfort', *Antiquity* 45, 251–61.

Savory, H.N. 1971b. *Excavations at Dinorben, 1965–9*, Cardiff: National Museum of Wales.

Savory, H.N. 1971c. 'A Neolithic Stone Axe and Wooden Handle from Port Talbot', *Antiquaries Journal* 51, 296–7.

Savory, H.N. 1972. 'Copper Age cists and cist graves in Wales: with special reference to Newton, Swansea, and other multiple cist cairns', in F.M. Lynch & C.B. Burgess (eds), 1972, 117–40.

Savory, H.N. 1973. 'Llyn Cerrig Bach thirty years later', *Transactions of the Anglesey Antiquarian Society*, 24–38.

Savory, H.N. 1974. 'An early Iron Age metalworkers mould from Worm's Head', *Archaeologia Cambrensis* 123, 170–4.

Savory, H.N. 1976a. 'Welsh hillforts: a reappraisal of recent research', in D.W. Harding (ed.), *Hillforts: later prehistoric earthworks in Britain and Ireland*, London: Academic Press, 237–92.

Savory, H.N. 1976b. *Guide Catalogue of the Early Iron Age Collections*, Cardiff: National Museum of Wales.

Savory, H.N. 1976c. 'The La Tène shield in Wales', in P.M. Duval & C.F.C. Hawkes (eds), 1976, *Celtic Art in Ancient Europe*, New York: Seminar Press, 185–99.

Savory, H.N. 1977. 'A new hoard of Bronze Age Gold Ornaments from Wales', *Archaeologia Atlantica* 2, 37–53.

Savory, H.N. 1980a. 'The Neolithic in Wales', in J.A. Taylor (ed.), 1980b, 207–31.

Savory, H.N. 1980b. *Guide Catalogue of the Bronze Age Collections*, Cardiff: National Museum of Wales.

Savory, H.N. 1980c. 'The Early Iron Age in Wales', in J.A. Taylor (ed.), 1980b, 287–310.

Savory, H.N. 1990. 'Review of Cunliffe 1988', *Archaeologia Cambrensis* 139, 82–3.

Schmidt, P.K. & Burgess, C.B. 1981. *The Axes of Scotland and Northern England*, Praehistorisches Bronzfunde. IX.7, Munich: UISSP, C.H. Beck'sche Verlag.

Schulting, R.J. 1996. 'Antlers, bone pins and flint blades: the Mesolithic cemeteries of Téviec and Hoëdic, Brittany', *Antiquity* 70, 335–50.

Schulting, R.J. 1998. 'Slighting the sea: stable isotope evidence for the transition to farming in northwestern Europe', *Documenta Praehistorica* 25, 203–18.

Schulting, R.J. & Richards, M.P. In press. 'The use of stable isotopes in studies of subsistence and seasonality in the British Mesolithic', in R. Young (ed.), *Current Research on the British and Irish Mesolithic*, Leicester: Leicester University Press

Scott, J.G. 1969. 'The Clyde Cairns of Scotland' and 'The Neolithic Period in Kintyre', in T.G.E. Powell *et al.*, 1969, 175–246.

Scott, N. & Murphy, K. 1992. 'Excavations at Pendinas Lochtyn, Llangranog, Dyfed, 1990–91', *Archaeology in Wales* 32, 9–10.

Scott, W.L. 1933. 'The Chambered Tomb of Pant y Saer, Anglesey', *Archaeologia Cambrensis* 88, 185–228.

Sell, S.H. 1998. 'Excavation of a Bronze Age settlement at the Atlantic Trading Estate, Barry, South Glamorgan', *Studia Celtica* 32, 1–26.

Shand, P. & Hodder, I. 1990. 'Haddenham', *Current Archaeology* 118, 339–44.

Shee-Twohig, E. 1981. *The Megalithic Art of Western Europe*, Oxford: Clarendon Press.

Shepherd, I.A.G. 1985. 'Jet, Amber, Faience', in D.V. Clarke *et al.*, 1985, 204–16.

Sheppard, T. 1941. 'The Parc y Meirch Hoard, St. George Parish, Denbighshire', *Archaeologia Cambrensis* 96, 1–10.

Sheridan, A. 1983. 'A Reconsideration of the Origins of Irish Metallurgy', *Journal of Irish Archeology* 1, 11–19.

Sheridan, A. 1986. 'Porcellanite artifacts: a new survey', *Ulster Journal of Archaeology* 49, 19–32.

Sheridan, A. & Davis, M. 1998. 'The Welsh "jet set" in prehistory: a case of keeping up with the Joneses', in A. Gibson & D.D.A. Simpson (eds), 1998, *Prehistoric Ritual and Religion: Essays presented to Aubrey Burl*, Stroud: Sutton Publishing, 148–62.

Sherratt, A. 1990. 'The genesis of megaliths: monumentality, ethnicity and social complexity in Neolithic north-west Europe', *World Archaeology* 22, 147–67.

Shotton, F.W. 1972. 'Large stone axes ascribed to north-west Pembrokeshire', in F.M. Lynch & C.B. Burgess (eds), 1972, 85–91.

Shotton, F.W., Chitty, L.F. & Seaby, W. 1951. 'A new centre of stone axe dispersal on the Welsh border', *Proceedings of the Prehistoric Society* 17, 135–53.

Sieveking, G. de G. 1971. 'The Kendrick's Cave mandible', *British Museum Quarterly* 35, 230–50.

Sieveking, G de G., Longworth, I.H. & Wilson, K.E. 1976. *Problems in Economic and Social Archaeology*, London: Duckworth.

Silvester, R.J. & Britnell, W.J. 1993. *Montgomeryshire Small Enclosures Project. Summary Report*, Welshpool: The Clwyd–Powys Archaeological Trust.

Simmons, I.G. 1996. *The Environmental Impact of Later Mesolithic Cultures: the Creation of Moorland Landscape in England and Wales*, Edinburgh: Edinburgh University Press.

Simmons, I.G. & Tooley, M. 1981. *The Environment in British Prehistory*, London: Duckworth.

Sims-Williams, P. 1998. 'Celtomania and Celtoscepticism', *Cambrian Medieval Celtic Studies* 36, 1–35.

Smith, C.A. 1974. 'A morphological analysis of late prehistoric and Romano-British settlements in north-west Wales', *Proceedings of the Prehistoric Society* 40, 157–69.

Smith, C.A. 1977. 'Late prehistoric and Romano-British enclosed homesteads in north-west Wales: an interpretation of their morphology', *Archaeologia Cambrensis* 126, 38–52.

Smith, C.A. 1987. 'Excavations at the Ty Mawr hut-circles, Holyhead, Anglesey. Part IV – Chronology and discussion', *Archaeologia Cambrensis* 126, 20–38.

Smith, C.A. 1992. 'The population of Late Upper Palaeolithic and Mesolithic Britain', *Proceedings of the Prehistoric Society* 58, 37–40.

Smith, C.A. & Lynch, F.M. 1987. *Trefignath and Din Dryfol: the Excavation of Two Megalithic Tombs in Anglesey*, Cardiff: Cambrian Archaeological Monographs 3.

Smith, F.H., Trinkaus, E., Pettitt, P.B., Karavanić, I. & Paunović, M. 1999. 'Direct radiocarbon dates for Vindija G1 and Velika Pećina late Pleistocene hominid remains', *Proceedings of the National Academy of Sciences* 96, no. 22, 12281–6.

Smith, I.F. 1979. 'The chronology of British stone implements', in T. Clough & W.A. Cummins, 1979, 13–22.

Smith, M.A. 1959. 'Some Somerset Hoards and their place in the Bronze Age of southern Britain', *Proceedings of the Prehistoric Society* 25, 144–87.

Spate, A. 1997. 'Karsting around for bones: Aborigines and karst caves in southeastern Australia', *Australian Archaeology* 45, 35–44.

Spencer, B. 1983. 'Limestone-tempered pottery from South Wales in the Late Iron Age and Early Roman period', *Bulletin of the Board of Celtic Studies* 30, 405–19.

Spoor, F., Wood, B. & Zonneveld, F. 1994. 'Implications of early hominid labyrinthine morphology for evolution of human bipedal motion', *Nature* 369, 645–8.

Spratling, M. 1966. 'The date of the Tal-y-Llyn hoard', *Antiquity* 40, 229–30.

Spurgeon, C.J. 1972. 'Enclosures of Iron Age Type in the Upper Severn Basin', in F.M. Lynch & C.B. Burgess (eds), 1972, 321–44.

St Joseph, J.K. 1980. 'Air reconnaisance: recent results', *Antiquity* 54, 47–51.

Stanford, S.C. 1972. 'Welsh Border Hill-forts', in C. Thomas (ed.), 1972, *The Iron Age in the Irish Sea Province*, London: Council for British Archaeology, Research Report 9, 25–36.

Stanford, S.C. 1974. *Croft Ambrey*, Hereford: privately printed.

Stanford, S.C. 1981. *Midsummer Hill: an Iron Age Hillfort on the Malverns*, Leominster: privately printed.

Stanford, S.C. 1982. 'Bromfield, Shropshire – Neolithic, Beaker and Bronze Age sites 1966–79', *Proceedings of the Prehistoric Society* 48, 279–320.

Stanley, W.O. & Way, A. 1868. 'Ancient Interments and Sepulchral Urns found in Anglesey and North Wales', *Archaeologia Cambrensis* 3rd series 14, 217–93.

Stanton, Y.C. 1984a. 'The Mesolithic Period: Early Post-Glacial hunter-gatherer communities in Glamorgan', in H.N. Savory (ed.), 1984, *Glamorgan County History Vol. II*, Cardiff: Glamorgan County History Trust Ltd, 33–121.

Stanton, Y.C. 1984b. 'The Hoard of South Wales or "Stogursey" axes from St Mellons, South Glamorgan: A Preliminary Statement', *Bulletin of the Board of Celtic Studies* 31, 191–5.

Startin, W. & Bradley, R.J. 1981. 'Some notes on work organisation and society in prehistoric Wessex', in C. Ruggles & A. Whittle (eds), 1981, *Astronomy and Society in Britain during the Period 4,000–1,500 BC*, Oxford: British Archaeological Reports, British Series 88, 289–96.

Stead, I.M. 1982. 'The Cerrig y Drudion "hanging bowl"', *Antiquaries Journal* 62, 221–34.

Stead, I.M. 1985. *Celtic Art in Britain before the Conquest*, London: British Museum Press.

Steele, J. 1999. 'Stone legacy of skilled hands', *Nature* 399, 24–5.

Stringer, C. & Gamble, C. 1993. *In Search of the Neanderthals*, London: Thames & Hudson.

Taylor, H. 1927. 'Second report on the excavations at King Arthur's Cave', *Proceedings of the University of Bristol Spelaeological Society* 3, 59–83.

Taylor, J.A. 1980a. 'Environmental changes in Wales during the Holocene period', in J.A. Taylor (ed.), 1980b, 101–30.

Taylor, J.A. (ed.), 1980b *Culture and Environment in Prehistoric Wales*, Oxford: British Archaeological Reports, British Series 76.

Taylor, J.J. 1980. *Bronze Age Goldwork of the British Isles*, Cambridge.

Thom, A., Thom, A.S. & Burl, A. 1980. *Megalithic Rings: Plans and Data for 229 Monuments in Britain*, Oxford: British Archaeological Reports, British Series 100.

Thorburn, J. 1990. 'Stone mining tools and the field evidence for early mining in Mid-Wales', in P. Crew & S. Crew (eds), 1990, 43–6.

Tierney, J.J. 1960. 'The Celtic Ethnography of Posidonius', *Proceedings of the Royal Irish Academy* 60C, 189–275.

Tilley, C. 1994. *A Phenomenology of Landscape: Places, Paths and Monuments*, Oxford: Berg.

Timberlake, S. 1990. 'Excavations and Fieldwork on Copa Hill, Cwmystwth, 1989', in P. Crew & S. Crew (eds), 1990, 22–9.

Timberlake, S. 1993. 'Copa Hill', *Archaeology in Wales* 33, 54–5.

Timberlake, S. 1995. 'Copa Hill', *Archaeology in Wales* 35, 39–43.

Timberlake, S. & Switsur, R. 1988. 'An archaeological excavation of early mineworkings on Copa Hill, Cwmystwyth: new evidence for prehistoric mining', *Proceedings of the Prehistoric Society* 54, 329–33.

Timberlake, S. & Mighall, T. 1992. 'Historic and Prehistoric Mining on Copa Hill, Cwmystwyth', *Archaeology in Wales* 32, 38–44.

Torrence, R. 1986. *Production and Exchange of Stone Tools*, Cambridge.

Trett, R. 1988. 'Newport Museum Recent Aquisitions', *Archaeology in Wales* 28, 56.

Trinkaus, E. 1983. *The Shanidar Neanderthals*, London: Academic Press.

Trinkaus, E. & Shipman, P. 1993. *The Neandertals: Changing the Image of Mankind*, London: Jonathan Cape.

Turner, A. 1992. 'Large carnivores and earliest European hominids: changing determinants of resource availability during the Lower and Middle Pleistocene', *Journal of Human Evolution* 22, 109–26.

Turner, J. 1970. 'Post-neolithic disturbance of British vegetation', in D. Walker & R.G. West (eds), 1970, *Studies in the Vegetational History of the British Isles*, Cambridge: Cambridge University Press, 1–96.

Turner, J. 1981. 'The Iron Age', in I.G. Simmons & M. Tooley, 1981, 250–81.

Varley, W.J. 1948. 'The hill-forts of the Welsh Marches', *Archaeological Journal* 105, 41–66.

Vyner, B.E. 1986. 'Woodbarn, Wiston: a Pembrokeshire rath', *Archaeologia Cambrensis* 125, 121–33.

de Waal, F.B.M. 1999. 'Cultural primatology comes of age', *Nature* 399, 635–6.

Wainwright, G.J. 1967. *Coygan Camp. A Prehistoric, Romano-British and Dark Age Settlement in Carmarthenshire*, Cardiff: Cambrian Archaeological Association.

Wainwright, G.J. 1971. 'The excavation of a fortified settlement at Walesland Rath, Pembrokeshire', *Britannia* 2: 48–108.

Walker, E.A 1996. 'A face from the tomb', in S. Aldhouse-Green (ed.), 1996, *Art, Ritual and Death*, Cardiff: National Museum of Wales, 11.

Walker, E.A. 1999. 'Island archaeology: a search for Middle Stone Age occupation on Burry Holms, Gower', *Amgueddfa 2: Yearbook 1998/99*, Cardiff: National Museums and Galleries of Wales, 31–33.

Walker, M.J.C. & Harkness, D.D. 1990. 'Radiocarbon dating the Quaternary in Britain: new evidence from Llanilid, South Wales', *Journal of Quaternary Science* 5, 135–44.

Walker, M.J.C., Griffiths, H.I., Ringwood, V. & Evans, J.G. 1993. 'An early Holocene pollen, mollusc and ostracod sequence from lake marl at Llangorse, U.K.', *The Holocene* 3, 138–49.

Ward, A.H. 1983. 'Excavation around two standing stones on Mynydd Llangyndeyrn, Dyfed', *Archaeologia Cambrensis* 132, 30–48.

Ward, A.H. 1988. 'Survey and Excavation of Ring Cairns in south-east Dyfed and on Gower, West Glamorgan', *Proceedings of the Prehistoric Society* 54, 153–72.

Ward, A.H. 1989. 'Cairns and "Cairnfields": evidence of early agriculture on Cefn Bryn, Gower, West Glamorgan', *Landscape History* 11, 5–18.

Ward, J. 1915. 'The St Nicholas Chambered Tumulus, Glamorgan', *Archaeologia Cambrensis* 69, 253–320.

Ward, J. 1916. 'The St Nicholas Chambered Tumulus, Glamorgan', *Archaeologia Cambrensis* 70, 239–67.

Ward, M. 1993. 'Pant late-prehistoric/Romano-British round-houses', *Archaeology in Wales* 33, 57.

Ward, P.A., Williams, G.H., Marshall, E.C. & Darke, I.M. 1987. 'The Glandy Cross Complex', *Archaeology in Wales* 27, 9–13.

Ward, R. & Stringer, C. 1997. 'A molecular handle on the Neanderthals', *Nature* 388, 225–6.

Wardle P. 1987. 'A review of the use of ceramic petrology in Wales', *Archaeology in Wales* 27, 16–17.

Warren, S.H. 1922. 'The Neolithic Stone axes of Graig Lwyd, Penmaenmawr', *Archaeologia Cambrensis* 77, 1–36.

Warrilow, W., Owen, G. & Britnell, W.J. 1986. 'Eight Ring-ditches at Four Crosses, Llandysilio, Powys, 1981–85', *Proceedings of the Prehistoric Society* 52, 53–87.

Waterman, D.M. 1997. *Excavations at Navan Fort 1961–71*, Belfast: Stationery Office.

Way, A. 1856. 'Notices of bronze celts and of celt moulds found in Wales', *Archaeologia Cambrensis* 3rd series 2, 120–31.

Webley, D.P. 1958. 'A Cairn Cemetery and Secondary Neolithic Dwelling on Cefn Cilsanws, Vaynor, Brecs.', *Bulletin of the Board of Celtic Studies* 18, 79–88.

Webley, D.P. 1976. 'How the West was won: prehistoric land-use in the southern Marches', in G.C. Boon & J.M. Lewis (eds), 1976, 19–35.

Webster, P. 1975. 'Roman and Iron Age Tankards in Western Britain', *Bulletin of the Board of Celtic Studies* 26, 231–6.

Wheeler, R.E. M. 1943. *Maiden Castle*, Oxford: Oxford University Press (for the Society of Antiquaries).

Wheeler, R.E.M. & Wheeler, T.V. 1932. *Report on the excavation of the prehistoric, Roman and Post-Roman site in Lydney Park, Gloucestershire*, Oxford: Oxford University Press (for the Society of Antiquaries).

Whimster, R. 1981. *Burial Practices in Iron Age Britain* 2 vols, Oxford: British Archaeological Reports, British Series 90.

Whimster, R. 1989. 'The Welsh Marches', in RCHME, 1989, *The Emerging Past: air photography and the buried landscape*, London, 35–65.

White, R.B. 1977. 'Rhosgoch to Stanlow Shell Oil Pipeline', *Bulletin of the Board of Celtic Studies* 27, 463–90.

White, R.B. 1978. 'Excavations at Trwyn Du, Anglesey, 1974', *Archaeologia Cambrensis* 127, 16–39.

White, S.I. & Smith, G. 1999. 'A Funerary and Ceremonial Centre at Capel Eithin, Gaerwen, Anglesey', *Transactions of the Anglesey Antiquarian Society*, 11–166.

Whiten, A., Goodall, J., McGrew, W.C., Nishida, T., Reynolds, V., Sugiyama, Y., Tutin, C.E.G., Wrangham, R.W. & Boesch, C. 1999. 'Cultures in Chimpanzees', *Nature* 399, 682–5.

Whittle, A.W.R. 1989. 'Two later bronze age occupations and an iron age channel on the Gwent foreshore', *Bulletin of the Board of Celtic Studies* 36, 200–23.

Whittle, A.W.R. 1997. *Europe in the Neolithic*, Cambridge: Cambridge University Press.

Whittle, A.W.R., Atkinson, R.J.C., Chambers, R. & Thomas, N. 1992. 'Excavations in the Neolithic and Bronze Age Complex at Dorchester-on-Thames, Oxfordshire, 1947–1952', *Proceedings of the Prehistoric Society* 58, 143–202.

Whittle, A.W.R. & Wysocki, M. 1998. 'Parc le Breos Cwm Transepted Long Cairn, Gower, West Glamorgan: Date, Contents and Context', *Proceedings of the Prehistoric Society* 64, 139–82.

Williams, A. 1939. 'Excavations at the Knave Promontory Fort, Rhossili, Glamorgan', *Archaeologia Cambrensis* 94, 210–19.

Williams, A. 1945. 'A Promontory Fort at Henllan, Cards.', *Archaeologia Cambrensis* 98, 226–40.

Williams, A. 1952. 'Clegyr Boia, St David's (Pembrokeshire): Excavations in 1943', *Archaeologia Cambrensis* 102, 20–47.

Williams, G. 1981. 'Survey and excavation on Pembrey Mountain', *Carmarthenshire Antiquary* 17, 3–32.

Williams, G. 1984. 'A Henge Monument at Ffynnon Newydd, Nantgaredig', *Bulletin of the Board of Celtic Studies* 31, 177–90.

Williams, G. 1985. 'An Iron Age cremation deposit from Castell Bucket, Letterston, Pembrokeshire', *Archaeology in Wales* 25, 13–15.

Williams, G. 1986. 'Recent work on Bronze Age sites in SW Wales', *Archaeology in Wales* 26, 11–14.

Williams, G. 1987. 'Bryn Maen Caerau, Cellan', *Archaeology in Wales* 27, 32–3.

Williams, G. 1988a. *The Standing Stones of Wales and South West England*, Oxford: British Archaeological Reports British Series 197.

Williams, G. 1988b. 'Recent work on rural settlement in later prehistoric and early historic Dyfed', *Antiquaries Journal* 68, 30–54.

Williams, G. 1989. 'Excavations in Longstone Field, St Ishmaels, Pembrokeshire', *Archaeologia Cambrensis* 138, 20–45.

Williams, G., Darke, I., Parry, C. & Isaac, J. 1988. 'Recent archaeological work on Merlin's Hill, Abergwili', *Carmarthenshire Antiquary* 24, 5–13.

Williams, G. & Mytum, H. 1998. *Llawhaden, Dyfed. Excavations on a group of small defended enclosures, 1980–4*, Oxford: British Archaeological Reports, British Series 275.

Williams, H. 1921. 'Excavation of a Bronze Age Tumulus near Gorsedd, Holywell, Flintshire', *Archaeologia Cambrensis* 76, 265–89.

Williams, H. 1924. 'A flat celt mould from the Lledr Valley', *Archaeologia Cambrensis* 79, 212–13.

Williams, J.Ll. & Jenkins, D.A. 1976. 'The use of petrographic, heavy mineral and arc spectrographic techniques in assessing the provenance of sediments used in ceramics', in D. Davidson & M. Shackley (eds), 1976, *Geoarchaeology*, London, 115–36.

Williams, J. Ll. & Jenkins, D.A. 1999. 'A Petrographic Investigation of a Corpus of Bronze Age Cinerary Urns from the Isle of Anglesey', *Proceedings of the Prehistoric Society* 65, 189–230.

Williams, J.Ll. & Davidson, A., with Flook, R., Jenkins, D.A., Muckle, P. & Roberts, T. 1998. 'Survey and Excavation at the Graig Lwyd Neolithic Axe-Factory, Penmaenmawr', *Archaeology in Wales* 38, 3–21.

Williams-Jones, K. 1976. *The Merioneth Lay Subsidy Roll, 1292–3*, Cardiff: University of Wales Press.

Wilson, D.R. 1991. 'Air reconnaisances of Roman Wales, 1969–88', in B.C. Burnham & J.L. Davies (eds), 1991, 10–18 (plates at back).

Wilson, J.C. 1983. 'The Standing Stones of Anglesey: a Discussion', *Bulletin of the Board of Celtic Studies* 30, 363–89.

Wood, B. 1994. 'The oldest hominid yet', *Nature* 371, 280–1.

Wood, B. & Collard, M. 1999a. 'Is *Homo* defined by culture?', in J. Coles, R. Bewley & P. Mellars (eds), 1999, *World Prehistory: Studies in memory of Grahame Clark*, London: British Academy, 11–23.

Wood, B. & Collard, M. 1999b. 'The human genus', *Science* 284, 65–71.

Woodman, P. 1985. *Excavations at Mount Sandel 1973–1977*, Belfast: Archaeological Research Monograph 2.

Woodward, A. 1992. *Book of Shrines and Sacrifice*, London: Batsford/English Heritage.

Wright, E.V. 1990. *The Ferriby Boats: Seacraft of the Bronze Age*, London: Routledge.

Wymer, J.J. 1996. *The Welsh Lower Palaeolithic Survey. A Supplement to the English Rivers Palaeolithic Survey*, Salisbury: Wessex Archaeology.

Wynn Williams, W. 1877. 'Bronze Implements and Copper Cake (Menai Bridge and elsewhere)', *Archaeologia Cambrensis* 4th series 8, 206–11.

Yalden, D. 1999. *History of the British Mammals*, London: T & AD Poyser Natural History.

Yellen. J.E. 1998. 'Barbed bone points: tradition and continuity in Saharan and sub-Saharan Africa', *African Archaeological Review* 15, 173–98.

INDEX